MW01248948

# Rites of Passage

*Member of Parliament H.M. Patel in a candid moment at Parliament House, 1976.*

# RITES OF PASSAGE

## A Civil Servant Remembers

H.M. PATEL

EDITED BY
Sucheta Mahajan

Rupa . Co

Published 2005 by

Rupa . Co

7/16, Ansari Road, Daryaganj,
New Delhi 110 002

*Sales Centres:*

Allahabad Bangalore Chandigarh Chennai
Hyderabad Jaipur Kathmandu
Kolkata Mumbai Pune



Typeset in 11 pts. Book Antiqua by
Nikita Overseas Pvt. Ltd.
1410 Chiranjiv Tower
43 Nehru Place
New Delhi 110 019

Printed in India by
Gopsons Papers Ltd.
A-14 Sector 60
Noida 201 301

Dedicated to SARDAR:
the steel core at
the heart of the steel frame
that guarded the early years
of the New Republic

# *Contents*

## III
## Appendices

# *Acknowledgements*

My first and only meeting with H.M. Patel was in May 1985 in Vallabh Vidyanagar near Anand at the office of the Charutar Vidya Mandal. I was part of a team of historians from the Jawaharlal Nehru University headed by Professor Bipan Chandra who went to interview him for an oral history project on the freedom movement. Two memories linger. One was how little of a brown sahib he was, given his being such a senior civil servant. The second was the absolute conviction with which he said that the Congress leaders had no option but to accept partition. I was thrilled to have such a powerful ally as I was then engaged in a polemical battle with fellow historians who said the Congress need not have done so.

The book may have remained unborn were it not for Amrita Patel. H.M. Patel's amazing capacity for work is, of course, legendary. Amrita must surely be her father's daughter in this respect. She, too, was relentless in her mission to secure public recognition of her father's work as a civil servant. I could call upon her at any time to provide information, check facts with her sisters, account personal impressions, or to send a book across from H.M. Patel's library. She sent across the entire set of volumes of the proceedings of the Partition Council and a rare copy of *My Submissions* by H.M. Patel.

I am grateful to the director, Nehru Memorial Museum and Library, New Delhi for granting me permission to consult the Mountbatten Papers. The library staff, especially Naveen Mahajan, were as always helpful with locating references and furnishing photocopies of documents on microfilm at short notice. I wish to thank Rajesh, Kalra and Sharma for efficient logistical support.

My primary debt of course remains to the Patel family for reposing confidence in me. I met 'the Patel daughters', as Maurice Zinkin described them, in 1998. For that visit to Vallabh Vidyanagar I had donned the hat of a maverick expert on Independence and Partition, whose brief was to look at H.M. Patel's papers and advise the family on how best to make them available for posterity. I prepared a list of files and their contents and made the suggestion that papers should ideally be placed in the Manuscript Section of the Nehru Memorial Museum and Library for scholarly and public access. This was, of course, a breathtakingly original suggestion, given that I had spent twenty years in that wonderful haven for students of history. So when I went to see Usha Katrak, I thought it was to be an exchange of pleasantries. As befitting a guest taking leave of gracious hosts, I not only praised the cooking and the fine hospitality, but also waxed eloquent about the importance of the papers and the incomplete manuscripts of memoirs of the scholarly world. Little did I realise then what I was getting into when I said I would have loved to have taken up the work of completing the manuscripts if I had not been neck deep in two books. My statement was taken at face value and sure enough, when one book was out of the way, H.M. Patel was in. And thus began this book, which I thought would be a pleasant summer interlude between serious history writing. It took over two years. During which H.M. Patel took over everything. Books, like memories, can sometimes be redolent of fragrances. This one, for instance, is pervaded by the lightly flavoured half sweet *kadhi* served at 'Savita', H.M. Patel's home in Vallabh Vidyanagar.

New Delhi, 2004 **Sucheta Mahajan**

# *Foreword*

It is a pleasure to write the Foreword to this book by H.M. Patel. The only time I met H.M. Patel was in 1985 when my colleagues and I interviewed him as part of a project on the history of the Indian National Congress. The meeting took place in his office in the Charutar Vidya Mandal in Anand. What struck me was that he was not the usual type of civil servant — he was a nationalist at heart and unusually down to earth. After holding high office as Cabinet secretary and finance and home minister he was content to devote his entire energy to the uplift of Charutar, the area he hailed from.

This extremely important book focuses our attention on the crucial years preceding, and following, the independence of our country from colonial rule. In one sense, it is in the tradition of books by other eminent civil servants, such as V.P. Menon's *Transfer of Power* and *Story of the Integration of the States*. Yet, it does not share the usual shortcomings of eyewitness accounts, namely, a tendency to put forth tall claims about the importance of the author, to the exclusion of other, as was particularly the case with the books such as *Freedom at Midnight*.

The memoirs recreate in rich detail, the life of a civil servant in the closing years of colonial rule, replete with challenges and trials. It goes on to describe how, after Independence, the Indian members of the ICS did not opt to retire with generous financial compensation.

They closed ranks with their erstwhile opponents, the nationalist political leaders, to put up a united front in nation building. One notable example of this cooperation is the manner in which the civil servants and political leadership joined hands to control the deteriorating law and order situation in Delhi in September 1947.

An important question H.M. Patel takes up is why the Congress accepted the partition of the country. It is sometimes argued that the Congress leaders accepted it because they were tired and hungry for power but they could have prevented it by forsaking the path of negotiations and launching a mass movement. In his view, the Congress had little option but to accept partition once the communal situation deteriorated to almost civil war and the Muslim League made the functioning of the Interim Government impossible. This view is especially significant coming from an important participant and a non-Congressman at that.

The book highlights many hitherto less known aspects of the Partition of India, which are often ignored in the literature available. For example, it is generally not recognized that the actual physical partition of the country into two independent functioning entities was a colossal task. It must have been no mean feat to arrive at an agreement on how assets and liabilities were to be divided when there was so much mistrust between the two countries. H.M. Patel recounts the working of the Partition Council in great detail. Whereas the published proceedings of the Partition Council merely record the decisions taken, H.M. Patel discusses the areas of disagreement and how and why resolution was achieved. This makes H.M. Patel's account of great value as a historical document.

**Prof. Bipan Chandra**
2004

# *Introduction*

## Modes of Remembering

The genre of memoirs is a variegated one. There are ruminations in the 'oh gentle reader' mode, sensational tell-it-alls, egoistical tales, recriminatory stories and of course, ringside views, straight from the arena. The memoirs of civil servants and political activists centred on the Independence and Partition of India are rich in their diversity. While Mountbatten is egoistical, Maulana Azad is both egoistical and recriminatory. H.M. Patel's memoirs are difficult to slot; they are partly in the genre of looking back and partly a ringside view, but related in an unhurried, factual style — reminiscent of a languid Test cricket commentary on the radio. This is in contrast to the evocative storytelling style of, for example, Malcolm Darling, ICS. Both men worked in the same region and both write of life in a district along the Indus — but it seems a different Indus. Darling's Indus is a romantic, majestic river on whose banks Porus faced Alexander, and which the young official looks upon with awe.[1] H.M. Patel's Indus is a practical, unruly river in spate at Shikarpur where his charge is to protect the people of the town from floods

1 Malcolm Darling, *Apprentice to Power, India, 1904-1908*, The Hogarth Press, London, 1966.

and even worse, brewing communal trouble. Contrast Patel's accounts of the river in flood with the dramatic representation of this episode by the son of his associate, Jaswant Singh Malik. H.M. presents it as an invaluable lesson in crisis management for a novice administrator while Malik's son recalls the sheer adventure of it all:[2]

> ...my father had received a telegram informing him of a record high level of the Indus at Attock; he had rushed to the Collector and asked for additional labour to guard the bunds on the right bank of the Indus for which he was responsible. The Collector had not only immediately agreed but had offered the services of his young Assistant Collector.
>
> ...the next three nights were the most exciting in my young life. After tea, we left immediately for an inspection bungalow on the bund. Already lights could be seen along the bund as hurricane lamps and improvised torches — rags stuck in bottles of kerosene oil — were hastily lit by the sturdy peasants who had left their homes to come and protect them from the threatening waters of the mighty Indus.
>
> In our car we had three powerful electric torches, which enabled the adults (Mr. Patel, my father and my mother) to inspect the landward side of the bund for tell-tale leakages. I was allowed — as a special concession — to stay in the car till midnight, while the adults went about encouraging the peasants and supervising their activity. Some leaks caused by the nefarious activities of rats in the dry season were spotted and sealed in time. Within the car, wakefulness and vigilance were maintained by telling jokes, setting riddles, competitions, in laughing and so on. I only saw one evening of this strenuous and very important activity but it went on for three successive nights till the peak of the flood had passed. Sind was saved that summer.

2 G. J. Malik, son of Jaswant Singh Malik, H.M. Patel's associate in Shikarpur, Sind. Malik was later in the Indian Foreign Service. pp. 61-62.

Memoirs of ICS administrators are often not merely reminiscences, but records — and records with a message. The theme could vary from racial equality between the races in an East meets West genre (Darling) to its counter point or, as in H.M.'s case, governing India, Gorwala style, within the 'paternalistic tradition'. A worthy memoir, like a worthy life, was recognised by the presence of a message. This was brought home strikingly by a cover blurb of an autobiography of an ICS official.[3]

> Bear-hunting in Bundelkhand, riding a yak through an 18000 foot pass into Chinese Turkistan, putting down mutiny in Peshawar, exchanges with Gandhi and Ghaffar Khan Lionel Jardine, as a British colonial officer in India, had plenty of the stuff of which autobiographies are made. But this book is not a string of windy reminiscences. Rather, in precise British understatement, it makes a specific point from the experience of Mr. Jardine — a point which is as pertinent for post-independent Indians and post-colonial British as it was in those turbulent days of 1914-1947. It is what made him a somewhat exceptional 'Impeccable imperialist'.

The editor adds, "His story, as reproduced in this book will add to the work of their lives".

This could as well be said of H.M. Patel's memoirs. There are none of the usual exploits and adventures in which the author plays a central role. Without stating it in so many words, the work exemplifies the life of a public man who upheld the principles of probity and integrity in a quiet and unassuming manner.

A distinction made by a perceptive psychoanalyst between Western and Indian autobiographies could explain the style of H.M. Patel's book.[4]

---

3 Lionel Jardine, *They Called me an Impeccable Imperialist*, Himmat Publications, Bombay, 1979.

4 Sudhir Kakar, *Shamans, Mystics and Doctors, A Psychological Inquiry into India and its Healing Traditions*, Delhi, 1982, pp. 7.

> A certain kind of introspection ... is a peculiarly Western trait, deeply rooted in Western culture ... the definitions of self and identity became contingent upon an active process of examining, sorting out and scrutinizing the 'events' and 'adventures' of one's own life .... This kind of introspection is simply not a feature of Indian culture and its literary traditions. Even today, in the essentially Western-inspired genre of autobiography, Indian writings often tend to have a curiously flat quality as far as the scrutiny of life in terms of a ruthless examination of motives and feelings are concerned. The section on childhood, whose ambivalences and ambiguities are the riveting content of a good autobiography, as well as the section on the turmoil of youth, are generally skipped over with driblets of information and conventional pieties such as 'Mother was loving,' 'Father was affectionate', 'Brothers were kind'. With rare exceptions, Indian autobiographies are evocations of places and accounts of careers, records of events from which the self has been excised."

In applying Kakar's yardstick to the autobiographies of eminent Indians, rare exceptions would be Jawaharlal Nehru's *Autobiography* and even Mahatma Gandhi's *My Experiments with Truth*, both ruthlessly self-indulgent and self-critical. A good example of an 'Indian' autobiography in Kakar's definition would be this book by H.M. Patel, which is an account of a career — a record of events. There is little of the self here. We do not even learn the names of his father, mother, brother, wife or daughters.[5] The father figures as a decision maker; there is little about his wife except that she came from a socially superior family of Sojitra and took to *khadi* and Harijan work, as, H.M. adds somewhat patronisingly, young girls at that time were wont to do.

---

5 It was from his daughters that I learnt that H.M. Patel's father was Muljibhai Jethabhai Patel and his mother Hiraba Muljibhai Patel. His brother's name was Manilal. He married Savitaben Hirubhai Patel. They had five children, Usha, Uma, Nisha, Sharad and Amrita.

For the person, his politics, we have to turn to his friends and family; "The house at Vallabh Vidyanagar is of unusual design, with H. M.'s study perched half-way between the ground and first floors, with a through draught and a view from above of the sitting-room. It is lined with books in English and Gujarati, with a few of German, French or Hindi. H.M. is an omnivorous reader, with books scattered over his bedroom as well as ranged on shelves in his study. When the rest of us are asleep, between 3 and 6 in the morning, H.M. is reading: may be papers and reports with which he must be familiar for the next day's work; may be studies of finance or defence in which he takes special interest; may be history or biography, such as Lord Wavell's diaries; or perhaps a detective story, by one of the old masters, Conan Doyle, Rex Stout or Agatha Christie, or by more recent writers such as Georges Simenon or Nicolas Freeling, whose regional stories appeal as he was based in Hamburg before 1939 as Trade Commissioner for Northern Europe."[6] Taya Zinkin tells us that his language skills were exceptional. Gujarati was his mother tongue and he was fluent in English, Hindi, Sindhi, Marathi, Persian, French and German. He translated from the Gujarati Narhari Parikh's *Life of Sardar Patel* and several novels of K.M. Munshi. On his relationship with his peers, a deputy economic adviser in the finance ministry who went on, like H.M., to become an eminent economic and financial administrator and institution builder himself, recalled "the complete sense of equality with which he treated every one, whether young or old, small or big."[7] The young son of his associate in Shikarpur, Jaswant Singh Malik, fondly reminisced in later years: "It was thus that Mr. H.M. Patel came into my life which he was to influence so profoundly. At the time I was overjoyed to meet someone half-way in age between my father and myself who was prepared to play with me, set me new puzzles, teach me boyish tricks and generally entertain a child in whom most adults took little

---

6 R.E.Hawkins, manager of Oxford University Press, Bombay.
7 I.G. Patel, former governor, Reserve Bank of India.

interest, if any." Nisha da Cunha, H.M's daughter, recalled, "For years I remember the scrape of the wheels on the gravel as he came home from office. Always in white, coming to a stop, taking off his bicycle clip that kept his trousers out of the way of the chain and his voice calling out for all of us, and what had we done all day?"

For H.M. Patel, the autobiography ironically was not focussed on the self of the individual; it was a narrative account of public events that he considered significant in his career. It was not a tell-all tale replete with the conspiracies and salacious gossip that people had always suspected. For H.M. Patel, the public self and work carried important lessons for posterity and appropriately his work is a mainly straightforward account of public action. This notion of writing for posterity was shared by contemporaries: K.B. Lall, ICS, wrote: "There is much in the life and work of HM and his colleagues which could help the present generation of civil servants to cope with contemporary constraints and help revitalise the polity and restore its credibility."[8]

In contrasting public figures in the 'West' and the 'East', Mines observes, "In the West, our fascination with individuality is elaborated in many ways: novels, biographies and autobiographies...All these various forms are also representations of self: expressions of idiosyncrasy and verbal or visual portraits of individuals that cause us to reflect on the interior person. Further, our interest in these many expressions stems from our own self-reflexive sense of who we are and how we act. Reflecting on others, each thinks about himself or herself."[9]

In the context of India Mines refers to the term, "individuality of eminence". This term could apply to H.M. This is an important distinction between an introspective individualism of the 'West' and

8 K.B. Lall, pp.149.

9 Mattison Mines, *Public Faces, Private Voices, Community and Individuality in South India*, University of California Press, Berkeley, 1994, pp.3.

an individuality measured by achievement. Socially significant individuality was based on preeminence, rather than on the more common premise of knowing oneself, through detailed examination of one's actions.[10]

It would appear then that eminent men were expected only to have public persona. Even while reminiscing, only weighty matters of public import were to be remembered — a personal note was to be avoided. H.M. Patel himself subscribed to this view. His memoirs are essentially an autobiography without the 'self'. It is an account of his times rather than an account of his life. Private spaces rarely figure; value is placed only in the public sphere. In his reminiscences of Sardar Patel, H.M. wrote almost apologetically: "I might end my reminiscences on a personal note -- but only because they illustrate facets of Sardar's nature and character."[11] About H.M. himself a colleague wrote: 'Shri Patel Saheb never dwelt in the past, except in matters relating to culture and human heritage. I never ever found him striking an autobiographical note'.[12]

## The Books and their Man

To begin with, this book was not intended by H.M. Patel to be *the* grand oeuvre, *the* magnum opus. H.M., as Patel was addressed by his contemporaries, conceived of two books — one, his memoirs and the other, a 'ringside' view of Partition, akin to V.P. Menon's books on the transfer of power and the integration of the princely states. He left the writing far too late in life, waiting for that moment of leisure, which never comes for a man of duty — furthermore for a man of public duty. Age and ill health cruelly caught up with him while he was dictating and redrafting the books through the

10 Mines, pp.106.

11 Reminiscences of Sardar Patel, 22-2-1976.

12 Hiren J Pandya, Department of Public Administration, South Gujarat University, Surat, commemoration volume, pp. 214.

1980s. When he died in 1993, a colleague in the ICS lamented, "My only complaint against him was that he did not listen to me in the matter of writing the history of the Partition. Nobody in India knew it as well as he did. I wish he had listened."[13] But Patel *had* listened. The history was there but in incomplete manuscript form. This is where I stepped in. It was in my *avatar* of a minor historian of Independence and Partition that the family invited me to Anand to look at H.M. Patel's papers. What began for me as a fairly simple brief of examining his private papers in order to decide where they may be placed, snowballed into an ambitious publication project with the discovery of two fascinating but incomplete manuscripts.

This book is based on H.M.'s manuscripts. It is made up of two parts. The first part, the memoirs, charts the familiar rites of passage in the life of a civil servant. In 1927, a civil servant is born; with his appointment as Cabinet secretary in 1946 he reaches the prime of life; the resignation in 1959 is a premature end to an illustrious life in the service.[14]

The chapters on the early years in the district in Sind are rich in detail and recall. It was obviously the period H.M. looked back on with nostalgia and even pride and which he contrasts with the present day when there is little accountability and when district officers rarely move out of headquarters and when they do, touring is by jeep: "The task of the civil servant was perhaps easier in my days in that he was left to carry out his duties without any interference, which unfortunately is not the case today. The accountability of the civil servant in the old days was complete. Today that is not the case." The young H.M. follows in the footsteps of his courageous and charismatic senior in the service, A.D. Gorwala, whose motto was

13 Uncle Bijju (B.K. Nehru) to Amrita Patel, 3 December 1993, Kasauli, Himachal Pradesh.

14 V.P. Menon recalls, "He advanced very rapidly in the service, and almost as far back as I remember he was handling important jobs. He entered the service in 1927, and by 1940 he had risen to a very high position in the Government of India."

'serving the people' and who dispensed justice without fear or favour: "It was Gorwala's endeavour to see that the poor received justice whenever it came to his notice that the well-to-do and powerful elements of the society sought to take advantage of him and to exploit him. .... This left such a very deep impression among the people that even to this day, some fifty years after he left Sind, people remember and long for what came to be known as Gorwala's justice!"

Of course, the reader might keep in mind that this picture of the district officer, who knew 'his district' well, and who was one with 'his people', is, like with other colonial civil servants, somewhat idealized.

In the chapters covering his years in the secretariat in Bombay in the 1930s, H.M. discusses the separation of Sind, which he was involved in: "Although this was not openly admitted the real underlying reason for seeking the separation of Sind from the rest of the Presidency of Bombay was without a doubt political." H.M. became part of the Finance Commerce pool in the ICS, a select group of officers with aptitude in economic and financial matters. In the late 1930s, H.M. was trade commissioner in Hamburg. He gives us an interesting eye-witness account of Hitler's persecution of the Jews, complete with a sharp critique of the weak policy of appeasement of Hitler by the Allies. Forced to return to England on the outbreak of the Second World War in 1939, H.M. lives through the dark hour of the early reverses in Dunkirk and then the resounding fightback masterminded by Churchill. He wrote: "This whole period was another astonishing period and gave me an opportunity of witnessing the British character at its best."

H.M. describes the impact of Gandhi on India's political life as "an extraordinary revolution" in his memoirs:

> Meantime, India was not standing still during the period I was away. Mahatma Gandhi's activities had commenced, and with them an extraordinary revolution had come about in the lives of

> the people of India, and in particular of the women of India, who had never stirred out of their houses, thought nothing of taking part in the picketing of liquor shops and of joining rallies and demonstrations. It was inevitable that young girls should be attracted by these movements and my wife too was drawn towards them, but mainly towards the wearing of khadi, and activities designed to help women of backward classes and particularly Harijans."

The phrase "extraordinary revolution" is a strong one from a man who was restraint and discretion personified and yet there is nothing in the memoirs on the impact of Gandhi on his own life. Intrigued by this, I asked his daughters what their father thought of Gandhi. They described him as an admirer of Gandhi. Usha, his eldest daughter, recalls: "I remember other "shaving" times when he would read to us extracts from "Harijan". During Gandhi's lifetime it had its occasional sparkle. He also taught me Gandhian bhajans like "Vaishnava Jan" and "Raghupati Raghav".

Maurice Zinkin, a British colleague wrote:

> (He was) a keen nationalist and it was he who gave me my best insight into the Gandhian point of view. I argued to him one day that khadi made economic nonsense, that it would never be possible to provide spinners with a reasonable living without an enormous subsidy. He had one of his little explosions — this counted as a private occasion. Then he explained that economics was not the point, that khadi was a symbol of the solidarity of those who were better off with the poor of the villages who were without work.
>
> This nationalism was never allowed to conflict with his duty as an Indian Civil Servant. His politics were, I suppose, those of Vallabhbhai Patel; he had the same combination of devotion to his country and understanding of how to make government work. He never concealed his belief that India should be independent,

but in the main before 1947, he accepted that the Government had to be run and that the better it was run, the better for the people. Perhaps the war eased any strain there may have been between his position as a civil servant and his Congress beliefs. The war had to be won and it was obvious that afterwards independence could not be long delayed .... above all, as a good Gandhian, he devoted himself to the uplift of the area from which his family had come."

The second part of the book focuses on the Partition of India. In the initial chapters on the important political developments in the years 1945 to 1947, H.M. points to the milestones on the road to transfer of power — the coming of the Labour Government to power in 1945, the sending out of the ministerial Cabinet Mission to India in 1946, the Interim Government in September 1946, the evolution of the 3 June Plan and the final countdown to 15 August 1947. While describing the atmosphere in Delhi on the swearing in of the Interim Government headed by Jawaharlal Nehru, he also hints at a subterranean communal sentiment: "There was tremendous excitement among the personnel in the various Departments of the Government of India, housed in the North Block and in hutments and hired buildings in various parts all over New and Old Delhi. Already because of the political discussions which had been going on in the country, during the previous couple of years, the civil servants of all ranks had become accustomed to discussing the current political developments with keen interest and with the clear realisation that these were not academic discussions, but would almost certainly lead to changes, which would affect them in a very far reaching and significant manner. Despite their general training to avoid political entanglement of any kind whatsoever, the general environment was such that few could maintain a completely objective stance. Even if not overtly, their sympathies did get involved, as more and more news began to be reported of communal disturbances."

In subsequent chapters in part two of the book, H.M. Patel describes in detail the elaborate machinery of partition – the Partition Council, the Arbitral Tribunal, the Expert Committees – and sketches the sequence of events by which agreement was achieved after much wrangling and in the midst of unprecedented communal strife. The account is invaluable as a ringside view, a first person account of the proceedings of the Partition Council.[15] We learn from a colleague in the ICS, L.K. Jha, that H. M. "devised the machinery [of partition] and ensured its smooth functioning .... The ultimate decisions were reached in direct personal negotiations between H. M. Patel and Chaudhri Mohammad Ali which were then ratified by the Partition Council." The Partition Council was at the top, then the Partition Secretariat and further there were Expert Committees to deal with specific areas and issues. The idea behind distributing the work to smaller committees was to prevent the Partition Council from getting mired in routine and controversy. To ensure that Indian representatives on one committee did not run into conflict with their counterparts in another committee, all Indian representatives on Expert Committees met informally every morning at H.M. Patel's house before office to work this out. H.M. mediated, if necessary. When he headed the group of civil servants who executed the complicated task of physical partition in a short time, he was only in his early forties. Amrita, the youngest daughter recalls, "I was born just a little before the time my father went smack into the middle of helping to break up India into two."[16]

As H.M. Patel writes about the Partition Council, "The magnitude of the task that had been accomplished has to this day not been fully appreciated. It has never occurred to anyone to this day to ask how had it become possible to arrive at agreements on controversial

---

15 Chaudhry Mahomed Ali, H.M.'s Pakistani counterpart in the Council, wrote an account but it is not easily accessible. He had sent a copy to H.M. which is in his papers in Vallabh Vidyanagar.

16 Amrita Patel, commemoration volume, pp. 68.

issues of such great significance, and importance in the midst of the surrounding atmosphere of great tension, violence and bitterness. That they were able to look at these problems with objectivity and moved only by the desire to ensure better understanding and friendliness in the future between the two countries reflects great credit on the members of the Partition Council."[17]

On the integration of the princely states he writes: "People had tended to assume at first that the problem of the Princely States would be relatively simple and not as challenging as it was soon found to be. Some states even went to the length of expressing a desire to remain completely independent and sovereign. Even a relatively small state like Travancore was among the first to take advantage of the fact that it was a coastal state and so could enter into independent agreement with other sovereign states."[18]

*

These are memoirs, not a chronicle of life and times, or even an autobiography. The story begins with the first decade of the twentieth century in Bombay where H.M. Patel grew up in a traditional Gujarati family. It spans the period of his time in the Indian Civil Service (ICS), the high points being his role in the Partition Council in 1947, the apex body which unraveled the physical partition of assets down to the last typewritten ribbon.[19] He went on to "saving Delhi" in September 1947 and building, block by block, some of the flagship institutions of new India. "At one time in 1947 he held simultaneously four jobs, each of which would have been quite enough for an able man. He was Cabinet Secretary, Establishment

17 See Section II.

18 See Section II.

19 Some issues dealt with by the Partition Council border on the inane. There is even a separate discussion on 'Division of Refrigerations' — 238 were in working order, Pakistan members demanded 55, Indian members offered 29 and the compromise reached by Expert Committee I was 33!

Officer, Member of the Central Committee for Refugees, the executive head of the Delhi Committee for restoring order in the Capital, and the Chief Indian Member of the Steering Committee whose function was to decide on the distribution of assets and liabilities between India and Pakistan." !

This book records his administrative career only and not his political career, which began when the first career ended. In keeping with the tone of his administrative career, the tone of the account is almost impersonal. There are no anecdotes, no confessions, no inside stories. It is a story told by a man who was discreet — a virtue inculcated and valued by the service he belonged to.

There are very few "later" accounts of independence. The period after Independence saw a number of 'ringside' views expressed in print. Most actors in the 'quit and divide' drama wrote their versions soon after the event. H.M. Patel's colleague, V.P. Menon's books, *Transfer of Power in India* and *Story of the Integration of the States* and Malcolm Darling's *At Freedom's Door*, published in 1949, are cases in point. Memoirs are generally the pastime of retirement, ostensibly written for the grandchildren but often to "put the record straight", in the case of public men, men of eminence. But in H.M.'s case, there was no retirement; only another life, and a fuller, public one at that. When he was writing these memoirs in the 1980s, distance allowed an impartial, even dispassionate view.

H.M. Patel's story is free from the obsessive self-preoccupation of most participant histories, especially the Mountbatten books (this includes those based on interviews with him, such as *Freedom at Midnight* and *Mountbatten and the Partition of India* and those written by his associates, Alan Campbell-Johnson and H.V. Hodson *(Mission with Mountbatten* and *The Great Divide* respectively).[20] H.M.'s task is

---

20 For 'participant histories' and their problems, see the Introduction to Sucheta Mahajan, *Independence and Partition, Erosion of Colonial Power in India*, Sage, New Delhi, 2000.

not to apportion responsibility or claim credit, it is to tell the story as he saw it. There are no heroes or villains and yet some figures are larger than life, for example, Vallabhbhai Patel, A.D. Gorwala, his mentor in the ICS, and somewhat surprisingly, Mountbatten. One would have thought as an insider, H.M. would have pointed to the negative consequences of the speedy transfer of power and partition. Other contemporaries were less circumspect. [21] In Patel's refusal to take sides, the view he expounds is somewhat sanitised.

H.M. was in some ways the quintessential civil servant. His paean to "Gorwala's justice" reveals that his, too, was a paternalistic ideal, in which the benevolent administrator was the *mai-bap* of the ordinary village folk. The years H.M. was a district officer in the Bombay Presidency [22] were years of political tumult, which even swayed men in the 'heaven born' service. Subhas Bose had resigned from the ICS, setting an example to others serving in the government. In H.M.'s native Gujarat, many had answered the call by Congress to give up jobs in the Government. Morarji Desai was one such official, coincidentally later to be H.M.'s political comrade in arms half a

21 B.K. Nehru criticizes Mountbatten: "He [Mountbatten] had taken a highly controversial decision to advance the date of the Independence of the two States by a whole year. It is on this account that many people hold him responsible for the holocaust which preceded and followed."

B.R. Nanda is sharply critical of the division of the services on a communal basis, which H.M. does not even draw attention to — "But the most critical decision, of which the full implications do not seem to have been realized at the time, was to divide the civil services and the armed forces between the two successor — states".... "This total 'communalization' of the services, including the police and the military which was in a sense the concomitant of the two nation theory and the establishment of a sovereign Pakistan, was a catastrophic decision. If government employees with their guaranteed terms and conditions of service, felt unsafe in a Dominion in which they belonged to the minority community, how could that community feel safe and stay on under the new regime?" ... "Jinnah did not heed Mountbatten's warning and insisted on the division of the armed forces and the administrative services". B.R. Nanda, *The Making of a Nation: India's Road to Independence*, New Delhi, 1998, pp. 307-8.

22 See Section I. Chapter 3 & 4.

century later.[23] H.M. makes no reference to the dilemma of the Indian civil servant when confronted with his own countrymen in revolt against a Raj of which he was a much-vaunted pillar. He was perhaps fortunate in that his postings were not in politically sensitive areas or departments. When the opportunity came, at the time of independence, to do his bit for his country, he did not hesitate. He put in everything he had to ensuring the best possible advantage to India in the administrative partition of the country.

And, as if this was not task enough, he took the initiative to approach the home minister to set up an Emergency Committee for Delhi to control the worsening situation in September 1947. This Committee initially met daily, such was the gravity of the situation. It was H.M.'s task to ensure the administrative implementation of the decisions taken. Samples of the minutes of the Emergency Committee have been printed as an Appendix to indicate the scope of this task.

The initial period of serving the nation was difficult but satisfying. The challenges were immense but his untiring efforts earned deep appreciation. He had the trust, and ear, of Vallabhbhai Patel.[24] He was Jawaharlal Nehru's choice for a "first class man here to look after Kashmir affairs". H.M.'s closeness to Sardar Patel in the years 1946 to 1950 was well known. His colleagues in the ICS, L.K. Jha, V. Shankar and B.K. Nehru[25] described H.M. Patel as Sardar Patel's "close confidant", the man chosen by the Sardar to head the partition team and again as the home minister's "obvious choice" to restore peace and normality in Delhi. H.M. himself recalled "being sent for by Sardar quite frequently and that he had begun discussing with

23 H.M. Patel was finance minister and then home minister in the Janata government, 1977-79, when Morarji Desai was prime minister.

24 H.M. Patel produced a film on him, *Sardar*, directed by well known film director, Ketan Mehta, with the money coming from fellow Gujaratis, especially NRIs, who were enjoined to give generously for a fitting memorial to Gujarat's worthy son.

25 Reminiscences of H.M. Patel in commemoration volume.

me matters which did not strictly fall within the field of my official responsibility."

His relationship with Nehru was never so close. H.M. felt let down by Nehru after the Mundhra controversy and this may have jaundiced his view of Nehru when looking back on his life. However, Nehru himself shared his home minister's high opinion of H.M.'s abilities and wished to place him in charge of Kashmir and the critical food situation. He wrote to Vallabhbhai Patel to this end on 3 February 1949.[26] The letter is quoted in some detail, as it is popularly believed that it was only Sardar Patel, and not Nehru, who put his trust in him.

> "I have spoken to you already about the necessity of our having some first-class man here to look after Kashmir affairs, more especially with the possibility of a plebiscite etc. Kashmir is a highly intricate problem and we play for high stakes there. We cannot afford to do this work in an inadequate and second-rate manner...
>
> I was thinking if it was possible for H.M. Patel to be relieved of his present work in the Defence Ministry and to undertake this Kashmir business for the next few months. He would be first-rate.
>
> There are two other highly important matters which require immediate attention. One is food. As we discussed this morning, we must set up some high-powered authority to deal with this food business. Again, the whole economic set-up requires, I think, a closer day to day (review) in a variety of Ministries. For this also H.M. Patel would be eminently suitable.

B.K. Nehru makes the significant point that Jawaharlal Nehru was converted to Sardar's way of thinking on the utility of the ICS fairly soon after Independence. This is especially important as civil servants

---

26 Sardar Patel's Correspondence, Vol. I edited by Durga Das, Navjivan, Ahmedabad.

generally lament the undervaluing of the civil service by Congress leaders, with the exception of Sardar Patel, in the years after Independence.

But the civil service itself was facing the challenge of working alongside and under a political class whose power was expanding. H.M. resigned from the ICS in 1959. He felt wronged at being made a scapegoat in the political tumult of the Mundhra affair. Despite being officially exonerated he chose to quit as he felt he did not have the whole-hearted confidence of his superiors.[27]

The role of the apolitical impartial civil servant was one that H.M. Patel was familiar with. The early years of freedom saw him continuing to give his best. He seemed to have made the transition to post-Independence quite easily and was much appreciated by Nehru and Vallabhbhai Patel. His mentor, Gorwala, had soon found himself out of sync with the new regime and chosen to retire and be a critic of the new order. H.M. Patel's resignation was different from Gorwala's on the face of it, in that it was virtually forced. He was left with little choice but to quit given the expression of distrust in him by the highest in the land. Yet, the values and emotions at stake were the same, the righteous, almost pugnacious, upholding of integrity. Both men resigned at the height of their careers because of differences with the political regime. Retirement only meant the beginning of new careers; Gorwala became a crusader for probity in public life and H.M. Patel pursued a political career along with building institutions. Maurice Zinkin has a different take: "His love of action in due course got him into trouble". Love of action is certainly not the hallmark of a typical civil servant,

At one level, H.M.'s resignation in the wake of the Mundhra affair can be seen as the clash between two conflicting notions of integrity,

27 The sense of being let down by the political establishment, and specifically by Jawaharlal Nehru, persisted in later years. In reply to my queries, H.M. Patel's daughters wrote, "He could be sharply critical of Nehru vis-a-vis his tolerance of sycophants".

reliability and honesty — the public and the bureaucratic — a distinction drawn by the social anthropologist, Mattison Mines. The honest bureaucrat is one who assiduously conforms to procedure, whereas a public servant is trusted with funds and secrets because he is known to be honest. In a society where reliability is rooted in relationships of trust, an honest person is one who is known to be so, it is a function of who a person is, rather than how he acts — in contrast in the bureaucracy the criteria for determining probity is that defined by the law, not a man's reputation. And it was an irony that an eminent civil servant became the victim of a bureaucratic interpretation of reliability. He was hoist on his own petard; he was charged with having "exceeded his brief", " he had not noted the advice or decision in writing" — all proverbial sins in bureaucratic eyes. It was no doubt a political scandal and he was the bureaucrat made the scapegoat — but by a fastidiously bureaucratic interpretation of the relationship between minister and secretary. H.M. went on to operate in a society, Vallabh Vidyanagar, where relationships were of trust, and became a charismatic community leader in Mines' words. It seems appropriate that the section in Mines' book is titled 'the "big-man" versus the bureaucrat'[28] — another name for big man would be chieftain, which is English for Sardar, and Sardar Patel was H.M.'s idol.

The ICS years behind him, H.M. went on to chart a new chapter in his life, this time as an educationist and public worker. He was the chairman of the Charutar Vidya Mandal and member of the several councils and committees of the Sardar Patel University. Reactions were mixed. V.P. Menon lamented that 'this remarkable career ended under a shadow' and that 'no proper use is made of the outstanding abilities of a man who is still in the prime of life'. In contrast, a British ICS colleague approvingly described his settling down in Charutar, the land of his ancestors, as the action of a true Gandhian. A colleague in Vallabh Vidyanagar was to later describe

28 Mines, pp. 35.

him as "almost like a chieftain among his clan".[29] After 1966, he got elected to the Gujarat Legislative assembly and Parliament on the Swatantra Party ticket. In 1977, he became finance minister and then home minister of India. For some, this last achievement seemed a vindication of a man wronged. I would rather see his becoming *sarpanch* of Vallabh Vidyanagar as the significant symbolic moment, the moment of inversion. The transformation from civil servant to public servant was complete in that bold distinctive stroke. It had been an amazing journey from subdivisional officer to *sarpanch*. The rest was detail and embellishment.

## Rethinking the History of 1947

### *The Transition and its Man: The civil service, nationalism and nation building*

On a first reading, H.M. Patel's story could be read simply as an ICS memoir or a partition story. Yet, there is more to it than that. His life story evades characterization as a civil servant memoir, a freedom saga or a 'ringside' view of partition. This is despite H.M. being an eminent civil servant whose moment of glory was in the late summer of 1947 when Independence and Partition took place. In fact, it is best read as a transition story, of a civil servant who served the Raj well and served free India even better during the transition from colony to free power. H.M. Patel's life story, where a civil servant goes on to play an important role in nation building, mirrors the story of transition from colonial to independent rule. Like all autobiographies of public figures, it closely follows the biography of the nation.

There is one feature of the Indian polity in the immediate aftermath of Independence and Partition, which never fails to amaze

29 B. Tarabai, an expert in Home Science at the Sardar Patel University, Vallabh Vidyanagar.

the observer. It is the way in which two very different sets of players, ICS officials and the political leaders, worked in tandem to set the new state on the rails. It was a feat that would have done a cohesive group trained in teamwork proud. The wonder is how the ICS official reconciled with serving under Congressmen, the avowed enemies of the Raj, of which he was a proverbial pillar. Did the imperial civil servant reinvent himself as a servant of the nation as claimed by many a hoary administrator? Or was it a sell out by the Congress, under influence of its right wing, who rallied the bureaucracy as a counterpoint to radical opinion in its ranks in order to ensure that the political agenda remained within safe conservative confines. H.M.'s experience, as related in this autobiography, suggests that there was not very much reconciling or reinventing to be done.[30]

When it came to dealing with the nationalist movement, H.M. Patel's loyalties do not appear to have been pulled in contrary directions, as was the case with many of his Indian colleagues in the ICS,[31] who were torn between their duty to the service and what many increasingly perceived as a greater duty to their country. B.K. Nehru, H.M.'s colleague and close friend, recounts how he joined the ICS at a time when another Nehru, his cousin Jawaharlal, was perceived by the colonial authority as an extremely dangerous threat to the very order, pax Britannica, it would be young B.K.'s mandate to maintain. Yet he seems to have had little problem getting into the ICS despite his notoriously political family. He was asked in his viva voce examination for the ICS why he wanted to join the

30 His rootedness in Indian tradition comes across in other contexts too. H.M. Patel's example suggests that even when Indian officials were dutiful servants of the Crown during their tenure in the heaven born service, they remained Indian in a larger cultural sense. In later years, when H.M. Patel spelt out his philosophy of governance, he did not, as one might expect of a colonial civil servant, propound the Benthamite ideal of the greatest good of the greatest number. He invoked the "ancient Hindu writers" who said the integrity of the ruler and the moral sense of the citizenry was crucial.

31 Indian ICS officials comprised half the numbers at Independence.

service when half his family was in jail. He answered that he wanted to see for himself whether his being in the ICS would help his people. If he found that it would not, he would resign. This got him 277 out of 300 marks. B.K. Nehru's explanation is that what was expected of an ICS officer was truth, courage, honesty and integrity and not cringing sycophancy. It would appear that the imperial masters understood such sympathies to be natural in Indian officials and were willing to turn a blind eye as long as such nationalist sympathies were expressed discreetly and privately.

Even the Indian civil servant who did not wear his nationalism on his sleeve, like H.M., was a nationalist in a more fundamental sense. He was part of the societal consensus on the nation building agenda — to forge a strong economy and an independent polity within the framework of democracy and socialism. The bureaucracy and the political class put past differences aside to push the national agenda. "It was just after Independence and an extraordinary spirit to accomplish results moved every officer, civil and military, high and low," recalled K.M. Munshi.

Lionel Jardine, ICS, who came from a family of old India hands, writes: "A former colleague of mine in India, who on retirement became a sheep farmer, came to the conclusion that the ICS was no preparation for any other occupation. Perhaps it was because we had too much power and too little need to build a teamwork". This may have been true of the British official who had little to go back to, though even the sheep farmer's experience in India of keeping the natives from straying may have helped with minding the flock. It was certainly not true of an Indian official like H.M. who now formed a formidable team with erstwhile opponents, the political class, for the task of nation building. It may have helped that in the case of H.M. "the guiding principle of his life ... [was] his obvious devotion to the national interest"[32] A Swiss consulting engineer who

32 B.K. Nehru, ICS., later governor, Gujarat, Commemoration Volume, 1994, pp. 138.

interacted with H.M. when he was secretary in the Defence ministry recalled that he was always for the wider interest of the country, not for the ministry or department he headed.[33]

H.M. Patel and Vallabhbhai Patel worked together to retain Indian ICS officials in the service by offering British and Indian ICS separate terms and conditions for compensation for termination of services. British officials were offered lump sum compensation but Indian officials were offered continuation of service. This action of retaining ICS officials often comes in for sharp flak. Radical critics of the post-Independence regime argue that the latter did not make a complete break with the colonial past and that the ICS worked as a conservative force. There is some point in this criticism but at that time the danger of an administrative void was greater than the danger of conservatism. Many arrangements of a temporary nature were made in the interests of a smooth transition to independence.

A perceptive political scientist writes: "India benefited in this phase from the presence of two very important institutions: a well-functioning civil service and a popular ruling party, the Indian National Congress (or Congress). The civil service constituted the heart of the state that India inherited from the colonial period, and India's "new" civil service was essentially based on this colonial base (Potter, 1986). This civil service contributed to effective government and imparted political stability."[34]

Harold R. Isaacs[35] described the ICS as a "pre-nationalist corps of *elite* Indian civil servants created by the British to help them

---

33 A. Gerber.

34 Introduction, in Atul Kohli edited, *The Success of India's Democracy*, Cambridge University Press, Cambridge, United Kingdom, 2001, pp. 6.

35 Harold R. Isaacs, "From Nationalist to Post-Nationalist: a Generation Gap" in *Say Not The Struggle, Essays In Honour Of A.D. Gorwala*, Second Edition, with an Appendix containing selections from *Opinion* during the Emergency, Delhi, Oxford University Press, 1978, pp. 250-1.

govern India". He could well have been describing men like Gorwala and H.M. Patel. According to him,[36]

> The function of an *elite* bureaucracy was to serve its political masters, whoever they might be. Ministers could come and go, permanent secretaries went on forever. Such civil servants have often, in India and elsewhere, continued to perform their necessary functions through tumultuous and turbulent transfers of power, keeping the public works working while the political system was being renovated....
>
> Some became nationalist minded themselves, for some of the same reasons that so many other Indians did, or perhaps because with independence some of them were finally going to be able at last to move beyond being underlings of the British and come to occupy the top positions themselves. Many more, probably, were ambivalent, or just fearful, and most, it seems fair to guess, just hoped, like all good bureaucrats everywhere, that the *status quo* would remain as quo as possible. The Hindu-Muslim conflict and the great partition cut in its own compelling way across all other pressures and counter-pressures, defining each individual's choice of allegiances. After the fact of independence, of course, many of these *elite* civil servants became the mainstays on both sides of the new national-communal frontier of whatever effective administration there was in the years that followed.

H.M. Patel's career was the 'bridge of service' that spanned political change.

*

Some themes in H.M. Patel's story would be of exceptional interest and import from the perspective of a student of the history and politics of Independence and Partition.

---

36 *Ibid*

## *Why Partition? Why the Congress Accepted Partition*

H.M. Patel's clarity of conviction on this much debated issue is what interested me in the manuscripts in the first place.

He is of the view that there was little option but to accept partition once the communal situation deteriorated and the Interim Government ground to a standstill with the non-cooperation of Muslim League ministers.

This view is particularly significant coming from a participant and a non-Congressman. It counters the view that the Congress could have averted partition but it hesitated to go in for a mass movement and chose the safe path of a negotiated transfer of power.[37] A corollary is that the Congress leaders were old, tired and hungry for power.

H.M. Patel is critical of the fallacy of hindsight. He is clear that partition could not be avoided and that civil war could have ensued.

> Whatever any one may say today and some people do say that partition could and should have been avoided at all cost, at that time, that is during May-June 1947, there was hardly any voice of dissent: communal trouble had reared its head in a really serious manner, and there was no knowing where it might lead the country to eventually....
>
> There are those who have no hesitation in saying that this was all unnecessary. There was no need for a partition. There was no need for panicking into envisaging a civil war. Whatever this hindsight might make some people think, there is not the slightest doubt that at the time these decisions were taken, all those who had to take the decision were thoroughly convinced that a right decision had been taken, and saw in the holocaust which ensued in the immediately following weeks a confirmation of what could have happened on a far bigger scale. Perhaps the most astonishing

---

37 For a critique, see my *Independence and Partition*, 2000.

of all has been the statements which are recorded in Maulana Azad's book, which certainly are not in accordance with facts. None of the Congress leaders, except Gandhiji and Khan Abdul Ghaffar Khan, had come out openly to denounce partition. Everyone in fact at that point of time said unhesitatingly that there was no alternative to what had been agreed upon.[38]

H.M. Patel went on to explain why the Congress leaders accepted partition.

Nehru's address (to the nation on 3 June 1947) makes it abundantly clear that he was commending the partition of the country with a heavy heart. He did not like it, nor did his colleagues. But the situation that had developed in the country had forced their hands. The alternative to partition was, they felt, a long drawn out communal conflict which may well lead to a civil war. Would it not be better to let a small part of the country go, so that we could get on with the far more important task of removing poverty from the rest of the country and set it on the path of development and growth. It was considerations of this kind which won the day, and made men like Nehru and Patel accept partition against which they had fought all their lives.

As one who lived during these fateful years, and had a good opportunity to see what was happening in the country among the political parties, considering the various options open to them, against the background of the communal holocaust towards which the country appeared to be drifting after the Muslim League's fateful decision to give up the path of constitutional development and take to Direct Action, I can bear testimony to the agony through which Congress leaders and others opposed to partition passed before they finally decided to accept it.

38 See Section II, Chapter 2.

More specifically on the 3 June Plan, also known as the Mountbatten Award, H.M. Patel writes that people were simply fed up and a decision was crucial, whatever it may be.

> The Statement was on the whole well received. The people had gradually worked themselves into a peculiar mental condition. They wanted the uncertainty to come to an end. They were therefore, in a frame of mind where all they wanted was a decision, even if it involved partition of the country.
>
> .... everyone for one reason or another [was] anxious to see the end of uncertainty and violence, the bureaucrats of every hue wanted the uncertainty to end; the politicians and the public generally longed for an end to violence in daily life....

## *Delhi, September 1947*

H.M.'s account of how the authorities rallied to bring the communal situation in Delhi in September 1947 under control is of great value as a historical document.[39] The capital city was in flames, swarms of Hindu and Sikh refugees looted property and occupied abandoned Muslim houses with impunity and the exodus of Muslims to Pakistan swelled menacingly threatening to submerge all Muslim residents of the city and neighbouring areas in its wake. H.M. writes of how civil servants took the initiative, backed to the hilt by the government, and restored order on an emergency footing. The change was perhaps as dramatic as that achieved by the Mahatma in Calcutta in August 1947 and later in Delhi in January. But stern official action has scarcely been the stuff sagas are made of! And yet it is an important moment in the annals of the secular Indian state — 'a newborn babe', in Jawaharlal Nehru's words.

---

39 H.M. Patel's version helped me to critique Gyanendra Pandey's account of Delhi in September 1947 in *Remembering Partition* in *The Book Review*, August 2002.

## *On Method*

My training as a student of history generally worked well while editing the manuscripts. Having analysed many accounts of this period while doing a book on Independence and Partition, it was easy to sift interpretation from latter day prejudice as well as distinguish between contemporaneous first hand impressions and retrospective assessment within the text. Further, I could evaluate the reliability of this account and assess H.M.'s judgements in the crucible of the reality they addressed in the context of other representations. By comparing the manuscripts with the original published proceedings of the Partition Council, the Transfer of Power volumes and the diary of Wavell, I could detect and correct some errors. Further, my familiarity with the national movement in Gujarat helped me in the process of editing, for example in making a distinction between the library movement and the labourers' movement.[40]

However, on occasion, my historical training has prevented me from wielding the proverbial editorial blue pencil ruthlessly. I was of the view that the fact that the memoirs are being presented to the public more than half a century after Independence and Partition, and posthumously at that, enjoins on the historian-as-editor an onerous responsibility of faithfully presenting the original text, retaining the original idiosyncrasy of idiom, the subtlety of the

---

40 A factual slip, "Motilal Amin of the labourers' movement in Baroda," had gone undetected despite many rounds of comparison with the original. It should have been library movement not labourers' movement. Such errors could be a function of the way the manuscripts were written. H.M. would write in his own hand or dictate to his stenotypist. Perhaps the stenographer heard library movement as labourers movement or worse, heard or read right but understood wrong. He may not have understood what a library movement was — library yes, movement yes, but library movement? Perhaps he fancied the hat of an editor rather than the more prosaic one of transcriber and quietly changed library movement to labourers' movement.

prejudice, restraining the tendency to make it politically correct. An example will suffice. H.M. Patel often refers to the "Pakistani side" or even the "Muslim view" in the Partition Council when referring to the members representing the interests of the future dominion of Pakistan. The views of the members representing the future dominion of India are referred to as the "non Muslim view". This could be read, as I did initially, as equating Muslim with Pakistan and non-Muslim with India. It suggested an understanding of society in communal digits, which was unexpected. The next set of questions was obvious. Was it a latent prejudice in a colonial civil servant, who was by definition impartial, a possible flaw in an otherwise perfectly fashioned 'modern' sensibility? Or was it a bias that crept in the Swatantra years, when he became increasingly anti-Congress, not merely in his private opinion, but in his public politics, and retrospectively coloured his impressions of the partition years?. Could it not have been that the use of the terms Muslim and non-Muslim was merely a literal, value free description, given that members on the Pakistan side were Muslim and members on the Indian side were generally non-Muslim? I have therefore let it stand in the text as it was without giving it a contemporary political slant or resonance. It is for the reader to form his own opinion.

This memoir is not all encompassing. The omissions in it are many. Among others, there is no reference to H.M.'s role in resettlement of refugees after Partition, to his being deputed by the Government of India to explore the possibility of settling refugees from East Bengal in Dandakaranya or to his setting up the National Defence Academy at Khadakwasla and the National Cadet Corps. Given that H.M. was central to his time, his silence on important matters, which he was directly involved in, can be frustrating. For his role in organizing the airlift of troops to Kashmir in October 1947 and army movement into Hyderabad in 1948, we have to turn to his contemporaries, V.P. Menon and K.M. Munshi who were closely involved in these events. Writing about the defence of Kashmir, Menon describes Patel's role.[41]

> In October the raiders from the Frontier entered Kashmir and advanced towards Srinagar. I was sent to get the Maharaja's signature to the accession, and as soon as I came back to Delhi I told H.M. that the plan was going through and we would have to send troops. He was given the job of arranging for their transport and supply. He commandeered all the aircraft within reach, concentrated them where the advance units of our force were to emplane, and the very next day the first battalion had been landed on the airfield at Srinagar. Other units duly followed them, and the force was kept properly supplied. Mountbatten, who is one of the world's best experts on this subject, said that it was a job requiring the highest organizational ability and one of the finest feats of the kind he had witnessed.

Patel's little known but critical role in the integration of Hyderabad into the Indian Union is attested to by K.M. Munshi:

> During 1948, I saw him at close quarters when I was the Agent-General of the Government of India in Hyderabad. H.M. as Defence Secretary, in association with Shri V.P. Menon, the States' Secretary, worked out and implemented the campaign leading to the police action against Hyderabad. It involved maintaining peace throughout India during the crisis which was expected to follow the police action. Hyderabad was surrounded by three States: Madhya Pradesh, Madras and Bombay. The movement of the army had to be coordinated with that of the civilian authorities

41 H.M. Patel was also sent by the Government of India to brief the British Cabinet on Kashmir. A colleague later wrote that "During one such visit, he had the unique opportunity of appearing before the British Cabinet in order to explain the Kashmir situation, as it then was, and the approach and policy of Government of India relating to it." H.M. Patel keeps his counsel.

in the three States, and H.M. had to shoulder the heavy responsibility of organising the movements, both civil and military. It was a very difficult task. It had to be carried out as far as possible in secrecy.

Despite holding key positions in important ministries during the war, H.M. is silent on how the war economy was financed by inflation or the nature and fate of controls, which others have written about.[42] Maurice Zinkin, then under-secretary in Textile Control in the Industries Ministry, based in Bombay, was honest that "The millowners had no great love for the government. The best of them were Congress by conviction, the worst were black-marketeers. Given the demands of the war, some inflation was inevitable, it was a question of how much?" T.N. Kaul was of the view that the black marketeers got away with their actions by making huge donations to the Viceroy's War Fund.[43] The Report of the Income-Tax Investigation Commission of 1948, noted that "the control regulations led dealers to conceal their most profitable transactions from the knowledge of the authorities."[44] Patel, however, is silent on these issues. In this silence he is, in good civil service tradition, following in the footsteps of others venerable administrators, who were exemplars of discretion.

## Memorial to a Father

It is this quality of 'the quintessential civil servant' in H.M.Patel that interested me in his memoirs in the first place. I met 'the Patel

42 Kamtekar, "A Different War Dance: State and Class in India, 1939-1945," in *Past and Present*, Number 176, 2002. Kamtekar draws on, among others, The Report of the Income-Tax Investigation Commission, 1948, Delhi, 1949, S.C. Aggarwal, *History of the Supply Department (1939-46)*, GOI Press, Delhi, 1947, C.D. Deshmukh, *Economic Developments in India, 1946-1956*, Bombay, 1957 and K. N. Raj, *The Monetary Policy of the Reserve Bank of India*, Bombay, 1948.

43 Cited in *Ibid*, pp. 202.

44 Delhi, 1949, pp. 4 cited in *Ibid*.

daughters', as Maurice Zinkin described them, in 1997. Usha Katrak was convalescing in the family home in Vallabh Vidyanagar in September 1998. For that visit, I had donned the hat of a maverick expert on Independence and Partition, whose brief was to take a look at H.M. Patel's papers and advise the family on how best to make them available for posterity. I prepared a list of the files and their contents and suggested that the papers should ideally be placed in the Manuscript Section of the Nehru Memorial Museum and Library for scholarly and public access. This was, of course, a breathtakingly original suggestion, given that I had spent the last twenty years in that wonderful haven for students of history. So when I went in to see Usha, I thought it was to be an exchange of pleasantries. As befitting a guest taking leave of gracious hosts, I not only praised the cooking and the fine hospitality, but also waxed eloquent about the importance of the papers and the incomplete manuscripts of memoirs for the scholarly world. Little did I realise then what I was getting into when I said I would have loved to have taken up the work of completing the manuscripts if I had not been neck deep in two books. My statement was taken at face value and sure enough, when one book was out of the way, the Patel sisters were back with their old world charm and persuasive ways. And thus began this book, which I thought would be a pleasant summer interlude between serious history writing. It took over two years. During which, H.M. Patel took over everything. Now that this book is done, ironically my next book is an anthology of another Patel's writings, H.M. Patel's idol and namesake, Vallabhbhai Patel.

With Nisha da Cunha, there was a meeting of minds. Both of us came to the same conclusion, but independently, that the best way to present her father's two incomplete and overlapping manuscripts was to amalgamate the memoirs of the ICS years and the story of partition into one book. The responsibility for the assessment remains mine, of course.

Stories of H.M. Patel's amazing capacity for work and ability to command and lead his colleagues are legion. His work in riot torn

Delhi in September 1947, which forms one of the most interesting episodes of the book, is ample testimony. Amrita Patel, H.M. Patel's youngest daughter, proved to be her father's daughter in this respect. She, too, was a relentless slave driver in her mission to secure public recognition of her father's work as a civil servant. Arranging the publication of his incomplete manuscripts to mark the centenary of his birth was part of this mission. A historian-editor's conception of the book was naturally different from that of a dutiful daughter and there were times when these conceptions clashed. I could call upon her at any time to provide information, check facts, recount personal impressions, or send a book across from H.M. Patel's library. Books, like memories, can sometimes be redolent of fragrances. This one, for instance, is pervaded by the lightly flavoured half sweet *kadhi* served at Amrita's table and the *mukhvas* that followed.

# I

## Memoirs

# 1

# Growing up in Bombay

I WAS BORN AND BROUGHT UP IN THE EARLY DECADES OF the twentieth century. Bombay was then a growing city and at that time did not extend northwards much beyond Dadar and Elphinstone Road. My first recollection is of a cottage in Lower Parel. My father must have come to the city only a few years earlier and was struggling to make both ends meet. However, he was evidently in his early twenties and thought nothing of working long hours and for several employers, teaching in one household or even two, keeping accounts for another two or three employers. Later, he seemed to have extended his activities to act as a broker in the real estate business. He would leave early in the morning and almost invariably return very late in the evening. In the meantime, there would always be some guests to look after, and this was my mother's responsibility. We children were as yet, too young to be of any help to her, we were indeed more of a hindrance and at an age when we needed looking after. Nevertheless, the household always had some guests, and most of them would look after themselves as most of them were in their twenties and thirties. They would all have come down in search of 'jobs' and had been, in the meantime, staying with us. We had the good fortune, apart from other things, to have by now a reasonably spacious house, the emphasis being on the 'spaciousness' in the conditions of those times. While most would remain with us for a few days, the stay of some would extend beyond a week or ten days, even longer. Most realised how scarce was the accommodation and how great the demand. There were constant newcomers and all expected to be welcomed, and were indeed welcome. Gujarat had just emerged from a disastrous famine and everyone who could move, moved to Bombay in the hope of employment; Bombay did provide them employment but they had to find accommodation somewhere. And they found that many of those who had come earlier were willing to give them temporary shelter.

My father had been one of the early comers to Bombay and had also had the good fortune to land on his feet almost immediately after his arrival in the city. However, he had to work hard, and seems to have had the right kind of temperament and ability to adapt, which helped him in winning the goodwill of his employers who as I came to know later, belonged to various communities, Hindus, Muslims and Parsis. It was because of this fact that he was also able to help many others who followed in his footsteps. As far as I can recall, this kind of more or less regular arrival of guests continued well into the next decade. I remember well how much of my brother's and my own time was spent in looking after such guests almost until the influenza epidemic of 1918 or so. During this period, my father's financial position must have gone on improving, though not in any spectacular manner. Thus, there was never any question of our being able to afford taxis. We moved about on foot, or in local trains. At the same time, there was never any problem of money not being available for all the manifold requirements of the household, however many the guests. My mother was in complete control of the household expenses. She looked after the guests and their many requirements, including at times 'advances' to them to move about in search of employment and till they were able to settle down. One lived economically but without making anyone feel that his reasonable requirements were ever neglected. My brother and I studied almost throughout in St Xavier's High School, though our household moved from Lower Parel to a multi-storied building in Sandhurst Road, and then for some years to a suburb as far away as Kandivli, beyond Malad and a little short of Borivli. When in Kandivli, we had to leave home well before ten and returned home by the train which left Marine Lines station at 5.45 p.m. When at Sandhurst Road, we would go everyday by road, covering two or three miles each way.

Some of our guests turned out occasionally to be academically oriented or even interested in matters spiritual. One of these persuaded me to accompany him regularly to a *pathshala* where a learned speaker spoke about the teachings of the Gita, Upanishads, and on occasions, even of such other discourses on ethics and other spiritual matters. Much of this was too abstruse for my limited understanding but I did almost unconsciously absorb a good deal that helped me later. One thing it certainly did for me was to make me learn by heart a good many chapters of the Gita. To this day I can repeat the 15th Adhyaya of the Gita without any difficulty. And all this happened when I was about nine or ten years old. My uncle and my father had both been primary school teachers, but their learning was profound. This was particularly the case with my uncle, in whose society I spent many of my early vacations.

In one way or another, thus my brother, who was only a couple of years older and I grew up in a most worthwhile atmosphere; where the academic side was not neglected and social duties were instilled in us without any special effort.

Another good fortune that came our way was the necessity, because of epidemics of various kinds to which the city fell victim, for our parents to send us away from Bombay to my uncle's and on one occasion to a model boarding house — modern for those days — where we came under influences of a totally different kind, where we were exposed to village life under proper guidance, and were also given an opportunity to live in a small town but not city or rather urban surroundings. Another unusual good influence came our way. Men of proven talent, poets, novelists and philosophers were also welcome in our Bombay home. Bhikshu Akandanand of Sastu Sahitya fame was a regular visitor, so were many men like the poet Kaun and a host of others whose books found their way soon after publication in my father's home. It is through them that I was able to get a glimpse of the great patriot Dadabhoy Naoroji in his house in Andheri. Men like Motibhai Amin who revolutionised the library movement in Baroda state, came frequently to our home in Bombay. All this in its own way played no small role in our upbringing.

Luck continued to play a surprising role in my life. My mother had to seek the help of doctors for herself as also for her numerous friends and relatives. Two of these doctors, a Dr. Rele and a Dr. Bhajekar became her friends, not just a patient-doctor relationship but that of family friends. It is because of this that when Dr. Bhajekar decided to go to England to arrange for his son's medical studies, he suggested to my mother that she should consider seriously if it would not be a good thing for one or both of her sons also to go along with his son to England. My brother was not keen on going, at least not at that stage. I had just got into the matric and because of the age restriction that was then in force, I would have had to spend two years in the matric class. This was held out as an inducement to me to go to England. There was also at the time, a special attraction for promising students to try and get into the Indian Civil Service (ICS), for which the examinations were held only in England. It was decided that I should attempt that exam, and my father showed readiness to set aside the necessary amount of money for the entire period of study.

As it turned out, this decision of his was most fortunate from my point of view. The idea of spending such a large amount at one time arose from the fact that foreign exchange was then more favourable to rupee holders, and my father was in a position to spare the cash.

Some four or more years later, my father got into financial difficulties, and he would have had much trouble in ensuring regular remittances to me. As it was, his troubles kept getting worse, and in what might have been my last year, assuming I was able to clear all my exams at first attempt, my Oxford 'Modern Greats', my London Commerce Degree as an external student, and the competitive examination for the ICS, my father's financial position became particularly critical. Once again Dr. Bhajekar came to our rescue. His son Madhav, who was in charge of my finances, told me how matters stood. He saw that my money was about to come to an end, and it was not known when additional money would come along. He resolved the immediate difficulty by sharing his allowance with me. Meantime, Dr. Bhajekar found a helper. He ran into a Mr. Dhavle (I learnt much later that he was an ICS officer) serving in Bihar, married to the daughter of one of India's greatest sons, Gopal Krishna Gokhale. Dr. Bhajekar met him by accident when he was on a short visit to Poona, and told him of my problem. Dr. Bhajekar vouched for me as a promising young student. This was truly very good of him, for at that stage I had my London matric first division as my only academic success to put forward. But Dr. Bhajekar's assessment seems to have weighed with Mr. Dhavle who expressed his willingness to help. He must have been a truly remarkable person, for he not only agreed to finance me for that one year's stay, but indicated further that he did not expect me to repay in financial terms but would accept my assurance that I would, in turn, help young and promising students to the maximum extent possible. What an amazing piece of generosity. Persons totally unknown to me were prepared to help me in this astonishing manner. Whatever other effect this incident had on me, one thing I had almost subconsciously adopted as a guiding principle for myself, to do whatever I could possibly do for anyone who stood in need of help. This was, apart from my unwritten undertaking, to help deserving students whenever and wherever possible. I can say without any hesitation whatsoever, that I have adhered to this undertaking. Once the decision was taken that I was to go abroad, and even the date of my departure fixed, and even the ship I was to travel by, *Loyalty* (a steamer that had very recently been acquired by Scindia Navigation Company Ltd.), my parents put it to me that I should agree to return after three or four years, marry, and go back to complete my studies, or marry at once and then go. I said that I would much rather marry immediately and return only after I had completed my studies. And this was what was decided. My marriage took place only some weeks before the date of my departure for England in June 1920.

Little did I then realise or have any idea of how great a good fortune this marriage was going to turn out for me. My father might quite easily have been persuaded to accept one of the several other proposals that were before him. He, however, chose to adhere to the one he had agreed upon long before it was decided that I was to go to England. There was, it appears, some opposition to this marriage but that was soon overcome by the determination of my brother-in-law to be, that his sister's marriage to me must be carried through, whatever the opposition from some of his relatives. All these petty incidents, petty in retrospect, come vividly to my mind. I had very little understanding of the cause for this opposition. I now know that these relatives felt that the marriage was, in their view, below the status of my wife's family. There is a complicated system by which the status of the various families is reckoned. First of all, the families must belong to the six villages to be accepted as among the best families. My village was among the first six as was my wife's, but within each village was a hierarchy and according to this, mine was thought among the top of my village, perhaps not quite the top, whereas my wife's was among the topmost of her village. Another point to be noted was that it was an unwritten law that there would be no marriages between persons belonging to the same village. My brother-in-law, who was then still a medical student, sought the assistance of all his fellow students, and with their help saw to it that the wedding celebrations went off smoothly. In those days, the bridegroom's party, running into a few hundred, would be guests at the bride's village for as many as three days. Altogether, marriages in those days were quite an expensive affair. In addition to the guests from outside, the bride's party would also have to feed almost the whole village for virtually the three days. The ornaments to be given to various members of each family and other family members were in addition to what had to be given to the bride herself, and this would depend on the family status. Fortunately, at this point of time, an undertaking had been reached strictly limiting the dowry to a sum of Rs.301. This understanding was binding to all the families of the six villages. Today, sadly, this understanding is totally ignored and the amount of dowry has become a matter of bargaining. The only special condition laid down by me or rather, my father, was that my wife should spend, during my absence in England, the greater part of her time with Dr. Bhajekar's family. It was hoped that this would enable her to acquire a certain amount of knowledge of English and some idea also of the way in which the slightly Anglicised families lived. Here again it will be seen that Dr. Bhajekar's interest in our family continued unabated.

Meantime, India was not standing still during the period I was away. Mahatma Gandhi's activities had commenced, and with them an extraordinary revolution had come about in the lives of the people of India, and in particular of the women of India, who had never stirred out of their houses, thought nothing of taking part in the picketing of liquor shops and of joining rallies and demonstrations. It was inevitable that young girls should be attracted by these movements and my wife too was drawn towards them, but mainly towards the wearing of *khadi*, and activities designed to help women of backward classes and particularly, Harijans.

When I look back on my marriage, it astonishes me that it never occurred to me to ask whom I was marrying. I accepted that what was being arranged by my parents must be the best and most satisfactory. I had barely a glimpse of my wife before I left for England. And this marriage worked out extraordinarily well. We were happy and never had any regrets. It is obvious that the major reason for the success was our understanding, our unquestioning acceptance of the institution and our determination to see that our marriage worked well. We learnt to adjust ourselves to each other. When the children came, there were never any differences about how they were to be brought up. Almost instinctively, we seemed to have agreed that they were to have the most liberal education possible, that to the extent our views counted when they grew up, while we would urge them to remain within our small circle, they would be free to make up their own minds. Where my wife discovered this approach for herself, I cannot say, but she did. She had no hesitation in saying what she would have preferred but having done so, she accepted her children's point of view.

# 2

# Preparing for the Indian Civil Service

I LEFT INDIA AS ARRANGED, BY THE SS *LOYALTY*, SCINDIA'S first passenger ship for England, in June 1920. The Bhajekar family had left earlier by a P&O ship, and with his usual considerateness, Dr. Bhajekar had arranged for me to travel with two of his friends. One of these, Karmarkar, the famous sculptor, was my cabin companion. Nothing particularly interesting happened during the voyage and we arrived in London to be met by Dr. Bhajekar. He had taken a spacious flat in St. John's Wood, Baker Street, and both Karmarkar and I began our stay in London in Dr. Bhajekar's flat. He had already been on the lookout for a good tutor to coach me for the London matric. Dr. Bhajekar found a Mr. Baker, a Cambridge Wrangler, who was taking five or six students every year for coaching for various entrance examinations, at Oxford, Cambridge, and London primarily. At the time I was accepted, there were at Mr. Baker's a couple of English students, two students from Thailand, one from the West Indies, one from Switzerland and now myself from India.

Accepting my tutor's advice, it was decided that I should prepare for the London matric and appear as soon as I was ready. Provisionally it was decided that I should appear for the exam by June-July 1921. As it was not practicable for me to have coaching arranged in Sanskrit, which was my second language in India, it was decided that I should offer Latin and French besides the other usual subjects like Maths and History. Mr. Baker himself was a mathematics student, but he was able easily to find really fine tutors for me in the other subjects. Mr. Baker had selected his residence in Felixstowe very wisely. The house had a large number of bedrooms and bathrooms, and it is my recollection that although Mr. and Mrs. Baker lived in the house along with a grown up son of theirs, we, his lodgers, were not inconvenienced in any way. Felixstowe, even those days had, besides a beach, a golf club, a swimming pool, and of course, several tennis clubs. I was the only one preparing for the London matric, and teaching facilities in various subjects had to be arranged only for me. I was very fortunate in the teachers selected for me. They were all very well qualified in their respective subjects and, what is more, were also excellent teachers. One was the vicar of a neighbouring parish, and had done English at Cambridge. He was an excellent guide for me. He encouraged me in reading a variety of books, which greatly enriched not merely my knowledge of English, but also gave me an insight into English character as also a broader view of other rich literature, French, Russian, German and Italian. I was also enabled to read something of Latin and Greek literature. A young lady, who had just done her History, Tripos was selected to help me in History. All my teachers were exceptionally qualified and loved teaching, even when teaching was not their normal profession. In this eminently fine atmosphere, I spent my first year-and-a-half in England. I had no idea how good my preparation for the London matric was but my teachers were satisfied. They had some doubt about my Latin, because I had not acquired sufficient familiarity with Latin literature, and consequently my knowledge of the language was very limited. I got over this difficulty for the purposes of this particular examination by learning by heart a glossary of a large number of words prescribed for the understanding of selected passages of 'unseen' Latin prose! All in all, my teachers felt reasonably confident of my success. I was successful and passed in the first division. I had not expected to do so well, but thanks to the first division, I had no difficulty in securing admission to Oxford and was accepted without any hesitation.

My stay at Felixstowe was almost continuous, except towards the end, when, through our Swiss friend's prompting, I decided to undertake a journey to Switzerland, first as my friend's guest, and then as soon as possible through his sister's help — the sister lived a few miles out of Geneva — with a suitable Swiss family. One of the English boys also decided to accompany me up to Paris, where we had planned to stay for a few days. The Paris visit was short and uneventful. My Swiss friend had been active in the meantime and arranged for me to stay with a family in Nyon, a few miles from Geneva on Lake Leman. Nyon was very conveniently situated between Geneva and Lausanne. The family I lived with had a lovely house on the lake itself and at the time I stayed there, the family consisted of the head of the family, a widow, with whom stayed her daughter, still unmarried, and three of her sons. It was a large family, two older sons stayed with their own families. The daughter did some occasional teaching, while two of the younger sons were still completing their education, both being students of engineering. The third and older son was already gainfully employed. Since they had a spare bedroom, they occasionally took paying guests and I happened to be the first one to come their way. I spent a very happy vacation lasting a little over two months with them.

There is no doubt that my stay in Nyon constituted a major landmark in my life. It was the first time in a manner of speaking that I was wholly on my own. Until then, I had always had the feeling that there was some 'elder' watching over me, if I stood in need of help. Here in Switzerland, in this small house in the town of Nyon, amidst complete strangers, however friendly they were, for the first time I felt I was really on my own, and thrown on my own resources. I began to think for myself. People were always asking questions about India, as if I were an expert on India, and could give them information about a country about which their information was, as even I began to realise, infinitely less than my own. Indeed, I was even asked to write about India by one of their leading newspapers! And I had the temerity to write for it, not worrying about how limited my own knowledge or information was. I must have written something that was clearly not wholly worthless, for it provoked some correspondence, which in turn necessitated my having to write again to substantiate or clarify what I had written initially. I am glad, however, that I knew my limitations and did not allow myself to be tempted into writing more about India. At that time, with the immaturity of the young, I was apt to be carried away by the woes of the downtrodden, the sufferings of nations dominated by the imperialists and generally felt oppressed by what appeared to be the hardships of the poor and the less fortunate.

I made quite a few friends. They were young, even though older than myself, and the circle among whom I moved were also all not only well-educated but also trained for some occupation or other, no one was outrageously wealthy, but no one also who was not moderately well off. Their wants seemed even to me not extraordinary but each one seemed to be never lacking for anything that he felt to be out of his reach. It was perhaps a good thing that the first glimpse I had of Europe was through Switzerland. The people were generally well off and had no grouse against anyone.

The next time I was in Europe was a year or so later, in Germany, which was then still in the process of recovering from the First World War, and its aftermath, the most heartrending of which was the period of terrible inflation. Even a description of what the people had to go through was sufficient to make one realise the extent of their suffering. The adoption of a new currency without undue delay helped the country as a whole. But it would take long for the people to forget what they had suffered and the hardships they had to endure. For some, this period of hardship was even now not wholly over.

What every German had to go through, the last vestiges of that period, I was still able to see for myself, when I visited that country in 1923. My main stay on this occasion was in Heidelberg. I lived with a family of an erstwhile professor at the University of Heidelberg. The family had been through very hard times during the war, and was now slowly regaining its normal balanced way of life. I was once again lucky to find myself a member of a German family of academically oriented individuals. They organised a number of walking tours for me. Sometimes one or other member of the family would accompany me. At other times, they would arrange for their friends to accompany me. Nothing could have been more delightful than these walks in the forests of Germany. I developed a taste for walking. One most unforgettable experience was a walking tour extending over almost a week through the Black Forest. The Germans, as a people, seemed addicted to walking. During these tours, I met an extraordinarily large number of people with rucksacks slung over their shoulders striding along and singing in chorus. Heidelberg is one of the oldest universities in Germany and its student population comprised of the studious as well as the fun loving. One characteristic feature of the German universities was their clubs. Every student was almost invariably a member of at least one of these. Beer drinking was almost universal and hardly anyone was not fond of it; women students were almost as keen on beer as men. Liking for work appeared to be another of their favourites. No one liked to be without something or other to occupy him or her. Even in those days, the industriousness of the Germans as a people could not but make us Indians ponder. And those were the days when our own people were relatively speaking, an industrious people.

But what one saw in Germany was something which exceeded anything that I saw in England or elsewhere in Europe, except perhaps Holland. The British, and more particularly the Swiss, were undoubtedly industrious, who liked work when it was necessary and did it well. With the Germans, however, there was a difference. I spent several vacations during later years in other parts of Germany and came in touch then with the German youth movement, an important wing of which was even at that time the nascent Hitler youth.

I spent every vacation in this manner, either going somewhere in Europe or some holiday spot in Great Britain, like the Isle of Wight, or to some village in Devonshire or Dorset. One vacation I spent in Scotland, in Edinburgh and its surroundings. All this was good education for me. I acquired confidence in myself besides coming to know, however briefly, a variety of people of different types, character, professions, and intellectual caliber.

During term time, I worked, but the system of tuition at Oxford was such that I was left very much on my own, to read as much or as little as I liked and the subjects I liked. As long as I did my 'tutorials' regularly and to my tutor's satisfaction, all would be well. The tutor would suggest each week the books I should read for the essay he would ask me to write on, which he would do his best to tear into pieces when I submitted it to him or give his enthusiastic approval if he thought the essay deserved it. He would indicate the manner in which the essay could be improved or pointed out why he felt I had neglected some relevant aspects of the subject, and because of that the essay lacked the clarity or thoroughness it required. This kind of teaching, and extensive reading suited me very well. While I read much that was relevant to the subjects of my choice, I also indulged in a great deal of reading just for pleasure, which in practice meant that my chosen subjects were sometimes neglected. One attended lectures relating to the subject, but again one was left to decide which lectures to attend, though the tutors would always be ready to help. If say, G.D.H. Cole was lecturing, we might decide to attend his lecture, as he was known to be an interesting lecturer in preference to some other lecturer. When the term began, a choice was made about the lectures to attend, and one usually chose quite a large number bearing in mind the various subjects one ought properly to attend. The lectures chosen depended on the known experience of the lecturer but quite often it was because the lecturer spoke well and attractively. As the term proceeded, the number of lectures one attended diminished, as one's interest in the subject or in the lecturer's own attractiveness as a lecturer diminished. I attended lectures fairly regularly but I had no hesitation in 'cutting' those that I found to be dull. In spite of so much freedom, somehow one managed to acquire quite a deal of knowledge of the various subjects selected, as also of extra-curricular matters.

If one was politically ambitious, there was plenty of scope for debating on all manner of subjects in the various clubs to which one belonged. The most important of these was the 'Union' where every so often, a major debate would take place in the presence of a distinguished visitor. The major Indian club was known as the 'Indian Majlis', where Indians debated regularly on subjects of Indian interest, and where interestingly enough, even candidates for the Indian Civil Service had no hesitation in criticising policies of the Government of India. The atmosphere of freedom was contagious. Oxford and Cambridge authorities took all such outpourings of students in their stride, for experience had shown them that only a very few meant all that they said so eloquently. In most cases, it was a sort of intellectual exercise. This was, in fact, a sensible way of dealing with such utterances. This does not mean that students were insincere, far from it, but during university debates and discussions, one tended to view most things in terms of an intellectual exercise, intended to rile others or get a rise out of them.

Finally, many also took part in games which took a good deal of one's time. I, for instance, played tennis on occasions but most afternoons I went for long walks with friends between lunch and teatime. The astonishing thing was that in spite of all such miscellaneous activities, one was able to put in quite a lot of work and to see that work did not suffer. At the same time, I must admit that the real work was done during vacations. That was when you were very much your own master, and free to work when in the mood. The greater part of each vacation I spent in my own company. I had made a few intimate friends and we spent a week or so of every vacation time together.

It was during the long summer vacation of 1925 that I came across an interesting person called Eric Dutt. He was a student of science. His father was at the time advocate general in what is now Madhya Pradesh then known as the Central Provinces. He was a person of considerable charm. We came together in Paris at a mutual friend's house. We spent a few days together and I watched him at work. He put forward an attractive proposition. I allowed myself to be tempted by it. I imagine that the ground had been prepared for it by the fact that I had, about that time, learnt that my funds were likely to be exhausted before long. If I want to provide myself with a justification for deciding to discontinue my studies at that late stage, shortly before I had to appear for my final examination at Oxford, that could be the only explanation that made sense. However, it may be, I did decide to throw myself in with Eric Dutt's proposition, and to return to Oxford only to inform the head of my college of my decision. He was quite shocked but failed to make me change my decision. He did, however, say that should I change my mind, I should not hesitate and return promptly. This is something that could happen only at Oxford. He had rightly sensed the possibility of my changing my mind. I did come to my senses within some three months, and resumed my studies, when barely three months were left before I would have to sit for the final examination at Oxford, and only a few more weeks, therefore, for the ICS competitive examination. I did not do too well at the schools at Oxford, but managed to do much better at the competitive examination for the ICS, sufficiently well to be among those who had been declared successful. I appeared for the B.Com. examination of London University as an external student a little later and was successful. The success at the ICS competitive examination meant a further stay of a year as a probationer. During this year, we were called upon to study, among other subjects, the Indian Penal Code, Indian Evidence Act, and the Criminal Procedure Code. We had to acquire some knowledge, however rudimentary, of the language of the province to which one was to be posted. We had also to qualify in riding. I was able to clear all these without any difficulty, and embarked on the P&O ship, SS *Rajputana*, I think and landed in Bombay some time in October 1927.

# 3

# District Officer in the Sindh Countryside

ON ARRIVAL IN INDIA IN OCTOBER 1927, I REPORTED AS I HAD been advised to in my letter of appointment to the Indian Civil Service, to the resident deputy secretary, government of Bombay. He turned out to be a much younger British officer than I had expected him to be. He was friendly enough, but strictly businesslike. He informed me that I was posted to Sind, and would receive my district posting from the commissioner in Sind. It was only when he asked if I knew the Sindhi language and added sympathetically that Sind was quite good and I would come to like it, that I began to suspect that it was perhaps, not a very popular posting. Not having any idea whatsoever of Sind or any of the other divisions of Bombay Presidency, I had no preferences. I, therefore, merely inquired how soon I was expected to report in Karachi and how best I could proceed there. I was advised to reach Karachi preferably by train as soon as possible and to inform before hand the assistant commissioner in Sind, when I proposed to arrive and report for orders of posting.

After consulting my parents and various friends, it was decided that I should give myself a fortnight or so before reporting for duty. I had to get myself some clothes, which I would almost certainly require for formal occasions, meet relatives and friends of my parents in Bombay and go to our ancestral village in Gujarat. My village was in, what was then, the princely state of Baroda. It is one of the more progressive villages and educationally was in the vanguard amongst the villages of the area known as Charotar. Most important of all, accompanied by my parents, I went to offer thanksgiving prayers to Goddess Ambaji on my safe return from the long overseas journey, in her most sacred abode in the north Gujarat princely state of Danta.

All these tasks and duties took some time to perform and it was therefore, almost three weeks after my landing in Bombay that I was able to report to the commissioner in Sind, a Mr. G.A. Thomas. I learnt later that he was known in the service as 'God Almighty Thomas', underlining his essential characteristic, not so much of arrogance, as of impatience with a difference of opinion or opposition. On my first meeting with him, he was most friendly. It was his assistant Sladen, the assistant commissioner, who was most helpful and full of very practical and useful advice. He informed me of my posting as supernumerary assistant collector, Larkana District. This meant that I would be attached to an experienced assistant collector, in this case A.D. Gorwala, who was at that time in charge of the Larkana sub-division of Larkana District in Upper Sind. Sladen told me to take my own time before going on to Larkana and to equip myself with the kind of clothes, etc., I would need as a touring officer. Upper Sind would be severely cold and I would have to do a good deal of riding, a horse or a camel. I was informed also of the departmental examinations that I would have to pass as also to acquire a certain degree of proficiency in spoken and written Sindhi language. I took his advice in every respect and remained a week in Karachi.

On my arrival in Karachi, I was met at the station by Manilal Mohanlal. He was a total stranger to my father and me, but had been asked by a friend of my father in Bombay to look after me during my stay in Karachi. He insisted on my staying at his house and just brushed aside any other suggestion. Manilalbhai must have been then in his late forties or early fifties. He had an export-import business and was quite obviously well to do. I was most fortunate in coming to know him immediately on my arrival in Sind. He had been in Karachi for many years and was highly respected among businessmen of all communities. He was straight, and lived in accordance to an extremely strict code of conduct. He was a remarkable person, simple in his habits and way of living. I was indeed fortunate in having been introduced to such a person in Sind. Throughout my stay in Sind, he was a source of great strength to me. Our relationship developed into friendship and I stayed at his home whenever I was in Karachi. He had been in Karachi for a large number of years and though a Gujarati, knew Sind and Sindhis very intimately. I discovered very soon that he was an exception to the generality of Indian businessmen, in that he, in all the years I knew him, never once seek any advantage for himself because of his acquaintance with me and through me of the large number of officers in high positions whom I came to know during the course of my service while I was in Sind, or even later when I was with the Government of India. Our relationship continued on that cordial basis until he passed away many years later in the late fifties in Bombay, where he had settled down after he had been forced to leave Karachi a year or so after Partition. He had continued to stay in Karachi after 15 August 1947 at my instance, for I had been optimistic enough at the time to think that Hindus would be treated well and welcomed as fellow citizens, once the initial emotional outburst had passed. I had felt certain that everything would function normally in spite of the initial holocaust. But I was wrong and it soon become impossible for Hindus to live in Karachi with safety to person and property.

Along with most others, Manilal and his family too left all they had behind in Karachi and moved to Bombay with what they could carry in their personal baggage. He never reproached me for my unwise and unsound advice. I was glad that he was able to reestablish himself to some small extent, thanks to the high reputation that he enjoyed in business circles.

Sind was, at that time, a part of Bombay Presidency. I served there in various positions for a little over eight years and it so happened that my last appointment was as Sind separation officer. The report that I prepared was for the separation of Sind from the Bombay Presidency, making Sind a separate state. I wrote that report very largely in Poona. It was accepted almost in its entirety and given effect fairly promptly.

The first of those eight years was entirely a training period during which I served first as a supernumerary assistant collector attached to the assistant collector, Larkana sub-division and after passing my first departmental examination was put in charge of one taluka (tehsil). After I passed my second departmental examination, I was given independent charge as assistant collector in-charge of a sub-division in Sukkur district. During the period of training, I was attached to A.D. Gorwala, who had himself at that time served for three years. He was an officer of outstanding ability, drive, and initiative.

It was one night's journey to Larkana from Karachi. Gorwala had sent his 'boy Dhanji' to meet me, as Gorwala himself was in 'Camp', several miles from Larkana. (Dhanji must have been at least thirty years old at the time, and had been with Gorwala ever since he joined service. He was to remain with Gorwala until he retired!) Dhanji told me that I was to join Gorwala. After ten o'clock, I was ready to leave for the 'Camp'. [I might explain here that it was the normal practice for every officer, in particular the ICS officer to have a learn in his service right from the day he joined his service. And if he suited his master he would certainly be with him till he married and then quite often may continue even afterwards till he retired if his wife was prepared to put up with him or he (boy) with his wife! One came to depend heavily on help like this.] Meantime, my 'boy' whose services I had engaged in Karachi, organised whatever I might need for camp life for days, clothes, bedding, etc. We travelled in a tonga and arrived at the camp about one in the afternoon. Gorwala had himself just returned from his morning inspection tour, and was emerging from his bath as I arrived. We met briefly and went straight for lunch. It was at lunch that we became acquainted, an acquaintance that developed into friendship, which lasted for years thereafter until his death at the age of eighty-nine in 1989.[1] This friendship may be said to be yet another stroke of luck for me. Gorwala was not just an outstanding administrator. He was thorough and meticulous in everything he did, and also carried out in everything he did, the teachings of the Gita — 'But thou, want not, ask not, find full reward of right in doing right. Let right duties be thy motive not the fruits thereof, and live in action, labour, make thy acts thy piety, condemning gain and merit, equable in good and ill' applied to him in every way.

Gorwala used to have quite a strenuous programme of work every day, Sunday included. He would leave for his field inspection on camel-back as soon as it was daylight around some time between six and seven. Land revenue in Sind was paid on the basis of the area and the crop sown. The village officer, known in Sind as tapedar, was expected to visit every cultivated field and record the nature of the crop. It was expected of the assistant collector that he would carry out an on-the-spot physical verification of a certain percentage of the tapedar's field book in which he was required to record the nature of the crops sown in each survey number in the villages for which he was responsible. In the course of the morning, the assistant collector would pass through several villages in each of which he would make a brief halt to meet the local gentry, discuss with them their immediate problems and take whatever action he

1 Born 9 December 1900, died 4 December 1989.

considered necessary in regard to those problems. At times, he would also go to the village school if the village had a school and inspect its working before proceeding further. Occasionally, it would be necessary for the assistant collector to inspect some reported encroachment of government land, in respect of which he might have received a complaint. He would also readily carry out other inspections as may be found to be necessary. The whole of the morning would thus be spent outdoors, and we would return to the camp towards 1 o'clock. On our return, we would bathe as that would help in removing our physical fatigue and sit down to our mid-day meal. Almost immediately after lunch Gorwala would proceed to do his files. The method of dealing with them was unusual, or at least to me it appeared unusual at that time. The head clerk would read the latest noting on a file and such other connected noting as would give a clear picture of what was at issue and Gorwala would dictate his recommendations or his orders. Thereafter, he would proceed to deal with the applications and complaints from people from all over the sub-division. He would direct appropriate action to be taken on each application. Sometimes, this might mean fixing another date for the respondent, that is the person complained against, to be called for a hearing of his side of the case. It was remarkable to see the large number of disputes that got settled in that manner. The number of applicants each day used to be quite phenomenally large.

In retrospect, I would say that no better method of training could have been devised. What the newcomer was presumed to have was reasonably trained intelligence. The new officer had to learn by watching his senior at work. He was, in effect, told right at the outset that what he learnt depended very much on himself and that he was expected to exercise initiative, to act with a sense of responsibility. Further, that he had to learn to judge the nature and character of the people with whom he had to work: those under one, those who were one's colleagues or superiors, and those whose welfare depended upon the soundness of his judgement. I, thus, proceeded to watch

Gorwala at work both in the office and in the field, ask questions and sought clarifications as I considered necessary. I accompanied Gorwala during his morning tour of field inspections, saw how he conversed with people, landowners, cultivators and others. As the local language was Sindhi, which at that point of time I did not know at all, I was therefore considerably handicapped. Gorwala had acquired mastery over the language. I decided to learn Sindhi as quickly as possible and as well as possible, for it was clear that without a satisfactory command over the language it would not be possible for me to discharge my duties adequately. The assistant commissioner in Sind had advised me to engage the services of a Sindhi teacher, which I did before leaving Karachi. It so happened the same teacher had taught Sindhi to Gorwala. I was fortunate indeed in my Sindhi teacher, for Kishan Singh was an outstanding teacher of languages. He had given me a few lessons while I was in Karachi and my subsequent instruction was through correspondence. It did not take me very long to understand the spoken language, but it took me quite some time before I was able to handle the language efficiently. (In those days, the government used to give rewards for passing extra language examinations at a higher level of proficiency, and I was able thus to win two rewards, one of Rs.500 and another of Rs.1000, quite a useful sum in those days.)

The two touring seasons from September — October to March — April of 1928 and 1929-30 were also most educative. I managed to visit every part of my sub-division and endeavoured to put into practice Gorwala's methods for sorting out the troubles of the poor. I met with considerable success. However, I also realised that whoever chose to utilise those methods, had to realise their limitations and above all had to develop a sensitivity which would enable him to judge where to stop and to let the normal course of law and justice play its part. During the period I was attached to him, he was appointed to officiate as collector of Larkana district. Fortunately for me, I remained attached to him, which enabled me to see him at work not only as an assistant collector of a sub-division, but also as a full-fledged collector of a district.

During the days that Gorwala acted as collector, I realised what great responsibilities a collector carried. For one thing, he was responsible for the entire district, which meant usually at last three sub-divisions, sometimes even four, each of which usually had three or four tehsils or talukas. He was responsible in the final resort for law and order though the district superintendent of police relieved him of the large number of responsibilities that were assigned to the police department. In the same way, he had to see that the lower magistracy functioned properly, and to the satisfaction of the district and sessions judge. The collector was, in an overall way, held responsible for ensuring that all facilities were available to the other district officers to be able to discharge their duties satisfactorily such as officers of the Irrigation and Public Works Department, Agriculture Department, Forest Department, Education Department and a host of other departments. This brief experience of seeing a collector at work proved very useful to me very soon afterwards when I was required to be in charge of my district for a short while during the very first year in which I was given independent charge of a sub-division, on completion of my training.

Gorwala's officiating charge brought to me an unexpected advantage. I had a glimpse of the way in which the British ICS officers recorded their confidential views on officers serving under them. The collector, a Mr. Acott who had proceeded on leave, had had only a few opportunities of seeing me and even less of seeing any of my work — I was only functioning as a magistrate who was entrusted with powers of a third class magistrate, that is, had power to sentence the guilty person to one month's imprisonment or a fifty rupee fine. I had only just been entrusted with the charge of a tehsil or a taluka. The collector had therefore, recorded that he had not much opportunity of seeing my work, but 'my wife considers that he has a nice manner'. I mention this only to indicate that where an ICS officer was concerned, it was considered important even to assess how he conducted himself socially and not just as a district officer. By the time the hot weather ended, that is sometime in October or soon afterwards, a permanent collector took charge. He was a totally different kind of officer, a Mr. Maclachlan, also a very experienced officer. He took quite a lot of interest in me and I too profited much from his accounts of some of his experiences in the different districts in which he had served during the eighteen to twenty years of his service.

It was very fortunate for me that I was attached to an officer such as A.D. Gorwala. He was not merely an officer with an extraordinarily high sense of values and a very strict code of conduct. He was exceptional in as much as he worked with only one objective, how best to serve the people. We are nowadays accustomed to see the expression 'to serve the people' being used loosely and rather frequently by politicians, in particular. When I use the expression, however, in respect of Gorwala, I do so in its very precise sense. He used his power, position and prestige that he enjoyed as an ICS officer to render assistance to the poor and the suffering cultivator. In Sind, at that time, zamindars owned large areas of land and paid land revenue, even at the then prevailing low rate running into thousands and even lakhs of rupees. The poor cultivator had right only to a small share of what he produced, with no certainty that he would be allowed to continue to cultivate the land from year to year. His position was very much at the mercy and whim of the zamindar. Not a few of the zamindars also, had no compunction in misbehaving with the womenfolk of the cultivators. It was sincerely surprising that moneylenders flourished and lands owned by smaller zamindars frequently passed into the hands of the unscrupulous moneylenders.

It was Gorwala's endeavour to see that the poor received justice whenever it came to his notice that the well-to-do and powerful elements of the society sought to take advantage of him and to exploit him. He dispensed his justice through persuasion, supplemented by judicious application of pressure. But the manner in which he worked certainly resulted in the dispensation of real justice. This left a very deep impression among the people that even to this day, some fifty years after he left Sind, people remember and long for what came to be known as Gorwala's justice!

This manner of functioning did make him unpopular with the big zamindars in particular, as well as the more wealthy and influential money-lending Hindu community. But Gorwala, caring neither for popularity nor for promotion, went his way doing what he considered to be the right thing to do. In a case, which became famous, Gorwala resisted all pressure to persuade him to drop proceedings against an extremely powerful personality, who had done an irreparable wrong to a small cultivator. There was reason even to believe that he was involved in encompassing the death of a cultivator whose wife, it was generally believed, he had kidnapped. The then commissioner in Sind conveyed to Gorwala a message he had received from a member of the viceroy's Executive Council in Delhi that the matter should be dropped. Gorwala replied unhesitatingly that it was out of the question since the matter had already gone too far. The commissioner, though in full agreement with Gorwala, advised him that it would be expedient to let the matter go no further. Gorwala was prepared to face the consequences, but would not accept the counsel of expediency.

This case provides a good illustration of the way in which officers worked in those days. The senior officers stood by their juniors in what they did in the course of their official duty. When on occasion, rare though they were, there was a difference of opinion, they would still allow the officer to go his own way if he chose to accept full responsibility for his actions. If the country wants good administration, then some such code of conduct will have to be accepted by our nascent democracy. Only then would officers function fearlessly and with integrity, and the politicians would be true to their loudly expressed loyalty to our constitution.

Even during the period I was with Gorwala, I saw for myself that a great many cultivators had their grievances redressed, both by his own direct action and because of the free access every cultivator had to his house or his camp. Most officers, however, could not emulate Gorwala's fervour, but all members of the ICS endeavoured to see that no identifiable injustice was allowed to take place and considered it their duty to help the deprived in this extra curricular manner. I cannot help thinking that this system of training was good and in conjunction with the normal practice of leaving a civil servant to work in the district for some ten years or so helped in securing for the government an experienced team of officers.

The civil servant was thoroughly trained in maintaining law and order, and what was always important, a rapid disposal of complaints. Grievances were not allowed to remain un-dealt with longer than was absolutely unavoidable. The coming of the jeep has, in some ways, made the officers treat touring as of far less importance than it used to be in my days. This is a great pity, for there is no substitute for the personal equation, the personal familiarity with every part of one's charge. Touring not only enables the administrator to get close to those whose well being it is his duty to ensure but also gives him valuable insight into the problems of the rural area which must necessarily be of immense value to him when he is called upon later in his career to hold higher positions in the bureaucratic hierarchy. The older ways helped the officer in knowing a great many of the persons who played a definite role in the lives of the people among whom they moved and did business. For a variety of reasons, that is no longer the case today. Officers are called upon to perform a great many duties, which take them away from the people, even though on the face of it, one would imagine that their duties take them close to the people. It was only a kind of frustration which led the late prime minister, Rajiv Gandhi to say that of every rupee sanctioned by the government for the people, barely a minute fraction reached the intended beneficiary. That can happen when there is not only corruption but also no administration. The task of the civil servant was perhaps easier in my days in that he was left to carry out his duties without any interference, which unfortunately is not the case today. The accountability of the civil servant in the old days was complete. Today, that is not the case.

Sind, in those days, was essentially an agricultural area except only in Karachi where there were some industries and these too were small ones. Agriculture was its main industry and was also dependent very much upon river Indus and the canals that had been built to take waters from that river out into surrounding areas. During this period, the completion of the Sukkur barrage gave a tremendous fillip to agricultural developments, but the use of chemical fertilizers was still some years away. Nevertheless, the land there was fertile and wherever there was adequate availability of water there were good crops. The method of cultivation was still of a traditional nature. But there was readiness to accept the use of both improved methods of cultivation as also of better seed or more organic manure.

These early years of my service in Sind were of great value to me. In the various positions of responsibility that I was called upon to fill, I learned valuable lessons in administration. I had the good fortune to see a number of able officers at work. Their methods of work differed greatly but they all believed in the importance of delegation, of hard work and attention to detail, of the value of justice and just attitude in administration and, above all, in providing full support to those working under them.

## Shikarpur, Sukkur, Sind

I did a fair amount of touring during that first winter, but didn't get round to all the tehsils in my charge. During the first summer, I was also able to see something of some of the main canals in my sub-division in the company of the executive engineer at Sukkur. He turned out to be another fine human being, a Sikh named Jaswant Singh Malik. We became lifelong friends. We did quite a lot of patrolling together along the canal roads, a patrolling, which is very necessary when the Indus river is in spate. Canals taking off the main river have to be watched day and night to see that wherever a 'leak' occurs for whatever reason, it is plugged at the earliest possible moment and before it develops into an uncontrollable breach. One of the peculiarities of the Indus river is that in Sind it flows above the level of the surrounding countryside. This makes it possible for most of its canals to be inundation canals. But while this is an advantage from the point of view of cultivation, it also carries with it the risk of the canals flooding the countryside in the event of a breach, which is a very real possibility during the summer months when the river and the canals taking off from it carry a vast volume of water. These breaches occur for many reasons, one of the most common of these arise from holes made by rats in the protection bunds lining the canals. That year, as luck would have it, several breaches occurred and some of these led to a flooding of large areas of my sub-division, necessitating in many cases the evacuation of a number of villages. That summer, thanks to one such breach, the Shikarpur town had to be evacuated, and the only place where such large number of refugees could be evacuated to was Sukkur itself. For several days I was engaged in the task, providing some accommodation to the refugees in school premises, in dharmshalas, and in any vacant space in which all available tentage could be put up. While we were struggling to cope with the floods and its consequences, some Congress workers chose to take out a procession through some crowded areas of Sukkur. In one such area, the Muslim residents protested, and on the processionists failing to pay heed, the authorities had an incipient communal trouble on their hands. This was particularly unfortunate, as most of the police available at district headquarters had had to be sent out to help the police and revenue authorities in coping with the large areas, which had become the victims of floods. And to cap all our troubles, the collector was away on a short 'Upper Sind Leave'. This, however, was soon remedied. The commissioner in Sind asked me to take over charge as acting collector and district magistrate and to do the best I could to cope with the situation.

In this way, I got my first acting charge within a few months of becoming a sub-divisional officer. I found myself heading the district, when I had hardly any experience of administration and none whatsoever of controlling disturbances, communal or otherwise and even less of organising refugee camps! My immediate duty was to see that law and order was restored in Sukkur itself and adequate protection was afforded to the refugees from Shikarpur who were spread out in various areas of the city. The district superintendent of police had, at the moment, a very minute police force at his disposal. Fortunately, Sukkur housed a large colony of railway officers, many of whom had received training by the Auxiliary Territorial Army. They were requested to place themselves at my disposal. Likewise, there were a large number of engineers and other personnel engaged in the construction of the Sukkur Barrage, who were housed in a colony adjacent to Sukkur city. I decided to request them to help me in the desperate situation in which I was placed. Both the organisations offered their help without hesitation. I requested those of them who had cars to come along with their cars and such firearms as they were in possession of. Groups of these were allotted areas of the city to patrol throughout the night and reassure the people that the situation was well in hand. I was also able to persuade the small group of soldiers who were there to ensure the safety of the bridge across the river Indus that joined Sukkur at one end and Rohri at the other. I had to ensure that trouble did not spread to Rohri and the rest of my district on the other side of the river. Meantime, I accompanied by the district superintendent of police, moved into the areas of the city where trouble was expected to assume serious proportions. Within minutes of my arriving at one place where trouble was expected, I found a large crowd of people from villages in the vicinity of Sukkur who had been told that their co-religionists were in trouble and had decided to come to their help. I asked their leaders to come forward so that I could explain to them what had happened and that there was nothing for them to do. These men were from villages where I had only very recently toured and many of them knew me by sight at least. I told them in Sindhi, which I could by that time speak fairly fluently, that the situation was completely under control and they would help me and the government if they went back to their villages. I assured them that there was in fact, no trouble in the city as they could see for themselves. Fortunately, the crowd from the villages saw sense and allowed themselves to be persuaded. I have little doubt that the fact that I had been only recently to their villages helped. Surprisingly, they responded and indeed I could see that the crowd's militancy had given way to shamefacedness.

It was possible in one way or another to stave off any serious trouble and to restore normalcy within a few days. I had been keeping the commissioner in Sind informed of the situation and the steps that were being taken for the restoration of law and order. He had, in the meantime, sent some police force to relieve those whom I had sent out to help in the flood affected areas. As soon as I informed him that the situation in Sukkur was under control, the commissioner decided to come to Sukkur along with the major general in charge of the Independent Brigade in Sind.

It was interesting to see how the commissioner went about his work. He met the heads of the organisations that had come to my help, the railway officers and the officers from Sukkur Barrage. He also met leaders of various local organisations. And naturally, he put the deputy superintendent of police and myself through a searching cross-examination. At the end of it all, he had no hesitation in complimenting me for the way in which I had handled the situation. The major general in charge of the Independent Brigade in Sind told me quite frankly that it was none of my business to have asked the small platoon in charge of the Sukkur-Rohri Bridge to come to my assistance. But while telling me off in this firm manner he told me as he was departing that I should not hesitate to call upon his men to help, if that was necessary, and they would respond readily. The commissioner in Sind expressed his satisfaction while promising to see that further police would be drafted to my district until the abnormal situation had been finally dealt with. He also said he would depute another ICS officer to help me during the period that the district was beset with floods. Thus, this difficult situation turned out to be another stroke of good luck for me. Right at the outset of my career, I was given an opportunity to deal with a difficult situation with nothing to guide me but my own common sense. It certainly added to my self-confidence. It also helped me in coming to know the entire district set-up very thoroughly. I was also able to see how the superior officers handled the situation in a way that gave confidence to the man on the spot, while encouraging him to use his initiative to the fullest extent. I remained in the district for a couple of years, during which, by a fortunate conjunction of circumstances, I got another opportunity of acting as collector.

## Life in the Districts of Sind

I ought to have made a mention of the great many shooting camps that used to be organised every year in Larkana district. There were many lakes of all sizes in the district, and in particular in Larkana sub-division, and these would be the venue for camps, which would be organised by some great zamindar or other (great because each one of such zamindars usually counted their holdings of land in terms of thousands of acres). To these camps would be invited a large number of people including government officers with all their retinue, who would over the course of three or four days account for literally thousands of birds, partridges and quails. A virtual newcomer to this pastime, I succeeded in bringing down a few at my very first attempt. There were birds in plenty and the slaughter would be immense. After Larkana, I never managed to get to one of these very pleasant interludes — pleasant except for the 'slaughter'. Fortunately, these camps were only organised during a relatively short season.

My first independent charge was Sukkur sub-division with my headquarters at Sukkur, which was also the headquarters of the district of Sukkur. My sub-division included one very important town, Shikarpur, which was the headquarters of one of its tehsils but which also provided a large number of rich Shroffs doing prosperous business of moneylending in Bombay and Karachi. On my arrival at Sukkur, I had the good fortune to find a fellow Gujarati ICS, an extraordinarily fine man, many years my senior and then a district and sessions judge. He was under orders of transfer to a Bombay Presidency station. He had been in Sukkur for the past couple of years as district and sessions judge. I met him some years later in Poona. Mr. Nanavati gave me much good advice before he left the district. He was also good enough to entrust me with the charge of his favourite horse 'Kim' along with its syce! I was told to see that he was well looked after, and if I ever decided to part with him, to see that he had a good home. I loved 'Kim' and parted company with him only when I left Sind finally in 1936 after I had completed my last assignment of separating Sind from Bombay.

My next posting was as officiating collector of Tharparkar with headquarters at Mirpur Khas for a short period. On the arrival of the permanent collector, I reverted as assistant collector. The conditions in this lower Sind district differed very much from those of the Upper Sind, such as Larkana and Sukkur and Jacobabad. A very large area was sandy desert with patches of cultivable land. It was large enough to constitute a whole sub-division, on the eastern side of the district, which bordered on the Rann of Kutch. The overwhelming majority of the people of this area were Gujarati speaking and professed to be Hindu in religion. They were hard working and it was astonishing to see what they managed to produce from an apparently most unpromising environment, adverse climatic conditions, from land extracted out of constantly encroaching sand, and with water available in extremely limited quantity. And yet, it was astonishing to see how clean and attractive the villages and houses of the residents of this area were, despite the fact that a great many of the residents belonged to what are now called scheduled castes. I had he opportunity to travel in this area on several occasions and on one in particular, when I had travelled along the whole of the area bordering the Rann of Kutch.

Some years after I had been transferred from Tharparkar, I was asked to undertake a special assignment by the Government of India in connection with the smuggling of silver from Sind into India via Gujarat. I had occasion then to travel along the Rann of Kutch bordering Gujarat crossing over thence via Nagarparkar (of Mirpurkhas district) and then travelling again along the Sind border, and crossed back into Gujarat at a point facing what was then the princely state of Kutch. I found the people on both sides of the Rann as also in the 'islands' in the Rann itself carrying on among themselves healthy and flourishing trade in cattle, agricultural produce and a variety of essential goods. A part of Tharparkar district was also colonised by farmers from the Punjab. They were good farmers and provided an object lesson in farming to the local farmers who were at that time somewhat backward and rather lackadaisical, and not as hard working as I am told they have now become.

From Sukkur, I was transferred to Tharparkar District of which Mirpurkhas was the headquarters. I was given charge of Mirpurkhas sub-division. Here again, I got an opportunity to act as collector for several months, during which I toured extensively, particularly in the sub-division which contained the desert talukas of Mithi, Diplo, Umarkot, and Nagarparkar. It was while moving from my camp from Mithi to Nagarparkar that I met with an accident that could easily have been fatal. I was riding 'Kim'. After I had finished my various inspections en route, and it was when only the last few miles remained to my next camp site at Nagarparkar, that I met with this accident. I decided to gallop when it seemed to me that there was good flat plain area before me. I suddenly found myself thrown to the ground, having run straight into a wire, which was supporting a telephone pole, and the morning sun gleamed so brightly that I could not see it and save myself. I was thrown to the ground on perhaps the 'only' rocky ground in the midst of the surrounding desert. When officers who were accompanying me and whom I had left some way behind caught up with me, they were naturally concerned to see me lying unconscious on the ground. They lifted me with great care and moved on to Nagarparkar, which was only a short distance away. By the time we reached the village, which was also the taluka headquarter, I had regained consciousness. I was in great pain from the injuries I had sustained during the fall. Fortunately, I had escaped any serious injury, and except for a fracture above my wrist, all other injuries were of a relatively minor nature. The fracture too could have been fixed very satisfactorily, had they left it to the local bonesetter to deal with. Instead, it was felt that someone as important as a collector must be treated by the local government doctor. The poor fellow had never had occasion to deal with such a fracture. He actually sought my assistance in determining the kind of fracture I had from the textbook illustration, which he held out for me to see! Anyhow, he did the best he could. By the time I could see the civil surgeon at Hyderabad (Sind) over a week had elapsed, nature had done its work. The civil surgeon did not think it advisable to attempt to reset the bones so as to remove the deformity, which had resulted. He assured me, however, that my wrist would be strong enough for any task it would be called upon to do. I did not wish to suffer any further pain and was quite happy to explain away my deformed wrist as a permanent souvenir of this particular incident. As it is, I continued to ride all the time I was in Sind and with great enjoyment. I parted with Kim only when I left Sind. I left him in the good hands of a deputy collector who loved riding and did so regularly on his own well cared for horse for pleasure.

After leaving Sind, all my subsequent service was either in the Secretariat or in special assignments. And it was my good fortune that all these assignments were not only important, but also most interesting.

## Smuggling of Silver

While I was still in Sind, I was sent on a special assignment to the Government of India. The government found that a great deal of silver was being smuggled into the country and suspected that this was happening by way of the Rann of Kutch, and asked the government of Bombay to depute a fairly senior civilian for a short deputation to suggest ways and means of plugging all likely areas through which the smuggling may be occurring. The government in Bombay selected me even though I was far short of the seniority in service that the Government of India had asked for. I was asked to proceed immediately to Simla where the Government of India had then migrated because of the hot weather to ascertain from the Central Board of Revenue what was expected of me. I met a senior member of the Board who gave me an idea of the problem for the solution of which they had asked for my deputation. I was asked to meet the customs and excise authorities in Bombay to get myself briefed further before setting about my task. Accordingly, I proceeded to Bombay and after discussion with the customs and excise authorities, I proceeded to Kharaghoda where I was met by their senior most resident excise officer. After further discussions and study of all available information, it was decided that we should cover the entire area covered by the Rann of Kutch, beginning with Kharagodha. After covering the western side of the Rann we were to double back at Nagarparkar and after inspecting the Sind side of the Rann, return back to Kharaghoda via the state of Kutch and along the Surendranagar side of the Rann. This was a most educative tour for me and I came to learn a good deal of this interesting part of the country. The tour lasted a good few weeks. I then drew up my report and was glad to learn later that the bulk of my recommendations had been accepted. How far they succeeded in stopping the smuggling of silver, I do not know. But they must have succeeded to some extent for there was no talk of it for some little time thereafter. I had been given six months to produce my report, but I had succeeded in completing it within less than three.

4

# The Secretariat in Bombay

## Separation of Sind from Bombay

IT HAD BEEN FELT FOR SOME TIME THAT TO ADMINISTER Sind from Bombay was difficult and, therefore, as a first experiment, the commissioner of Sind was vested with greater powers than the ordinary commissioner. This was indicated by his being designated commissioner in Sind instead of the usual designation of a commissioner of a division. Even so, it was felt that Sind was not receiving all the attention it merited, and it would receive a fairer deal if it were separated from Bombay. Although this was not openly admitted, the real underlying reason for seeking the separation of Sind from the rest of the Presidency of Bombay was without a doubt political. Therefore, as soon as political considerations gathered sufficient strength, the decision was taken to separate Sind from Bombay and given the status of a separate province. Once this decision was taken, it became necessary to work out the administrative implications and for this purpose, the post of a Sind separation officer was created. I was appointed to this position. Because of its geographic location, the actual task of hiving off Sind from the rest of Bombay presented no great difficulty and the work resolved itself mainly into creating a separate administrative organisation for Sind. I started work on my new assignment in Bombay and then proceeded to Poona to complete my report. The task was relatively simple in that I was not expected to ascertain the public's wishes in the matter but only to see that a new province was created, what should its area be, and what resources it should have out of the resources of the Bombay Presidency of which it had hitherto formed a part. The report was expected to suggest its form of government, how its legislature should be constituted, and the kind of governmental machinery with which it should start work as an independent state. It did not take me long, therefore, to complete this duty and I was able to submit my report within a few months.

### 'Ways and Means'

I was then deputed by the government of Bombay to join a group of officers, one from each of the various provinces of India, for receiving training in the 'ways and means' work. As a result of the decision by the Government of India to give the provinces of India greater autonomy, it became necessary for each province to shoulder the responsibility for looking after its own 'ways and means' position. To enable them to do so efficiently, the government considered it advisable to give special training to selected officers from each province in the 'ways and means' work. Each selected officer was attached for a few weeks to the accountant general of his province and was then asked to proceed to the Office of the Controller of Currency at Calcutta. Planning the availability and utilisation of funds in such a way that funds needed for administering the province were available for payments as they fell due, was not a particularly difficult operation. Apart from obtaining a better understanding of the manner in which the finances of our provinces and of the country were managed, the main advantage that I obtained was to get to know more intimately officers from other provinces, some of whom were of outstanding ability and brilliance. One such officer, for instance, was C.D. Deshmukh, who later became the first Indian governor of the Reserve Bank and later on, after Independence, finance minister of India. I certainly helped myself copiously from Deshmukh's notes and prepared a useful 'ways and means ' guide for the Bombay state. Quite apart from this, I must admit that I benefited much from this training. As happens not infrequently in our country, by the time I returned to Bombay to take over my duty as deputy secretary in the Finance Department, it had been decided that I was to proceed within a few months to Europe to take over duties as trade commissioner for India in northern Europe, with headquarters at Hamburg.

## Stock Exchange Inquiry Committee

In the period that remained before I was to go abroad, I was appointed member secretary of Morison Stock Exchange Inquiry Committee. The Bombay Stock Exchange had been going through a troubled period owing to excessive speculation and consequent payment and clearance difficulties. With a view to controlling speculation and ensuring that the country's major stock exchange was better regulated, the government of Bombay decided on the appointment of a committee, and selected as its chairman a senior member of the London Stock Exchange. The other members were Sir Ibrahim Rahimtulla, Sir Sorab Pochkhanawala who was the head of the Central Bank of India and K.R.P. Shroff, chairman of the Bombay Stock Exchange. This was, thus, an important appointment from my point of view. Since I would have left India by the time this assignment was completed, I was asked to see that a 'ways and means' handbook was prepared for the guidance of the officers who would actually be called upon to look after the affairs after I had left. Both these tasks of preparing the handbook as well as drawing up of the report of the stock exchange were interesting, and enriched both my theoretical as well as practical knowledge in directions which later proved of not inconsiderable value.

# 5

# Europe, the Hitler Years

## Trade Commissioner in Hamburg 1937-1940

IN THOSE DAYS, ONE STILL HAD TO TRAVEL BY SEA. IT TOOK all of twenty-one days to get to London. The P&O liners were most comfortable. My wife and three children were all travelling together in this leisurely manner for the first time ever. We made some interesting friends and with some, matured into much more than just a sea-journey friendship. Altogether, this particular journey remained an unforgettable memory.

We spent a few days in London during which we engaged the services of a 'governess' who could see to the education of my two elder daughters. It was my intention to put them in a boarding school, and until that could be arranged satisfactorily, I was anxious that their education should not suffer during their stay in Hamburg.

I spent most of my time, while in London, at India House, where the office of the trade commissioner was located. The trade commissioner was senior in rank, and the Indian trade commissioner of both northern and southern Europe reported to him for advice and general guidance. The office of the trade commissioner, northern Europe was set up by my predecessor, a senior ICS officer.

I was met by my deputy trade commissioner, an officer who had earlier served in a junior capacity in the British Commonwealth, on arrival in Hamburg. He spoke German fluently. My office was very small, consisting of my deputy, a stenographer who also worked as my private secretary, one typist clerk and myself. The office was very well located, on the Alster Lake, which is a fairly large lake in an important part of the city. I was fortunate enough to obtain a flat in a house located at one end of the lake. It was possible for me to walk comfortably early morning and evening from my flat to my office and back.

Hamburg was both an important part of Germany, and an important business centre. It is also very well connected by rail and road (and now by air), though not to as great an extent as today, with the rest of Germany and other countries of Europe. The selection of Hamburg as the headquarters of the office of the Indian Trade Commission was, therefore, a sound decision. It was also within easy reach of Berlin.

The work of the Trade Commissioner's Office was two-fold. It was expected to deal with any complaints received from Indian businessmen or businessmen of the countries who approached him for information and guidance. The second duty of the commissioner was to keep the Government of India informed of any important development in the countries he was responsible for, which was likely to affect India to its advantage or otherwise, and to suggest possible ways of dealing with them whenever this was called for. It was this latter duty that kept the Indian trade commissioner pretty fully occupied. The complaints from Indian businessmen were not many, and those from their counterparts, even fewer. But what both sought was a great deal of general information about Indian laws and credit-worthiness of an individual businessman or a company. It was clear that I had to acquaint myself with each country and establish relations, which would enable me to obtain any information I stood in need of. And this is what I proceeded to do as soon as I was well settled at Hamburg and established contacts with both businessmen and German officialdom. Thereafter, I visited other countries in my jurisdiction. This was a lengthy process, as I had to keep returning to Hamburg after a few days spent in other capitals. I first visited France, Belgium and Holland, because India had already some business relations with them, and there were quite a few Indian citizens who lived in those countries. The other countries I went to as and when time permitted. And I thus went to Norway, Sweden and Denmark during the first year of my stay in Hamburg. The following year, that is in 1938, I was able to go to Austria and Czechoslovakia, and later to Poland.

The years I spent as trade commissioner were years in which great developments had begun to take place, which soon made trade and business take second place. Hitler's ascendancy was soon to be complete and with it also the persecution of the Jews. I witnessed the aftermath of several such pogroms. It was tragic. From talks I had with a large number of Germans, it appeared to me that their sympathies lay with their fellow Jewish citizens, whom most of them had known for generations. But the Hitler movement and the fear it seems to have inspired had sealed the mouths of most Germans. During 1938 and 1939, and particularly after the Neville Chamberlain accord, Hitler's prestige grew enormously. Hitler's projected entry into Austria and Czechoslovakia became clear and virtually unhindered. And with this, the misery of the Jews became incredibly greater. The Allies could only watch helplessly at what was happening, for they were unable to make up their minds, whether to come to the help of those whose security they had guaranteed. It was only when Poland was attacked that the Allies' hand was forced.

Meantime, the average citizen could only watch events without being able to help those whose freedom was being trampled upon. In these circumstances, the smooth functioning of the economy was impossible. It was just a question of marking time.

When things became particularly critical, I decided to put my two elder daughters in a boarding school. I was recommended a school in Bristol. I visited this school, a fairly well-known school called

Badminton School. It turned out to be first rate and as long as my daughters were there, they had a happy time, quite apart from whatever they might have absorbed educationally.

Sometime later I decided to take the rest of my family to England, and the first few months of the stay were spent in Bristol. Later, the family moved to London where a friend had placed his house at our disposal. This was in 1940, after I had myself to move to London on the declaration of war by England against Germany.

I arrived in Hamburg in the latter half of 1937. Europe was already under the spell of Hitler and his national socialism. Speculation was rife as to the future and men had begun to ask whether peace would continue to reign or war was unavoidable. As trade commissioner for India, my concern was with economic conditions in the countries I would be accredited to in particular, and in Europe in general. I was expected to see that trade relations prospered between India and countries of north Europe, that is, Germany, the northern half of France, Belgium, Holland, Denmark, Sweden and Norway, and the Baltic countries, Estonia, Lithuania, and Latvia, Poland, Czechoslovakia and Austria. Though the area I was concerned with was large, our trade with these countries was not of any particular magnitude. Trade with Germany alone was of any significance, and in regard to which there were interesting possibilities. With all other countries, the scope for expansion of exports from India was not very great because we were at that time in a position only to export agricultural products, and in the absence of industrialisation or any policy for industrial development, the scope even for the development of imports from these countries was very limited.

Very soon after I assumed charge of my office in Hamburg, I met the British consul general in Hamburg. He was good enough to give me a general idea of conditions in Germany and advised me to meet the British ambassador in Berlin, which I did. He made arrangements for me to see the commerce minister's office. On returning to Hamburg, I met German officialdom in Hamburg, and then met a number of German businessmen who were engaged in trade with India. My predecessor, also an ICS officer, but of considerable seniority was the first trade commissioner of India in northern Europe, and left a fairly exhaustive note of whatever he had done in Hamburg and the rest of his charge. He had a deputy in charge of the office, who was a senior officer recruited from the British Consulate Office in Germany. He was a German by birth but had acquired British citizenship. There were two other persons on the staff of my office. One of these was my personal secretary, who was a first rate stenotypist and a general clerk. My predecessor had established a practice of sending a monthly report, giving the commerce minister a general idea of developments of an economic and commerce nature in the large area my office was expected to cover. This meant keeping myself informed of happenings in each of the various countries for which I was responsible. The countries that mattered at that time to Indian trade and industry were, Germany, Czechoslovakia, Holland, Belgium, Sweden, to a much lesser extent Poland, Austria, France, while the Baltic States did not count for much. Nevertheless, one had to keep oneself informed and I did my best. The years between 1937 and 1940 were years of great unease for Europe.

During the little over three years that I spent in Hamburg as trade commissioner, I did a great deal of travelling. I went to Norway, Sweden, Denmark, Holland and Belgium. I visited France on more than one occasion, I travelled to Austria and to Czechoslovakia and though I could not go to the Baltic States of Estonia, Lithuania and Latvia, I did manage to go to Poland. In each of these states, I met both officials and businessmen who were in some way connected with India as exporters or importers, or who were anxious to develop trade relations with India. I also had the opportunity to meet organisations that were anxious to learn something about India's political and social conditions. Wherever possible, I managed to find time to visit the opera or theatre. My wife accompanied me sometimes. She enjoyed these visits, even though she was handicapped by the fact that her knowledge of English was limited, and she knew nothing of French or German, the knowledge of which languages helped me greatly during these travels.

During the two-and-a-half years or so until the outbreak of War in September 1939, I visited at least the capitals of all these countries and travelled extensively in a few. Apart from obtaining a first-hand idea of the economies of these countries and future possibilities, I was able to learn a great deal about their cultural development. A tour of the great museums in Amsterdam and Rotterdam was an experience in itself. One was able to see remarkably fine plays in France and Germany and listen to some superb music in Vienna, Paris and Cologne. I was able to see a superb exhibition, which to that date was the largest in terms of the countries represented and the variety displayed.

The situation in Europe, however, had already become uncertain and abnormal by the time I was able to get to Austria, Czechoslovakia and Poland. My arrival in Vienna, for instance, coincided with the march into Vienna by Nazis, and indeed I found myself all but isolated in the hotel in which Schussnig, the head of the Austrian state, was detained. Similarly, my first visit to Prague coincided with the over-running of Czechoslovakia by the Nazis. In the case of Warsaw, my visit was in circumstances which were outwardly normal but which, as it turned out, was only a few weeks away from the invasion of Poland by Germany. Because India had many business contacts in Hamburg and because I lived there, I was able to see in Hamburg how the German government functioned, and what roles were played in the lives of the average citizen by the 'brown' and the 'black' shirts. In Hamburg, Berlin and in one or two German cities, I had occasion to see the manner in which Jewish business had begun to be throttled.

Moreover, though outwardly everything was normal and orderly, throughout these three years one realised that there was an undercurrent of apprehension, that of trouble because of the forces of fascism in Italy and Nazism in Germany which were beginning steadily to gain ground in the countries of their birth and spreading their influence in other countries of Europe. The persecution of the Jews had already begun, but it was still not carried out in a blatant manner. This persecution, however, had begun to gather momentum by 1939. And most outsiders and as yet, a large number of Germans, felt horrified at what was taking place, in this the twentieth century. The amazing thing was that the people in the rest of the world, particularly in Europe and America, appeared to think that this was only a temporary aberration. A great deal of sympathy was expressed with the suffering Jews, and those who were able to come out were treated with sympathy. But there was little condemnation of Hitler or the German government. For whatever reasons, good or bad, Britain and France had decided upon a policy of appeasement. The first results of that policy were soon seen. First Austria was run over and then Czechoslovakia. Both Britain and France realised that the policy of appeasement had failed. If it was adopted to buy time, that too had failed, because Germany was in no mood to relent. Soon Poland was threatened, and Britain and France could no longer continue to be spectators and were forced to declare war.

Thus, the period I spent in Hamburg as trade commissioner was an abnormal period. There was almost never a day when something had not occurred which caused anxiety to the ordinary people. First, there was the attempt by Hitler to get to power in Germany, and when that was substantially achieved, Hitler began his diplomatic or semi-diplomatic attempts to browbeat his neighbours. He knew that some of these states had been promised assistance by Britain and France but seemed to have a better idea than most people of the degree to which the rulers of Britain and France would be prepared to go before accepting his challenge. In spite of these abnormal circumstances, my main functions as trade commissioner were not neglected. However, because of these circumstances, it was inevitable that commerce and trade should take a lower place in men's minds, which were dominated more by the uncertainty of the future.

Even so, I must note that inquiries regarding trade came in quite a large number both from India and from many of the European countries to which I was assigned. Thus, we had quite a lively volume of inquiries from Germany, France, Belgium, Holland, Denmark, Sweden and Norway, and similarly quite a considerable number of Indian businessmen asked for information of various kinds and in respect of various firms resident in these countries. Towards the end of my stay, a great deal of interest was displayed by some persons, who were interested in developing a market for tobacco as a raw material, and a fairly good response was forthcoming particularly from Germany. I met a number of Indians who had settled down in Antwerp and were doing quite a considerable volume of business in diamonds. I came in touch with a number of Indian businessmen who had made their home in Berlin and Paris. But on the whole, the total number in all these countries was small. It was good for the country to have a representative of India in these countries. The ordinary men in these countries have, as a consequence, a little better idea of India and its peoples. Also, the Indian government for its part acquires a little better understanding of the people of the various countries with which we wished to enter into trade relations. For the rest, there was only one occasion when an Indian member of the Viceroy's Executive Council visited Germany, the late Shri Zaffrulla Khan. I accompanied him to his meeting with the German minister of commerce and industry, alongwith an officer of the British Embassy. My one impression of this visit is that our minister showed himself to great advantage. He knew his stuff, he knew what he wanted and saw to it that it was communicated very clearly. The German minister, whose name does not come to my mind now, also had come prepared with the result that this official meeting was one of the most fruitful ones that I have attended – and I have had occasion to be present at a great many. While in Hamburg, I naturally met the British representatives whenever possible, and from them I received the fullest cooperation and help.

I can say in retrospect that my stay in Hamburg was of great value and interest to me personally, but it cannot be said to have been of much value in terms of my official duties. I was impressed with the great goodwill that the people of all these countries had towards India both in the official as also in the non-official world. A surprising number of people knew something of Rabindranath Tagore and of Mahatma Gandhi, but the people generally knew very little about India. I was gratified to see, however, that on the whole those who had been doing business with India had very rarely to complain about their dealings. Occasionally, of course, there were some complaints about the quality of goods being different from what they had been led to expect. But generally speaking, they had a high regard for the honesty and straightforward behaviour of their counterparts. There were very few resident Indian businessmen in most of these countries. Only in Antwerp in Belgium, there were a fair number of Indians in the diamond trade. In all other countries, the number of resident Indian businessmen was extremely small. There were of course, in Germany in particular and in France, a number of Indian students.

This might suggest that there was not a full day's work in the appointment of the trade commissioner, northern Europe. This would be true if the incumbent had very little interest other than in his own assignment.

I was disappointed when the situation deteriorated after the illusory agreement between Neville Chamberlain and Hitler in 1938. When War broke out, I had only to make arrangements for my family and myself and to hand over my belongings to the care of the British consul general who was then diplomatically responsible for India. I was asked to continue in London until further instructions were received.

The few months that I was in England in 1940 were spent usefully. I worked both as deputy trade commissioner in UK and later as trade commissioner. Unlike the European countries, India had a flourishing trade with the United Kingdom. Both its exports to, as well as its imports from, the United Kingdom were substantial in volume and variety as well as in value. A fair number of British firms were interested in trade with India and quite a few Indian firms had also either opened their branch offices or had representatives in that country. Because of the political relationship between the two countries, India's purchases of manufactured goods as well as of machinery, chemicals, and equipment required for Indian nascent industries came very largely from the United Kingdom, which for its part absorbed in return a large volume of commodities which entered India's exports trade. It was not as if UK consumed all that it imported from India but it was a major entreport trade centre. A great many of the commodities imported from India such as tea, coffee, tobacco, oilcakes, etc., were re-exported to the European countries, the British ports and London in particular, functioning as entreport trade centres. European importers of Indian goods preferred to do so through London rather than directly, chiefly because their imports from India were not of any great magnitude in relation with their total imports.

At that time, there was a majority of Indian students going to universities in UK for higher studies. Only a very few went to European countries. It was obviously more convenient for the students to go to UK because of their familiarity with English. One would have thought that Indian students would have gone in larger numbers to the United States of America, but in those days they did not do so very largely because of the high cost of living. Another reason, of course, was that the British degrees were more highly recognised from the point of view of employment.

Though War had been declared formally by the United Kingdom and Germany with each other, actual hostilities did not commence for several months. During this period of dormant warfare, the United Kingdom was preparing actively for economic warfare, and I was able to obtain a glimpse of this as I was called upon to attend a number of meetings at the ministry of economic warfare as representative of the Government of India. It was interesting to find how the activities of the ministries connected with war in the United Kingdom were also galvanised into feverish activity only after active warfare began. I had the opportunity to see the way in which people of that country as well as the officialdom reacted to the great setbacks that Britain and France suffered at the outset. The setbacks were so shattering that a recovery seemed initially to be utterly impossible. But the nation, valuing its independence, made up its mind to resist to the bitter end, and geared itself into a tremendously purposive machine. Grim determination could be seen on every face. Those were the days of disasters, and each fresh disaster seemed only to add to the determination of the people to hang on grimly and to defeat the Nazis. Hitler had grievously underestimated Britain. Churchill gave eloquent expression to this grim and unshakable determination to fight on till victory was won. It was a great experience to see the patriotism and the spirit that so visibly moved the British people during this period. And even the French, though initially they gave in almost without a fight, soon showed that they too were made of a different mettle and gave Germans no peace even though nominally they had made themselves masters of France.

The Government of India, as was only to be expected, was unable to take a speedy decision, and as things were expected to become difficult in England, for everyone expected that Germany would before long subject England to severe air attack, I decided to send my family back to India. I was able to obtain accommodation for them on a P&O sailing, and I saw them off at Portsmouth. I knew this would be hard on my wife, as she would have to look after four children, one of them barely a year old, and the eldest one only eleven. A submarine attack was an ever-present risk. The German submarines had begun by then to operate most efficiently. They dealt severe blows to British shipping. As in the First World War, the British fashioned an efficient convoy system that certainly succeeded in reducing the rate of the loss. As the number of frigates and destroyers necessary for such convoys was limited, the British took the risk of letting their fast moving steamers go independently. The P&O ship's speed was expected to help in the event of an attack as it could out-manoeuvre any submarine. As it happened, the ship had to take on board a number of women and children who were on their way to Australia and had the misfortune to be torpedoed. It was indeed very brave of my wife to have agreed to travel in the circumstances without any friend or assistance. Her ship had, as was inevitable those days, to go round the Cape of Good Hope and thence make for Ceylon. As it turned out, I need not have sent them ahead of me, for, within days I received orders of my posting and was directed to return to India without delay. Whereas it had taken several weeks to arrange for my family's departure, I was offered a passage almost immediately, though from Liverpool. As luck would have it, my ship, as it was not made to go to Ceylon, was able to get to Bombay some days before my wife's arrival in Ceylon. My wife and children had to remain some days in Colombo while one of my daughters recovered from an infection she had acquired on the ship.

On my return to India, I was posted in the newly created Supply Department as deputy secretary under a very outstandingly able secretary, Evans Jenkins. Soon afterwards, there was created a new organisation called the Eastern Group Supply Council at which there were representatives of the United Kingdom, Australia, New Zealand, Holland, South Africa and India. I was invited to join the Secretariat of that Council as deputy secretary. Appointments of this nature give one unique opportunities for acquiring very valuable experience and knowledge which would have been almost impossible to obtain in the usual kinds of appointments in the Government of India, as also enlarging the field of one's activities by coming into contact with a great many people with experience of a wide and varied nature. Because of the War, many new kinds of problems began to develop, the most important among them was that relating to supply of essential commodities and rise in prices of such commodities. The Government of India decided to create a new

Department of Industry and Civil Supplies and I was asked to join that Department as joint secretary. For the first time, economic controls had to be instituted and it fell upon me to both plan such controls and organise their implementation. It may be said that these controls worked quite smoothly and well, and so far as I was concerned, I had enough opportunity through them of acquiring knowledge and experience of a very wide field of the economy of this country.

# 6

# India and the Second World War

I PROCEEDED TO SIMLA WITHOUT WAITING FOR MY FAMILY, to report for duty as deputy secretary in the Supply Department, a department created after the Second World War. The main duty of the department was to mobilise the industrial capacity of the country to the maximum extent possible in the interest of the country's war effort. During this period, I acquired a very good idea of what the country was capable of manufacturing and what new items it could undertake to produce, given an assured market. As the purchaser was the government, the product had to comply with rigid requirements in terms of quality. In the main, since there was not much corruption at this initial stage, the supplier had to take good care to comply with the required specifications. I was not, however, left too long in this appointment and was soon posted to another organisation newly created to coordinate the requirements of the allies from the dominions of Australia and New Zealand, Indonesia (which had by then been overrun by the Japanese) and Hong Kong. The war had begun in earnest, the allies were being driven back at an unholy speed and India became the major supply base of the allies. Very soon, this was recognised in a concrete manner with the establishment in India of what was designated as the Eastern Group Supply Council. Australia, New Zealand, Indonesia, Hong Kong and Great Britain were its members. I was appointed deputy secretary of this Council and worked on it until it almost ceased functioning.

I was then brought back to the Supply Department in a higher capacity, returning as deputy director general of supply and functioned in that capacity until I was moved to another department that was created to meet certain consequences of the war for the economy of the country. This department was named the Department of Industry and Civil Supplies. Sir Akbar Hydari, who was a member from India on the Eastern Group Supply Council, was placed in charge of it, and I joined it initially as joint secretary and later as its secretary.

One of the department's major duties was to take steps necessary to control prices of commodities, which the common man used. One of the most important of these was cotton textiles. Thanks to the large need of the army, the prices had risen abnormally, so much so that there was an outcry from the average citizen. We decided to bring together magnates of the cotton industry and asked them to help us find an answer to the problem. The first important control order initiated by the department was in respect of that industry. This was followed up by controls on various other items such as aluminium utensils, paper, and footwear. An attempt was made even to control prices of drugs and medicines. On the whole, it may be said that our attempts met with considerable success chiefly because we endeavoured to effect control through the industry itself, and we received full support of the industry in each case. It is also important to note that we did not endeavour to do too much. In each case, we were content to see that prices were sought to be pegged at the levels they had already reached or a little below that level, and also to ensure in each case that the commodity would be available at that price. Only in some cases did we try actually to bring prices down to a substantial extent, but always so that we would ensure that the prices remained frozen at that level. In the case of cotton textiles, we even attempted to produce a standard cloth that would result in a sufficient supply of cloth in general demand, being available to meet the needs of the vast majority of the people. Anyhow, in retrospect, it would be fair to claim that these initial efforts of ours met with success, chiefly because we did not try to do too much and knew our limitations and sought to do only as much as we could successfully enforce. This important point has too often been forgotten. A control order which cannot be enforced has not only no value, but can even prove very harmful.

This new Civil Supplies Department had a very short existence. It was decided to merge it with the Supply Department, when Sir Akbar Hydari was appointed first as a member of the Executive Council and thereafter as governor of Assam. I took over from him until the formal merger took place in April 1946, and then moved over to the newly created Cabinet Secretariat as a joint secretary.

I may mention for purposes of record that the government, as a token of its appreciation, conferred on me the C.I.E. in the New Year awards of 1946. There were no further awards thereafter by the British government, while the Government of India had decided in its earlier wisdom to do away with all titles and awards. Later, Pandit Jawaharlal Nehru found a way out despite strong protests from the purists who had succeeded in securing this decision when the Constitution was being discussed. And gradually, what was specifically urged at the beginning was also accepted in practice, namely that the awards should be prefixed to the name of the awardee. It is interesting to note the number of issues that the Congress government strongly condemned at the outset, have all been readmitted later.

7

# At the Centre: The Cabinet Secretariat

AFTER THE CRIPPS' MISSION AND THE INCARCERATION OF the Indian political leaders in 1942, there had been a complete lull in the political scene. An awakening began soon after Mahatma Gandhi's release in 1944 when it was felt that he was seriously ill and it was desirable to release him. However, as soon as his health improved within a few weeks, Gandhiji was active and suggested various ways in which things could be made to move forward. He put it to the new viceroy whether the British government would be prepared to promise independence to the people of India if he invited the people to give up the path of confrontation and civil disobedience and so on. This was, at first, not acceptable to the authorities. Gandhiji then, possibly under the influence of Rajaji, moved in another direction and that was to see if a way could be found out of satisfying Mohammad Ali Jinnah and bring the Muslim League once again along with the Congress to press for the freedom of the country. He had several meetings with Jinnah. This particular move of Gandhiji was not liked by a number of his principal followers but Gandhiji said that it was of the utmost importance that every effort was made to remove the apprehensions and fears of the Muslims who were an important part of the Indian people. The talks with Jinnah failed and it was felt that this move made by Gandhiji had perhaps, worsened the situation. He had not succeeded in removing Muslim apprehensions and, if anything, had hardened them in their conviction that partition and Pakistan was the only answer to their problems. Lord Wavell, who had succeeded Lord Linlithgow as viceroy, had come to the conclusion meanwhile, that an effort must be made to reactivate the political scene. He felt that an effort had to be made to bring the League and the Congress together and a move forward brought about in the political atmosphere. His ideas, however, ran along the lines of bringing the Indian leaders into his Executive Council in the first instance and to this end, he decided to invite the political leaders to a conference. The British government was not particularly receptive but Lord Wavell, nevertheless, decided to go forward along these lines and he arranged for the leaders to meet him in a conference in Simla. The conference, however, failed in its object. Lord Wavell persisted in his efforts thereafter and put forward certain quite imaginative proposals to the British government. As it now appears at the time, however, this was not generally known and the popular feeling was that there was little possibility of progress.

Already in 1945, the Government of India had started giving serious thought to problems that could arise as and when the Transfer of Power to the representatives of the people of India was finally decided upon. One such problem related to the setting up of a Cabinet Secretariat on the model of the Cabinet Secretariat in the United Kingdom. In India, at that time, the governor general's Executive Council was served by the Law Department, the secretary of that department functioning as the secretary to the Executive Council. Once, however, power was transferred to a popular government formed more or less along the lines of the British government, it was felt that it would be more satisfactory for that government to have its secretariat organised along the lines of the

British Cabinet Secretariat. It was decided accordingly, to organise such a secretariat right away in anticipation of the transfer, which quite clearly was expected at that point of time to take place within a matter of months. Sir Eric Coates, who was then the head of Military Finance, was appointed as Cabinet secretary and entrusted with the task of organising an efficiently functioning secretariat.

The functions of the Cabinet Secretariat were to be comprehensive in nature. It would, for example, be assigned the duty of ensuring that decisions taken by the Cabinet were implemented expeditiously. Likewise, it would also be expected to act on its own initiative to see to it that departments do not deviate from priorities laid down by the Cabinet in some important respects. It would be functioning, in a very real sense, as a friendly guide to the departments themselves and to the ministers. For this reason, a Cabinet Secretariat has to be staffed with officers of experience and initiative. Initially, it was decided that the Secretariat should have one joint secretary, a couple of deputy secretaries, and four or five under secretaries as found necessary.

I was informed early in 1946 that as soon as I could be relieved from my present appointment, that of officiating secretary, Department of Industry and Civil Supplies, I would be required to take over as joint secretary in the new secretariat. It had been decided already that, that department was to be wound up by April or so and its functions taken over by the Supply Department. During British rule, there used to be a senior officer designated as establishment officer whose duty it was to keep track of the ICS officers throughout the country and earmark such of them as in his view were good material for filling the senior appointments at the Centre. As a corollary, he had to see that these officers were tried out appropriately in suitable junior appointments. I was assigned this responsibility during 1946 and 1947 along with my duties in the Secretariat. Indeed, I continued to remain in charge of these duties even after I became Cabinet secretary on the retirement of Sir Eric Coates, the first Cabinet secretary.

One major change was the incorporation of a military wing in the Cabinet Secretariat. This was, in a way, the herald of the big changes to come. Until the Transfer of Power, there was a big divide between the civil and military sides of the government, which was then known as the War Department under the commander-in-chief and functioned at the time almost as if it was a separate organisation, independent of the civilian government whose various departments had very little contact with the War Department. From an administrative point of view, the contact was maintained primarily through the officers of the Accounts and Audit Department, who alone of civilian officers had some fairly good understanding of the functioning of the military organisation. Following the British model, it was considered advisable for senior officers of the Cabinet Secretariat to have some understanding of the functioning of the defence organisation. With that objective in view, the then commander-in-chief, Sir Claude Auchinleck, drew up a plan for me to go around the country and see the various defence installations and obtain a good idea of military organisation.

It was in accordance with this plan that I spent a couple of months in 1946 visiting various defence installations of the Army, Navy and Air Force in the country. My guide was Major Bewoor, who later became the Chief of Army Staff in independent India. Such training was not necessary for Sir Eric Coates as his earlier appointment was that of officer in charge of Military Assets in the War Department. It was perhaps not a coincidence that the member of the Steering Committee of the Partition Council on Pakistan's side was Chaudhry Mohammad Ali, who had succeeded Sir Eric Coates in that appointment, when Coates was made the first Cabinet secretary. The member of the Steering Committee of the Partition Council on the Indian side was myself.

With my appointment to the Cabinet Secretariat, I did not realise at the time that a new chapter in my life had begun. The country was expected to have a popular government in some form, and the Secretariat was being set up in anticipation of that possibility. Its main function would be to serve as the Secretariat of the Cabinet or the Executive Council of the government. The military cell would keep track of matters military, since defence would be a major responsibility of the government hereafter. The Secretariat was also designed to ensure that the decisions taken by the Executive Council were carried out by the various ministries. In effect, it was to serve as a proper Secretariat and not as was the case hitherto, serve as an organisation to keep a record of what happened at each Executive Council meeting. It was naturally quite some time before the Secretariat was able to perform all these functions. Right from the outset, the Secretariat had justified its formation and been of help to popularly elected members of the government.

As it turned out, my tenure as Cabinet secretary was also brief, ending in October/November of 1947. However, during that brief tenure I was called upon to discharge a vast variety of duties and responsibilities, all of exceptional importance. Thus, when it was decided in June 1947 that the country was to be[1] partitioned, and that there were to be two dominions, a Partition Council was set up with the directive that it must ensure that the country was divided into two dominions on the lines agreed upon within a matter of some seventy-odd days. The Cabinet Secretariat had to play an important role, although of course a separate Partition Secretariat had been set up, with myself as Partition Secretary in addition to my duties as Cabinet secretary. But that was not all; I was in addition required to work as a member of the two-member Steering Committee on behalf of the Indian Dominion to be. The Steering Committee was required to perform a very important role in the work of the Partition Council set up to divide the existing country India into two Dominions. After Partition, and as soon as the Boundary Commission had reported, communal disturbances broke out resulting in a mass movement of population from one dominion to the other. The Government of India called upon Mountbatten who was governor

1 This is discussed in greater detail in Part II.

general of the Indian Dominion to give them the benefit of his experience. An Emergency Committee of the Cabinet was then set up, with Mountbatten in the Chair. Mountbatten's personal secretary recorded the minutes of the Committee but it fell to the Cabinet Secretariat to ensure that the decisions taken by the Emergency Committee of the Cabinet were duly carried out by those concerned. Delhi itself, was soon affected by the mass movement of population. At the instance of the home minister, Sardar Patel, the Emergency Committee of the Cabinet constituted a Special Emergency Committee for Delhi. This became necessary chiefly because of a conjunction of certain circumstances. The chief commissioner of Delhi was a competent Muslim officer of the ICS while his deputy was a Sikh, also an ICS officer of merit. However, both of these officers were suspect in the eyes of the people at large and in particular, the Muslim and Sikh refugees. Without disturbing these two officers, it was considered best to set up this Delhi Emergency Committee. The arrangement turned out to be satisfactory, as the Delhi administration was called upon to tackle a whole host of special problems. Over a hundred thousand Muslim refugees had to be housed in Purana Qila and a slightly lesser number in Humayun's Tomb. A fairly significant number of persons had also found shelter in Jama Masjid and in Idgah. Matters were further complicated by the fact that rationing was then in force, and this added to the responsibility of the authorities, who had already on their hands the very serious problem to see that no epidemics started among the large number of refugees who had to be housed in conditions that could only with difficulty be provided workable sanitary conditions. As deputy chairman of the Emergency Delhi Committee, the responsibility devolved on me. Fortunately, I had very able deputies to share my load in men like L.K. Jha and K.B. Lall and a number of other experienced officers of the ICS with executive experience.

The Cabinet Secretariat was called upon to play during 1947, a very varied role. Towards the end of 1947, I was asked by Pandit Nehru and Sardar to take over as secretary of the Defence Ministry as they felt that that ministry for all practical purposes needed to be established afresh. I was thus required to agree to a voluntary demotion, for Cabinet secretaryship was considered to be a senior position.

As joint secretary, I was required along with the secretary to be present at every Executive Council Meeting. My task was to record the minutes of each such meeting. This was no easy task, for discussions tended sometimes to be long and lively. The chairman also rarely attempted to sum up a discussion, much less indicate what he considered the decision arrived at. The minute-writer had to exercise his judgement and discover for himself what he considered was finally decided at the end of a rambling discussion. I am glad to say that rarely was any fault found with the decisions I had recorded.

# 8

# On the Threshold of Freedom

WE WERE FORTUNATELY NOT INVOLVED IN ANY WAY WITH the political discussions that were then in progress, and which led before long to the induction of the 'Interim Government' in September 1946. Originally, it was expected to be a government of the Congress and the League, but in the end it was a government formed entirely by the Congress.

I still recall one interesting incident. With the usual desire of the British to be as correct as possible in matters of protocol, the viceroy was anxious to ensure that inter-se seniority of the Congress ministers was observed and every minister was correctly seated at the Cabinet table. I was asked to ascertain the position from Pandit Nehru. I fixed an appointment and met Pandit Nehru on the day before the swearing-in-ceremony was to take place. I posed my problem, which seemed greatly to amuse Pandit Nehru. He burst out laughing. Instead of relieving me of my anxiety, he asked me to go to Sardar Patel for the answer. This I did. The Sardar was also amused on hearing my problem, but this time, my problem was immediately solved. Sardar had no hesitation in indicating the relative seniority of his colleagues. My problem solved, I sought permission to go. I was instead asked to stay on and give some further information about what was expected to take place on the following day. I gave him some further information that I thought might be useful and added that I was always at his disposal to furnish any information or assistance he might need.

This was my first meeting with Pandit Nehru and with Sardar Patel. I had never met them before, and now began a period during which I was required by my official duties to meet them often.

There was tremendous excitement about the formation of the Interim Government among the personnel in the various departments of the Government of India, housed in the North Block and in hutments and hired buildings in various parts all over new and old Delhi. Already, because of the political discussions which had been going on in the country, during the previous couple of years, the civil servants of all ranks had become accustomed to discussing the current political developments with keen interest and with the clear realisation that these were not academic discussions, but would almost certainly lead to changes which would affect them in a very far reaching and significant manner. Despite their general training to avoid political entanglement of any kind whatsoever, the general environment was such that few could maintain a completely objective stance. Even if not overtly, their sympathies did get involved, as more and more news began to be reported of communal disturbances. The constitution of the Interim Government with the representatives of only one major political party was not designed to create a calm atmosphere. Fortunately, the Muslim League realised before long that it was not in its interest to keep out of the government for long.

In the years 1945 and 1946, which were years of great political activity in the country, the discussions whenever civil servants met among themselves inevitably centred on what developments were likely to take place. When India became independent, would India obtain dominion status? Would the Congress and the League come to an understanding and if so, on what basis? Was a partition of the country inevitable? All these questions were discussed fully and thoroughly and yet, no one was able to either come to any conclusion or formulate their own ideas in regard to what could happen or what ought to happen. There were a few who considered that a partition of the country was unavoidable. There was a larger group that felt that an understanding between the Congress and the League was so important that every effort must be made to meet the League's apprehensions and even if it became necessary to ensure that they had a sense of security to go to the maximum length possible without the actual partitioning of the country. All these discussions were a consequence of what was taking place among the political circles and among the official circles in the Government of India and in the country generally.

These were also stirring times. Political discussions were continuing which one knew would result in a definite political advance. The Cabinet Mission had left, but their work had resulted in a plan that though not acceptable in its entirety to either side, had at any rate led to the formation of an 'Interim Government' without the Muslim League, which had decided not to come in. One knew that the League may change its mind and then there would be further developments. Meanwhile, the Muslim League had sent out its call for 'direct action' which it said was sent out because they had found that the constitutional methods had led nowhere. The League could not have been unaware of what the direct action call was bound to result in. And sure enough, it led to what could only be described as a holocaust. It is true that initially, the holocaust was confined to one city, the city of Calcutta, but it was certain to have repercussions, and these were not long in coming. The communal trouble spread to other states. The League leader Jinnah disclaimed that he or the League had any such intention in mind. But no one believed such disclaimers, and the whole political atmosphere was once again thoroughly vitiated. The viceroy continued nevertheless to be optimistic and persisted in his efforts to make the League come into the 'Interim Government'. His efforts did succeed eventually and Jinnah named the League's representatives for the government. By staying out of the Interim Government, they soon realised that they were losing ground in the country and hastened, realists that they were, to repair their error. The League quite naturally desired that they should have a proper share of the more important portfolios. After some considerable difficulty, the League agreed to be content with finance and commerce. But the arguments which prevailed with the League, were the ones urged by their shrewd adviser, Chaudhry Mohammad Ali. The League's object in coming into the government was not to provide the people with a government which would look after its interests, but to further its own political demand, the partition of the country. The result was that practically from the outset, the government was divided into two groups, which met separately before meeting as a Cabinet under the viceroy, each group formulating its own separate policies. After the first budget, things came to a head, and there was an open rift. The situation reached a climax when the budget presented by the League finance member was found, by the Congress, to be totally unacceptable. It was a clever budget. The Muslim League finance minister had suddenly become a socialist determined to clip the capitalist wings. An impossible situation would openly be created if the Congress decided to oppose the budget in the Assembly.

The government, for all practical purposes, came to a halt. It was at this stage that the British government decided to initiate a new policy and to send out a new viceroy to implement it.

Wavell, it was generally admitted by the Congress as well as the League, had tried hard to bring about an understanding between the Congress and the League. Unfortunately, success had eluded his efforts. I have gone carefully through the viceroy's journal. This makes it very clear indeed that whatever his own predilections, he was always anxious to do whatever was fair and just in the circumstances. I had a small personal experience of his desire, indeed his anxiety, to see that the fair thing was done. Towards the end of 1946 and early in 1947, Sir Eric Coates, the Cabinet secretary proceeded on short leave. Normally in such cases, the practice invariably has been to appoint the person next in seniority in the department to officiate. Instead, on this occasion, the then home secretary was invited to officiate in addition to his own duties. I considered this to be rather strange. I mentioned my feelings quite casually, to the viceroy's private secretary, George Abell. It would seem he had reported this casual conversation to the viceroy. The viceroy, who had then gone to Simla for a brief rest, desired that I should proceed to Simla. I had no idea at the time of the purpose of my being summoned. It turned out to be in respect of the complaint I had voiced to his private secretary. The viceroy came straight to the point and said that a Cabinet secretary had to deal with the secretaries to government, and many of them were fairly senior, and were certainly my seniors. Therefore, it was felt that it would be best to let a senior secretary officiate. I told him that this argument had never been held to have any weight in vacancies of this kind. Moreover, the viceroy's own secretary was a case in point. Apart from this, I was brought to the Cabinet Secretariat on the tacit understanding that I would be considered for Cabinet secretaryship when Sir Eric Coates left, unless I was found wanting. Wavell replied promptly that he was fully satisfied with my work. He wanted only to explain to me why he had decided that the home secretary should officiate on this occasion. It is interesting to note that Sir Eric Coates decided to retire very shortly after this. Wavell himself appointed me as permanent Cabinet secretary. He was quite honest when he had told me during our Simla interview that he was quite satisfied with my work. He had to leave soon afterwards and he was not able to see for himself how I fared in the appointment.

Wavell had done his best to see that the country remained united. It was one of his earnest suggestions that the British intention to leave India at the end of a fixed period of time should be made public. Wavell was not going back because he had been unsuccessful, but because the British government had decided to formulate and announce a new policy, and it was felt that a new viceroy would have a greater chance of success.

Meantime, the communal situation had worsened in the country as a whole but more particularly in the two provinces of Bengal and Punjab. Clashes were almost a daily occurrence in different parts of these provinces and the figures of casualties reported soon increased to disturbingly high figures. The time to take some innovative and bold action had come. Lord Wavell turned his mind in India to the consideration of plans for the safe withdrawal of the large British community in India. The British government was reluctant to accept the line of action that the viceroy appeared to favour and came to the conclusion that a new bold policy was needed. The Congress and the League, the two major parties should be forced to face facts and this could best be done by announcing a definite date by which the British would leave the country, whether an arrangement had been reached between the representatives or not. The British would do their best to bring about an agreement among the various political parties. They would prefer that but if no such understanding could be reached before the fixed date, they would still leave the country, whatever the ensuing situation in India. That would be the responsibility of the people of India. The anarchic conditions that would ensue were to be regretted. The ordinary people would suffer unimaginable hardship. But the responsibility would be that of the political leaders for their failure to arrive at a reasonable understanding. The British announced a policy more or less along these lines on 20 February 1947. Prime Minister Attlee also announced the appointment of a new viceroy, Lord Mountbatten. The underlying thinking undoubtedly being that he might obtain greater cooperation from the political leaders, as he would start without any preconceived ideas and with a determination to bring about an understanding before the final date. A time limit, not later than June 1948, having been fixed, it was hoped that a sense of urgency would prevail in everyone's mind as also a desire to find a solution. As things developed, a decision was taken within a matter of weeks to transfer power to a partitioned India, to two dominions, India and Pakistan by 15 August 1947.

The new viceroy arrived on 22 March. The oath-taking ceremony was quite spectacular. Departing from all normal procedure, Mountbatten made a short speech, as he seems instinctively to have felt that in the special circumstances of his acceptance of the office of viceroy something of the nature was called for. He asked for the cooperation of all concerned and promised his own cooperation in their united search for an understanding which would enable the British to leave the country with the feeling that it had been left safely in the hands of the people of the country. The new viceroy got down to business without delay. He started almost immediately after he had taken the oath of office to meet political leaders. And he kept up a terrific pace, day in and day out. One care the new viceroy had taken was to obtain the British government's approval to bringing with him besides a group of officers, personal private secretaries and steno-typists. He wanted to ensure that no information should leak out of his talks and discussions. It was only towards the end that he admitted to his inner circle of advisers men like V.P. Menon. Even I, as Cabinet secretary, met him only at meetings of the Executive Council. This was so even when I functioned along with Chaudhry Mohammad Ali on the Steering Committee to the Partition Council, and vast powers had been vested in us. I think this was a wise precaution, and did ensure that there were no 'leaks' and few rumours. It certainly helped greatly as all parties had the clear and justified assurance that none would enjoy any special privilege.

It would be useful to recall the kind of atmosphere that obtained at that time in the country as a whole and in Delhi, more particularly in the government circles. Ever since it had become fairly evident that the British authorities had decided upon leaving India as soon as they were able to devise a fairly satisfactory formula for transferring power to the people of India, all manner of speculations had begun to be voiced and discussed. This had the effect of creating a sense of uncertainty and unease. Everyone understandably asked himself the question what the effect would be of this major revolutionary change on him and whatever area he was working in. The communal situation had also become extremely tense because the Muslims, under the leadership of Jinnah, were being goaded into adopting an extreme stance, if what they wanted was not agreed to. They threatened direct action without any clear indication of precisely what that direct action involved. The efficiency of the district administration had also begun to suffer. To some extent this deterioration was expected with the departure of the British officers, who had hitherto controlled administration at every significant level. A certain measure of laxity was inevitable with less experienced hands replacing them. A foretaste had been experienced by the people during recent years during which popular administration had been installed in the provinces. Members of the Secretary of State's Services, the ICS and the IPS in particular, were naturally concerned and uncertain of their future prospects. Left to themselves, most British officers would have decided to leave. Some Indian officers of these services were also not certain whether they would be wanted when the new government came in. In this state of uncertainty, it was inevitable that administration should suffer. Nevertheless, the installation of the Interim Government had a certain reassuring effect. It made at least this clear that some progress was being achieved towards the eventual transfer of power.

Having regard to the very limited time available, a bare seventy days till 15 August, the date fixed for the transfer of power, Mountbatten suggested to the Interim Government that not a day should be lost and instead of waiting until Bengal and Punjab had formally decided to agree to the partitioning of their respective states on the basis of majority community areas, the present Interim Cabinet on which both the Congress and the League were represented should agree to the constitution of a Special Partition Committee. This committee, he suggested, should complete as much of the preliminary work as possible, before handing over the task to a regularly constituted Partition Council along with all the bodies to assist it in its task of dividing the country along with the assets and liabilities that it was agreed should go with them. The Special Committee would begin work straightaway, and agree upon, for instance the kind of Partition Council that should be set up together with the attendant partition machinery, agree upon the manner in which the existing staff of the Government of India should be divided to staff the new dominions and so on.

The Interim Government readily agreed to Mountbatten's suggestion and accordingly the Special Committee (Partition) was immediately constituted. This was to consist of Sardar Patel and Dr. Rajendra Prasad on the Congress side, and Liaqat Ali Khan and Sardar Abdur Rab Nishtar on the Muslim League side. When eventually the Partition Council was formed, only one change was made in this Committee, Jinnah coming in on the League side in place of Nishtar and Rajaji and Nishtar were nominated as alternatives in the event of one of the two regular members of the Council being unable to be present for any reason. It was agreed that Mountbatten would act as the neutral chairman, his role being that of a conciliator, having no right to vote. It may be stated right away that Mountbatten performed this role most admirably – he never allowed any issue to reach the stage of a stalemate: some compromise, some formula, some skilful bypassing was invariably evolved and in this effort, he was helped to an extent not only by his own staff, but also by what even he perhaps never fully realised, by the role played by the Steering Committee Members, who did their utmost jointly to see that their principals, that is, Sardar Patel and Jinnah, understood fully all implications and therefore in their turn did all they could to avoid a breaking point from being reached.

The first meeting of the Special Committee actually met on 6 June itself. There were four meetings in all before the Partition Council took over on 27 June. And during these four meetings, the Special Committee gave final shape to the partition machinery. The Partition Council was to be served by a Steering Committee of two members, who were to be, Messrs H.M. Patel and Mohammad Ali (I was at the time the Cabinet secretary and the latter was finance member,

Military Accounts). The Steering Committee was to be assisted by ten expert committees, each of which dealt with different groups of subjects, such as organisation, records, personnel, assets and liabilities, central revenues, contracts, currency and exchange, budget and accounts, economic relations, domicile, foreign relations, and Armed Forces Reconstitution Committee. These expert committees were in their turn assisted by sub-committees. Each of these committees had on them an equal number of Muslims and non-Muslims, except the Armed Forces Committee on which there had of necessity to be a number of British officers. The Steering Committee's functions were very wide. It was expected to see to it that decisions were taken which would ensure that there came into being a virtually functioning Pakistan government on 14 August 1947. In other words, the Steering Committee had also to make certain that a certain minimum of decisions were taken and implemented. To achieve this, the Steering Committee had also to see that every Expert Committee functioned and took the requisite number of decisions to enable various departments or ministries to come into being and be capable of carrying on its minimum essential duties. It was thus, one of its major duties to see to it that every expert committee produced concrete proposals, and as far as possible agreed proposals. In any event, it had to ensure that its proposals were formulated in a manner that would enable the Partition Council to evolve agreed proposals or decisions. In addition, the Steering Committee members had to keep in close touch with the Partition Council members. It was because of this that they were able to help in getting a great many issues cleared before they became disturbingly insoluble. Certainly the Steering Committee members helped greatly in avoiding issues from becoming emotionally surcharged, thus rendering an eventual solution impossible.

It was astonishing to see the speed with which information, that would ordinarily have taken weeks to collect, was made available in a matter of days. Everyone recognised that there was a race against time, and everyone was determined to see that everything necessary to bring into being the two dominions was achieved before 15 August. The persons on whom fell the maximum responsibility were, without a doubt, the two leading members on the Partition Council, namely Sardar Patel and Mohammad Ali Jinnah. They had to bear in mind the fact that on every issue handled by them, they would be committing their respective governments. And next only to them the major burden was carried by the two members of the Steering Committee. It was for them to see that the entire machinery of the government operated smoothly so that every Expert Committee in its turn could function in the most efficient manner possible. Moreover, it was their duty also to see that the Expert Committees made agreed recommendations to the maximum extent possible and were couched in language free from ambiguity, and when differences could not be reconciled, that these too were couched in an unambiguous manner, and indeed wherever possible indicating also a possible meeting ground. As a Steering Committee member, I used to meet Sardar Patel every evening, apprise him of the progress made by various Expert Committees, indicate wherever it looked as if they may find it difficult to reach an agreement, and prepare him for the items on the agenda of the forthcoming Partition Council meeting where there was no agreement, and suggest possible lines along which a settlement may be attempted. In short, as a Steering Committee member I had to ensure that the Sardar was never taken unawares in the Council and was fully prepared for any eventuality. My counterpart must also have functioned in a similar manner. And for both of us, our task was made easier by the fact that we enjoyed the fullest possible confidence of our principals. It was amazing what enormous amount of work was done during those fateful seventy odd days, what a mass of data relevant to every issue under consideration was made available, and how all this was accomplished during a period in which all around us there obtained an atmosphere of violence, hostility and suspicion. Great credit was due to all these people who strove single-mindedly towards the accomplishment of a goal set to them.

# 9

# Delhi Riots, September 1947

## I

SURPRISINGLY, FEW PEOPLE KNOW HOW NEAR THE BRINK of disaster Delhi was during those critical early days of Independence. One had anticipated unrest and disorder in the Punjab, West and East, and in particular in the areas, which were to constitute the further boundary between East and West Punjab, between Pakistan and India. And steps were taken, which it was hoped, would prove adequate to prevent any major outbreak and to keep it in check should there nevertheless be trouble. The Boundary Force of a mixed composition under British Commanding General Rees, was constituted. But events moved swiftly and pretty soon were beyond the capacity of the force to hold in check. This is not the place to describe those developments, but their effect was felt in a most unexpected manner in Delhi. A brief account of it here is not out of place, not only because it was an important episode in itself, but even more because it brings out facets of the character of our people which are most refreshing and heartening. Even when evil passions seemed to triumph, so many were found who were desirous of doing the right thing and who acted fearlessly and fairly. When

I find current events depressing, I look back on this among a few other episodes to draw fresh inspiration.

## II

What many had feared, and for the prevention of which, it was felt, adequate precautionary measures had been taken, nevertheless occurred. Little incidents led on to bigger ones and, slowly but surely, the extreme elements got the upper hand. They succeeded in working up communal bitterness to a frenzied pitch, and soon, all restraint was thrown to the winds. The average law-abiding citizen was either swept off his feet into participating in actions which he would not ordinarily have dreamt of committing, or was cowed into remaining a silent spectator of the most unholy massacre of the members of the minority community — the musclemen of the Indian side of the Punjab and the Hindus and Sikhs on the Pakistan side. As the reports of these occurrences reached Delhi, followed soon after by the refugees from the Western Punjab, the atmosphere of the capital, which was still full of the glow of Independence, was rapidly transformed first, into an atmosphere of anxiety and bewilderment and then of horror and anger. A seemingly increasing tide of refugees kept pouring into Delhi. They came by air, by train, by bus and in private cars — and later, much later, in foot convoys too. In the beginning, the movement was but a trickle, but very soon it developed into a flood which, sweeping through the Punjab, engulfed the city and province of Delhi and overflowed into the western districts of UP.

The uprooted millions were in a terrible mental state. They had been driven from their hearths and homes under conditions of indescribable horror. Not many had then the time to plan their evacuation; most had to move out at the shortest possible notice. They had experienced bestial cruelty. Their womenfolk were subjected to terrible indignities. Their near and dear ones were hacked to pieces before their eyes. Their houses were ransacked, looted and set on fire by their own neighbours, and none had come to their rescue or relief. They had no alternative but to seek safety in flight. Their one objective was to reach the frontier, somehow or the other. Once across the border, they felt safe. They were full of wrath for what they had seen and full of anguish for numberless missing kinsmen who were still stranded in Pakistan and for their womenfolk who had been abducted.

All classes of people joined the stream of refugees. There were rich persons who had been reduced overnight to poverty and penury. There were petty tradesmen and office-workers for which the future was, if anything, very uncertain and there were the Sikhs who had borne the main brunt of Muslim fury. They had all one thing in common; none had the wherewithal to sustain life in flight or to start it afresh. One and all needed food, shelter and also means to earn a living in due course.

The plight of the refugees stirred the people of Delhi into an impressive effort. A number of relief committees were quickly formed. The Arya Samaj established the Hindu Sahayata Committee. The Hindu Mahasabha formed a relief committee of their own, while the Gurudwara Prabhandak Committee organised distribution of cooked food on a large scale. This was not enough. Mrs. Sucheta Kripalani, who worked indefatigably all through the emergency, hastened to organise a Central Refugees Relief Committee, but by 28 August even her organisation proved to be inadequate. The chief commissioner therefore, took steps to bring into being the Provincial Refugees Relief Committee, which was composed of officials and non-officials and aimed at coordinating the work of all the relief committees then in existence. The Wavell Canteen near the Railway Station was taken over by the Kripalani Committee. The canteen served as a transit camp. Sucheta Kripalani also organised a number of refugee camps, one at Kingsway and the other at Kalkaji, both precursors of the refugee colonies now in existence at these sites. The Diwan Hall near the Red Fort was also used to give food and shelter to the incoming refugees.

While panic-stricken refugees poured into Delhi, the capital buzzed with rumours of a deep laid, long-prepared Muslim conspiracy to overthrow the new government of free India and to seize the capital. In retrospect, the rumours look, if not baseless, at least extremely improbable, but so credulous had the people become that they were very widely believed. Was not Delhi, before the advent of the British, the seat of Muslim empires for centuries? Was not the capital the cradle of Muslim culture? Almost half of its population professed the Muslim faith and they enjoyed great influence both in the city and in the local administration. There was a time when many a Muslim had followed nationalist leaders like Ansari and Ajmal Khan, but the number of their followers had dwindled to a mere fraction and for many years before Partition, the vast majority of Muslims of Delhi had lent their powerful support to Jinnah. The Muslim League high command functioned from Delhi and it was from Delhi that the campaign of direct action had been organised and conducted throughout the length and breadth of the country. The militant National Guards had a well-knit organisation in the city and Khaksars too boasted of a number of adherents. A determined effort had been made, before the announcement of the Mountbatten plan, to organise and equip the Muslim community for communal violence. The majority of the ammunition dealers in the city were Muslims and they found it easy to help their co-religionists in obtaining a wide variety of weapons and ammunition. Muslim blacksmiths and arms repairers also played their part. Their shops had been converted into miniature arsenals for fabricating country-made bombs, mortars and other ammunition. There is little doubt that the Muslims in the city had been fully prepared for a major showdown. But Pakistan was achieved without having to fire a shot. The militant National Guards and Khaksars were left in a quandary; they did not know how to conduct themselves in a partitioned India. It was not unnatural for them to be led away by stories of an imminent effort to annex Delhi as a part of the new Muslim kingdom.

The Hindus of Delhi represented, so to say, the third force. Their hearts were warm with the glow of freedom. They were frankly jubilant. For days they remained completely ignorant of what Partition had meant to their co-religionists in Pakistan. Nor could they appreciate the feelings of the average Muslim in Delhi, much less have even a glimmer of the plans of the militant Muslims.

It was perhaps not surprising in the circumstances that the first recorded communal incident in Delhi took place in a predominantly Muslim locality. On 21 August 1947, an explosion took place in a house belonging to a Muslim science student. It is believed that he was trying to prepare a bomb. It is again significant that a few days later the first stabbing was reported from the vicinity of the Diwan Hall and the Wavell Canteen, the two places where the Central Relief Committee had arranged the reception of the incoming refugees. On 25 August, an altercation ensued between a Hindu worker and a Muslim worker in the Birla Mills, which led to a free fight, but the police were able to control it and restore order quickly. Meantime, reports of stray incidents kept coming in from the countryside also.

The local administration was faced with a task far beyond its capacity. Many of its Muslim officers had opted to serve Pakistan. Their withdrawal caused almost a crippling depletion of the officer-cadres. More than fifty per cent of the police force was drawn from amongst the Muslims and all of them had opted for Pakistan. They could not obviously be relied upon in an emergency. In fact, there were persistent rumours of their plans to go over to the rioters along with their firearms. Many of the Hindu policemen were drawn from the Punjab and they had heard of what had happened to their friends and relations in the West Punjab. Few of them were in a fit mental state to take strong action against rioters. Only a handful of troops were present in the capital and these could not be reinforced quickly because many of the formations that had fallen to the share of India were still locked up in the northwest in Pakistan. In an effort to preserve order with the help of the limited manpower at his disposal, the district magistrate, Delhi imposed an extended curfew from the afternoon of 28 August to the early hours of 1 September. The old city seemed peaceful and quiet during this period but as was discovered later, forces bent on mischief were busy making offensive and defensive preparations on a large scale in areas which were either predominantly inhabited by Muslims or into which the refugees had penetrated. On the morning of 4 September, the explosion of a bomb in a Hindu locality in Karol Bagh was the signal for a serious outbreak of rioting in many parts of the town and there occurred numerous isolated cases of arson, looting and stabbing in all parts of the city. Muslim and Hindu localities were so intermingled that each locality feared an attack from its neighbour. An atmosphere of nervousness and apprehension pervaded the entire capital.

In the beginning, the use of firearms was the exception. But on 7 September, some Muslims shot and killed a few of their Hindu opponents: their action was probably only defensive. It was, however, provocative in the tense atmosphere that prevailed. Trouble broke out afresh on a large scale, in which firearms were freely used particularly in the Subzimandi, Karol Bagh and Sadar Bazaar areas. Some houses in the locality were converted into powerful bastions, where firearms from the neighbourhood were collected and stored for use. One of these houses was later found to contain considerable subterranean stores of arms and ammunition. In a situation such as this, the small police force was completely helpless. A police picket was surrounded inside the Turkman Gate, and was rescued only with the greatest difficulty. A sub-inspector was shot dead in the Subzimandi area. Troops had to be called upon to assist in quelling the riots, and even with their help, order was not easy to restore. If it had only been a question of protecting the few against the onslaughts of the many, perhaps the troops, even though small in number, might have proved equal to the task. But here, both sides seemed well provided with firearms and were equally well organised and determined and operated in guerilla fashion. The task of restoring law and order called for patience, perseverance and a degree of ruthlessness.

Organised rioting apart, sporadic and isolated incidents of looting, stabbing and arson were rampant in many parts of the city. Muslim shops situated in predominantly Hindu areas were the chief targets and needy refugees were the chief beneficiaries. The police force was much too small to protect each shop and to remain on duty all day and all night. Whenever a police party appeared on the scene, the looters would disappear into the by-lanes; and as soon as it withdrew, they would reassemble and resume their operations.

Stabbing was developed into an art and it seemed to provide a natural outlet for the over-powering urge to wreak vengeance. For the most part, it was women, children and the aged, who were the victims. But stabbing did not take place only in alleys. Groups of blood-thirsty refugees would even rush into houses and drag people out to be stabbed. Roving bands of Sikh refugees struck so much terror even in New Delhi that it became necessary to evacuate Muslim servants into refugee camps so as to ensure their safety. For days together, no effective protection could be given against treacherous, sneaking and silent killing by individuals impelled by an uncontrollable urge to settle the score: they sought an eye for an eye, a tooth for a tooth.

The passion for revenge found its expression in many ways, and arson was one of them. Delhi had six fire engines and all of them were kept more than busy; they had scores of small and big fires to attend to. On the night of 7-8 September one could see from roof-tops in New Delhi red clouds and smoke curling up from numberless points in the old city.

Not all had, however, lost their balance; indeed, there were numerous instances of brave and defiant conduct by individuals in defence of the helpless. When a mob attacked a Muslim family, a Congressman intervened and dared them to kill him before laying their blood stained hands on the Muslim family. Hundreds of Hindus took their Muslim neighbours into their protective care and escorted them to refugee camps. Many institutions mounted guard to protect their Muslim members. A sweeper family moved into their Muslim master's house to protect him against threatened attacks by refugees in the neighbourhod.

Verily, only a thin line divides the man from the beasts — and order from chaos. Even though not more than a small section of the population had been directly involved in the riots, the uncertainty of the moment, the prevailing atmosphere of nervousness and apprehension, and the fear of one's own neighbour, all but paralysed the normal life of the old town. While Muslims from the disturbed areas were fleeing to refugee camps in search of security, others, Muslims and non-Muslims alike, were unwilling or unable to leave their homes. Their families would not let them go because they did not know what might befall them on the road. The breadwinner hesitated to go out because he was afraid of what might happen to his family in his absence. And so for days together, shops remained unopened, offices ceased to function, health services were disrupted and communications were disorganised.

Conditions in New Delhi never deteriorated to so serious an extent. It too, however, experienced some lawlessness. A number of shops in Connaught Place were looted and stray cases of stabbing too occurred. Sufficient feeling of uncertainty was created to make it necessary to move out almost the entire Muslim population of New Delhi to refugee camps. Nor was there a sense of security among the Hindus. The concentration of Muslims, particularly the turbulent Meos from the neighbouring villages roundabout the Lodi Road area, was a potential source of trouble. The lurid glow of fires in the horizon, the screaming and shrieking of victims and all-night shouting and shooting, even though at a distance, were enough to unnerve anyone. Food and milk were scarce and the majority of staff absented themselves from the Central Government offices. Telephones worked fitfully and for two days the mail was not delivered at all. Airports too were not spared by the rioters and air-services were badly interrupted.

In the areas surrounding Delhi too, in the villages of the neighbouring states of Alwar and Bharatpur, and of the adjoining districts of Uttar Pradesh and East Punjab, there took place serious disturbances, and a large number of people, mostly Muslims, trekked into Delhi and greatly added to the already complex problem of protecting the local Muslim population.

The authorities were, thus, faced with much more than quelling disturbances. They had to restore not just law and order, but also that intangible essential – the sense of security. The ordinary citizen had to be assured that he could continue to live his every day humdrum life!

## III

The local administration was quite obviously overwhelmed, and some extraordinary and imaginative action was called for. Mountbatten, Nehru and Sardar were all concerned, for they realised the supreme psychological importance of prompt restoration of normalcy in the capital. But they had a plethora of problems on their hands.

I remember still with what shock I first learnt of the angry crowds of Sikhs and Hindus moving about after dark, even in New Delhi in areas where government servants' houses were located. I felt immediately that it was necessary to ascertain the latest position and what was being done by the Delhi administration to come to grips with the situation. It was immediately clear that something needed to be done without delay. The bulk of the Delhi Police Force opted for service in Pakistan, and could no longer be trusted to look with sympathy on the woes of the Hindus and Sikhs in West Punjab, much less the refugees. To make matters more difficult, the chief commissioner of Delhi at the time happened to be a Muslim ICS officer and the deputy commissioner, a Sikh, both officers with blameless record, but liable in the heavily charged atmosphere to be 'suspect'. I put my anxieties to several of my colleagues and then discussed the matter with V.P. Menon. We (V.P. and some other civil servants used to meet almost every day during that critical period) decided that the home minister should be apprised of my fears immediately and the need therefore, for some special arrangements without delay. He suggested that we might put A.D. Gorwala in charge of the city. (He was then stationed in Delhi as chairman of the Commodities Prices Board and was thus, most easily available). But would that not mean suppression of the local administration? And in any case, would he have the necessary weight and authority? A high level committee appointed by the Emergency Committee of the Cabinet might have greater credibility and would also not involve any suppression. This suggestion was put to Sardar who approved of it and put it immediately to the Emergency Committee of the Cabinet the very next day. On 9 September, it was decided to set up an ad hoc committee. The committee was to be composed of Bhabha — a Cabinet minister as the chairman, and I myself was appointed as vice-chairman. The chief commissioner and the deputy commissioner of Delhi were to be members and K.B. Lall, who was then working as deputy secretary in the Partition Secretariat under me, and an old resident of Delhi, appointed secretary of the Committee. It was further agreed that any Cabinet minister interested may be co-opted, and initially Shyamaprasad Mukherjee and Shri Niyogi said they were interested. The main responsibility naturally devolved on me, as the only civil servant on the committee, and as one who could also provide a ready link as Cabinet secretary with the Emergency Committee of the Cabinet. The plan was bold and yet extraordinarily simple. It recognised that the local administration had broken down. It envisaged that emergency arrangements had to be improvised and yet no new centralised administration could be built up because of the paucity of personnel and breakdown of communications. The city was therefore to be divided into five zones; each zone was to be entrusted to an administrator to be drawn from amongst the senior officers of the Government of

India. The administrators were to be allowed their respective quotas of men and material. Each zonal group was to be asked to rely on its own initiative and resources to do what appeared to be the best in the circumstances and only keep the headquarters informed every four hours of the situation and regional requirements if any. To begin with, a skeleton headquarters organisation was to be located at the Town Hall with only a mobile reserve at its disposal and with wireless facilities to maintain contact with zonal administrators. The idea was to secure maximum decentralisation and effective coordination with a view to making the best possible use of the limited manpower available at the time. It may be mentioned here that the plan was subjected to close scrutiny. It was urged that it was wrong to change horses mid-stream and that any arrangements of the nature proposed would destroy the little confidence among local administration that still remained. Before any decision could be reached, news was received that some Muslims on the Ajmeri Gate side armed with automatic weapons had run amuck and were shooting down Hindus at a site in the Minto Road Area. A feeling of helplessness appeared to overwhelm all. Members and I proceeded to Sardar's residence. Our report depressed Sardar beyond words. There were signs of deep anguish on his face but he did not speak. Just then, someone brought in the news that a few Hindus had been killed by Meos in the Lodi Road area and a minute later a man rushed in to say that a Muslim had been butchered not very far from the minister's residence. The Sardar was visibly shaken and in a voice charged with deep emotion, he exclaimed: What is the point in waiting and discussing here? Get on with the committee as already approved. The new committee proceeded immediately to meet in the Town Hall, situated in the heart of the old city. The situation was briefly reviewed at the meeting of the Central Emergency Committee that approved of the arrangements made. Thus, was born the Delhi Emergency Committee, which rescued the capital from chaos and brought it back to normal life within a matter of days.

## IV

A kind of zonal system that was devised essentially as an emergency device, was designed to secure limited objectives in the shortest possible time. It was put into effect on 11 September and it soon yielded fairly quick and good dividends. The zonal administrators succeeded very largely in putting a stop to large-scale rioting. Of necessity, they had to concentrate on dangerous spots. These they neutralised successfully. The calls, however, were too numerous for them to attend to each promptly or effectively. They could not, therefore, restore confidence in the Muslims to induce them to stay on in their homes, particularly in the worse affected zones. Zonal officers, therefore, did the next best thing and arranged to escort them safely to refugee camps. In the less-affected zones, particularly the Jama Masjid and the Kashmere Gate areas, greater success was achieved and the Muslims felt sufficiently reassured to stay on in their homes.

Decentralisation was vital to success, and without entering upon any academic discussion as to any definite plan of action, the committee under my active guidance proceeded to divide the Old and New Delhi areas into four zones and to constitute the rural area into a fifth zone. It was also decided that maximum possible coordination between the magistracy and the police as also other organs of local administration, should be achieved at the zonal level. K.B. Lall and L.K. Jha were appointed secretaries to the committee.

The committee set up its headquarters at the Town Hall. It was rapidly organised into a most efficient 'Central Control Room', as it came to be known. From here were issued directives and instructions to zonal organisations and workers over the wide area of old and new Delhi and surrounding villages, which became the responsibility of this young organisation to administer, and into which flowed an almost unending stream of demands and requirements for assistance of every conceivable kind from all sections of the public and other official and semi-official bodies.

I have a very vivid recollection even to this day of the first visit to the Town Hall where the control room was located, as soon as the Emergency Committee of the Cabinet sanctioned the creation of the Delhi Emergency Committee. Mr. Bhabha and I (along with Shyamaprasad Mukherjee and Niyogi who were Cabinet ministers and had expressed a desire to obtain an idea of the latest position) proceeded to the Control Room to form an idea of the situation as it then stood. The normally extremely busy areas such as Daryaganj, Jama Masjid and Chandni Chowk presented an incredibly deserted view at 11.30 or so in the morning, when it should ordinarily be humming with activity. As we approached the Town Hall, we were shocked to find a small crowd gathered around some poor devil who had fallen a victim to a miscreant's knife. The chief commissioner and the deputy commissioner met us at the Control Room, and they gave us a quick review of the situation, and broadly the steps that they had taken to cope with it. It was clear immediately that the Control Room needed to be strengthened forthwith. The responsibilities of the government had increased in several directions. Thus, one immediate task that had to be faced was that of cleaning up the city very thoroughly. It had been unswept and uncleaned for several days. There were areas in which, we were informed, even corpses had not been removed. After a general assessment of the tasks that needed immediate attention, the ministers left, leaving me to see to it that whatever called for immediate implementation was taken up for appropriate action. I took immediate action to strengthen the Control Room.

This is not the place to describe in detail the working of the Control Room. I can only hope that it will one day be written, for it not only did a magnificent job, as it seemed to me, looking on largely from the outside. The Control Room called upon many of the officers of the Government of India of all services and ranks during this period to take on some job or other. What came into existence was an amazing mechanism — improvised and developed but perfected in the space of a few days by a group of enthusiastic young men and women, officials and non-officials, under my leadership. The Emergency Committee, as such, virtually ceased to exist after the first two days, during which it made a general survey of the situation and decided to leave all further action to me, the vice-chairman. Members of the committee in their individual capacity continued throughout to assist the Central Control Room in every conceivable way and gave each in his own way, his personal support. The chairman, in turn, gave full authority and discretion to me. I was not in a position to give my entire attention to this task, as I was also the Cabinet secretary and concerned with Partition matters, neither of which duties I could hand over to any one else. However, in K.B. Lall and L.K. Jha we had found remarkably able and self-reliant lieutenants. Lall had great drive and initiative and he soon welded the mixed crowd of volunteers, officials and non-officials, men and women, into a wonderful team. Late every evening, a meeting would be held under my chairmanship at which all the day's occurrences and experiences, unsolved problems and difficulties, would be reviewed and suitable instructions issued and solutions found. That same day, however, late it might be, I would make a brief oral report to Bhabha and Sardar. The following morning, Bhabha would inform the Central Emergency Committee of the principal activities and events in the city during the previous day. Bhabha and I would then clear up their doubts, give any new information on some occurrence or event, and make known our requirements whether of men, equipment or materials. Nothing that was required was considered to be too small for this supreme authority, and directions were promptly given to whomsoever was regarded as capable of meeting that need.

Nothing was more inspiring and nothing cheered one so much as the spontaneous way in which men and women of all ages, classes and shades of opinions, came forward to work at all hours — if need be, round the clock — in a disciplined manner for a task, which they realised was of great humanity. The committee's need was for men and women of determination and devotion to duty, who would readily undertake any task, however disagreeable, and who would shirk nothing even if physical risk was involved; and the committee found them – thanks to K.B. Lall's old contacts with political and social workers and with professional men in different walks of life. Within twenty-four hours, more than enough had come forward. Trained administrators were also essential, and there my pivotal position as Cabinet secretary proved a boon. I was able to obtain from the Cabinet the power to requisition the services of any Central Government officer I wanted. This power was used freely, though with discretion. A number of young officers were detailed for full-time duty with the committee, while quite a number of officers volunteered to perform part-time duties. (Incidentally, one of these officers, K.S. Mishra, then working as joint secretary in the Ministry of Food, was shot dead by a rioter while on duty at Mehrauli.) IAS probationers, then under training at the Administrative Training School, were also pressed into service and they showed extraordinary enthusiasm and were undoubtedly effective. They too lost one of their very promising young men.

The strength of the armed forces at the disposal of the Emergency Committee was very limited. Reinforcements were expected to come in much later. Only a small number of Gurkhas and Madras paratroopers could be made available quickly. Madhya Pradesh contributed a contingent of armed police. For the rest, the committee had to rely on the citizens of Delhi. Every possible source of trained and disciplined manpower was tapped. The OTC were the first to be called in; they performed their duties most keenly and in the process sustained a few casualties. The Territorials were also given certain escort duties. They proved particularly helpful in evacuating stranded Muslim families. Scouts Organisations were called upon to make their contribution. The Jamiat-ul-Ulema contributed a band of very energetic Muslim workers who, dressed in red shirts, cheerfully performed unpleasant tasks at great risks to themselves. Sher Jung, an ex-revolutionary, organised a small corps of Congress volunteers who were armed by the Emergency

Committee with shotguns. This corps rendered useful service in reviving the confidence of the minority community in the desire and ability of the authorities to provide security to every man and woman irrespective of his or her religion. Each of these separate organisations had its accredited representative in the Control Room and it was through him that each organisation made a daily report of its performance and received daily orders regarding disposition of its resources in men and material.

All the Service Departments and organisations were represented at the Control Room. Each of the three Municipal Committees was represented in the Control Room and so also the Health Department and the Food Department. The Communications Department too was represented as also the Railway Board, the Delhi Transport Organisation and social welfare organisations including the Relief Committees. Each important organisation or department was given a separate table in the Control Room and the representative sitting at this table was expected to function as the liaison officer between the Control Room and the parent organisation.

As far as practicable, broad assignments were given to the different organisations and each was expected to raise its own resources, take its own decisions and to fulfil its assignment, only keeping the Central Office of the Control Room informed of the extent of success achieved and stating its requirements if any from other organisations. However, most of the tasks involved a pooling of the resources of a number of departments and organisations, and only a few could be performed except on a basis of cooperative and coordinated endeavour. The detailed planning of assignments, allocation of resources of all kinds was Lall's responsibility assisted by Jha. This they discharged with consummate skill and with an almost inestimable bonhomie that won them complete and devoted cooperation. But, however careful and detailed the planning, it was inevitable that in the prevailing disorder and confusion, things should go wrong sometimes. Even so straightforward a job as the supply of bags of foodgrains to refugee camps could be held up if a Sikh driver succeeded in feigning illness or a clerk in the foodgrains store declined to honour the Control Room's order. It was therefore, very necessary to chase each operation from hour to hour and to see that each organisation and each officer performed the allotted task. A corps of chasers was specially organised and each chaser was given a set of operations to monitor. He was required to watch on an hourly basis, the progress of each operation and to bring immediately to the Control Room's notice any difficulties or obstacles that were encountered. Solutions for these difficulties were improvised on the spot. No operation was allowed to be delayed; overriding importance was attached to results. Within seventy-two hours of the organisation of the Control Room, the reported performance was as high as could be desired.

## V

Communications constituted perhaps the most important single basic problem. The normal means of transport were no longer available. The public transport system was virtually at a standstill, while tonga drivers out of prudence, kept their tongas off the road. Only a few ventured to go out on cycles or on foot; even the voluntary workers of the Control Room had to be picked up from their respective homes and be transported to and from their place of work in government vehicles. Transport for essential workers represented only a small percentage of the total requirements. For each job or operation, as it was somewhat grandiloquently called, depended for its speedy execution on the availability of adequate and reliable transport.

When the trouble started, the local authorities requisitioned a few public vehicles. But these soon proved to be too few and later even concerted attempts at requisitioning yielded disappointing results. Two requisitioning squads were organised, each under a magistrate, but both experienced difficulties in locating car owners, and when owners were located, drivers were missing, and when both could be traced, requisitioning officers found it impossible to drive away in the vehicle because someone had cleverly removed an essential part or two. The Control Room soon devised ingenious ways for countering the tricks employed by recalcitrant owners. The insistence on roadworthy vehicles was abandoned: instead it was decided to accept, extract or acquire from every possible source everything that could be of any use to the transport organisation. Stocks of spare parts were commandeered from automobile shops. People were invited to donate essential spare parts. The Control authorities just helped themselves to abandoned vehicles on the road. An enterprising officer managed to take delivery of a consignment of batteries lying at the railway station. Another worker in the organisation was able to fly out a consignment from Bombay. An appeal for volunteer drivers was made and lastly, trained mechanics were literally rounded up from their homes. Muslim mechanics were brought from refugee camps to improvised workshops where their personal safety was guaranteed. Soon a large number of vehicles were on the road. But more were needed. Workers in the organisation were asked to use their own or their friends' vehicles, and many owner-drivers were encouraged by the offer of extra coupons of petrol for private use to volunteer their transport for the use of the control authorities for part of the day. The Defence Department made strenuous efforts to make good the deficiency in trucks and jeeps. Disposal stocks were re-examined in search of roadworthy vehicles, and trucks were spared for short periods from regular formations. Bit by bit, an impressive transport fleet was thus, built up.

A rigorous method of allocation was devised. The transport requirement of each job was carefully assessed. The assessment and the allocation were reviewed from day-to-day. The wastage of transport was very largely eliminated but the drivers, many of whom were themselves refugees from Pakistan, gave an infinite amount of trouble. They had no heart in working for the welfare of the Muslim refugees, and they would pretend to lose their way if they were sent to a Muslim mohalla or vehicles entrusted to their care would develop engine trouble on the way to a Muslim refugee camp. It took sometime to overcome this type of malingering. It was not until student volunteers, drawn from the OTC, had been drafted to perform escort duties on vehicles manned by these drivers that a satisfactory rate of performance of the requisitioned vehicles could be attained.

## VI

Sanitation was our next big problem. Sanitary arrangements, especially in the old town, broke down completely. For over a week, the municipal conservancy staff and private sweepers stayed away from their work. A week's accumulation of filth is enough to cause despair to any health authority; loot and arson multiplied the problem tenfold, while rotting dead bodies brought death nearer to the living. Urgent and decisive action was essential. Inhabitants of each locality were called upon to organise voluntary squads and assist in cleaning up the streets and to pile up the filth at comparatively accessible points wherever it could be removed or destroyed on the spot. Once a beginning was made, it soon acquired momentum. It took a much longer time and greater effort to persuade the sweepers to rejoin duty, and even when they came back to work, they were inclined to tarry over each heap to search for valuables. A large number of volunteers drawn from the Congress, the Jamiat-e-ulema-Hind, the student unions and scouts had to be drafted to assist them. These volunteers rendered invaluable service; they not only did the greater part of the cleaning up themselves, but they also succeeded by their example in making others including the sweepers to join in and speed the completion of this vital task. Special motorised transport was made available for the removal of dead bodies and filth and services of batches of sweepers were also requisitioned from the neighbouring towns in the United Provinces. Cleaning units consisting of transport, sweepers, and volunteers were organised and the work of removal of filth and of cleaning up the lanes was taken up systematically one area at a time. Later, the Army was able to place at the disposal of the Control Authority a Hygiene Squad, which made it possible for the badly affected parts of the town to be thoroughly disinfected. The work went on twenty-four hours, by day as well as by night. It was only after a week of sustained effort that it could be said that the city had been averted from the danger of epidemics.

## VII

Food distribution arrangements were thoroughly disorganised for over a week. Ration shops remained closed; authorised ration distributors were unwilling to stir out of their houses to replenish their stocks and those who ventured out found difficulty in drawing money from their banks and in securing necessary transport to carry the stocks to their shops. The Control Room organised, without delay, a system for delivering rationed food grains to shopkeepers at their shops. Salt too was similarly supplied. For the first couple of days, unfortunately, the authorities overlooked the need for making arrangements for the delivery of fuel, and this caused the people serious inconvenience in some areas. It is only in times of disorder and disorganisation that one realises how critically important small things can become; many a family had to forego a meal because there was no fuel in the house. Fortunately, the Control Authorities did not have to worry too much about the supplies of essential goods themselves. There were enough stocks of food grains available to meet the city's requirements for a month or more. Salt and fuel were in short supply and these had to be brought in rapidly to replenish the reserve. However, when the special trains arrived bringing in the additional supply, fresh difficulties arose in the shape of labour and transport to unload and move the stocks. The Control Room machinery proved its effectiveness; the required transport was readily diverted from less essential jobs and one of the local cloth mills was directed to provide the labour.

Given adequate supplies and the will to help themselves, it should not have been difficult for the evacuees to build themselves a rudimentary cooperative organisation to look after their daily needs. But none was in a fit psychological state to give the lead or to lend a helping hand. Each was overwhelmed with their problems and all had been dazed with the rapidity of the tragic events. The Pakistan high commissioner tried, in the beginning, to look after the requirements of the refugees in the Purana Qila. But the job was too big for him and his limited staff. The local administration had also its hands full with manifold responsibilities and the efforts it made were understandably but nonetheless, pitifully inadequate. None but a brave official or a foreigner could dare to set foot. So high was the tension in these Muslim concentrations that the inmates were prepared to beat up even those who came only to help. When a Sikh driver, carrying food grains from the Control Room, was persuaded to drive his jeep into the Purana Qila so that the food grains could be delivered inside the camp, he was surrounded by a furious mob and it was with the greatest difficulty that he could be rescued from the refugees who were determined to kill him. For days, only known and identifiable foreigners and Muslims could enter the camps, and fortunately, also a few Hindu senior officials.

The Control Room had to act with speed here also. The basic requirements of over a hundred thousand persons had to be met; and the numbers went on increasing. Arrangements for the regular and adequate supply of food, filtered water, sanitary and medical facilities were quickly improvised. Three officers of the ICS were detailed to work as camp commandants; the Indian Administrative Service Training School supplied them with a few deputies. Many non-officials joined in. Assistance was also rendered to the official organisation by a devoted band of women, wives of Indian and foreign officials. Their liaison at the Control Room, Taya Zinkin and Fori Nehru, played a notable part with their amazing zeal and energy. Foreign missions contributed a number of volunteers and many ladies, who came to make enquiries about their servants, stayed on to serve in the camps. Lady Smith, wife of General Sir Arthur Smith, led a band of workers to look after hospital arrangements at one of the camps and the tireless manner in which she worked was indeed inspiring. Help came from various social welfare organisations in Delhi and Christian missions also contributed volunteers. Lady Mountbatten was a frequent visitor; she not only gave help from her own household but did not rest content until, bit by bit, the enormous requirements of the camps had been put together from different sources. A band of nationalist Muslim workers led by Dr. Zakir Hussain and reinforced by volunteers from the Jamia Milia made tremendous efforts to revive the morale of the refugees and to instill in them a desire to help themselves. This was no easy task and their success, although slow and not complete, was yet striking and greatly helped those who were anxious to assist the refugees.

Every foot of the covered accommodation in the Purana Qila and Humayun Tomb was occupied. Scores of tents were pitched and every possible contrivance was used to improvise shelter. So great was the congestion that even space for locating the administrative sections could be found with great difficulty. The Air Force lent command trailers for the use of camp commandants. But although the semblance of an office was set up on the first day, the camp commandants had no means to communicate with the vast mass of humanity placed under their charge, until the Navy provided them with loud hailers (it is interesting to recall that the procurement of these hailers figured on the agenda of the Central Emergency Committee presided over by Lord Mountbatten and the speed with which they arrived on the scene owed not a little to the existence of that machinery) and a loud speaker system had been rigged up from civilian sources. No lighting arrangements were available for the first two nights, but thereafter, powerful searchlights were erected with the help of the Army. The only water available was unfiltered. The Military Engineering Service and the Central PWD helped to lay on a water system and steps were taken to put in an emergency telephone connection.

Labour and equipment were required for every conceivable purpose and in the early stages these were simply not available. There were tents to be pitched, drains to be cleared, sanitation to be looked after and volunteers were needed for the distribution of food grains and to maintain law and order. To set an example, the camp commandant and his officers themselves went round the camps with shovels, filling up a drain here and digging a trench there. There was no job, which was too mean or too specialised for the volunteers. The ornamental fountains in Humayun's Tomb became a mass of stinking water within the first few days; the volunteers filled them up with sand to prevent further stagnation. The slit trench latrines were flooded by heavy rains and these too had to be filled up. The supplies, which rolled in from the city had to be unloaded, stacked and guarded; water had to be transported; food grains to be brought and distributed each day and those who had fallen ill had to be nursed back to health. And when an epidemic threatened to break out, mass inoculations had to be resorted to. There were not enough trained hands to do the job, but student volunteers soon learnt the drill and had statistics been kept, they would probably have shown that never before had so many men, women and children been inoculated or vaccinated in so short a time.

An efficient supply and services organisation at the Control Room made it possible to cope with such a variety and unending stream of demands from so many sources, and all of the highest priority. The camps sent in their indents every day, and every evening, the camp commandants discussed their problems and difficulties with the authorities at the Headquarters. It was by no means an easy task to raise the hundred and one things that were required when the complex machinery that ordinarily kept the city itself going had ceased to function. Somehow, by improvising, ingenious and simple but effective little organisations were created so that every essential job was done and every necessity met. Every possible source was tapped. A portion of the supplies required came by way of donations. Stocks from godowns and shops were freely requisitioned. The PWD stores were ransacked to supply the enormous numbers of picks and shovels that were required. When no one was able to obtain refuse bins from anywhere, one of the camp commandants, who happened to see a stock of empty tar barrels in an open space loaded up the barrels on to his pick-up and drove to his camp. Another officer systematically removed refuse bins from the roads in New Delhi and later gratefully made acknowledgement to the NDMC for the loan of these bins. Thus, in diverse ways the varied and enormous requirements of over a lakh people were met within a week. Life in the camps became a little more organised and a little more tolerable.

Even nature was merciless and added to the suffering of the refugees. The late September rains were exceptionally heavy that year. Few could keep dry under such improvised shelters as existed and the influx of refugees into the camps continued. At one time, it was thought that another refugee camp might have to be organised. But the efforts of the Delhi Emergency Committee to stamp out lawlessness were also meeting with success in the meantime, and in at least two areas in the town, sufficient confidence was reinstalled in the minds of the Muslim inhabitants to make them stay on, rather than leave their homes.

Thought was given all this time to the future of those who had sought safety in numbers, in camps. Obviously, they could not stay there indefinitely. It was explained over the loud speaker system that those Muslims who wished to stay on in Delhi were welcome to do so and a number responded. But those who were keen to go to Pakistan were in a majority, and demanded that facilities should be provided for them to move on to Pakistan immediately. With the cooperation of the railway authorities, special trains were arranged and a large number left each day. But far more trains were required than could be made available and the camp authorities had to face enormous difficulties in deciding upon who should go and who stay behind.

## VIII

We were able to bring the situation in Delhi and immediate surrounding areas under control in so far as law and order was concerned, though here too as I soon realised there was no room for complacency. I remember how on one occasion during this period, I stated in the Emergency Committee of the Cabinet that the situation in Delhi was completely under control. To my discomfiture, I had to admit the very next day that during the night a crowd from a neighbouring village had burst into the Safdarjung Hospital and killed a number of riot-affected patients in the hospital. This, however, was the last incident of lawlessness.

Within less than two weeks, the Special Emergency Committee had achieved its main object — the restoration of normal conditions in the city. The sense of insecurity among the Muslims took longer to disappear, though it would be correct to say that by the first week of October, a Muslim could move about the city without any real danger to his life or limb. So long as the great camps in Purana Qila and Humayun's Tomb remained, the Control Room too had to remain, for there was no other organisation which could have taken over from it the responsibility of running these two camps with their population of over a lakh and a half. Gradually, the camps emptied; a certain number went to Pakistan, and the remainder returned to their homes in Delhi and the neighbouring areas.

One other duty the Control Room staff had undertaken, which deserves a passing mention was the custodianship of evacuee property of the refugees. Like all other tasks, this too was discharged with efficiency and sympathy. This duty was handed over to the regular custodian organisation as soon as it was created during October.

When the time came for the organisation to be wound up, Bhabha wrote to thank all those who had worked under him in his organisation for their truly magnificent work. No other word could more appropriately describe what was done. The manner of their doing it, and tremendous devotion to duty and the humanitarianism that inspired it will always be an unforgettable memory to all those who likewise were privileged to get a glimpse of it. It is the knowledge of such episodes that made Sardar say in 1949 in the Lok Sabha —

> "... I wish to record in this House that if, during the last two or three years, most of the members of the services had not behaved patriotically with loyalty, the Union would have collapsed... They are the men who served selflessly and devotedly and deserve the affection of the people."

# 10

# Serving the New Nation, 1947 to 1958

## Changes in the Defence Organisation Consequent on Partition

IT BECAME CLEAR DURING DISCUSSIONS ON MATTERS relating to the partition of the Armed Forces that the entire defence organisation would have to be thoroughly overhauled. Even the armed forces themselves as also their officers would have to adapt themselves to a very radically altered set up. Sardar Patel asked me to help in this task and desired that I move over to the Defence Department as early as possible. My selection for this task was in some ways an obvious one because I was among the very few officers on the civil side who had acquired some worthwhile experience of defence matters. As I have mentioned earlier, on my appointment to the Cabinet Secretariat, I was taken on a conducted tour and given a more than bird's eye view of the defence organisation and the various important installations of the three services. And thereafter, during the Partition discussions, as a member of the Steering Committee, I had to go through all the proposals recommended to the Partition Council by the Armed Forces Reconstitution Committee presided over by the supreme commander-in-chief.

It is interesting to note at this stage that both the India and Pakistan representatives showed very lively and keen interest in the manner in which the question of division of armed forces was to be tackled. Neither had any understanding of the problems involved, but both were anxious that the division should be carried through as quickly as possible. Both sides curiously enough were suspicious of the role the British commander-in-chief and the British officers might play. The only civilian of some standing and experience of military matters was Sir Chandulal Trivedi, an ICS officer, who was at the time functioning as governor of Orissa, and who had been War secretary during the immediately preceding period. Both sides and the British had high regard for Sir Chandulal and it was decided therefore that he should be invited to act in an advisory capacity. He was actually offered membership of the Partition Council for defence matters, but he declined as he felt his other duties would not enable him to discharge his duties as a member of the Partition Council that had to function from day to day. Fortunately, there were available very experienced finance officers, with long experience of the armed forces, and these were associated with the main Army, Navy and Air Force committees. Most of the units were mixed, and the division had to be affected in such a way that the overall efficiency of the armed forces was not adversely affected. Despite many difficulties, the task was carried out, on the whole, to the satisfaction of both the sides, and the British officers deserve great credit for this as also their Muslim and non-Muslim colleagues, who showed a creditable sense of reality.

It is worth noting also that when Partition took place, the highest position to which any Indian officer had reached was that of brigadier. It was inevitable therefore, that our first services chiefs were all British and continued to be so for some years, particularly in the Navy and the Air Force. All policy decisions were taken in the War

Office in Whitehall. Moreover, as the commander-in-chief was also the Defence member of the Executive Council, for all practical purposes, the Defence Ministry functioned as a mere post office. All this had to now change. The Defence minister would have to play a significant role, and the Defence Ministry (all departments were after partition converted into ministries) had also correspondingly to function like all other ministries of the Government of India, and while playing a distinctive coordinating role among the three services, to make its own appraisal of the recommendations of the three services headquarters. My immediate task as Defence secretary was to see that the defence ministry was organised so as to be able to play this role. Thanks to the cooperative attitude of the officers concerned, this presented no serious difficulty. In fact, it was good to see how quickly the middle-level officers accepted the position that in the new set-up it was necessary for the civil services to play a very different role, and that it was up to them to see that the officers of the Defence Ministry learnt to appreciate their point of view. The officials responded suitably and did not press their point of view unduly, until they had obtained adequate insight into defence problems.

The most important change made by the government in regard to the three services was that each of the three services should have its own chief. This was a significant change and was made in order to ensure that each service could develop as rapidly as possible, and this the Navy and Air Force could do best under its own chief of staff and other high grade officials belonging to its own service. Inevitably, the Army would have to continue to play a predominant role, but the other two services had also to play their own proper and distinctive role, and their development also would have to proceed, bearing that in mind. It is noteworthy therefore, that in the committee of the chief of staff, the chairmanship of the committee went according to seniority of the chief of staff. At the same time, wherever it was felt that common service arrangements would be advantageous, it was ensured that that advantage was not allowed to be lost. Thus, certain services operated in common for the three services, such as the medical and engineering services, inspection organisation, the scientific research organisation and the like.

Until Independence, it was not necessary for India to develop its own weapons, and therefore no attention was given to creating an efficient scientific organisation. Indeed, India relied for its weapons also on the War Office in UK. This had now to change and change as rapidly as possible. The scientific organisation was the first to be taken in hand. Dr. Kothari, a distinguished physicist from Delhi University, was entrusted with this task, under the guidance of such extremely able and talented persons such as Dr. Homi Bhabha, Dr. Bhatnagar and P.M.S. Blackett (who had done some remarkable work during the Second World War).

We sought guidance from the Swiss in regard to setting up a defence industry. We were advised and I think, rightly, to set up an organisation that would enable us to produce components and accordingly it was decided to set up an Ordnance Factory at Ambernath for the purposes. This helped us greatly and made it possible for us to develop other defence factories to enable the country to develop weapons. Parenthetically, I may mention that this same Swiss organisation helped us to establish a similar factory named Hindustan Machine Tools, which has a brilliant record in the development of civilian industries. India had inherited a number of ordnance factories where ammunition for various purposes was produced, and where a certain amount of repairs and maintenance work in respect of defence weapons was carried out.

## Secretary, Ministry of Food and Agriculture

After about six years in the Defence Ministry, the government transferred me to take over as secretary, Ministry of Food and Agriculture, at that time considered of great importance. I found the work of the Ministry to be most interesting and rewarding. All manner of special problems kept arising and called for urgent solution. For instance, Sindri Fertiliser Company started production just about this time, and the question before the government was how to popularise the use of chemical fertiliser among farmers. It seemed to everyone that for this purpose, it was essential to ensure that the fertilizers were made available at the same price in every part of the country. It would clearly not be right to give the farmers who had the good fortune to live close to the factory in Bihar unfair advantage over the farmers who had the misfortune to be located far away, say in Tamil Nadu. I decided therefore, to discuss with the Railway Ministry and see if arrangements could be made which would enable fertilisers to be carried over the whole country at a uniform price, and thus neutralise the advantage of being located close to the factory. I was able to make such an arrangement and succeeded in making the Sindri fertiliser available at a uniform price throughout the country. This was, at the time, rightly considered a major achievement of great value to farmers. It must be remembered also that the problem was an urgent one, for the need to popularise the use of the fertiliser throughout the country was urgent; also because from the fertiliser factory's point of view it was of the utmost importance that the take-off should keep pace with the quantity produced.

But apart from problems of this nature, there was a need also to keep under review long-term policies. The inspector general of forests brought up one such problem. He was rightly of the view that the entire forest policy needed to be thoroughly overhauled. The forest policy had been in force for a very long time. A new policy, more in consonance with the country's long-term interests, needed to be evolved urgently. One of the fresh decisions taken was to see that a thorough policy revision was carried out and concurrence obtained of all concerned. In this connection, I travelled over considerable areas of the country, including Andaman and Nicobar, which contained some of the most magnificent forests of the country. The most revolutionary of all was the decision taken by Rafi Ahmed Kidwai, who was for a short while our minister. He was a remarkable personality and it was interesting to have had an opportunity of working with him. He was a strong advocate of the free movement of foodgrains throughout the country. He was confident that this would help the consumer and not harm the farmer. His instinct was fully justified.

While in the Food and Agriculture Ministry, I was asked by Dr. Rajendra Prasad, then the president of the country, to work as his secretary. I could not very well refuse, whatever my personal inclination. At the same time, I had become very deeply interested in the work of the Food and Agriculture Ministry. I, therefore, requested the president most earnestly to let me carry on in the Agriculture Ministry. He was gracious enough to agree. I may mention that I liked Dr. Rajendra Prasad very much, for I had had an opportunity to work with him on several occasions. I was, however, genuinely interested in having an opportunity to tackle the numerous problems that faced the Agriculture Ministry. We had just then received the report of the Rural Credit Survey, whose recommendations needed to be given effect to very promptly. I must admit that I did not regret my decision not to go as the president's secretary. I continued in the Food and Agriculture Ministry and finished the various tasks that needed to be taken up.

The Rural Credit Survey was one of the most important surveys that had been undertaken. It was the work of a high-powered committee appointed by the Reserve Bank of India and created a considerable stir. Its message was that the cooperative credit had failed but cooperative credit must succeed. Its recommendations needed consideration without delay. I am glad to say that I was able to help in ensuring this. The sooner effect was given to them the better it would be for the country. Thus, for instance one of the recommendations was that the Imperial Bank should be nationalised. The first chairmanship was offered to, and accepted by, Dr. John Mathai. It was most important that rural areas should be provided the benefits of banking. The government was persuaded to accept this revolutionary recommendation. As State Bank, the new bank took up the challenge and succeeded in a very short time in organising a large number of branches in district and taluka headquarters. This opening of branches in semi-urban and rural areas had a remarkable effect on development in rural areas. This process has since been further accelerated. A related recommendation sought to facilitate the farmer's ability to hold on to his crop until a more worthwhile price became available. The government was prevailed upon to accept this also.

One of the committee's major recommendations was that a warehousing corporation should be set up to help the farmer not to have to sell his crop when prices were not to his advantage. The recommendation was accepted and appropriate legislation was passed as well as necessary finance provided to start the constitution of a warehousing corporation. This readiness of the government to act speedily once the recommendations of a committee were accepted was a particularly significant characteristic of the government in those days. Admittedly, there had to be requisite civil service cooperation at that time. And though I say it myself, I was able to provide it with the help of a number of my colleagues. When the idea of starting a State Trading Corporation was first mooted, I was a strong opponent of it unless care was taken to limit such trading to areas where, for a variety of reasons, private trading was likely to place the local user at a disadvantage. I also sounded a note of warning that particular care would have to be taken to see that only those officers were appointed who had a proven record of honesty, for this was an area in which temptation to go wrong abounded. I remember, in fact, that on one occasion I had to take up a strong stand in regard to this when the whole question was being discussed, and of all persons this happened when the then home minister, Pandit Govind Vallabh Pant held a somewhat different view.

It so happened, however, that early in 1956 I was asked to move into the Finance Ministry as secretary, Economic Affairs. I had once again to decide whether I should request to be left in the Food and Agriculture Ministry or agree to go over to Finance. This time I decided to let things take their own course. Thus, my stay in the Agriculture Ministry was for a relatively short period, but it had nevertheless been long enough to enable me to make quite a useful contribution to the Ministry.

## Secretary, Economic Affairs, the Ministry of Finance, 1956

I took over charge as secretary, Economic Affairs, in the Ministry of Finance some time in 1956. The finance minister, Deshmukh, in welcoming me, drew my attention pointedly to one item of work, which he said, had been pending in the Ministry for quite some time, despite the fact that the government attached considerable importance to it. The government had come to the conclusion that on broad general grounds, the insurance industry ought not to remain in private hands. It was an important source of funds that could be ploughed into industrial development. To the extent that the investment was made wisely no risk would be involved to the policy holders, in as much as the insurance company would have funds needed to meet claims on policies when they matured. And it was clearly of vital importance that the policy holder should not have the need to turn to anybody other than the company with whom he had insured his life. But if the insurance company invests its funds unwisely or so as to serve some individual interest, the policy holders stand to suffer. That should not be allowed to happen, having regard to the vital importance of insurance as an industry, and even more from the point of view of the individual, anxious to safeguard his own or his family's future. The government's anxiety regarding the sound functioning of this industry, therefore was understandable, the more so as a number of insurance companies had failed and thus, let down their policy holders.

I took up the matter in right earnest. I called the Controller of Insurance whose office was in Simla to come to Delhi as early as possible and brief me fully on what had so far been done in regard to this matter, and how it was proposed to proceed further. It appeared that very little real progress had been made as it was felt that nationalisation would be very difficult to achieve. I decided to take up the whole question without delay. The number of companies involved was large, and their soundness varied very greatly. Some were very sound indeed, and followed a reasonably well-conceived investment policy. A great many, however, were administered so as to further the interests of those who controlled the companies. I held many sessions with the controller and his deputies, and soon came to grips with the problem. It was clear that the greatest secrecy would have to be maintained. No company should have the time to 'doctor' its books as soon as it became known the government intended to nationalise the industry. It was also realised that it would be necessary to decide what compensation should be paid. We were anxious to see that a fair compensation scheme should be devised, fair to the companies, fair to the policy holders, and fair to the government. The question of foreign companies complicated matters, but only in as much as they would need not only a different treatment, but also a treatment which they would have to agree was fair to the point of being generous. All these and other relevant matters were soon tackled. And there remained only the question of how the decision to nationalise was to be announced, and what steps would need to be taken to ensure that the management of all the Indian companies changed hands immediately on the day that the decision to nationalise was announced. This was not an easy task to organise but we were successful in finding an answer even to this problem, which meant that persons would have to be selected for every company and the person would be informed only on the day of the takeover, which company he was to be in charge of. I must say that the entire operation was carried out remarkably smoothly. The company managements as well as the outside world became aware of the nationalisation only after it had been given effect. Within a year or so of my taking change of the Ministry, I was able thus to complete the first major task given to me. I must admit, of course, that while I provided the drive and necessary decisions, the controller of insurance and his organization did the detailed work. The finance minister was very pleased that the scheme had been carried through so competently and so expeditiously. His public announcement, too, had been drafted carefully and laid down all the basic principles relating to the scheme of nationalisation.

The objective of nationalisation had been amply realised, but they were not fully understood by the large majority of the people. It was not merely a question of securing for development purposes the vast sums of money that would be realised as premiums. With greater understanding of the principles of insurance, it was hoped that the message of insurance and its intrinsic value would reach every citizen. It was hoped to be able to achieve other advantages also. Stock exchanges, for instance, were liable every now and again to be in difficulties through speculative activities and consequent overtrading. At such times, an institution like the Insurance Corporation with large funds at its disposal could come to the rescue of the investing public and minimise the consequences of such overtrading. This was, at that time, difficult for most people to realise, but is now generally appreciated and greatly valued. Apart from the fact that more and more people have begun to realise the virtues of insurance, not only as a means of safeguarding one's own and one's family's future, it is also a great encouragement to saving. It is not generally realised what an enormous source of public saving the corporation is. Thus, during one month alone in the year 1972, the Life Insurance Corporation invested Rs.517 crores in Central Government Securities, advanced Rs.1.52 crores to Apex Cooperative Housing Finance Securities and Rs.0.5 crores to Industrial Estates, and advanced term loans amounting to Rs. 9.49 crores to eleven companies in the public and private sectors. This one corporation is thus, able to advance over Rs.6000 crores every year to various government securities, government organisations, besides providing insurance cover to hundreds of thousands of individuals.

I must also mention that the taking over of the insurance companies did not end the task of nationalisation. As the first chairman of the Life Insurance Corporation, (I was asked to do this in addition to my duties as secretary, Economic Affairs), I had to see that staff of the various companies were assimilated into a single service. This was a difficult task, which was very competently performed by a committee that had been specially constituted for the purpose. The investments of the companies were scrutinised and diverted into sound channels, the types of policies and policy premia rationalised. The insurance companies had invested their funds in real estate also and it became necessary to establish a competent estate and maintenance department. All these tasks were substantially achieved or begun during the few months that I remained as the chairman of the corporation, before handing the task over to a whole time chairman. It was understood of course, that a permanent chairman would be appointed as soon as these major problems had been dealt with. My successor was appointed without much delay. As secretary, Economic Affairs, my relationship with the corporation continued. As luck would have it, it led to a very significant 'crisis' both in the affairs of the corporation, at the government level in the future relationship between ministers and secretaries and for me personally.

# 11

# An End and a Beginning

## Resignation from Service[1]

WHILE WAITING FOR THE FINDINGS OF THE PUBLIC SERVICE Commission, I had enough time to think of the future. On one point, I was quite clear. I would not consider continuing in the Civil Service, even if, as I confidently hoped would be the case, the finding would be in my favour and exonerate me completely of the charges framed against me. I wrote in reply to the Home Ministry's letter, after the Public Service Commission had pronounced in my favour,

1 In 1957, when H.M. Patel was principal secretary, Finance Ministry, investments made by the Life Insurance Corporation became the subject of a major public controversy, which came to be known popularly as the 'Mundra affair'. Jagmohan Mundra, a businessman, held large stocks of joint stock companies and in a depressed market, the Life Insurance Corporation was persuaded to buy his stocks, at the behest of the finance minister, to shore up the market. But when news of huge losses to the corporation became public, H.M. Patel was singled out for favouring Mundra politically and financially (allegedly for the latter's favours to the Congress party). The finance minister, T.T. Krishnamachari, denied any knowledge and responsibility for the deal and accused H.M. Patel of lying and cheating the corporation by abusing his position. For details of the 'Mundhra Affair', see Appendix No.1.

that I should rejoin, that it would be best for me to be allowed to resign, as the government would have in fairness to appoint me to a senior appointment and I would find it difficult to do justice to it as I would not enjoy the wholehearted confidence of my superiors, which at that level would be necessary.

I was fairly certain that there might be tempting offers from the industry; these I proposed to turn down. I had all but made up my mind to go into rural India and there see in what way I could put my experience to some worthwhile use. Fortunately for me, there was one such offer already made to me and which was very much to my liking.

Having decided to resign, once the government accepted the recommendation of the UPSC, the question of what I should do next was looming large in front of me. This fortunately, presented no problem at all. I had been invited sometime earlier to take charge of an educational organisation located in a rural area. This was a challenging task and therefore I welcomed it. This organisation had been created in order to make available to persons living in rural areas, an opportunity for higher education. Hitherto, every one had to go to a metropolitan city, for all educational institutions imparting higher education were located there. This made it difficult for promising students in rural areas to arrange for funds necessary for such education. It occurred to an engineer of all persons to think of locating institutions of higher education in a rural area. He put his idea before the people and was successful in receiving sufficient initial support to go ahead with his scheme. He suggested that he should be given a fairly large area of land on condition that for every bigha of land (1 ¾ bighas constituted an acre) he was given, he would return the giver 3/8 in the shape of a plot in a township that would be developed in the land given; the 5/8 of the land given would be utilised for the educational institution and hostels that would be developed. His offer was accepted. The organisation received sufficient land for the educational institutions and the hostels and those who gave the land obtained building plots in a township that was developed, which have appreciated so greatly that everyone who gave land has benefitted far beyond anything that the most optimist giver may have expected. The organisers were able to obtain as much land as they wished for at that initial stage.

What I had not reckoned on at the time was of any other direction from which offers might be forthcoming. One such came from a direction I had least expected. And this was an offer from FAO to head a group they had decided to send out to Nigeria. I cannot now say what I would have done had this offer come before I had already decided in favour of the education trust. I might have been tempted but as it was, I had gone too far. I had actually taken charge of the trust when the Nigeria offer came along. Thereafter, another tempting proposition was put to me, though some months later. This was to consider taking charge of the Electricity Board that was to be constituted to look after the power problems of the new state of Gujarat that was to be set up on the division of the Bombay presidency into the state of Maharastra and Gujarat. I informed the chief minister designate of the new state, Dr. Jivraj Mehta of my difficulty. I had already given my word to the education trust people. If he was prepared to accept me on a part-time basis, I would be willing to accept the responsibility and give him the assurance that I would be able to cope adequately with the work of the new Electricity Board. Dr. Jivraj Mehta decided to take the risk and made me the chairman of the Gujarat Electricity Board, in which capacity I continued for six years. During that period, I had the satisfaction of ensuring that the Board was well-established, with a power generation capability designed to take care of the state's immediate needs as also of its growing needs for the next few years. The state was also by then well provided with transmission lines capable of carrying the power generated to most parts, besides being well staffed and well organised. Not only would further production be looked after, but it had also become well equipped for generating additional capacity as required by the state. I was sorry I had to leave the Board, but as I had decided to enter politics I had no choice, particularly as I had decided to join the newly created Swatantra Party and to become a moderately active member of it.

This fortunately, came in the way of my activities only to a very limited extent. I was devoting most of my time to the trust activities. The colleges that were already in existence when I took charge, an arts and science college, an engineering college and a commerce college had already become extremely popular. And the immediate question I had to apply my mind to was that the arts and science college had to be bifurcated into two separate colleges. What is more, the University that had been established three years before my arrival was now beginning to be well housed and to perform its functions confidently and competently. The township — Vallabh Vidyanagar — was also beginning to look more like a township; some fifty-odd buildings had come up where not even ten existed when I came. But what is more, an industrial estate had started coming up, adjoining the township soon to be known as Vithal Udyognagar.

The famous sculptor, Karmarkar's statue of Vitthalbhai Patel, a duplicate of that at Chowpatty in Bombay, was very kindly donated by Karmarkar in memory of our journey to England in the second voyage of S.S. *Loyalty* of Scindia Steam Navigation. The magnificent statue stands at the entrance to the Industrial Estate, just as the very fine statue of Sardar Patel sculpted by the then budding sculptor Kantibhai Amin stands at the entrance to the township of learning, Vallabh Vidyanagar. The development of the industrial estate helped greatly in the development of Vallabh Vidyanagar. Those who owned building plots there, began to realise that if they utilised their plots, it would be possible for them to find tenants without any difficulty. The industrial estate also had a flying start. The industrial units had no problem in finding skilled workers and executives to come because they found that the problem of their children's education would not exist, as the University provided facilities for education from nursery to the post-graduate degree stage. During term time, the student population of the township had already grown into well over ten thousand.

# II

# The Partition of India

# 1

# The Beginnings

I MUST CONFESS I AM DISTRESSED – THOUGH BY NOW I should have become wiser – whenever I come across people who are not only ignorant of the history of this country, in say, the decade preceding Independence but are also utterly indifferent to it. Especially the history of the couple of years immediately preceding 15 August 1947, when discussions took place and events occurred, which converted Congress leaders finally to the view that the creation of Pakistan was no longer avoidable, and when it became clear to all the parties, the British, the Congress and the Muslim League that the sooner the Partition took place, the greater the likelihood of its being carried through without violence. And yet, all this history is relevant to a proper understanding of the relationship that has subsisted between our two countries. One major attempt then made to ensure that the parting took place in a friendly atmosphere and with the conviction that everything had been arranged fairly, was the manner in which the entire process of allocating to the two new states the resources of united India took place so that both could start functioning more or less equally well or ill equipped. Unfortunately, the immediate outbreak of violence on a totally unexpected scale, leading to the transfer of hundreds of thousands of people under conditions of great suffering and hardship, followed very shortly afterwards by tribals from Pakistan 'invading' Kashmir, destroyed whatever goodwill that had been generated by the spirit of give and take that had inspired those who manned the partition machinery. In fact, it is remarkable how strong was the influence of that spirit, for it still obtained on 1 December 1947, when the two members of the Steering Committee worked out formulae for agreement on all the various issues on which no agreement had been possible till then and it had, in fact, been decided by the Partition Council earlier to remit to the Arbitral Tribunal. One wishes fondly that that kind of spirit, if it was possible to generate it then in the midst of a period of great tension, could perhaps have been generated once again to help in the solution of the problems that plague our two countries today. But alas, that was not to be or at any rate that has not happened so far.

In any case, the vast majority of the people appeared to have lost interest in the mechanics of partition as also in what finally emerged as the two dominions. It is not surprising, therefore, to note that very few people have fully appreciated what was involved in the actual partition of the country. Certain things are obvious, such as the division of the Armed Forces or the division of the assets and liabilities. But even in respect of these matters, few have realised the great complexities involved and even more, the limited period of time that was available in which these complex problems had to be resolved and acceptable formulas evolved. Thus, even a person like V.P. Menon, who was intimately associated with everything that led to the partition of the country and witnessed also both the actual process of partitioning and the aftermath of the Partition, considered some four pages or so of his authoritative book on the *Transfer of Power* sufficient for compressing the information on the work that was done by the Partition Council and its machinery. Unfortunately, even such matters relating to partition as are occasionally referred to, because of their intrinsic importance or because of their relationship with other important matters, are not dealt with in a way that would give some idea of the work done and that had to be done in this area. No attempt whatever has hitherto been made to give anything like a comprehensive idea of the various issues and problems that had to be considered and resolved, and the process by which solutions were found. My object in referring to this aspect is only to emphasise the fact that the task that had been entrusted to the Partition Council and its supporting executive machinery for its accomplishment within a period of little over sixty days was well nigh impossible. That it was, in fact, accomplished nevertheless within the time allotted, and the few items that were left over because no agreement could be reached in respect of them did not have to be referred to the Arbitral Tribunal, but were settled by the Partition Council itself by the beginning of December 1947, was something for which all concerned may well feel extremely gratified and the two countries thank their stars, for a vast area of potential conflict and dissatisfaction was removed from the potential arena of disputes and confrontations by discussion, and to the satisfaction of both the countries.

How did this become possible? As I see it, the conjunction of many factors made it possible to accomplish this all but impossible task. In the first place, the Council had as its chairman, a person with character, experience and qualities, like Lord Mountbatten. It is significant that he declined to act as an arbitrator. He visualised his role as that of a persuader. As chairman of the Partition Council, he acted with great skill and imagination. He managed things in such a way that in no matter was a stalemate reached: he saw to it that in one way or another, differences were frankly discussed and argued over until some formula acceptable to both the sides emerged. No less fortunate was the character and status of the members of the Partition Council. They had the power to get what they agreed, accepted by their political colleagues. Apart from that, they were men of strong and determined personalities, who were realistic enough to recognise the great value in the future of agreed solutions being found to all the issues under discussion.

No matter how vehemently they may have discussed an issue in the Council, they had no hesitation in accepting solutions that were obviously based on compromise. The Expert Committees also made their contribution. They were manned by officers who were thorough, conscientious and able and who also had sufficient imagination to realise the importance of the injunction of the Partition Council that they should work on the general principle of securing the greatest good of the new states. They rarely, therefore, took up a rigid stance but left room for adjustment. It was also fortunate that the members of the Steering Committee, who on the one hand, enjoyed the respect and confidence of the members of the Expert Committees, and who also trusted each other, had complete confidence in each other's integrity. The Steering Committee had a critical role to play. They had not only to find solutions for matters in respect of which the Expert Committees failed to arrive at an agreement, but at times had also to anticipate the possibility of their failing to do so and hence, to begin their task of reconciliation even while the matter was under discussion and study by the Expert Committees. Their intervention in the discussions of the Expert Committees at crucial stages helped the latter in ironing out, or at any rate, in narrowing their differences. It was essential also for the members of the Steering Committee to enjoy the complete confidence of their political chiefs. It was their duty to keep them fully informed of the progress of the discussions within the Expert Committees and of the nature of their possible differences and how they could be resolved. My duty, thus, was to see that members for India on the Council were kept fully informed and to obtain their instructions and guidance. In practice, I used to meet only Sardar Patel, as Rajendra Prasad and Rajaji appeared to have entrusted this entire task to him. Sardar Patel was able to give me time whenever I wanted — how he managed it I do not know — and his ability to concentrate and to grasp the issues put to him was so remarkable that he rarely had to be explained the position twice.

He appeared to have a sure instinct and would put his finger infallibly on the weak link: he would then ask me merely to look at the matter anew, and I may say without exaggeration that his suggestion for a re-examination was found almost always to be worthwhile. Sardar's approach to every matter was to ensure fairness, never to take advantage. And this became, therefore, the approach of all on the India side. The Muslim members of the Expert Committees and my opposite number on the Pakistan side, Mohammad Ali appeared also, on the whole, to desire solutions. It seems to me that what enabled agreements to be reached over the wide area involved was due to this spirit that appears to have moved us all in varying degree. Nothing else can explain the fantastic hours of work that we were able to put in day after day until everything was tidied up. And it must be realised that most of us and in particular, the members of the Partition Council and of the Steering Committee, had a great many other responsibilities also to discharge during this very period, and all of these were also of an urgent nature and such as called for decisive action.

It is interesting to note how little has been written about the actual Partition of the country. There existed one integrated administration of British India. That integrated administration was responsible for administering a vast variety of subjects, organisations and installations. A new country had to be created complete with a fully functioning administration and its share of all the facilities, equipments, requirements, amenities and institutions that existed in the country that was to be partitioned. The precise basis of this partition had to be decided. The division of personnel both of civil administration and of the Armed Forces had to be done in a manner, which should be just and fair and workable. Lots of problems had to be resolved that would arise in respect of currencies, cash balances, provident funds, public debt; organisations like railways, post and telegraph facilities had all to be shared in an equitable manner and what is more, the sharing should be determined so that the minimum possible disturbance was caused to their efficient functioning.

Problems of domicile had also to be clearly set out so that the residents of the two countries were put to the minimum possible inconvenience. And all this work had to be completed within less than seventy days. The task would have been challenging enough in normal times but on this occasion it had to be done against an extraordinary background. The relations between the leaders of the two new countries that would be created were as tense and as bad as they could be. The relations between the two major communities, which were to reside in the two countries were at their worst and were to become even more disturbed immediately after the actual transfer of power — a period within which the more important problems regarding assets and liabilities that were unresolved on 15th August 1947, were to be discussed and settled if possible. However impossible the conditions were, these problems were overcome and agreements were reached on all matters. A matter of even particular satisfaction was that the decisions reached in respect of these complicated matters had never been questioned by either side. Yet for some reason, those who have studied this period and what occurred during that period have not asked the question, which was necessary for them to ask — what was it that made this possible? To whom should the credit go? Although the task seemed basically simple, was it difficult for the task to be accomplished? As in fact, it was. Even a simple problem like that of domicile had many angles to be examined in depth before taking decisions. The terms of reference of the Expert Committee on domicile and nationality were as follows: To examine and make recommendations on the implications of partition with reference to domicile and nationality of the inhabitants of British India and in the position as Indian nationals abroad. The report of this Committee was one of the first to be ready and was quite short. The legal position that existed before the creation of the two new dominions would remain the same because the inhabitants would continue to be the subjects of the British as they were before partition. A question, however, arose whether for the purpose of public service the common status of British subjects would be sufficient. Partition by itself would affect no change in nationality and therefore there was no need for the Partition Council to take any decision except in regard to public service. The view taken was that persons presently domiciled or permanently residing in one dominion were not to be eligible for public service in the other dominion.

The domicile of an individual is again becoming relevant under the Indian Succession Act 1925. The question whether the inhabitants of one dominion will need to have a passport to the other had also to be considered. The simplest solution it was felt would be by suitable adaptation of the passport rules to exempt the inhabitants of each dominion from passport regulations of the other at least at the start, and until passport restrictions were introduced by the two dominions. The Committee came to the conclusion that the Partition Council decides to restrict entry into the public service in the manner suggested by the Expert Committee and left it to the two dominion governments to take whatever action they consider proper later, in regard to introducing any restrictions. I have referred to this report at this stage only to emphasise that even a relatively straightforward method needed careful examination and that had necessarily to be carried out within the time available in such a way that no avoidable difficulties were created for the governments, residents or inhabitants of the two countries. Financial questions gave rise to many problems and their solutions were not easy. The representatives of the new country could not wholly disabuse themselves of the fear that the representatives of the larger dominion would not give them their just share. The representatives of the latter for their part appeared at times unable to disabuse themselves of the feeling that the representatives of Pakistan were seeking to have the better of them. While such suspicions were general, they were not well founded as they caused a delay in arriving at agreed solutions. They were not allowed in the main to lead to a stalemate. That this became possible at all was due, to my mind, partly to the fact that the experts on both sides were people who had worked together as colleagues for a number of years and had generally been on friendly terms and subsequently because the representatives of both dominions were big men, men with vision and finally because the Partition Council had the good fortune of being presided over by a genuine neutral chairman who interpreted his neutrality to mean complete inactivity. Indeed, he took it upon himself to ensure that whatever differences arose were never allowed to lead to a stalemate and he often offered various suggestions for possible ways of arriving at an understanding.

The way in which, for instance, he prevented a breakdown in the case of 'unique' institutions, provided a good example of the conservationist and objective role he played. He did this by emphasising the need for not breaking up an existing institution so it becomes useless for both sides. He recommended that it be retained by the dominion in which the unique institution was located but the other dominion be given access to the service that institution provided during the period that dominion could create that institution for itself. It was with regard to the printing press that this difficulty first arose. The solution found was for India to let Pakistan utilise the full capacity of one press for a definite period, within which it was felt reasonably that a new printing press could be established.

# 2

# The Partition

WITH THE COMING INTO POWER OF THE LABOUR PARTY and Churchill's defeat in the general elections in the United Kingdom in 1945, a radical change came over the British government's attitude towards India. Clement Attlee, who had been the main proponent of decisive action in regard to the Indian political situation in Churchill's government, now became prime minister and it seems as if he was determined to show that something definite was being done in regard to the Indian situation. An informal decision appeared to have been taken that the British should leave India at an early date after handing over the reins of power to the people of India. This was reflected in certain measures of administrative reorganisation that the Government of India decided upon and started giving effect to from 1945 onwards. One such measure related to the creation of the Cabinet Secretariat.

It was the practice till then for the governor general's Executive Council to be serviced secretarially by the Law Department of the Government of India. The law secretary used to function in addition to his other duties as secretary to the Executive Council of the Government of India. It appears to have been assumed that India would almost certainly adopt a Constitution after the transfer of power based on one of the several forms of parliamentary governments that were then actually functioning. Whatever the form, the government would have to be served by a Secretariat. Accordingly, a Cabinet Secretariat was organised very largely along the lines of the one then in existence in UK to take over the secretarial functions of the secretary to the governor general's Executive Council. Sir Eric Coates, a senior member of the ICS, who had been working at that time as financial advisor to the War Department of the Government of India was appointed the first Cabinet secretary of the government, and the responsibility devolved on him to organise a Cabinet Secretariat to provide the elected ministers with the kind of expert service, information and advice that would enable them to discharge their duties efficiently. Within a matter of months of my joining the Cabinet Secretariat, Sir Eric Coates retired from service and I succeeded him as Cabinet secretary in February 1947.

During British rule, the War Department (renamed Defence Department after Independence) enjoyed a special status, and its head, the commander-in-chief's relationship with the viceroy and the governor general was very different from that of the rest of the Executive Council of the Government of India. This special position and the special relationship would cease as soon as the power was transferred to the representatives of the people. Anticipating that change, a couple of military officers were included in the new Cabinet Secretariat. This was an important innovation, for until then, there was virtually no direct point of contact between the Civil Departments and the War Department, which used to be headed by the commander-in-chief, who worked directly under the viceroy and the governor general of India.

I mention this at the outset to underline the fact that discussions regarding the transfer of power to the people of India, were being held during these years at a political level both in London and in India in all urgency and seriousness. The authorities had evidently come to the conclusion that a definitive arrangement was certain to emerge as a result of these discussions, which would lead to power being transferred within the shortest possible time to duly recognised representatives of the people. Of course, the assumption at that stage was in terms of the transfer of power of the country as a whole. There was sufficient optimism even at that date of the possibility of the Congress and the Muslim League arriving at some understanding.

The British government had sent out to India early in 1946, three members of its Cabinet under the secretary of state for India to evolve with the assistance of the viceroy a suitable and acceptable scheme. The Cabinet Mission was composed of Secretary of State for India Lord Pethick Lawrence, Sir Stafford Cripps and A.V. Alexander. The Cabinet Mission, as it came to be known, held discussions with political leaders but was unable to evolve any formula that was acceptable both to the Congress and the League. So, it drew up a scheme that it considered would be the fairest in the circumstances then prevailing and announced it. If the Congress and the Muslim League accepted the scheme, an Interim Government was to be formed.

The majority provinces, the provinces where there was Hindu majority, would be one group, the provinces where the Muslims were in the majority would form another group and a third group would be where the position was not particularly clear.[1] Provinces would have the right to make up their own mind. The subjects under the Central Government would be defence, external affairs and communication. For the rest, the provinces would be autonomous. This plan, however, was not acceptable either to the Congress or to the League. The preliminary step to this kind of grouping would be the general elections followed by the formation of a government of the political leaders based on the results of the elections, the portfolios being given according to the formula of equal numbers

1 Section A comprised Madras, Bombay, United Provinces, Bihar, Central Provinces and Orissa; Section B comprised Punjab, Sind and NWFP and Section C comprised Bengal and Assam. Sucheta Mahajan, *Independence and Partition*, pp.151.

of Hindus and Muslims and representation to the other minorities. The formula was five, five and three. The government would also set up a Constituent Assembly for the drawing up of a constitution. This formula was, in a way, acceptable to the political parties but it foundered because the League insisted upon all the Muslim members being appointed by and named by itself and no place should be given to the nationalist Muslims. This formula was not acceptable to the Congress because of the Muslim League's position. The Congress, on the other hand, was of the view that nationalist Muslims must be included in the seats reserved for the Muslims. Lord Wavell and the Mission were determined that a popular government should be formed and a modified plan was evolved. If that was accepted, Lord Wavell could proceed to form the government.

The Scheme formulated by the Cabinet Mission in May, 1946 and which the Mission thought had received general acceptance of the two major political parties, the Indian National Congress and the Muslim League, envisaged the setting up of an Interim Government, composed of the representatives of the Congress and the Muslim League, under the chairmanship of the viceroy and governor general. Both the Congress and the League had, however, laid down certain conditions subject to which only they were prepared to accept the Cabinet Mission's statement of 16 May. The governor general took the view that the conditions laid down by the Congress were not such as would nullify its acceptance of the statement and therefore decided to invite them to join the Interim Government. The League's attitude as indicated by the conditions they had laid down could not be treated as virtual acceptance and since the League was in no mood to modify their conditions, it could not be invited to join the Interim Government. Even the intimation by the viceroy that he had decided to invite the Congress even if the League persisted in its stand and declined the invitation to come into the Interim Government had no effect. The viceroy accordingly invited the Congress to join the Interim Government, which they did on 2 September 1946.

The 2nd of September 1946 was a historic day for India. That was the day on which the Interim Government was ushered in. The formation of the Interim Government was part of the scheme put forward by the Cabinet Mission. The Muslim League had, for its own reasons, declined the viceroy's invitation to come into the government, and therefore, the government that assumed power on that day was that only of Congressmen and others supporting them. Nehru was informally accepted as the vice chairman of the Executive Council, the viceroy being the chairman. It was only during the latter part of October that the viceroy, Lord Wavell, succeeded in persuading the League to come in. By that time, the Muslim League had itself also realised its mistake in refusing the viceroy's invitation to join the Interim Government, which it indeed was. The Congress, understandably, did not like this development. The Congress would have preferred that the viceroy should let the League itself seek another invitation. The viceroy, however, was anxious to bring the League into the government as early as possible. Their coming in late was bound to create all manner of problems such as the redistribution of portfolios. Neither Nehru nor Sardar Patel was prepared to give up external affairs or home. Fortunately, the League agreed to accept the finance portfolio, which the League had been advised by their chief civil service adviser Mohammad Ali, would enable the League to have a good view of the functioning of all other ministries. Unlike the Congress, the League had been in close touch with the Muslim civil servants, obtaining their valuable guidance in matters relating to administration and to finance. With their help, the League ministers were successful in adopting tactics that enabled them to bring the government to a virtual halt. It is pertinent to add here that the Congress ministers had not established or even attempted to establish a similar relationship with the non-Muslim civil servants.

The viceroy, for his part, was determined to make the Cabinet Mission Plan work. He had succeeded in bringing the Congress and the League together in forming a government. But unfortunately for him, and for the country, the Congress and the League right from the outset made no attempt to work as a team. The budget for the year 1947-48, provided the League with an opportunity that it was seeking to embarrass the Congress. The taxation proposals in the new budget were designed to hit the industrialists hard. They had been, and were, active supporters of the Congress. The proposals were not in themselves particularly unreasonable, but the Congress was convinced that the proposals were designed to place them in an embarrassing position. A virtual impasse was thus reached. The differences in respect of the budget were only indicative of the inability of the Congress and League to work together in the interest of the country. The members of the Congress met separately to consider the agenda of each meeting of the Cabinet. And this was also what members of the Muslim League in the Cabinet did. The two groups came together only at the meeting of the Cabinet, which was presided over by the viceroy. The situation was precipitated by the budget, which made it clear that some other way would have to be found to get the League and the Congress to work together. Though Lord Wavell was still keen on the Interim Government, the British government felt that the time had come for finding some other way of tackling the problem.

Before it came into the Interim Government, the Muslim League had decided formally on 16 August 1946 to launch, what it called, Direct Action. In fact, the call for Direct Action was interpreted as the call for communal disturbances wherever possible. The consequences of the announcement of such a policy were thoroughly predictable. Communal violence erupted in many places. It manifested itself at its fiercest in Calcutta, the capital of Bengal, where a Muslim League chief minister headed the government. The death toll was of a magnitude until then unknown. The mob behaved with extraordinary ferocity and cruelty. Soon thereafter, communal riots broke out in Noakhali and other parts of Bengal, in the city of Bombay to a limited extent and in other states, such as Bihar, NWFP and in many districts of the Punjab. It looked as if the country would soon be plunged into a fierce and bloody civil war. This was the background against which in the early months of 1947, the British, on the one hand, and the major political parties in India, on the other, had to make up their minds as to the lines along which they wished political developments to proceed — along the path of discussion, persuasion and compromise or along the path of conflict and immense human suffering.

From documents that have now been published, it is clear that the viceroy and his advisers had about this period of time come to the conclusion that it would be advisable for the British to leave India by a definite date. The British prime minister and his advisors had also come independently to a similar conclusion.

Since there were two major parties claiming to represent the people — the Congress, which claimed to represent the people of India as a whole and the Muslim League to dispute their claim to represent the Muslims — the problem for the British was to decide to whom power was to be transferred. They claimed that they were anxious to hand over power so that the unity of the country could be ensured. Only if this appeared impossible, would they have to consider the feasibility of forcing the Indian political parties to be realistic. One such course would be to announce a definite date by which the British would leave India, irrespective of whether an agreed solution had been arrived at between the various political parties or not. Neither the Congress nor the League, it was obvious, would find it to their advantage to inherit a country in a state of anarchy. While they still had some choice, the various parties faced, fairly and squarely, the realities of the situation and agreed to discuss the partition of the country in principle, however much they disliked the very idea. So far as the League was concerned, its leaders too would prefer to avoid a civil war, the outcome of which would be uncertain, and accept a reasonable compromise.

On 20 February 1947, the British prime minister, Attlee, announced a new policy regarding India in the House of Commons. The first and most important change from the policy that had been pursued hitherto was the announcement of a definite date for transferring to Indian hands the responsibility for the Government of British India, namely June 1948. An attempt would be made, in the meantime, to ensure the unity of India. However, it had now been decided not merely to accept the possibility of a partition of the country, but if need be, even to leave the country without handing over formally the reins of power to anyone. With this change in policy, the British prime minister stated that it was decided also to appoint a new viceroy, for it was felt that the present viceroy, even though he had discharged his duties well and efficiently, was likely to be looked upon by the Indian political parties for no fault of his own to be committed to certain ideas and policies. The new viceroy would start with a clean slate.

What was not announced publicly and what was not generally known then was the fact that Lord Mountbatten, the new viceroy, had been given virtually full freedom to make whatever modifications he deemed necessary in the policy announced by the British government if he felt that the changes would make it more acceptable to leaders of the main political parties in India. As legislation in the British Parliament would be necessary to give effect to whatever new plan was evolved for the transfer of power to Indian political parties, Lord Mountbatten had also taken the precaution before coming to India of seeking the support of Churchill, who was the leader of the Opposition, for any legislative proposals that may have to be brought before the Parliament as a result of the fresh approach he (Lord Mountbatten) might find it necessary to make.

The 20 February announcement was on the whole welcomed in India. The general feeling in India at the time was that the retiring viceroy had done a good job, in the face of the very heavy odds against which he had to operate, but people were prepared to welcome the new viceroy, in the hope that he might have greater success in finding a solution.

The new viceroy arrived in India on 22 March 1947. Both he and Lady Mountbatten were seen in their full regalia at an impressive swearing-in-ceremony held in the Darbar Hall of the Rashtrapati Bhavan. Besides the members of the Interim Government, there were present a large number of princes in their glittering dresses and uniforms, as also many top ranking personnel of the armed forces and distinguished citizens. The new viceroy made a departure from the normal procedure and delivered a short and quite effective speech. 'This is not a normal Viceroyalty on which I am embarking,' said Mountbatten. 'His Majesty's Government are resolved to transfer power by June 1948, and since new constitutional arrangements must be made and many complicated questions of administration resolved — all of which will take time to put into effect — this means that a solution must be reached within the next few months. I feel certain that every political leader in India realises as I do the urgent nature of the task before us. I hope soon to be in close consultation with them and I will give them all the help I can. In the meantime, everyone of us must do what he can to avoid any word or action which might lead to further bitterness.

'It will be no easy matter to succeed Lord Wavell who has done so much to take India along the path to self-government. I have always had great admiration for him and I shall devote myself to finishing the work, which he has begun. I am under no illusion about the difficulties of my task. I shall need the greatest goodwill of the greatest possible number and I am asking India today for that goodwill.' This speech made a tremendous impression on his immediate audience and later, in the country generally. It was masterly.

Mountbatten got going immediately after he was sworn in. His first visitor was the Nawab of Bhopal, followed by the Maharaja of Bikaner. Both these princes had kept away from the swearing-in-ceremony and they seem to have felt it necessary to explain to the viceroy why they had done so at the earliest possible moment. From what they said, it became clear to Mountbatten that the princes were going to be divided. Bhopal denied that he had any intention of joining the Muslim League, much less Pakistan, while Bikaner explained why he and a number of his friends, like Jaipur, Jodhpur,

Patiala, Gwalior and Baroda had already decided to join the Constituent Assembly. Both Bhopal and Bikaner tried to ascertain if there was any chance of the British decision to leave India by June 1948 being changed or extended. They appeared to have convinced themselves that the British were not in earnest and were therefore, surprised at Mountbatten's very firm reply that there was no possibility of a change in the decision. After the interviews with Bhopal and Bikaner were over, Mountbatten met, one after the other, Nehru and Liaquat Ali Khan. Later in the day, Mountbatten held his first staff meeting. His very first day in office was typical of the relentless way in which he drove himself and his staff throughout his viceroyalty until 15 August 1947.

Mountbatten had very wisely taken the precaution of bringing with him to India not only his own private secretaries, besides the senior advisors, Lord Ismay and Sir Eric Mieville, but had even brought with him British stenographers and typists. He was anxious to ensure that nothing that was discussed or that took place in his personal office should leak out and the only sure way of ensuring this was to have around him in his personal office only British staff. Mountbatten kept on, of course, the British staff he inherited from his predecessor. Indeed, he increased their number as he found it necessary to do. This was a wise precaution, for however trustworthy the Indian personnel may have been, they would have always been suspect. On balance, therefore, Mountbatten may be said to have acted wisely, even though this meant that he had to deprive himself of the wisdom and experience of some very outstanding Indians. Towards the end, however, he was compelled to depart from this self-denying ordinance, and openly sought advice of men like V.P. Menon, the reforms commissioner and Sir B.N. Rau, a distinguished member of the ICS.

Lord Mountbatten's mission was to arrange the transfer of power from the British to the people of India at the earliest possible moment, the target date being June 1948. Who could be said to represent the people of India? The Congress laid claim to do so.

The Muslim League, who claimed to represent the Muslim population of India, contested this. Mountbatten's first objective was to persuade these two political parties to arrive at an understanding so that India's unity could be maintained. The Muslim League under its leader Jinnah, however, sought the creation of another state out of the contiguously situated provinces of Sind, Punjab and NWFP, on the one hand, and Bengal and Assam on the other. Mountbatten's first task therefore, was to meet the leaders of these two major parties, as also the leaders of all other political parties representing Sikhs, Christians and others. As these talks proceeded, Mountbatten realised that he had arrived upon the scene when attitudes had hardened to a very serious extent. Jinnah was determined to have his Pakistan and had no use for the unity of India. Even when it was pointed out to him that on the contiguous area principle, he might have to give up big chunks of Punjab, Bengal and Assam — though he protested at the extension of the continuity principle in this way — he was not deterred from pressing his point for a Pakistan. Mountbatten was also beginning to realise that the Sikhs too had a problem and their demand for the safeguarding of their interests had to be considered. Likewise, Mountbatten could not ignore the repercussions of the holocaust of August 1946 in the form of communal violence breaking out in various states of India. Mountbatten seemed to have realised that there was not much time to lose, and he must find an acceptable solution with the utmost possible speed.

Mountbatten's attention was throughout being drawn to the deteriorating communal situation, which the Congress leaders complained to him, was worsening because of the blatantly partial attitude of the British ICS officials. The Congress leaders also kept drawing his attention to, what was according to them, the mischievous attitude of the officers of the Political Department. He could not also ignore the fact that his government was hopelessly split and had virtually come to a halt. Meantime, his talks with the political leaders, in particular of the Congress and the League, had led him to only one conclusion — that there was no chance of persuading Jinnah to give up his demand for Pakistan, and that therefore the possibility of leaving behind them a united India was, for all practical purposes, non-existent. Nevertheless, he felt he must make an attempt. And this led Mountbatten and his advisers to go back to the formulation, which had appealed to the Cabinet Mission. In that formulation, the provinces were divided into groups, and it was made permissible for a province in one group to decide to move into another group without affecting the unity of the Centre. Eventually a formula was evolved, which Mountbatten felt would be acceptable to both parties. Mountbatten decided to forward his scheme to the British prime minister. In order to hasten matters, he decided to send Ismay, his senior adviser, and George Abell, his private secretary, to England along with his plan to satisfy Attlee and his colleagues why the plan was the best that could have been devised.

After having despatched his scheme to England, Mountbatten had decided to seek a little rest in Simla. But he knew well, that it may not be a real rest, for on a 'hunch', he had invited Nehru also to come to Simla as his guest. And while there, he further decided to show Nehru the scheme that London was considering. Nehru reacted strongly to the proposed scheme, which he unhesitatingly described as designed to balkanise India and one to which the Congress could never agree. Mountbatten was taken aback at such a reaction, and being a realist did not waste any time in persuading Nehru to think coolly, but instead sought V.P. Menon's assistance to draw up a fresh scheme without delay. It was also fortunate that Mountbatten had asked Menon to come to Simla along with some of his other special staff. Menon had a plan ready, which he had earlier placed before Wavell. That plan he now presented to Mountbatten and with his concurrence, before Nehru, who to everyone's relief, expressed his willingness to consider it if it was also acceptable to Sardar Patel. Nehru was prepared to consider this even though the revised proposals meant virtual acceptance of the

Partition of the country. Both Nehru and Sardar Patel had by now come to the conclusion that since Jinnah was adamant and the League had made clear their call for direct action that they had no scruples about the country drifting into a civil war, it would be better to accept partition on a well-considered basis than to make the country go through an era of serious communal trouble amounting almost to a civil war. Whatever any one may say today and some people do say that partition could and should have been avoided at all cost, at that time, that is during May-June 1947, there was hardly any voice of dissent; communal trouble had reared its head in a really serious manner, and there was no knowing where it might eventually lead the country.

Mountbatten was determined to see that a new formula should be evolved, which would be acceptable to both the major political parties. Menon's suggested new formula had the merit that it might be acceptable to Congress spokesmen, Nehru and Sardar. It would not then be difficult to get the Muslim League to agree, for even under the new formula they would be getting the substance of what they wanted. The Congress would be accepting the concept of partition, provided the League were prepared to accept the division of Punjab and Bengal on the same principle of partition, namely contiguous majority areas would go to the majority community. It was along these lines that eventually a formula was evolved, which became acceptable to all concerned including the British government.

Mountbatten and Menon both had to go to England to present his new plan.

Before leaving for UK, Mountbatten had very wisely taken the precaution of obtaining the formal assent of the Congress, Sikh and the League leaders to the broad outline of the new plan, which, in effect, involved the acceptance in principle of the partition of the country. There was no time for drawing up the new plan in all its detail, and so Menon was asked to prepare a summary of the plan in the form of 'Heads of Agreement'. He then showed the draft of these 'Heads of Agreement' to Nehru, Patel and Baldev Singh, on the one hand, and Sir Eric Mieville (one of the two senior advisers to Mountbatten, the other being Lord Ismay) to Jinnah and Liaquat Ali, on the other. After they had had time to ponder over the draft, Mountbatten discussed the scheme with all of them. On their oral concurrence being received, Mountbatten requested them to give him their acceptance in writing. While Nehru readily agreed and so did Baldev Singh, Jinnah as usual avoided doing so.

Briefly, the new plan envisaged the coming into being of two sovereign states in India, on a dominion status basis. The transfer of power would be on the basis of the Government of India Act of 1935, modified to conform to the dominion status of the two new countries. The governor general could be common to both the dominions, if they so desired. A commission would be appointed for the demarcation of the boundaries in the event of a decision in favour of partition of the two provinces of Bengal and Punjab and to a small extent of Assam. The governors of the provinces within each dominion would be appointed on the recommendation of the respective Central Governments. The Armed Forces of India would also be reconstituted on an agreed basis, units being allocated according to the territorial basis of recruitment. In the case of mixed units, the separation and redistribution would be carried out by a committee consisting of Field Marshal Sir Claude Auchinleck, the supreme commander-in-chief and the chiefs of staff of the two dominions, besides the governor general and the two defence ministers.

The British government fortunately found the new plan acceptable, as it did not go against any of the basic principles they had already accepted. The one major consequence of the new proposals was that it speeded up the entire process and brought substantially forward the date of the transfer of power. In a way, since the viceroy had already tentatively discussed the revised proposals with the Indian leaders and obtained their broad approval, so far as he was concerned, he stood committed, while the British government had no better alternative to put forward. The new scheme was therefore accepted, with some minor amendments, and it was agreed to issue a statement announcing the new scheme. The viceroy was to return to India to obtain the formal concurrence of the Indian leaders to the announcement of the new scheme in the form accepted by the British government. The latter was to announce the new proposals as soon as they received the agreement of the Indian leaders.

Accordingly, Mountbatten returned to India on 30 May and proceeded immediately to meet the Indian leaders. He discovered on his return, that during the few days that he was in England pleading for the acceptance of his new proposals, Jinnah had put forward a demand publicly for a 'corridor' to unite West and East Pakistan. As was only to be expected, the immediate reaction of the Congress and other parties was extremely hostile. Jinnah must have known that it was a demand that would be rejected out of hand by the Congress, and possibly also by the British. His object in making it could only have been to show how difficult he could be, if he had a mind to be. Mountbatten was able to make Jinnah see, without much loss of time, the un-wisdom even from the Muslim point of view of pressing this new demand. Jinnah was shrewd enough to realise that the new proposals gave him the substance of what he had been asking, and that it would be wise to make certain of that.

Mountbatten then invited the Congress, the Sikh and the Muslim leaders on 2 June to meet and discuss the full implications of the new scheme as outlined in a statement, which was to be made by Prime Minister Attlee in the British Parliament and asked them to inform him in writing of their acceptance on that very day. Again, while the assent was received from the Congress and the Sikhs, Jinnah asked for a discussion that evening in the course of which he said that while the statement was acceptable, he was not authorised by his Council to give anything in writing. Mountbatten used a subtle technique on this occasion. He asked Jinnah to state what he wished the British prime minister to be informed, whether he would like him to make in Parliament the statement, which he had shown him (Jinnah) and the other Indian leaders.

Accordingly, on 3 June 1947, a pronouncement was made in the House of Commons by Attlee, the British prime minister to the effect that, His Majesty's Government proposed to introduce legislation during the current session for the transfer of power this year on a dominion status basis to one or two successor authorities according to the decisions taken as a result of the announcement. The right of the two Constituent Assemblies to decide in due course whether or not to remain within the British Commonwealth would not be prejudiced in any way. The die was cast. India was to be divided. There would be two new dominions, the dominion of Pakistan and the dominion of the rest of India.

Later the same evening, Nehru addressed the nation on All India Radio: 'Today I am speaking to you on another historic occasion when a vital change affecting the future of India is proposed. You have just heard an announcement by the British prime minister. The announcement lays down a procedure for self-determination in certain areas of India. It envisages on the one hand, the possibility of these areas seceding from India; on the other, it promises a big advance towards complete independence. Such a big change must have the full concurrence of the people before effect is given to it, for it must always be remembered that the future of India can only be decided by the people of India and not by any outside authority, however friendly.

'These proposals will be placed before representative assemblies of the people for consideration. But meanwhile the sands of time run out and decisions cannot await the normal course of events. While we must necessarily abide by what the people finally decide, we have to come to certain decisions ourselves and recommend them to the people for acceptance. We have, therefore, decided to accept these proposals and recommend to our larger committees that they do likewise.

'It is with no joy in my heart that I commend these proposals to you, though I have no doubt in my mind that this is the right course. For generations we have dreamt and struggled for a free, independent united India. The proposals to allow certain parts to secede, if they so will, is painful for any of us to contemplate. Nevertheless, I am convinced that our present decision is the right one from the larger viewpoint.

'.... On this the eve of great changes in India, we have to make a fresh start with (a) clear vision and a firm mind, with steadfastness and tolerance and a stout heart. We should not wish ill to anyone, but think always of every Indian as our brother and comrade. The good of the 400,000,000 people of India must be our supreme objective. We shall seek to build new relations with England on a friendly and cooperative basis, forgetting the past, which has lain so heavily upon us. I should like to express on this occasion my deep appreciation of the labours of the Viceroy Lord Mountbatten, ever since his arrival here at a critical juncture in our history.

'Invariably on every occasion of crisis and difficulty we think of our great leader, Mahatma Gandhi, who has led us unfalteringly for over a generation through darkness and sorrow, to the threshold of our freedom, to him we once more pay our homage. His blessing and wise counsel will happily be with us in the momentous years to come as always. With firm faith in our future I appeal to you to cooperate in the great task ahead and to march together to the haven of freedom for all in India. Jai Hind.'

Nehru's address makes it abundantly clear that he was commending the partition of the country with a heavy heart. He did not like it, nor did his colleagues. But the situation that had developed in the country had forced their hands. The alternative to partition was, they felt, a long drawn out communal conflict, which may well lead to a civil war. Would it not be better to let a small part of the country go, so that we could get on with the far more important task of removing poverty from the rest of the country and set it on the path of development and growth? It was considerations of this kind that won the day, and made men like Nehru and Patel accept partition against which they had fought all their lives. The immediate task before the country therefore, was to make a success of the partition. The administrative consequences of partition were serious, and so also were the consequences of the end of paramountcy, which made every princely state in the country, an independent sovereign state. If the country were to be saved from utter fragmentation, immediate steps would need to be taken to persuade the princely states to accept a suitable standstill agreement before 15 August, the date on which paramountcy was to cease. Further negotiations for a more permanent and lasting solution could then be negotiated at leisure. People had tended to assume at first that the problem of the princely states would be relatively simple and not as challenging as it was soon found to be. Some states even went to the length of expressing a desire to remain completely independent and sovereign. Even a relatively small state like Travancore was among the first to take advantage of the fact that it was a coastal state and so could enter into independent agreement with other sovereign states. It is a futile exercise, which some people wish to indulge in to believe that partition could have been avoided. Those who wish to do so must put themselves in the situation that existed in 1945, 1946 and 1947. They did not have the benefit of hindsight and had to act on the basis of the conditions that existed then. As one who lived during these fateful years, and had a good opportunity to see what was happening in the country among the political parties, considering the various options open to them, against the background of the communal holocaust towards which the country appeared to be drifting after the Muslim League's fateful decision to give up the path of constitutional development and take to Direct Action, I can bear testimony to the agony through which the Congress leaders and others opposed to partition passed before they finally decided to accept it.

It was clear that Mountbatten had made up his mind to hasten the entire process at a break-neck speed. For the further developments thereafter, Mountbatten was responsible. On his own responsibility, he announced on 6 June, that the power would be transferred to the two dominions on 15 August. The plan had to be accepted by the people of India and this was done by the acceptance of the 3 June Plan by the three main political parties, the Congress, the Muslim League and the Sikhs. The verdict of the Provinces, Bengal, Punjab, NWFP, Sind, Baluchistan and Sylhet was received during the month of June. In anticipation of the verdict of the provinces, Mountbatten had proceeded to draw up a note on the administrative consequences of partition. This note was prepared by W.H.J. Christie, ICS, additional private secretary to the viceroy. He had done this on the basis of discussions he had held with a number of officers of the Government of India, including Chaudhari Mohammad Ali and myself. This was the document, which Mountbatten placed before his Cabinet, when they realised the magnitude of the task before them. To achieve such a task within a matter of weeks would have been regarded as impossible. It would call for some years, certainly not less than a year to accomplish, and yet it was in fact achieved. There were a number of other tasks that had to be accomplished. There had to be a Boundary Commission to draw up a workable boundary line between Pakistan and the rest of India. Then there was the task of an India Independence Bill that had to be drawn up for presentation in Parliament that Mountbatten had sought for the Indian leaders to see for comments before it was presented to Parliament in July. Likewise, the consequences of the termination of British Paramountcy on the relations between the Indian states and the two new dominions were to be worked out so that the process of transition was peaceful and orderly.

The 3 June scheme envisaged in the first instance, the acceptance of the people of India represented by the major political parties, namely the Congress, the Muslim League and the Sikhs. Once the broad acceptance of the scheme became available, the provinces that were affected had to indicate what their wishes were. These provinces were the Punjab, Bengal, Sind, Baluchistan, NWFP and to a small extent Assam. Their verdict was secured very speedily. Then would follow the formal constitution of the Partition Council, the Arbitral Tribunal, the arrangements for the division of the Armed Forces, the arrangements necessary to be made consequent upon the lapses of paramountcy, making all the Indian princely states, big and small, independent sovereign states. All these various steps, measures and arrangements and many more had to be accomplished within a matter of seventy-odd days. It would have been impossible to achieve all this, but one has to accept it because all this was, in fact, accomplished. For this, credit must go to only one fact, the fixing of 15 August as the date for the transfer of power. Mountbatten was clearly moved by one consideration, and that was that the transfer must take place as early as possible, if trouble was to be averted. He received maximum possible cooperation because everyone was, for one reason or another, anxious to see the end of uncertainty and violence; bureaucrats of every hue wanted the uncertainty to end; the politicians and the public generally longed for an end to violence in daily life. One must also give credit to Mountbatten's staff. They were experts in ensuring coordination and in dovetailing the various programmes so that none had to wait till someone had completed the task assigned to him.

In a way, the Partition Council played a major role, because its approval meant the approval of the successor governments and until that was forthcoming, no action could be taken. And the Partition Council meant from a practical point of view the Steering Committee, which among all its other responsibilities was entrusted with the task of ensuring that all action be taken, following upon the Partition Council's decision, necessary for the purpose of ensuring that a Pakistan government was ready in every respect to start functioning from the 14 of August. The Partition Council, therefore, had to be composed of persons on both sides who could be trusted to commit the future dominions. On the Muslim side, it was composed of Mohammad Ali Jinnah, and Liaquat Ali, with Abdur Rab Nishtar as an alternate in the event of either of the two not being available.

On the Congress side, it was composed of Sardar Patel, Rajendra Prasad, with Rajaji as the alternate. Thus, both sides were represented at a very high level. Mountbatten was the neutral chairman, without a vote, but expected to ensure that discussion on no subject reached a stalemate. The Steering Committee was composed of Chaudhari Mohammad Ali and myself and we both enjoyed the fullest confidence of their respective principals on the one hand, and of the civil servants on the other.

Under the Steering Committee were the Expert Committees, composed of civil servants representing the notional Pakistan and the notional Rest of India. The Expert Committees were constituted to deal with ten matters, which virtually covered the entire relevant field namely (1) organisation and records; (2) assets and liabilities (3) central revenues (4) contracts (5) currency and coinage (6) economic relations (7) trade and controls (8) domicile (9) foreign relations and (10) armed forces.

Given the possibility of an agreement not being reached on some issues, a provision for an Arbitral Tribunal was also made.

In accordance with the 3 June announcement, two Boundary Commissions had to be set up, one to deal with the partition of Bengal and the separation of Sylhet from Assam and the other to deal with the partition of the Punjab. Each commission was to have a chairman and four members, two nominated by the Congress and two by the League. With the consent of the Congress and the League, Sir Cyril Radcliffe was appointed chairman of both the commissions. The terms of reference of the two commissions were to demarcate the boundaries of the two parts of the respective provinces on the basis of ascertaining the contiguous majority areas of Muslims and non-Muslims. The Bengal Commission had, in addition, to demarcate the Muslim majority area of Sylhet from the rest of Assam.

In the Punjab, the Congress had the special duty of ensuring protection of the cultural and religious life of the Sikhs, besides other considerations such as economic and rational distribution of the irrigation system, river waters, canal colonies, and of course considerations relating to security of the two dominions. The Sikhs themselves put in their claims, which had to be given full consideration by the Punjab Boundary Commission.

As was only to be expected, the Boundary Award satisfied neither side, but it was an exercise that had to be undertaken and completed by 15 August.

Mountbatten therefore, managed to ensure that practically everything necessary to be done to facilitate the transfer of power by the British was completed on time. Its consequences unfolded themselves within no time at all. Every one anticipated some trouble, but no one had anticipated quite what actually took place. Every precaution for dealing with what was anticipated had been taken. Thus, there had been created a Joint Boundary Force, and it helped for a while, but pretty soon situations developed, which were impossible for it to control. As soon as the full implications of what had taken place was realised by the average citizen, all appeals issued jointly by leaders on both sides fell on deaf ears, and law and order had ceased to exist in the Punjab, West and East and in East Bengal. What everyone had hoped would be averted, could not be averted. There began an astonishing movement on a massive scale of non-Muslim population from the NWFP and western districts of Punjab towards the India border, that is East Punjab, and a similar movement of Muslims from the districts of East Punjab towards West Punjab. This had its repurcussions in Delhi and surrounding areas whose Muslim residents moved out of their homes and sought refuge in camps that were hastily organised in various parts of Delhi. A similar movement of Hindu population from East Bengal was on a continuous scale for a considerable time.

There are those who have no hesitation in saying that this was all unnecessary. There was no need for a partition. There was no need for panicking into envisaging a civil war. Whatever this hindsight might make some people think, there is not the slightest doubt that at the time these decisions were taken, all those who had to take the decision were thoroughly convinced that a right decision had been taken, and saw in the holocaust, which ensued in the immediately following weeks, a confirmation of what could have happened on a far bigger scale. Perhaps the most astonishing of all has been the statements, which are recorded in Maulana Azad's book, which certainly are not in accordance with facts. None of the Congress leaders, except Gandhi and Khan Abdul Ghaffar Khan, had come out openly to denounce partition. Everyone, in fact, at that point of time said unhesitatingly that there was no alternative to what had been agreed upon. Naturally, there was dissatisfaction with aspects of the boundary award.

# 3

# The 3 June Statement, and Machinery for Partition

I THINK IT DESIRABLE TO QUOTE HERE FROM THE STATEMENT, which is remarkably succinct and clear:

> 3. It has always been the desire of His Majesty's Government that power should be transferred in accordance with the wishes of the Indian people themselves. This task would have been greatly facilitated if there had been agreement among the Indian political parties. In the absence of such agreement, the task of devising a method by which the wishes of the Indian people can be ascertained has devolved upon His Majesty's Government. After full consultation with political leaders in India, His Majesty's Government has decided to adopt for this purpose the plan set out below. His Majesty's Government wishes to make it clear that they have no intention of attempting to frame any ultimate Constitution for India; this is a matter for the Indians themselves. Nor is there anything in this plan to preclude negotiations between communities for a united India.

4. *The issues to be decided:*

It is not the intention of His Majesty's Government to interrupt the work of the existing Constituent Assembly. Now that provision is made for certain Provinces specified below, His Majesty's Government trust that, as a consequence of this announcement, the Muslim League representatives of those Provinces, a majority of whose representatives are already participating in it, will now take their due share in its labours. At the same time, it is clear that any Constitution framed by this Assembly cannot apply to those parts of the country, which are unwilling to accept it. His Majesty's Government are satisfied that the procedure outlined below embodies the best practical method of ascertaining the wishes of the people of such areas on the issue whether their Constitution is to be framed:-

(a) in the existing Constituent Assembly; or
(b) in a new and separate Constituent Assembly consisting of the representatives of those areas which decide not to participate in the existing Constituent Assembly.

When this has been done, it will be possible to determine the authority or authorities to whom power should be transferred.

5. *Bengal and the Punjab:*

The Provincial Legislative Assemblies of Bengal and the Punjab (excluding the European members) will, therefore, each be asked to meet in two parts, one representing the Muslim majority districts and the other the rest of the Provinces. For the purpose of determining the population of districts, the 1941 census figures will be taken as authoritative. The Muslim majority districts in these two Provinces are set out in the Appendix to this announcement.

6. The members of the two parts of each Legislative Assembly sitting separately will be empowered to vote whether or not the Province should be partitioned. If a simple majority of either

part decided in favour of partition, division will take place and arrangements will be made accordingly.

7. Before the question as to the partition is decided, it is desirable that the representatives of each part should know in advance which Constituent Assembly the Province as a whole would join in the event of the two parts subsequently deciding to remain united. Therefore, if any member of either Legislative Assembly so demands, there shall be held a meeting of all members of the Legislative Assembly (other than Europeans) at which the decision will be taken on the issue as to which Constituent Assembly the Province as a whole would join if it were decided by the two parts to remain united.

8. In the event of partition being decided upon, each part of the Legislative Assembly will, on behalf of the areas they represent, decide which of the alternatives in paragraph 4 above to adopt.

9. For the immediate purpose of deciding on the issue of partition, the members of the Legislative Assemblies of Bengal and the Punjab will sit in two parts according to Muslim majority districts (as laid down in the Appendix) and non-Muslim majority districts. This is only a preliminary step of a purely temporary nature as it is evident that for the purposes of a final partition of these Provinces a detailed investigation of boundary questions will be needed; and, as soon as a decision involving partition has been taken for either Province, a Boundary Commission will be set up by the governor general, the membership and terms of reference of which will be settled in consultation with those concerned. It will be instructed to demarcate the boundaries of the two parts of the Punjab on the basis of ascertaining the contiguous majority areas of Muslims and Non-Muslims. It will also be instructed to take into account other factors. Similar instructions will be given to the Bengal Boundary Commission. Until the report of a

Boundary Commission has been put into effect, the provisional boundaries indicated in the Appendix will be used.

10. The Legislative Assembly of Sind (excluding the European members) will at a special meeting also take its own decision on the alternatives in paragraph 4 above.

11. *North West Frontier Province:*

The position of the North West Frontier Province is exceptional. Two of the three representatives of this Province are already participating in the existing Constituent Assembly. But it is clear, in view of its geographical situation, and other considerations, that if the whole or any part of the Punjab decides not to join the existing Constituent Assembly, it will be necessary to give the North West Frontier Province an opportunity to reconsider its position. Accordingly, in such an event, a referendum will be made to the electors of the present Legislative Assembly in the North West Frontier Province to choose which of the alternatives mentioned in paragraph 4 above they wish to adopt. The referendum will be held under the aegis of the governor general and in consultation with the Provincial Government.

12. *British Baluchistan:*

British Baluchistan has elected a member, but he has not taken his seat in the existing Constituent Assembly. In view of its geographical situation, this Province will also be given an opportunity to reconsider its position and to choose which of the alternatives in paragraph 4 above to adopt. His Excellency the Governor General is examining how this can most appropriately be done.

13. *Assam:*

Though Assam is predominantly a non-Muslim Province, the district of Sylhet, which is contiguous to Bengal, is predominantly Muslim. There has been a demand that, in the event of the partition of Bengal, Sylhet should be amalgamated with the Muslim part of Bengal. Accordingly, if it is decided that Bengal should be partitioned, a referendum will be held in Sylhet district under the aegis of the governor general and in consultation with the Assam Provincial Government to decide whether the district of Sylhet should continue to form part of the Assam Province or should be amalgamated with the new Province of Eastern Bengal, if that Province agrees. If the referendum results in favour of amalgamation with Eastern Bengal, a Boundary Commission with terms of reference similar to those for the Punjab and Bengal will be set up to demarcate the Muslim majority areas of Sylhet district and contiguous Muslim majority areas of adjoining districts, which will then be transferred to Eastern Bengal. The rest of the Assam Province will in any case continue to participate in the proceedings of the existing Constituent Assembly.

16. *Administrative Matters:*

Negotiations will have to be initiated as soon as possible on the administrative consequences of any partition that may have been decided upon:-

(a) Between the representatives of the respective successor authorities about all subjects now dealt with by the Central Government, including Defence, Finance and Communications.

(b) Between different successor authorities and His Majesty's Government for treaties in regard to matters arising out of the transfer of power.

(c) In the case of Provinces that may be partitioned, as to the administration of all provincial subjects such as the division of assets and liabilities, the police and other services, the High Court, provincial institutions, etc.

17. *The Tribes of the North West Frontier:*

The agreements with tribes of the North West Frontier of India will have to be negotiated by the appropriate successor authority.

18. *The States:*

His Majesty's Government wishes to make it clear that the decisions announced above relate only to British India and that their policy towards Indian States contained in the Cabinet Mission Memorandum of 12 May 1946 remain unchanged.

19. *Necessity for Speed:*

In order that the successor authorities may have time to prepare themselves to take over power, it is important that all the above processes should be completed as quickly as possible. To avoid delay, the different Provinces or parts of Provinces will proceed independently as far as practicable within the conditions of this Plan. The existing Constituent Assembly and the new Constituent Assembly (if formed) will proceed to frame Constitutions for their respective territories: they will of course be free to frame their own rules.

20. *Immediate Transfer of Power:*

The major political parties have repeatedly emphasised their desire that there should be the earliest possible transfer of power in India. With this desire His Majesty's Government are in full sympathy, and they are willing to anticipate the date of June 1948 for the handing over of power by the setting up of an independent Indian government or governments at an even earlier date. Accordingly, as the most expeditious, and indeed the only practicable way of meeting this desire, His Majesty's Government propose to introduce legislation during the current session for the transfer of power this year on a dominion status basis to one or two successor authorities according to the decisions taken as a result of this announcement. This will be without prejudice to the right of the Indian Constituent Assemblies to decide in due course whether or not the part of India in respect of which they have authority will remain within the British Commonwealth.

Within the shortest possible time, British India was to be divided into two states with dominion status. And at the same time

> that the power was transferred to these two states, the princely states would also become independent sovereign states. The Indian Armed Forces were also to be reconstituted into two Armed Forces.

The statement was, on the whole, well received. The people had gradually worked themselves into a peculiar mental condition. They wanted the uncertainty to come to an end and were in a frame of mind where all they wanted was a decision, even if it involved partition of the country. It is doubtful if even the leaders fully appreciated the implications of the plan they were prepared to accept. Certainly, very few understood the significance of the princely states becoming sovereign states. Likewise, very few had any idea of the large number of decisions that would have to be taken within less than two and a half months. That was all the time we would have since 15 August had been virtually decided as the date on which power would be transferred to the two dominions.

Lord Mountbatten may himself have had only a very general idea of the problems to be faced. But he certainly had sufficient experience of administration to know how many administrative and other related questions would arise because of partition and would have to be tackled. He therefore, had a paper drawn up entitled 'The Administrative Consequences of Partition', and had entrusted the task to Christie, a member of his own staff. He was a member of the ICS and additional private secretary to the viceroy. This, however, was not something that Christie could do by himself. He realised, being an administrator himself, that if the question was to be tackled with adequate thoroughness, it would have to be considered in consultation with experienced administrators in the Government of India, both Muslims and non-Muslims. This was also what Menon advised. And so they arranged a discussion with Mohammad Ali and myself. The people to be consulted had deliberately been restricted to the minimum possible. Our discussions were fairly thorough. While we had no difficulty in spelling out what needed to be done and how it was to be done, we made it clear that it would be essential to set up a body capable of taking certain basic decisions, which would be binding on both India and Pakistan. Barely seventy days would be available within which not only would decisions have to be taken on an enormous number of issues, but a great many of them would also have to be implemented before the actual date so that the Pakistan government could start assuming its responsibilities from from that very date itself. Having regard to the very limited time available, the very complicated and wide ranging onerous task could be attempted with some reasonable chance of success, only if firm and final decisions could be taken on a number of preliminary issues by the two 'potential' governments in the first fortnight or so. Indeed, even decisions on other issues too, however, complex or controversial, would have to be taken without loss of time.

Christie drew up a paper on the basis of conclusions reached at these discussions, which came to be known as 'The Administrative Consequences of Partition'. It was placed before the Cabinet on 6 June 1947. Mountbatten, while doing so, drew attention to the fact that the entire task had to be completed within a very short period of time. Because of the paucity of time, he had taken the liberty of placing this paper before the leaders of the political parties to ascertain their political reactions on the way in which it was proposed to go about the work that would have to be accomplished in the available time. Decisions would have to be taken on various issues as they were concretised on behalf of the two new governments that would come into being on 15 August. Their representatives on the Partition Council would have to be given plenipotentiary powers. They would therefore, have to be persons enjoying the fullest confidence of the two political parties, namely the Congress and the Muslim League, which were expected to constitute the new governments. In suggesting that he work as the chairman of the Partition Council, his object was to put himself in a position to be able to help most effectively in ensuring that decisions were reached and reached speedily, and stalemates were avoided. He made it quite clear that he would not, under any circumstances, allow himself to become an arbitrator.

The Partition Council could be constituted only after the essential preliminaries were completed. Mountbatten, for obvious reasons could not afford any delay, having regard to the shortness of the total time available, barely seventy days. He prevailed upon the Congress and the League leaders to start work with an organisation almost as representative as the Partition Council eventually would be, namely a Special Committee of the Cabinet. Four meetings of the Special Committee were held during the interim period, the first of them being held on 6 June and the last on 26 of the month. As soon as the preliminaries were completed, the Partition Council was constituted and started working on 27th of June. The Special Committee did important work in the four meetings that were held during its existence. Accordingly, in the first meeting of the Special Committee, the Muslim League representatives named were Liaquat Ali Khan and Abdur Rab Nishtar and from the non-Muslim side Sardar Vallabhbhai Patel and Dr. Rajendra Prasad. After all the preliminaries in regard to the provinces and territorial areas that now constituted Pakistan were completed, the regular Partition Council could be constituted. And as Mountbatten anticipated, the regular Partition Council was practically the same as the Special Committee of the Cabinet, except for one change, Mohammad Ali Jinnah coming in instead of Abdur Rab Nishtar. The latter was designated the alternative should either of the two regular colleagues not be available. The non-Muslim side was unaltered, Rajaji being added as the alternate member.

At its second meeting, the Special Committee agreed that the Provincial Separation Committees should be constituted more or less on the same lines as at the centre. It further took the important decision to appoint a Steering Committee of two, namely Chaudhary Mohammad Ali, (financial adviser, Military Accounts) on behalf of Pakistan and H.M. Patel, Cabinet secretary on behalf of India. The significance of the Steering Committee to the whole process of partition lay in their terms of reference, which were in a way extraordinary; the terms of reference were:

(a) To ensure that concrete proposals were evolved in time by the Expert Committee,
(b) To ensure that these proposals adequately dove-tail each other and form a comprehensive whole,
(c) To ensure that the recommendations of the various Expert Committees are presented to the Partition Committee in a suitable form,
(d) To ensure that the decisions reached are implemented in time.

The Steering Committee was further directed —

(1) Subject to the terms of reference that may be laid down for each of the Expert Committees, to provide day to day guidance, advice and direction to the Expert Committees; and
(2) To keep in close touch with the members of the Special Committee (and later of the Partition Council when it was set up).

The Steering Committee was further directed in consultation with the various departments concerned to make recommendations in regard to –

(a) the various Expert Committees to be set up,
(b) the terms of reference of each Expert Committee, and
(c) the personnel of each Expert Committee.

The Partition Council was to be serviced by the Steering Committee. Ten Expert Committees were to be constituted to deal with important groups of subjects and on each there were to be equal number of representatives of the two future dominions to be. One of the Expert Committees was to deal with matters relating to armed forces and it was understood that on this committee, besides the representatives of the two dominions to be, there would be senior British officers as neutral advisors. The commander-in-chief was expected to keep the defence minister acquainted with whatever steps he took; it was likewise expected that he would keep in close touch with the Steering Committee and the Partition Council.

The Expert Committees were required to submit their report to the Partition Council through the Steering Committee, among whose duties was the very important one of seeing to it that the Expert Committees also reached agreements on the various matters dealt with by them. One of the Steering Committee's main functions was to put matters before the Partition Council in a most suitable and constructive form.

The Steering Committee had thus, to play a very vital role in the whole system of things. It was the Steering Committee that was asked to formulate the terms of reference of the various Expert Committees as also the persons who should constitute the latter. When these proposals came before the Partition Council, wherever there were any differences between the members of the Steering Committee, the Partition Council called upon the members of the former to find some suitable solution. The Steering Committee members clearly were able to discharge their duties satisfactorily only because they enjoyed the fullest confidence of their principals, i.e. the members representing the two future dominions to be.

At its second meeting on the 12th of June, the Special Committee decided that every government servant should be given the opportunity to select the government he wished to serve within ten days and in case he felt later that he had erred in deciding, he was to be told that he could alter his decision within six months. The Steering Committee was required to see that this decision was given effect to.

Finally, the Steering Committee was to see that every reasonable assistance was given for the training of Muslim officers in the work of departments of which no Muslim officer had any knowledge.

At the third meeting of the Special Committee, the Steering Committee presented its proposals in regard to the Expert Committees other than the Armed Forces Committee, the proposed terms of reference of each Expert Committee and of its personnel.

It was unfortunate that the Steering Committee was unable to present agreed terms of reference in respect of all the Expert Committees.

A foretaste of the kind of difference and difficulties that would arise during the following sixty odd days was provided when in respect of the Expert Committees Nos. I and II, the members of the Steering Committee were not able to agree on their respective terms of reference. Each of the members therefore, set out the terms of reference, which he considered reasonable and appropriate, and these were then placed before the Council. The differences in these two cases indicated the differences in attitudes and outlooks that were going to lead to disagreements on most issues during the ensuing days. The way in which they were resolved provides equally a good example of the tact and sensitivity displayed by all concerned, the chairman as well as the members of the Partition Council. For these reasons, a detailed account of these differences and their resolution would be useful.

In so far as Expert Committee No. I was concerned, the difference was only in regard to item (d) of the term of reference.

### A. Expert Committee No. I (Organisation, Records & Personnel)

| *As proposed by Mr. H.M. Patel* | *As proposed by Mr. Mohammad Ali* |
|---|---|
| 1. To obtain and submit proposals for the administrative machinery required for Pakistan including | 1. To submit plans for the organisation of departments, offices and services so that two successor governments have the necessary administrative machinery including |
| (a) the various kinds and grades of staff, | (a) the various kinds and grades of staff |
| (b) the necessary office equipment, furniture, stores, etc. | |

(c) the necessary records, documents, international agreements etc. (which should be separated or duplicated)

(d) for the consequential adjustments required in the administrative machinery of the rest of India.

(b) the necessary office equipment, furniture, stores etc.

(c) the necessary records, documents, international agreements, etc. (which should be separated or duplicated).

The difference in the two drafts arises from the Muslim anxiety to emphasise that both the states were identically situated. Yet, that was not the case in this respect. The entire administrative machinery for Pakistan had to be brought into being from scratch: India, on the other hand, would have its administrative machinery in place, except that it would need to be rearranged and balanced so as to make good the gaps left on the departure from each department and office of the officers and staff who would have opted for Pakistan.

In regard to Expert Committee No. 2 also, alternative drafts were submitted.

These are set out below:

## A. Expert Committee No. II (Assets and Liabilities)

*As proposed by Mr. H.M. Patel*

1. To compile lists of assets by broad categories showing value and present location.
2. To make recommendations as to the division of assets between the two successor governments keeping in

*As proposed by Mr. Mohammad Ali*

1. To compile lists of assets by broad categories showing value and present location.
2. To make recommendations for the physical division of assets between the two successor governments

view the following broad principles –

(i) Fixed assets like railway lines, buildings and public works, telegraph and telephone lines etc. should be regarded as the property of the Government in whose jurisdiction they lie.

(ii) Moveable assets like rolling stock, reserves and maintenance stores, equipment relative to the fixed assets in (I) where applicable should be divided in such manner as would enable the respective governments to be currently self-sufficient and maintain the utilities efficiently.

(iii) Assets like plant and machinery in workshops, factories and other installations and equipment in institutions of an all-India character may, subject to needs of the jurisdiction in which they lie, be shared by the other government bearing in mind the objective that as far as practicable –

(a) the services in the two governments run with the same degree of efficiency.

(b) the two governments are self-sufficient to the maximum degree.

*Explanatory Note:*

There are certain categories of assets such as irrigation, canals, railway lines, telegraph lines, buildings which will be taken over by the government in whose territory they are located. On the other hand, there are other categories of assets such as stores, equipment, rolling stock, workshops and industrial installations which can and should be divided between the two governments irrespective of their present locations so that both governments have their due share of such assets. This division should not be such as to destroy their utility to either government except of course the temporary loss of production during the period of transportation and in some to assist the latter to be self-sufficient as far as practicable.

3. When division is impracticable, to make recommendation either for mutual assisance or for joint administration or for any other arrangement for such period as may be necessary.
4. To make recommendations in regard to the financial settlement between the two governments arising from the above as well as from an allocation of the public debt, pensions and other liabilities.
5. To recommend measures for giving effect to any transfer of assets after the recommendations have been accepted by the Partition Council.

*Note:* Departmental Sub-Committees and the Armed Forces Committee will submit reports to the Expert Committee in regard to assets falling within their purview.

cases of dismantling and re-erection.

The difference between the two drafts raised a fundamental issue. The differences brought out by the members of the Steering Committee were indicative of the basic difference — who was parting from whom? The author's view was that normally material assets must be left where they are. In ordinary times, it is not only a simple arrangement but positively advantageous in certain ways. It proceeds from the truth that division and physical transfer of material assets generally impairs its total value. This, in fact, is a well-established principle, and was adopted first when Burma was separated from India and was followed subsequently in the separation of Sind from Bombay and Orissa from Bihar. In the then existing state of scarcity of capital goods, however, a certain measure of physical transfer, it was realised, might be necessary in order that the government lacking in a particular resource may not be unduly inconvenienced in that service for a prolonged period. For that reason, in the author's draft it has been stated that in such cases subject to the jurisdiction in which they lie, negotiated arrangements may be reached.

Jinnah's view, on the other hand, was that the accident of geographical location should not have priority over the just and equitable distribution of assets like workshops and industrial installations between the two successor governments. The separation of Burma did not provide a parallel since owing to its geographical isolation, services there were very largely self-contained. It is only fair that both the successor governments should in the matter of efficiency of services start on as equal a footing as possible. Inevitably, Pakistan will be comparatively worse off in industrial equipment, which is at present in short supply throughout the world. This disadvantage should not be further accentuated.

It is significant that in their attempt to reconsider these two points of view in regard to the formulation of the terms of reference of the two important Expert Committees, the Council virtually avoided a clear-cut decision. In regard to the first Expert Committee, it advised that the terms of reference should be settled after the British government had announced their decision regarding the successor to the present government for purposes of continuity of foreign representation etc. In so far as the second Expert Committee was concerned, it merely exhorted the Steering Committee to evolve agreed terms of reference and if they failed, to let the Expert Committee II proceed with the work bearing in mind the broad principle of securing the greatest good of the two states. This was, no doubt, a wise course to adopt in the tense atmosphere that then existed and feelings ran high. The Council was anxious to find a way to get on with the task even if that involved a skirting of some differences and leaving over their resolution to a later date when the atmosphere would be more congenial.

This illustration also indicates clearly that, however well-conceived the machinery for implementing the decision to partition the country, its successful functioning had necessarily to depend upon the quality and temperaments of the individuals manning it and the spirit and motivation inspiring them. In this case, the individuals involved on both sides, whether they represented Muslims or non-Muslims, India or Pakistan, were unquestionably able and expert in the fields they were called upon to work in and advise. What was no less important, they were all keen on seeing to it that the task was accomplished within the allotted time. They scarcely needed Mountbatten's repeated emphasis on the sixty-odd days available at the outset to goad them into working unremittingly and purposefully. Everyone worked most zealously. And now the further exhortation by the Council to see to it that the partition work was carried out in a spirit of friendship and goodwill and with a sincere desire to part as friends merely confirmed their own decision to work in a constructive spirit.

While it was true that by making known that this was the Council's view, valuable psychological pressure would be exercised on the Expert Committees, the members of these committees hardly needed any external inducement or incentive. The work of partition was to be undertaken both in a spirit of friendship and goodwill, and also with the desire to give a fair deal to both sides. This spirit so far as the members of the Council themselves were concerned manifested itself when they agreed without much ado:

(1) To the setting up of the Expert Committees with the personnel recommended in the note prepared by the Steering Committee.

(2) That, as a special case, Sir Ghulam Mohammad though a non-official, should be allowed to serve on Expert Committee No. II, which dealt with Assets and Liabilities. (Sir Ghulam Mohammad was a distinguished member of the Indian Audit Service and had retired fairly recently with a high reputation as an expert in financial matters).

(3) That the terms of reference of the Committees should be as recommended by the Steering Committee except in regard to Expert Committee No. I and No. II. And the differences among the members of the Steering Committee in regard to the terms of reference of these two Committees were resolved virtually by throwing the responsibility back into their laps. They were to see to it that the work of the Expert Committees was not held up because of their differences and that the Steering Committee would endeavour to give suitable instructions to enable the Expert Committees and their sub-committees to get on with their work! And the Steering Committee was also to see to the fact that the Expert Committees I and II worked in accordance with the broad principle of securing the greatest good of the two states.

(4) That every government servant should be given the opportunity to elect which government he wished to serve. This option should be exercised within a period of, say, ten days. If, however, any government servant so desired, exercising his right to reconsider his decision, he could make a specific request to that effect at the time he made his choice and he would then be allowed six months in which to make his final choice. When the option had been exercised, the cadres would be separated accordingly. But actual physical transfer would

have to be arranged over a period of time, and in the meantime a stand still agreement would operate so that the efficiency of the organisations may be preserved.

(5) That changes in the personnel of the Expert Committees could be made by the Steering Committee subject to the approval of the members of the Partition Council.

The Council had thus made known its attitude towards the task that was entrusted to it. It clearly meant business — its attitude towards problems posed to it was going to be of a constructive, and positive nature — it had also indicated in no uncertain terms that it intended to work with speed, and that it would repose full confidence in its main instrument, the Steering Committee.

Quite fortuitously, at the very first meeting of the Council, the Steering Committee had sought approval to a procedure for the transfer of officers and personnel from Delhi to Karachi in order to set up the Pakistan government. Liaquat Ali Khan, a member of the council, submitted another note at the meeting in which he advocated a slightly different procedure. It was decided:

(1) That the procedure should be as indicated in paragraph 2 and 3 of the Steering Committee's note; and

(2) That members of the Partition Council would be entitled to bring up matters directly before the Council, it being understood that, as far as possible, the Steering Committee be given sufficient time before the meeting to enable them to examine the proposals in question, and to brief, where necessary, members of the Council on such subjects.

The object, clearly, was to ensure that the Council should be taking decisions on those problems that had been thoroughly examined by the Steering Committee and it would be for them to marshal arguments for and against as objectively as possible. This could only be ensured if whatever came to the Council did so only after it had been considered carefully by the Steering Committee.

On behalf of the League, the members nominated by the League were:

Mr. M.A. Jinnah
Mr. Liaquat Ali Khan
And on behalf of the Congress,
Sardar Vallabhbhai Patel, and
Dr. Rajendra Prasad.

A third member who would be entitled to attend in the absence of any one of its two members was permitted to both the League and the Congress. The person nominated by the League was Abdur Rab Nishtar, and by the Congress, C. Rajagopalachari. The viceroy presided. In addition, there were always present the chief of the officers' staff, principal secretary to His Excellency the Viceroy, Chaudhuri Mohamad Ali and myself. It may be reiterated that Lord Mountbatten as chairman of the Partition Council expressly desisted from expressing any views, but only intervened to help in finding a compromise solution where an acceptable compromise had to be found. The representation at the political level was clearly at the highest level possible from the point of view of taking binding decisions.

The work of partitioning the country into two fully functioning countries within a matter of seventy-two days was the task assumed by Mountbatten and the leaders of the main political parties, who would be called upon to assume responsibility for the governance of the two new countries, which would come into being at the end of those sixty days. (If we calculated from 3 June to 15 August there would be seventy-two days: by the time, first the Special Committee of the Cabinet and later the Partition Council was constituted, there were left barely sixty odd days) They accepted this responsibility without having any clear concept of what the task involved. Their attention was concentrated on the political solution, and they appear to have assumed that other matters would be tied up somehow or other whatever the time available for the purpose. And since speed was of the essence, it was just as well that this was the case; they were all forced to face the situation in a realistic manner.

The paper entitled 'The Administrative Consequences of the Partition' provided the first glimpse to them of the magnitude of the task. Fortunately, the two sides had selected as their representatives, on the Partition Council, men of outstanding ability and character. What they lacked in direct experience they made up by their ability, imagination and sense of realism. These four men — Vallabhbhai Patel and Rajendra Prasad on the one side, and Jinnah and Liaquat Ali Khan on the other, (and similarly also the two alternative members, Rajagopalachari (Rajaji) and Abdur Rab Nishtar) realised that they had to come to grips with the issues placed before them, that they had to forget the past conflicts and bitterness engendered, and that they had to find some solutions for the various problems posed within the limited time available. It is true that an Arbitral Tribunal had been provided, which could take decisions on issues on which the two sides could not themselves come to an agreement. However, it would not do to leave over too many matters to be pronounced upon by the Tribunal if the two governments were to be in a position to function even moderately efficiently after 15 August. They were all strong men and men of determination, but they were also realists. They knew therefore, where to stop before a breaking point was reached. They were all anxious also to get on with the task of running their governments for the benefit of their people and it was this anxiety of theirs which I have no doubt was at the end responsible for their agreement to abide by what the two members of the Steering Committee, whom by that time they had come to trust, would agree on issues on which agreement had not been reached and which it had been decided to refer to the Tribunal. And the two did not fail them; they were able to forge agreements on every one of the outstanding issues.

# 4

# The Expert Committees at Work

THE CONSTITUTION OF THE EXPERT COMMITTEES AND THEIR terms of reference were sanctioned on 16 June. They were asked to submit their reports by the third week of July. The volume of work involved and the complexity of a great many issues made compliance with the completion date almost impossible. Yet, every committee tried its utmost and in most cases, came close to success. A number of issues could not be agreed upon by the due date and many could be taken up for consideration well after 15 August 1947.

Having regard to the very limited time that was available, what had to be ensured was that the committee did not get stuck at any point so that any further progress would be held up. The two members of the Steering Committee made it a point to meet the members on the various Expert Committees to help the process towards agreement. Where they felt the differences were too great, they would meet and discuss among themselves. In this manner, over a very large area they were able to arrive at agreed decisions. There were, of course, matters in respect of which the two members of the Steering Committee would find it necessary to consult their 'principals' so as to make certain that in their anxiety to procure agreement they did not accept something that might be politically unacceptable. All these consultations meant that everyone involved in this process was heavily overworked. Their day would start very early, well before sunrise, and conclude well after sunset. But they did succeed in getting through an enormous volume of work.

An outline of the terms of reference of the ten Expert Committees will give a broad view of the variety of matters in respect of which the Partition Council was called upon to take decisions during the short period of seventy days. They are as follows:

## Expert Committee No. I – Organisation, Records and Personnel

(i) *Terms of Reference:*

(a) To obtain and submit proposals in regard to the organisational consequences of partition in respect of the administrative machinery, including:-
- (1) the various kinds and grades of staff,
- (2) the necessary office equipment, furniture, stores, etc.
- (3) the necessary records, documents, international agreements, etc., (which should be separated or duplicated).

(b) To make recommendations regarding the division in accordance with the general directive given below as far as possible, and where this may not be possible, to suggest the basis of division, of the following:
- (1) officers of the superior services.
- (2) the staff of the departments of the Government of India and of the attached and subordinate offices,
- (3) the staff of the regional organisations, for example, the various railways, P & T circles, and income-tax circles.
- (c) Where it is not possible to effect a complete separation of functions by the partition date, to recommend interim arrangements for carrying out the functions concerned in the two areas.

(d) To recommend measures for giving effect to the decisions taken on the recommendations in (a), (b) and (c) by the Partition Council.

DIRECTIVE

Every government servant should be given the opportunity to select the government he wishes to serve. The cadres will then be separated accordingly, but the actual transfers will have to be arranged over a period of time and in the meanwhile, a standstill agreement should be arranged so that the efficiency of the organisations may be preserved.

*(ii) Departmental Sub-Committees of Expert Committee No. 1:*

(a) TERMS OF REFERENCE OF SUB-COMMITTEES:

Each of the departmental sub-committees will report to the main committee and its terms of reference will be as for the Expert Committee No. 1 suitably modified to meet the requirements of the departments concerned. In the case of the Departmental Sub-committee for Agriculture and Food, the following additional clause will be added to the terms of reference:

> 'to make recommendations for the division of All-India organisations such as the ICAR*, and Agricultural Commodity Committees or for their continuance as joint organisations for such periods as may be considered necessary.'

And, in the case of the Departmental Sub-Committees for Communications and Railways the following clause will be added:

> 'to make recommendations for such arrangements as may be necessary for the interchange of traffic between the territories of the two future governments.'

---

* Indian Council of Agricultural Research. Ed.

And, in the case of Departmental Sub-committees for Home/ Legislative Department, the following clause will be added:

'to consider and make recommendations regarding the consequences of partition on the work being done in the Secretariat of the G.G.[1] (Public) and Secretariat of G.G. (Reforms).'

**Expert Committee No. II — Assets and Liabilities**

(i) *Terms of reference:*

(1) To compile lists of assets by broad categories showing value and present location.

(2) To make recommendations as to the division of assets between the two successor governments. The general principle should be to secure the greatest good of the two states, but if there are disputed claims for fixed assets, like plant and machinery, the removal of which might be detrimental to the interests of the other government, the facts of each case should be reported for consideration by the Partition Council.

(3) When division is impracticable, to make recommendation either for mutual assistance or for joint administration or for any other arrangement for such period as may be necessary.

(4) To make recommendations in regard to the financial settlement between the two governments arising from the above as well as from an allocation of the public debt, pensions and other liabilities.

(5) To recommend measures for giving effect to any transfer of assets after the recommendations have been accepted by the Partition Council.

Note: Departmental sub-committees and the Armed Forces Committee will submit reports to the Expert Committee in regard to assets falling within their purview.

1 Governor General

*(ii) Departmental sub-committees of Expert Committee No. II:*

Note No. I: In regard to all other departments, the departmental sub-committees of Expert Committee No. 1 will also function in the same capacity for Expert Committee No. II.

Note No. II: Departmental Sub-Committee No. 12 (Political) should make recommendations regarding the assets and liabilities created in connection with the functions of H.E.[1] the Crown Representative.

## Expert Committee No. III (i) – Central Revenues

(i) *Terms of Reference:*

(1) To make recommendations for the collection and allocation between the two governments of revenues from customs, central excises, income tax, salt, opium and stamps for the current year.

(2) To make recommendations regarding the relations between the two successor governments in the matter of customs, income tax, etc., in future.

## Expert Committee No. III (ii) – Miscellaneous Revenues

*(i) Terms of reference:*

(1) To make recommendations for the collection and allocation between the two governments of revenues other than customs, central excises, income tax, salt, opium and stamps for the current year.

(2) To make recommendations regarding the relations between the two successor governments in matters of revenues other than customs, income tax, etc., in future.

1 His Excellency

## Expert Committee No. IV – Contracts

(i) *Terms of reference:*
To make recommendations regarding the allocation of the liability, including contingent liability, such as pending litigation for contracts entered into by the present Government of India.

## Expert Committee No. V (i) – Currency, Coinage and Exchange

*(i) Terms of reference:*
(1) To make recommendations regarding currency and coinage arrangements consequent on partition for the two governments.
(2) Consistent with the recommendations under (1) above, to formulate proposals in regard to the division of the assets and liabilities of the Reserve Bank of India and the organisational consequences of partition in respect of its administrative machinery.
(3) To make recommendations consequent on partition regarding exchange control for the two states.
(4) To report on the position of the two states consequent on partition in regard to the membership of the International Monetary Fund and the International Bank.

## Expert Committee No. V (ii) – Budget and Accounts

*(i) Terms of reference:*
To make recommendations –
(1) regarding the financial, budgetary, accounting and auditing arrangements for the two governments for the current financial year.
(2) regarding the adjustments between the two governments in respect of services rendered in future by one government to the other.

(ii) *Departmental sub-committees of Expert Committee No. V (ii) to deal with (1) Railways and (2) P. & T.:*

(a) *Terms of reference:*

To make recommendations—

(1) regarding the financial, budgetary and accounting arrangements for the Railway/P&T systems for the two governments for the current financial year.

(2) regarding adjustments between the two governments in future in respect of traffic running over both states and of services rendered by one government to the other.

## Expert Committee No. VI – Economic Relations (Controls)

*(i) Terms of reference:*

To examine the effect of partition on the administration of existing controls and to make recommendations regarding alternative arrangements if necessary.

## Expert Committee No. VII – Economic Relations (Trade)

*(i) Terms of reference:*

To examine matters regarding all trade and movement between the territories of the two successor governments.

## Expert Committee No. VIII – Domicile

(i) To examine and make recommendations on the implications of partition with reference to domicile and nationality of the inhabitants of British India and on the position of Indian nationals abroad.

## Expert Committee No. IX – Foreign Relations

*(i) Terms of reference:*

To examine and make recommendations on the effect of partition—

(1) on the relations of the successor governments with each other and with other countries (including the countries of the British Commonwealth and border tribes),

(2) on the position of Indian nationals abroad,
(3) on India's diplomatic representation,
(4) on the existing treaties and engagements between India and other countries and tribes,
(5) on India's membership of international organisations.

**Expert Committee No.X — Armed Forces Reconstitution Committee**

*(i) Terms of reference:*
It should, in close consultation with the Steering Committee, acting under orders of the Partition Council, make proposals for the division of the existing Armed Forces of India, namely, the Royal Indian Navy, the Indian Army, and the Royal Indian Air Force (including various installations, establishments and stores owned by the present Defence Department of the Government of India).

(a) *Special sub-committee for financial matters:*
The following four officers (who are members of the Army, Navy and / or Air Force Sub-Committees) acting together will constitute a Special Sub-Committee of the Armed Forces Reconstitution Committee to make recommendations regarding the financial adjustments consequent on the division of the assets of the armed forces. The recommendations of this sub-committee in this respect will be submitted to the main Expert Committee No. II (Assets and Liabilities) through the Armed Forces Reconstitution Committee.

The machinery that was set up was simple and yet sound. It ensured that all issues would be studied in depth by those who were competent to undertake such a study, i.e., the Expert Committees. Their recommendations were to be subjected to a further scrutiny by two persons, who, besides being experts, had commonsense, patience and judgement. Only thereafter would the recommendations made be placed before the Partition Council, which was to take the final decisions, binding the two new governments.

At the level of the study by the experts, it was further ensured that both sides would be adequately represented so that not only would the study be by professionals but the professionals would also bring to bear upon each problem the outlook of the two sides. It might appear at first sight that this kind of arrangement would make agreement difficult. However, it was just contrary to that. While every issue was considered from the point of view of each side, the underlying approach of both sides was to seek out ways of arriving at an understanding on a reasonable and fair basis, if that was at all possible. The two members of the Steering Committee were expected to help the Expert Committees in arriving at an understanding on every issue, their endeavour being to emphasise the essentials in each issue and to persuade all concerned to disregard minor aspects or issues, which did not affect the substance of what was at stake. Such combined effort made it possible for formulae to be evolved, which led to acceptable compromise solutions. The result was that it was only on a limited number of issues that agreements could not be reached by the date that power was to be transferred.

While therefore it had to be decided formally by the Partition Council to refer such issues to the Arbitral Tribunal, efforts continued even after the Transfer of Power to find compromise solutions on the outstanding issues. The relationship that had developed between the representatives of the two potential governments on the Partition Council and in particular, the two members of the Steering Committee and some of the key experts on each side during the few weeks that they had worked together on the problems of partitioning the assets and liabilities of the country, had brought them sufficiently close together for them to trust each other's sense of fairness. This made it easier for an understanding to be reached even on the remaining outstanding issues. These outstanding issues were undoubtedly extremely important issues in so far as the financial implications were concerned. Nevertheless, an understanding was evolved on all the issues by the Steering Committee at the end, so that nothing remained to be remitted to the Arbitral Tribunal.

In this sense, therefore, it may be said that the machinery that had been evolved had proved its worth. But it was also clear that, however good the machinery, if the individuals who had to work it were not of the right kind and caliber, success would not have been easy or even possible. While, therefore, one may justly praise the machinery that was evolved and those who evolved it, much credit should go to the individuals who laboured for an understanding. They mattered most.

It is quite clear to me that had there not been as chairman of the Partition Council a person of the caliber of Mountbatten, success would have been difficult. He had a good understanding of the issues, he thought with remarkable clarity and speed and he had quite an astonishing capacity for preventing stalemates. The fact that he enjoyed the confidence of the British government to an extraordinary degree made it possible for him to offer assistance from the British government of the appropriate type, which, on more than one occasion helped in a solution being found to problems, which at that moment had appeared to be insoluble. His determination to see that nothing should come in the way of power being transferred as planned certainly helped most. Everyone else also became equally infected with that spirit, though understandably the motivation varied.

The Partition Council was also fortunate in the nature of the individuals who had been deputed by each side to represent it. The leaders on each side, Jinnah on Pakistan's side and Sardar Vallabhbhai Patel on India's side, were both men capable of taking big decisions without hesitation and their contribution to these discussions in the Council showed them to be farsighted men of vision. They had as their colleagues, men of complementary qualities, shrewd, clear thinking, and thorough. None of them ever appeared during this period to have lost sight of the goal. Both sides were thus, fully equipped to look at every problem in a thorough and comprehensive manner and yet with a full understanding of the issues at stake.

They were also men big enough to repose complete confidence in their main advisors, the two members of the Steering Committee. It was because of their faith in their judgement, their thoroughness and imaginative understanding of the problems that it became possible to dispose of the vast volume of work with speed and with thoroughness. The Steering Committee, in turn, was underpinned by men who were not only experts in the particular problems that they had to deal with but were also genuinely moved by the same spirit, the same determination to arrive at decisions which were fair to both sides.

With all this, on 6 August, it had to be admitted that a number of important matters remained in respect of which no agreement had been reached. Understanding on sufficient issues had been reached to make it possible for power to be transferred and the two governments to come into being. At the same time, it was also realised that efforts to arrive at an understanding on outstanding issues had to be continued even after the transfer of power. And so, even after deciding to remit the outstanding issues to the Arbitral Tribunal, the Partition Council decided to continue in being, with changed personnel and without a chairman. It met on four occasions, on 25 August 1947, 8 September, 29 October and on 1 December of the same year. A large number of matters of relatively minor importance were settled but all the major issues that it had decided to remit to the Arbitral Tribunal had proved too tough to resolve until the meeting on 1 December.

At this time, India was still represented by the same personnel as before the transfer of power, while Pakistan was represented by two persons who enjoyed the fullest confidence of those who had represented Pakistan at the Partition Council before the transfer of power. Jinnah and Liaquat Ali Khan were no longer available for the work of the Partition Council. The former had become the governor general of Pakistan and the latter its prime minister. They had deputed Ghulam Mohammad, who later became the governor general. It will be recalled that Mohammad, though a non-official, had been specially permitted by the Partition Council to work on the important Expert Committee No. II, the Committee, which dealt with all the most complicated financial issues. He was held in high respect in undivided India for his expertise on matters financial. Of the others, one was Sir Archibald Rowlands, finance minister of Pakistan and who had also been finance minister of undivided India during British rule. And the other was Zahid Hussain, Pakistan's high commissioner in India and a man of great ability and financial acumen, greatly respected.

After discussion had gone on for a little while, Sardar Patel sprang a surprise. He intervened to observe that there was little chance of arriving at any agreement if they continued arguing the way they were doing. He suggested that the two persons who had gone into the merits of all the outstanding issues most thoroughly were the two members of the Steering Committee. He had full confidence in their competence, judgement and fairmindedness. He would be prepared to leave it to them to evolve solutions to the remaining issues. Ghulam Mohammad responded without hesitation and said he too was equally prepared to repose full trust and confidence in the two members of the Steering Committee.

After this expression of confidence and faith, they were asked to retire and return with agreed solutions. The members of the Steering Committee went out into an adjoining room in Sardar Patel's house and proceeded to tackle the task assigned to them. They were, of course, familiar with each of the issues and knew every argument for and against any proposition. In most cases, it was for them merely a question of how far they could go in an endeavour to arrive at an agreement. The gap in every case had been reduced to the narrowest possible proportions. They called in their respective expert advisors and considered how far towards an agreement each side could move. Because of their own understanding of the issues involved, the two members of the Steering Committee did not have much difficulty in reaching an understanding on every issue. The details, of course, had to be worked out later. And when they reported the agreements to the Council, the Council accepted them without the slightest of hesitation. It was indeed a triumph of faith in each other's sense of fairness.

It was clear from the outset that the task set to the Partition Council was of such magnitude and with such potentiality for raising controversies and disagreements that even if the Council had far more time at its disposal, the task would have been extremely difficult to accomplish: it is no exaggeration to say that it was well nigh impossible to achieve. And yet it was accomplished. And because it was accomplished, there has not been much thought given to the achievement or the reasons for it. Every time the Council met, points arose which aroused controversy and a stalemate seemed unavoidable: but it was somehow avoided, sidestepped or circumvented. At the time, we, who at those meetings could only watch, ruminate but speak only when called upon to do so, could not help wondering how progress at the rate necessary was going to be achieved.

It is curious, but as I cast my mind back, I recall distinctly that we never seemed to have thought that we would not succeed! Somehow the two of us, the two members of the Steering Committee had convinced ourselves that the task would be accomplished, no matter what the obstacles. I do not think we ever expressed ourselves in those terms. Nevertheless, we discussed the problems, planned our work, strove to resolve differences brought before us by the Expert Committees, always with the confidence that differences and difficulties notwithstanding, we would find a way of overcoming them. Where did that confidence come from? Speaking for myself, I would say that it was basically from my own conviction that we had no alternative but to succeed. But my conviction alone would not have been the deciding factor. It was necessary that all others engaged in this task should also be working with that same type of conviction. It certainly obtained in Sardar Patel, who led the three-men Indian team on the Partition Council. I had reason to believe that my colleague on the Steering Committee had also the same outlook and attitude as mine and the Muslim members on the Council, Jinnah, Liaquat Ali Khan, and Abdur Rab Nishtar conducted themselves in the course of the discussions in the Partition Council as if they too had made up their minds to make the Council successful if they found the other side similarly disposed.

The magnitude of the task that had been accomplished has, to this day, not been fully appreciated. It has never occurred to anyone to ask how had it become possible to arrive at agreements on controversial issues of such great significance and importance in the midst of the surrounding atmosphere of great tension, violence and bitterness. That these men were able to look at these problems with objectivity and moved only by the desire to ensure better understanding and friendliness in the future between the two countries, reflects great credit on the members of the Partition Council.

## The Working of the Expert Committees

The Expert Committee No. II, the Committee on Assets and Liabilities was found to be the most heavily burdened committee of all the Expert Committees appointed. It was not only dealing with various items but had to deal with a number of problems of great complexity. Moreover, the time available for the task that had been assigned to them was far too short. In the circumstances, what the committee was able to achieve was not particularly remarkable, unfortunately because of the shortness of time and also because of the complexity of the difference of opinion that existed between the two sides. They left an enormous amount of unsettled area for the Steering Committee and the Partition Council to resolve.

This committee was composed of Sir Ghulam Mohammad who later became governor general of Pakistan, Narharirao (who had been auditor general), B.S. Sunderam, S. Ratnam Shoable and Mumtaz Hasan. N.V. Rangacharya and Anvar Ali serviced the committee.

The committee appointed two sub-committees, specially for Railways and All India Radio. For all the other departments, the sub-committees of Expert Committee No. I were assigned to deal with matters relating to Expert Committee No. II.

*The terms of reference of the Expert Committee No. II were:*

1. To compile lists of assets by broad categories showing value and present location.
2. To make recommendations as to the division of assets between the two successor governments. The general principle should be to secure the greatest good of the two states, but if there are disputed claims for fixed assets, like plant and machinery, the removal of which might be detrimental to the interests of the other government, the facts of each case should be reported for consideration by the Partition Council.
3. When division is impracticable, to make recommendation either for mutual assistance or for joint administration or for any other arrangement for such period as may be necessary.
4. To make recommendations in regard to the financial settlement between the two governments arising from the above as well as from an allocation of the public debt, pensions and other liabilities.
5. To recommend measures for giving effect to any transfer of assets after the accommendations have been accepted by the Partition Council.

It is evident that this committee was entrusted with the task of resolving by far the most difficult and complicated problems relating to the division of assets and liabilities. Even in what might appear to be the simplest of tasks, that of listing and valuing assets, they were faced with immense problems. As they have themselves stated 'a proper listing of assets as required by Para 1 of the Terms of Reference was an almost impossible task in the time at the committee's disposal.' The assets of the Government of India fell into the following broad categories:

(a) Capitalised assets of a productive character, e.g., railways.
(b) Capitalised assets of a non-productive character, e.g., New Delhi capital.
(c) Capital assets acquired out of revenue and borne on charge:
  (i) with values, e.g., buildings, stores, Ordnance Factories, etc.
  (ii) without values, e.g., stores and Ordnance Depots.
(d) Assets acquired out of revenue, not borne on charge, e.g., shop tools and consumable stores drawn for current use.
(e) Assets not paid for by the Government of India, but received as gifts, etc.
(f) In addition to the above, there are buildings, stores, etc., belonging to His Majesty's Government, in the Government of India's custody, and there are also assets taken over from the American Army under a special arrangement.

The main difficulties in preparing the lists were:
(a) the complete absence of records in some cases;
(b) the fact that where inventories are maintained, they are not necessarily complete or fully priced;
(c) the lists had to be prepared with reference to a date in the past although the financial settlement between the two successor governments would naturally have to be based on the facts as on 15 August 1947;
(d) the immensity of the task of listing out the very large number of items involved, particularly in the defence services;
(e) the impracticability of determining values allocable to the two dominions where the same asset extends over the territories of both dominions and figures are not available for each portion of the asset separately.

Faced, as they were, with a task of immense magnitude and complexity, the committee approached it in a realistic and practical manner. Thus, when considering the problems involved in listing and valuing stationery and furniture they decided that for such items, a broad financial adjustment would suffice without going in for elaborate checks. When actual values were not easily available the committee adopted a per item scale; a portable typewriter would be taken to cost Rs.250 and a standard typewriter Rs.375, an officer's furniture Rs.150 and that of a clerk Rs.50. Since values had to be given in all cases, it directed that book values should normally be adopted; unless good reasons exist for adopting some other basis. The book value was taken as cost recorded without depreciation, except when a depreciation fund is maintained, the value would be the original cost less the amount so credited in the fund.

The committee was able to make good progress because of this attitude. Even so, on all major issues the committee was not able to produce agreed recommendations before 15 August 1947. This was so in regard to items such as sterling balances, lend-lease silver, cash balances, uncovered debt, financial settlement, certain aspects of railways — all these were settled on 1 December. Then too it became possible because both Mohammad Ali and I had been discussing the questions over days and had considered every possible formula. The important thing to note is that a solution in fact was found.

The difficulties that had to be faced in coming to an agreed decision may be appreciated more clearly if I give a somewhat detailed account of how decisions had actually been reached in a few matters. One of the most important of these relate to the question of the uncovered debt. In its report, Expert Committee No. II stated that the two sides were agreed that the liability for this type of debt had to be allocated between the two governments in a proportion based on considerations of a general character. The view of the Muslim members was that the allocation of this liability should be in proportion to the contributions made by the areas which would be included in the Dominions of India and Pakistan to the revenues of the present Central Government. This, according to the Pakistan members, was the basis adopted by the Amery Tribunal appointed to advise on the formulation of financial settlement between India and Burma when Burma was separated from India.

The non-Muslim members did not agree that the uncovered debt should be allocated solely or even primarily on the basis of revenue contributions. They were of the opinion that the population was the most important single consideration for determining the basis of division of these liabilities. Contribution to the Central revenue was also an important consideration, as also were several other factors. All these they spelt out in a detailed note, which they prepared. The Muslim members also submitted a detailed note to support their line of thinking. According to the Muslim members, Pakistan's share of the uncovered debt should not exceed seven per cent while the non-Muslim members raised it to twenty per cent. In order to determine the respective contributions to the Central coffers by areas, which were expected to form Pakistan and those remaining that would constitute the Indian dominion, the Expert Committee requested Professor B.P. Adarkar and Dr. A.I. Qureshi, the two economists attached to the Finance Department to examine the matter on certain basis indicated to them by the committee and to submit their report. Subject to certain modifications, the Muslim members of the committee accepted the conclusions reached by the two economists.

The Partition Council after careful consideration of all factors decided that Pakistan's share of the uncovered debt should be fixed at 17½%. This percentage would also apply to all cases such as liability for pensions, allocation of the sale-proceeds of surplus stores, etc., in which it has been agreed assets or liabilities are to be divided, they should be divided in the ratio of the uncovered debt.

A further difference between the two sides pertained to the discharge of public debt. The Pakistani members felt that 'the public debt of India as on 15 August 1947 will consist of a number of rupee and sterling loans with varying rates of interest and maturities. Sterling loans will be liquidated as part of the sterling balances settlement with HMG.' On the question of the manner in which the liabilities of the present government to the bond-holders should be discharged by the two successor governments, two alternatives were suggested. First, each bond will be replaced by two bonds to be issued by Pakistan and the Indian dominion respectively, (the amount of each bond representing the proportion in which the two governments share the public debt).

The second alternative would be the responsibility for the whole of the debt may be assumed by one government, the other government becoming its debtor to the extent of its share of the debt. In such a case, the liability of the debtor government to the creditor government will be discharged on a mutually agreed basis such as by payment of annuities. The first alternative would not only involve an immense amount of work but would also entail the issue of bonds for comparatively small and meticulously calculated amounts and would cause inconvenience to the bond-holders. The second alternative, however, would not be consistent with the sovereignty of the government, which assumes a debtor status and would not be linked with any inherent necessity of the situation.

This issue could not be resolved before 15 August and was one of those that was agreed upon between the two sides to refer to the Arbitral Tribunal. The two members of the Steering Committee decided the matter on 1 December 1947 and their decision was that the Indian dominion was to take over the entire responsibility of the public debt dovetailing Pakistan with the amount of its share of the public debt.

It will be seen thus, that in this very important matter the final decision was reached in a spirit of give and take. And yet, it was not as arbitrary as it would appear at first sight. It was on a careful weighing of all the arguments that had been urged in the course of the examination of the question by the economists, and by the experts from the two sides that the compromise arrangement was determined.

The fourth point of the terms of reference, that relating to the financial settlement between two governments, turned out to be an extremely difficult point and on almost all points of issue, the opinions of the members of the Indian and Muslim group differed very greatly. Thus, for instance in regard to terminable loans, the opinion of Indian members was that the present value of the repayable principal plus the present value of the interest payable during the life of the loan should be considered. The Muslim members did not agree. In their opinion, the question of valuation of loans would have arisen if Pakistan's share of existing debt of the Government of India were converted into an inter-governmental debt to be discharged by means of payments. Another group of cases in which a few differences existed in the Expert Committee No. II relates to the adjustment of liability in respect of pensions both actual and accrued. While both sides were agreed that the accrued pensions in respect of joint service, that is service up to 14 August 1947, should be estimated actuarially and added to the uncovered debt and divided as part thereof, there was difference of opinion as to the adjustment of liability in respect of pensions taking effect on or before that date. The Pakistan members were in favour of adjusting the liability of these pensions year by year or at short intervals on the basis of actual payments certified by the auditor general of either dominion in the same ratio as the uncovered debt. The Indian side preferred actuarial estimate being made of the liability on account of these pensions also and the liability being adjusted once and for all as part of the uncovered debt.

Briefly, Pakistan's view was that their proposal had the merit of absolute accuracy without involving actuarial forecast of future duration and without necessitating medical examination of existing pensioners, without which determination of average expectation of longevity, impaired or otherwise, would not be easily practicable with any reasonable degree of exactness. The Pakistan members considered that the political pensions were of the same nature as pensions in the course of payment.

The Indian side was prepared to accept a settlement based upon actual payment for some time, say, till 30 September 1948 at the latest; they were against accepting a settlement on the basis of actual payment as a permanent measure. They were definitely of the view that actuarial estimate of the current pensions, that is, payments taking effect on or before 14 August should be made and the necessary adjustments made between the two governments on the basis of such actuarial estimate. As regards political and territorial pensions, they considered that they should be allocated on a territorial basis wherever possible and then capitalised. Their capitalised value may be added to the uncovered debt.

This matter too was resolved finally in the Partition Council meeting on 1 December 1947 along the lines commended by the two members of the Steering Committee. The Steering Committee submitted a note on the question of sharing the pensionary liability soon after 15 August. Their note ran as follows:

1. Para 11 (2) of the Indian Independence (Rights, Properties and Liabilities) Order, 1947, has placed on the Indian Dominion the initial liability for the pensions which on the date immediately preceding the partition were the liability of the Governor General in Council, subject under para. 13(2) of the order, to Pakistan making such just and equitable contribution as may be agreed upon or in the absence of agreement determined by the Arbitral Tribunal.
2. In the discussions at the Expert Committee complete agreement could not be reached regarding the allocation of the liability for pensions.
3. The liability for pensions falls into two categories:
   (a) liability in respect of serving officers for services under the combined Government upto 14 August 1947.
   (b) liability for pensions of officers who had retired from service on or before 14 August 1947, or who retire from service after that date but without opting for service under either Dominion.
4. During the discussion in the Expert Committee, it was agreed in regard to (a) that the liability should be assessed

actuarially and shared between the two dominions in the ratio determined for the allocation of the uncovered debt:

In regard to (b) that the India members considered that the same arrangement should be followed, the Pakistan members suggested that this liability should not be capitalised; Pakistan should share the current expenditure in the ratio of her share of the unallocated debt. The difference of opinion is, therefore, not in regard to the relative share of the liability but the method of discharging it.

5. It is suggested that the following proposals may be put before the Partition Council —
   (a) The liability in regard to both serving and retired officers should be capitalised, the work being entrusted to two actuaries one nominated by each with an umpire to resolve any difference between the two actuaries.
   (b) The liability should be allocated between the two dominions in the ratio of the unallocated debt.
   (c) Each dominion should then assume the liability for the pensions paid in its territory and for the serving officers who have been taken over by it. If the capitalised value of the pensions paid in Pakistan and for personnel taken over by Pakistan is more than its share of the total liability under (b) the excess should be taken in reduction of the debt resulting from the partition.
   (d) The existing facilities for the transfer of pensions should be discontinued as between the two dominions. (If the facility is maintained after the partition for a short period as a matter of convenience, it should be subject to the usual financial adjustments.)

6. This note does not relate to 'political' pensions which are dealt with separately.

A note was submitted by the India side for the consideration of the Partition Council with reference to the fourth term. The note stated that:

> 'There was no agreement in the Political Department Sub-Committee or the Expert Committee about the allocation of Political Pensions.'

The Pakistan representatives on the Expert Committee suggested that these pensions should be treated as common and the current payments shared in the agreed proportion by the two dominions, while all future pensions will be the liability of the sanctioning dominion.

The Indian side proposed that these pensions should be capitalised and treated in the same way as service pensions, the total capitalised value being added to the debt of the undivided government, each side will accept liability for pensions which could be allocated to it on a territorial basis and the balance that cannot be so allocated will automatically be shared as part of the uncovered debt.

On the question of political pensions the Steering Committee submitted another short note:[1]

> "The position at the moment is that the liability for the political pensions has not been taken over by the Central Government under para. 4 of the Crown Representatives' (Transfer of Properties and Liabilities) Order 1947 and does not therefore come within the purview of para. 11 (2) of the Indian Independence (Rights, Property and Liabilities) Order, 1947. The allocation of liability to these pensions between India and Pakistan has not yet been determined by the Partition Council who have, however, expressed the view that it would be open to the two dominions to examine on its merits the question of continuing such of the pensions

1 Meeting on 1 December 1947.

as are now being paid. Until the question of liability is settled, it seems that some interim arrangement on the following lines would be necessary:

(a) Each of the dominions should agree to continue the payments, which have been made in its territory on the date of partition.
(b) Until the question of liability is settled, no transfer of pensions from one dominion to the other should be allowed.
(c) Each dominion should provisionally carry against its balance the pensions paid by it pending final settlement.
(d) Each dominion should examine the question of the continuance of the pensions paid by it, the other dominion being consulted in cases in which it is considered from the history of the pension that it relates to territories which are now included in both the dominions.

The interim arrangements suggested by the Steering Committee were approved by the Partition Council in October 1947."[1]

On the allocation of political pensions the Partition Council decided that:

> Political Pensions will be capitalised in the same manner as the civil pensions and the liabilities shared between the two Dominions in the ratio of the uncovered debt. Each Dominion will continue to disburse the pensions in payment in its area and the necessary financial adjustment will be made as in the case of civil pensions. This does not affect the right of either Dominion to terminate the grant of any political pension.

It will be seen that here again the final decision by the Partition Council followed well-accepted financial practices; simply conceived, practical and yet fair to both sides.

---

1 Meeting, 29 October 1947.

Expert Committee No. III (i) was asked –

1. to make recommendations for the collection and allocation between the two governments of revenue customs and central excise, income tax, salt, opium, and stamps for the current year, that is 1947-48, and
2. to make recommendations regarding the relations between the two successor governments in the matter of these sources of revenue, income tax, customs, etc., in future.

The committee had no difficulty in reporting on the first part of its first term of reference unanimously; that as the collections under the revenue heads mentioned up to 14 August 1947, would already have been or would be credited to the joint account of the undivided Government of India, no question of the allocation to the two dominions of the revenues under these heads until 14 August would arise.

As regards collections during the remaining period of the financial year, i.e., from 15 August 1947 to 31 March 1948, there was difference of opinion between the two sides. The non-Muslim members were of the opinion that each country should keep the revenues that it actually collected and that there should be no pooling and division of the revenues of the two countries. This would be in accordance with normal practice between two independent countries, namely that each country keeps what it collects. Any departure from this normal practice would be justified only if such departure was clearly to the advantage of both the countries. If there was to be a pooling and division of revenues, the country, which was to make net payment to the other country from the revenues that it had actually collected, would have to derive some substantial advantage in return for such payment. The non-Muslim members were of the view that no such advantage was likely to arise for the country, which would have to make a net payment on the division of revenues from these sources.

The Muslim members, however, viewed the matter in a totally different manner. They considered that in the special and quite extraordinary circumstances in which the Partition of India was taking place, pooling of the revenues of the two states in respect of income tax, customs and central excise for the financial year from 15 August 1947 onwards and their division after the end of the year on an agreed basis was the only practicable, sound and just way of proceeding in this matter. By keeping the revenues actually collected, each dominion will not necessarily secure what it is entitled to for this period in respect of these heads of income. Among the arguments they urged in support of this contention, were the following:

(i) These items of revenue are assessed for the whole year and not a portion of the year. The financial year is the basis for the assessment. The progress of assessments and collections in different areas cannot be assumed to be uniform, and the income tax, etc., collected by each dominion after 14 August would, therefore, not correctly represent the revenue due to each.

(ii) These taxes are assessable on the basis of the income of the previous year. As the income for the previous year was derived from India as a whole, assessment and collections should continue on joint account.

(iii) India is considered as a unit for the purpose of this assessment and in many cases, a resident of one province is assessed in another province. Business houses are assessed in the area in which they are situated or in the area in which the principal office of the business house is situated. Due to concentration of business in big cities, many people are assessed at Calcutta and Bombay although their branches functioned in other provinces and their activities covered different areas. It will be practically impossible for such assessees at this stage to prepare their accounts of the previous year to show separately income accruing or arising in the territories of Pakistan and the rest of India respectively.

Several other arguments, on more or less the same lines, were urged with a view to establishing the reasonableness of their request for the income from these various taxes and duties to be pooled and then divided on an agreed basis. The non-Muslim members also put forward other arguments, which were cogent enough and yet, did not carry conviction to their fellow members on the committee. Thus, they claimed that the very first point of the Muslim members was almost a non sequitur. The fact that income tax is assessed on the income of the whole of the previous accounting year and not on that of a portion of that year only, did not affect the proposition that the tax, which is collected by each country during the remainder of the current financial year should be retained by each country. In united India, income tax was at times collected by income tax officers of a particular province or district irrespective of whether the whole of the income or even a portion of it actually arose or accrued, or could be deemed to have arisen or accrued in that particular province or district. From 15 August 1947 onwards, each country would assess the entire income, which arose or accrued or was deemed to have arisen or accrued within the respective areas irrespective of whether the same income will also be wholly or partially assessed to income tax in the other country, subject, of course, to the assessee being given such relief from double income tax as is agreed upon between the governments of the two countries. Though, in actual practice, all business houses of any considerable size do keep branch accounting separately for purposes of control and management, the inconvenience that will be caused to the assessees who had already furnished their returns of income to the income tax officers of one country, that is the country where the head office is located, will be considerable if they were again asked to make a separate return of income in respect of their branch earnings. The division of India into two independent countries must inevitably bring in its wake certain disadvantages and these have to be faced. The residents of both countries will thus have to face the inconvenience of double taxation. On balance, there did not appear to be any overwhelming force in either view, and when the Partition

Council came to consider the matter, it decided that the matter should be left to the two governments to settle by negotiation.

In regard to revenues from customs and central excise too, there was a difference of opinion between the Muslim and the non-Muslim members. The Muslim members advanced the following arguments: The geographical and economic position of the two dominions with lengthy common land frontiers, established channels of trade and a single transport, communication and currency system is such that goods subject to customs and excise duties are distributed in areas under one or the other dominion irrespective of the dominion, which collected the duties. In order that these dominions receive the revenues to which each is entitled under these heads, it is essential that goods intended for and passing for consumption into the territory of one dominion should not be taxed by the other domonion. A 'collect and keep' basis that the non-Muslim members favoured was absolutely unscientific. Influenced by considerations of common good of the two dominions and by the complications that would be created by restrictions on trade, like, customs barriers and the adoption of divergent policies in matters of tariff duties, etc., the Expert Committee (Trade) had recommended that as far as possible, the status quo regarding all matters affecting trade and movement of goods between the two dominions should be maintained up to 29 February 1948. In particular, it had recommended that customs barriers should not be imposed between the two dominions. The only logical conclusion was that the revenues under customs and excise should be pooled and allocated on an agreed basis: with free trade between the two dominions, the dominion collecting the duties on goods passing freely into the territory of the other, would be depriving the other of its legitimate dues. Excisable goods exported to foreign countries were either duty free or refunds and drawbacks were granted. But with free trade between the two dominions, excise duties would continue to be levied by each dominion on goods exported into the other territory, with the result that an anomalous and unfair situation would be created. That would also be the case in regard to customs. Import duties collected at Karachi and Calcutta on goods passing into India and Pakistan would remain with the collecting governments. It would be impossible for the two dominions to create the land customs frontier by 15 August 1947, which was necessary to secure to each dominion its legitimate and proper share of revenue under these heads.

The non-Muslim members were of the view that the customs and central excise revenues must be collected by the country where they accrue or arise and there can be no question of another country having a share of these revenues on the ground that a portion of such revenue is derived from articles that might be eventually consumed in the latter's area. What the non-Muslim members strongly recommended was free trade between the two independent countries, an agreement being reached between them regarding the terms and conditions under which goods imported at a port situated in one country could be despatched by land to the other country, and goods produced in one country could be sent across either for consumption or for export by sea. The terms and conditions of the agreement would depend on economic and other conditions, but an agreement could certainly be reached to the advantage of both the countries. Finally, the net amount that is likely to be involved for payment by either side for the period 15 August 1947 to 31 March 1948 in respect of customs and excise would be relatively small and unlikely to be appreciable enough to necessitate or warrant any special adjustments. Certainly it would not justify the pooling and division of the entire customs and central excise revenues of the two countries.

The second term of reference of the committee was to make recommendations regarding the relations between the two successor governments in the matter of income tax, customs, etc., for the future. In regard to this, the committee unanimously recommended that (a) there should be no sharing of revenue after 1 April 1948 (although as regards the period from 15 August 1947 to 31 March 1948 there existed a difference of opinion among the Muslim and non-Muslim members to which reference has been made earlier);

(b) There should be no joint administrative control of the collection of revenue after 15 August 1947; (c) the two governments should give all such facilities to each other as are provided in the Sea Customs Act and Central Excises Act of united India and made available to foreign countries in accordance with international conventions; (d) other matters such as exemption from duties on articles of indigenous produce or manufacture in one country when exported to the other country and the establishment of 'most favoured nation' treatment between the two countries in the matter of tariff policies should be left to the two governments to decide after such time as each may take to consider the problems in the light of circumstances as they develop after Independence; (e) the two governments should incorporate in the appropriate Income-Tax Act provisions for the avoidance of double income tax along the lines suggested in a draft note, which may be agreed upon.

It will be seen that while there was agreement on certain general principles regarding the policy, which may be pursued by the two governments vis-à-vis each other in the future, there was considerable difference of opinion in regard to the sharing of collections of income tax, customs and excise before and after 15 August. The Steering Committee was also unable to reach an agreement on this point. The Partition Council, however, agreed that all the assets and liabilities existing prior to 15 August were subject to division between the two dominions. The question of sharing future revenues, that is revenues arising on or after that date, was a matter for free negotiation between the two dominions or for submission by agreement to the Arbitral Tribunal. The Council was also of the view that income tax due for the period up to and including 14 August 1947 and not paid by that date, that is covering both arrears of assessment and of demand should be divided between the two dominion governments on the same basis as assets of the present Government of India. There should be no sharing of revenue after 1 April 1948.

The Expert Committee No. III (ii) submitted an agreed report regarding collection and allocation between the two governments of various items of miscellaneous revenues, that is revenues other than those derived from customs, central excise, income tax, salt, opium and stamps and to make recommendations regarding relations between the successor governments in respect of the miscellaneous revenues in future. There were several, and agreement was reached in respect of all of them. Mention may be made here of some of them to indicate the nature of these items of revenue and the manner in which it was agreed to deal with them. The committee agreed and recommended that as a general rule and subject to certain qualifications: (a) receipts falling due after 14 August 1947 should be retained by the dominion in whose jurisdiction they arose; (b) receipts relating to the period ending 14 August 1947, if realised after that date, should be booked to the joint account of the present Government of India in accordance with the procedure which had been recommended by the Expert Committee on Budget and Accounts.

Among the various items of miscellaneous revenues, there was the item of revenue accruing from lighthouses and ports. Receipts from the major ports falling due after separation would accrue to the dominion in which the port was situated; receipts from the Bengal Pilot Service would accrue to the Indian dominion if Calcutta was with that dominion; receipts from lighthouses and lightships due after 14 August would accrue to the dominion in which the lighthouses were situated. Similarly, in regard to receipts from aviation, which would mainly consist of licence fees and landing fees, it was recommended that in respect of fees covering the period of a full year no re-adjustment should be made; in respect of the period after 14 August 1947, each dominion should retain whatever fees it collected.

In so far as receipts from currency and mints were concerned, it was decided that the allocation of surplus profits of the Reserve Bank and the profits from the circulation of small coins should be in accordance with arrangements recommended by the Expert Committee on Currency and Coinage. Miscellaneous revenue from the mints such as receipts from the disposal of scrap, etc., should be retained by the dominion owning the mints.

There were a number of other sources of miscellaneous revenue and it was recommended in effect that each type of revenue should be dealt with on its merits. The Steering Committee and the Partition Council accepted this to be the correct approach.

The terms of reference of Expert Committee No. IV were to make recommendations regarding allocation of the liability including contingent liability such as pending litigations for contracts entered into by the undivided Government of India. The work that this committee had to do is illustrative of the enormous variety of problems that had to be gone into by the Partition Council. And even though this committee was concerned only with contracts of the nature covered by Section 175 of the Government of India Act, 1935, there remained another vast group of contracts such as G.P. Notes, Post Office Cash Certificates, Post Office Insurance Policies, etc., which did not fall within the ambit of its responsibility. Contracts entered into under Section 175 of the Government of India Act broadly covered the following categories:

(a) Contracts pertaining to immovable property.
(b) Contracts pertaining to supplies to be made and services to be performed by the public or to be rendered to the public.
(c) Contracts pertaining to the personal services of government servants.
(d) Contracts pertaining to the sale of surplus, waste and obsolete stores.

The committee was able to produce an agreed report, its main recommendations being:

(1) Contracts relating to immovable property should be deemed to have been made by the dominion in which the property is situated.

(2) Contracts relating to supplies and services to be made by or rendered to the public exclusively for the purpose of either dominion should be deemed to have been entered into by that dominion. This would cover all contracts placed for stores which are of purely local interest and which have not been placed abroad.

(3) Contracts pertaining to government servants should be deemed to have been made by the dominion under which the government servant serves after 15 August 1947. A government servant who has opted for India but is temporarily serving in Pakistan would be regarded as serving the Government of India and on deputation to Pakistan. Accordingly, his contract would be deemed to be with the Government of India.

(4) Contracts of the types falling under 1, 2, and 3 above but excluding contracts for the supply of stores, dealt with later, will, when they are being performed for the purposes of both the dominions, be deemed to have been made separately by the two dominions in respect of the areas falling within their respective jurisdiction. Thus, a catering contract entered into by the North-Western Railway for the system as a whole will be deemed to have been entered into separately with the two dominions in respect of the railway system lying within the territory of each.

(5) Contracts pertaining to the purchase in India of stores intended for the purpose of both dominions should be deemed to have been made with the dominion in whose territory the consignee under the contract is located. If there are several consignees, some located within the territory of one dominion and others within the territory of the other dominion, the contract will be deemed to be severed and to have been entered into separately with the two dominions in respect of stores to be delivered to the consignees within their respective jurisdiction. If no consignee has been specified

in the contract, it would be deemed to have been entered into by the dominion within whose territory the place of performance of the contract is situated.

(6) The contracts entered into by the director general, India Stores Department, Blackpool, UK and the India Supply Mission, Washington, should be deemed to have been made by the dominion of India which will be under an obligation to deliver to the dominion of Pakistan, with suitable financial adjustments, such portions of the goods forthcoming as were originally intended for the requirements of the area under that dominion or for a consignee or consignees within its territory.

(7) Rights and obligations under contracts made upto 15 August should be deemed to have been made by the dominion in whose territory the stores are.

(8) Rights and obligations under contracts made upto 15 August will, after that date, follow the location of the contracts as proposed above between the two dominions provided that in respect of contracts falling under 5, 6, and 7 above there will be a sharing of such rights and obligations including losses and damages between the two dominions in accordance with the benefits each derives from such contracts.

There were certain other comparatively minor matters such as the rights of a contractor to sue. These and other matters of detail were embodied in a Draft Order in Council. The committee recommended that the draft order, suitably modified by the draftsman as directed by the Partition Council, should be issued before 15 August 1947.

The Steering Committee recommended the acceptance of the basis of allocation between the two dominions proposed by the Expert Committee No. IV and consequential action in regard to allocating, determining, severing and modifying contracts and sharing out the stores coming forward against joint purpose contracts to be taken on lines recommended by the committee. The Partition Council accepted the recommendations of the Steering Committee and directed the issue of the Draft Order in Council with suitable modifications before 15 August 1947.

When we look at the terms of reference of the Expert Committee No. V (i), we realise the great variety of problems that existed, which needed to be tackled. The experts had been set, most of them, on an all but impossible task. And yet, problems were tackled and a real effort made in every case to find ways to reach an agreement. This committee's terms of reference were:

(1) to make recommendations regarding the currency and coinage arrangements consequent on partition for the two governments;

(2) consistent with the recommendations in (1) above to formulate proposals in regard to the division of the assets and liabilities of the Reserve Bank of India and the organisational consequences of Partition in respect of its administrative machinery;

(3) to make recommendations consequent on partition regarding exchange control for the two states; and

(4) to report on the position of the two states consequent on partition in regard to the membership of the International Monetary Fund and the International Bank.

A great deal of discussion ensued on every single point. Thus, even with regard to the question of the membership of the International Monetary Fund and the International Bank for Reconstruction & Development, agreement could not be reached because it was looked at from the point of view of prestige. The non-Muslim members expressed the view that India's identity could not disappear because a part has gone out from it, and India, even after Partition, as the successor government, would continue to remain a member of the International Monetary Fund and the Bank and that Pakistan will have to apply for membership. The Muslim view was that both India and Pakistan were successor governments and both should therefore jointly approach the IMF and the International Bank for membership and a division of the existing quota. This issue was resolved by the need to take a decision and act according to it before the next meeting of the International Monetary Fund and of the Bank: either to take a practical view which would secure membership for Pakistan without delay or to go on wrangling over a theoretical issue. The Muslims were sufficiently realistic to realise that to persist in their stand was more a prestige issue and that it would be better to apply for membership of the Fund and the Bank and obtain it with India's support. The point raised was nevertheless not given up and remained an unresolved issue until the very last meeting of the Partition Council.

On the basis of information supplied by the Reserve Bank and the Mint Masters, the Muslim members considered that it would be possible to have all the treasuries and sub-treasuries in Pakistan stocked with the country's full requirements of over-printed Pakistan notes effective from 1 April 1948. As Pakistan notes could be put into circulation from 1 April 1948, from that date no further India notes should be issued in Pakistan territory. Minting of Pakistan's new design coins would have to be started, according to Muslim members, from 1 March 1948 and even earlier if possible. Taking these views into consideration, the committee suggested that the programme for the separation of currency and coinage should be as follows:

(1) The existing currency and coinage should remain common to both the areas upto 31 March 1948;
(2) From 1 April to 30 September 1948 there would be a transitional period during which, (a) both Pakistan and 'Indian' coins will be issued in Pakistan areas (Pakistan coins will be issued upto the extent available and 'Indian' coins will be issued only to supply any excess of demand for coins in the Pakistan area over the supply of Pakistan coins); (b) only Pakistan over-printed notes will be issued, but 'Indian' notes will continue to remain legal tender in the Pakistan area.

It is with this programme in mind that the committee proceeded to make recommendations regarding the arrangements for currency and coinage for the transitional period. There was only one Currency Note Press in undivided India, at Nasik. (The question whether any physical division of the press was possible was considered separately by the Partition Council and rejected.) Assuming the final decision to be against the physical division of the Press and realising that it would take the Pakistan government between three to five years to establish its own press, the Partition Council decided that during the intervening period, the Nasik press should continue to print notes for Pakistan with the same security arrangements, the same priority and the same rates as for India.

In so far as the coinage was concerned, there were at the time three mints located at Bombay, Calcutta, and Lahore. The Partition Council took the view that until the Lahore mint was in a position to take up the responsibility for Pakistan coinage, the existing arrangements whereby coinage requirements were spread over all the three mints should continue. The work for Pakistan at Bombay and Calcutta during this period would be on a no-profit basis.

The Expert Committee No. V (i) was thus able to reach agreements on the first term of reference. However, there still remained the other terms of reference and here they were faced with difficulties, which they found to be insuperable on several issues. The Steering Committee recommended to the Partition Council the acceptance of all matters on which the Expert Committee were agreed and as regards the remaining, itself recommended that (1) the request for foreign exchange to import equipment for a security press would be considered along with Pakistan's claim for a special allotment of foreign exchange to import equipment required for duplicating some of the 'unique' institutions located at present in India; (2) the bulk of the capacity of the Bombay and Calcutta mints be made available to Pakistan for six to nine months; the remainder also to be released for the use of the Pakistan government if it was not required by the Indian government; (3) the supply of the nickel blanks from the Alipore Mint for Pakistan's coinage should be made available, subject to India's own requirement; (4) the Reserve Bank should, during the interim period ending 30 September 1948, function as the currency authority and as banker of the Pakistan government; (5) should the Pakistan government find it necessary to have their currency administered even after 30 September 1948 by the Reserve Bank for a further period, it should be possible to do so by agreement with India; (6) (i) it will not be appropriate for a deputy governor to be appointed by the Pakistan government, but there would be no objection to the appointment by the Pakistan government of an officer on special duty for maintaining contact with the Reserve Bank of India; (ii) it will not be necessary to amend the Reserve Bank of India Act, if the Government of India could agree to nominate Pakistan government's nominees to two of the four seats reserved on the Central Board for nomination; (7) it was in the interest of both the dominions not to encourage unnecessary expansion of currency: the overall limit should not exceed rupees sixty crores. And having regard to the requirements of the situation, it was suggested that a ceiling of rupees twenty crores for Pakistan and rupees forty crores for India would be reasonable; (8) remittances should be allowed to move by sea which will overcome the need for armed guards, etc; (9) the provisional date for the final allocation of assets should be 31 March 1949 but if it appeared on or about 1 January 1949, that Indian notes were still returning from Pakistan to a significant extent the final date could be extended up to 30 September 1949 by agreement; (10) it was hoped to be able to circulate Pakistan's one rupee notes by March 1948: the Steering Committee agreed to the suggestion that allocation of liability for one rupee notes should be dropped on the understanding that holders of Indian notes would be asked to exchange them for Pakistan notes before 30 September 1948 and that India notes will cease to be legal tender in Pakistan as on 30 September 1948; (11) the question of the membership of the International Monetary Fund and the Bank would be taken up along with the general question of membership of international organisations. For purposes of division of assets, it was agreed that as soon as Pakistan became

HM's father, Muljibhai.

HM's mother, Hiraba.

Oxford, 1922-23.

With his Oxford contemporaries, 1923.

HM in his Jodhpurs after his routine early morning *chukkar* in Sindh.

HM and his wife Savitaben outside their bungalow in Sindh at the start of his career as collector.

HM with Savitaben and daughters Nisha, Uma and Usha (clockwise) on the *P & O* liner to England.

HM with his two eldest daughters in the garden of his bungalow in Sindh.

On a very rare holiday.

As trade commissioner in Hamburg in 1938, with wife Savitaben and daughters.

HM'S closest friend and mentor A.D. Gorwala.

Relaxing with his elder brother Manubhai at the latter's Jogeshwari residence. Daughter Sharad is at extreme right.

Eight-year-old HM with his uncle.

Standing beside A.D. Gorwala during ICS week, in Sindh in the mid-1920s. (Second and third from right)

Two pilgrims at Cape Comorin, ready after a dip in the sea to go to the famous temple of Kanyakumari.

Emergency Committee Control Room, Delhi, September 1947. HM is at extreme right. Mrs. B.K. Nehru sits at the head of the table.

Standing behind HM (extreme left) are the first Indian Air Vice Marshal Mukherjee (left) and the hero of Kashmir, General Kulwant Singh (centre).

In the War Room planning the Kashmir campaign. With HM are Prime Minister Jawaharlal Nehru and Defence Minister Baldev Singh. Second from left, a very young Field Marshal Sam Manekshaw.

HM as secretary-Defence, entertains wounded veterans from Kashmir at his residence in New Delhi, in October 1948.

Visiting a border post.

During his Defence secretary days, with the first Indian Commander-in-Chief, General Cariappa, (centre), December 1951.

The 1951 Indian Medical Service dinner at the Army Mess, conducted with great panache and in full regalia. (HM far left)

An autographed picture given to HM by Commander-in-Chief General Rajendra Singh.

The swearing-in ceremony of the first Cabinet of Independent India. HM is to the left in the dark suit near the pillar.

HM as Defence secretary, accompanied by General Kulwant Singh, being shown the Oerlikon Machine Tool Works by Dr. Gerber in Switzerland (centre).

The family at 1 Safdarjung Road, Delhi.

While serving as trade commissioner for Northern Europe (1936), HM photographs his daughters with their mother in the balcony of their home in Hamburg (Germany).

Savitaben with her second daughter Uma, in front of the collector's bungalow in Sindh.

Wife Savitaben and daughter Sharad in a London park during World War II, when HM was trade commissioner for British India.

A family photograph taken by HM on holiday at Bournemouth, England.

The Patel family in the garden of their bungalow, 2 Roberts Road, later renamed Teen Murti Marg, in New Delhi.

a member of the IMF and the International Bank, the dominion of India would make available to Pakistan its share of the gold and dollar assets or equivalent foreign exchange assets acceptable to the Fund and the Bank.

The Partition Council accepted the recommendation of the Steering Committee in all respects. The Council reached the decision on sterling balances on 1 December 1947.

The terms of reference of Expert Committee No. V (ii) were: (1) regarding the financial, budgetary accounting and auditing arrangements for the two governments for the current financial year, and (2) regarding the adjustment between the two governments in respect of services rendered in future by one government to the other. Two sub-committees, one dealing with the railways and the other with posts and telegraphs were appointed to assist the committee in its work.

The committee recommended that the finances of the two dominions will be completely separate with effect from 15 August 1947. The closing balance of the Central Government with the Reserve Bank on 14 August 1947 will be allocated between the two dominions on a basis to be decided by the Expert Committee dealing with the division of the assets and liabilities. After that date, transactions occurring in each dominion will be carried against its balance subject to the recommendations in subsequent paragraphs.

The sanctioned budget for the current year will cease to be operative from 15 August 1947 when the two new dominion governments start functioning. It will be for the new governments to prepare separate budgets for the remaining period of the current financial year and obtain the approval of their legislatures. As this is likely to take some time, we recommend that steps should be taken by the new governments as soon as possible after they are set up to authorise incurring of the expenditure in anticipation of the sanction of funds. So far as the collection of revenue is concerned, we presume that the necessary authority to continue collection of the existing taxes and duties by the two dominions till other arrangements are made by the government of each dominion will be secured by the adaptation of the existing laws.

As the present Central Government will cease on 14 August 1947, the committee considers it necessary that the accounts of the Government of India in India and abroad, civil, military, railways and posts and telegraphs should be closed on 14 August 1947, as if it were the end of a financial year. We recommend that necessary steps should be taken in this regard. Detailed proposals for the matter are contained in the Interim Report issued by us on the tenth instant.

It will be necessary to keep the accounts of the Central Government open for some time after 15 August 1947 so that as far as possible transactions relating to the combined government occurring after that date may be formally incorporated. This arrangement cannot obviously be for an indefinite period and from the point of view of both the dominions it is desirable to ignore minor transactions after a certain period. We, accordingly, propose that the accounts for the period 1 April 1947 to 14 August 1947 should be finally closed on 31 March 1948 and that after 31 December 1947 only transactions exceeding Rs.1 lakh should be adjusted against the combined account. We wish to make it clear, however, that our recommendation, which has been concurred with by the Expert Committee dealing with Assets and Liabilities, does not rule out any recommendations that may be made by the other Expert Committees about the allocation between the two dominions of receipts and payments. Some provision for the sharing of the receipts and payments will be necessary in respect of items like payments in respect of de-mobilised personnel, leave salaries of government servants who proceeded on leave prior to 15 August 1947, realisation from surplus stores and so on. We would, however, like to stress the point that in the interest of simplicity of accounting such arrangements between the two dominions should, as far as possible, be limited to transactions involving substantial amounts.

We would also suggest that Administrative Departments should issue instructions to subordinate authorities in both the dominions that all receipts and payments concerning them are relatable to the period before 15 August 1947 and correctly classified. The responsibilities for the accounting and auditing of all transactions occurring in each dominion after 14 August 1947 should fall on that dominion subject, in the case of transactions affecting the combined account of the present government to the facilities provided to the auditor general of the other dominion to satisfy himself that they have been correctly audited and accounted for as suggested in the Interim Report. Although the organisations may be separated we feel that at least for the rest of the current year the existing procedure for accounting and audit should be continued with as little change as possible in both the dominions. The closing of the accounts on 14 August 1947, the separation of the records and vouchers relating to the Pakistan area and vice versa and the physical division of some of the accounts offices will throw a considerable strain on the staff of both sides and we would strongly advise against any procedural change until the staff had had time to find their feet after the Partition.

In our view the audit of the transactions of each dominion occurring in the United Kingdom should, as soon as possible, be directly subject to the audit of the auditor general of the Dominion in the same way as the rest of the expenditure of that dominion. We recommend that steps should be taken, as soon as practicable, to terminate the present arrangement.

We suggest that the receipts and expenditure authorised by the Joint Defence Council and of the organisations subordinate to the Council incurred in each dominion should be initially taken against the balance of that dominion, that the transactions should be distinct in the accounts from the other transactions and that periodical adjustments should be made between the two dominions. As regards the actual machinery for accounting and audit, the Expert Committee was unable to reach an agreed conclusion.

The Steering Committee recommended the acceptance of the report of the Expert Committee No. V (ii) on Budget and Accounts and of its Railway and P&T Committees. It referred to the fact that the report of the Expert Committee raised the issue of reorganisation of the Military Finance and Military Accounts organisation needed in respect of the activities controlled by the Joint Defence Council and the Supreme Commander. In a circulation note submitting the recommendation it promised at a later date a separate note containing its recommendation in this matter of reorganisation of the Military Finance and Military Accounts Departments. The Partition Council approved the recommendation of the Steering Committee on the Report of Expert Committee No. V (ii) on Budget and Accounts.

In its note on reorganisation of the Military Finance and Military Accounts Departments, consequent on the establishment of the two dominions, the Steering Committee, after examining various alternatives, recommended that the supreme commander's headquarters should be served by the existing Military Finance Department (less the personnel withdrawn by the two dominions to man their Finance Departments) irrespective of the fact that the department includes personnel who have elected for India as well as those who have elected for Pakistan, i.e., it should, like the supreme commander's headquarters, be an integrated organisation. At the head of this organisation would be two officers of equal status, one each from the Finance Departments of the two dominions. It was out of the question to have a completely duplicated organisation as this was unnecessary and would have been unworkable even if there were no shortage of trained manpower.

The respective charges held by the officers now working in the Military Finance Department will not be disturbed except that the deputy financial adviser (Navy), an officer who had opted for Pakistan, would, at as early a date as possible, be asked to take over instead, the present charge of the deputy financial adviser (Q). It is proposed that the financial adviser (India) from the Dominion Finance

Department will be the officer from India who will be one of the two heads of the joint organisation, i.e., he will be common to the 'India' and the 'Joint' organisation. The services of any other officer of the joint organisation required for making advice available to the Dominion Headquarters will be arranged in consultation between the two financial advisers.

It is further recommended that in future both the financial advisors (FAs) should be members of the supreme commander's committee. Cases requiring the decision of the Joint Defence Council having financial implications will be prepared in consultation with both the FAs. If the two FAs are not in agreement they will prepare a joint note setting forth the matters in issue and their respective viewpoints for the decision of the Joint Defence Council.

For purposes of discipline and administration, the Steering Committee proposed that the FA drawn from India should be the head. He would, however, except in routine matters, ascertain first the views of his colleague. Decisions on the transfer of or the institution of disciplinary proceedings against personnel who have opted for Pakistan will be taken only in consultation with the FA drawn from the Pakistan Finance Department.

Military Accounts offices which are on a territorial basis should be taken over by the dominion concerned, i.e., controllers of military accounts, Eastern Command and Southern Command should continue under the military accountant general (India) and the functions of the controller of military accounts, Northern Command (with suitable adjustment regarding his territorial jurisdiction) be taken over by the military accountant general of the Dominion of Pakistan. In regard to other offices, namely, field controller of military accounts (Other Ranks), field controller of military accounts (Officers and Clearing House), chief controller of factory accounts and the controller of military accounts (Pensions) which will serve the need of both the Dominion Forces until the reconstitution is completed (or the office in question, for example, the office of the controller of pensions, is divided, if this is earlier), a special arrangement is recommended, namely, they should be directly under the administrative control of the joint military finance organisation serving the supreme commander's headquarters. For practical reasons, however, copies of all references made from these offices to the joint military finance headquarters, which are of general interest, will be supplied to the military accountants general of both the dominions.

Work regarding pay accounts in the common offices, which shall have to be divided ultimately, should be segregated on the basis of units which are to be finally allotted to Pakistan, by the creation of one or more cells in each office. Steps will be taken to transfer to these cells progressively all work in respect of units allotted to Pakistan and to man these cells by officers and men who have opted for Pakistan.

To ensure that the Military Accounts Departments of both the dominions deal with joint expenditure correctly, the following arrangements are suggested:

1) The decisions of the Joint Defence Council having financial implications to be transmitted to the Military Accounts Department through the respective financial advisors just as administrative decisions will be transmitted through the joint secretaries to the Joint Defence Council.
2) The classification of joint expenditure and its subsequent allocation between the two dominions, whether arising out of the decisions of the Joint Defence Council or of the subordinate authorities, should be checked by the auditor general. India should accept the certificate of the auditor general of Pakistan in respect of joint expenditure incurred by the Military Accounts Department of Pakistan and Pakistan should similarly accept the certificate of the auditor general of India. If this is considered necessary, each dominion will be at liberty to send test audit parties to the Military Accounts offices of the other dominion to examine the accounts of joint expenditure.

The recommendations of the Steering Committee on the reorganisation of the Military Finance and Military Accounts Departments were accepted by the Joint Defence Council.

Expert Committee No. VI was set up in order to examine the effect of partition on the administration of existing controls and to make recommendations regarding alternative arrangements if necessary. Although the wording would suggest that the committee was expected to examine all control measures in force at that time, the Expert Committee assumed, and rightly, that it was expected to deal only with controls of an economic nature. Statutory authority for the exercise of these controls sprang from four enactments: (1) The Essential Supplies (Temporary Powers) Act, 1946; (2) The Railways (Transport of Goods) Act, 1947; (3) The Capital Issues (Continuation of Control) Act, 1947; and (4) The Imports and Exports (Control) Act, 1947. The committee again correctly assumed that its function was to suggest interim arrangements for a short period, during which the dominions of India and Pakistan would be able to arrive at agreements of a more enduring nature and accordingly recommended that these interim arrangements should not go beyond 31 March 1948. It recommended also that even these arrangements could be superseded, if other arrangements were agreed upon by the two dominions in the meantime.

The articles of control under the Essential Supplies (Temporary Powers) Act were divided into three Groups: Group A consisting of foodstuffs, cotton textiles, coal, iron and steel, paper; Group B consisting of petroleum and petroleum products, spare parts of mechanically propelled vessels; and Group C consisting of mica. Group A commodities were not only vital commodities but were also commodities which were in short supply at that time in the country. The need for them was so vital and their supply position so uncertain that the continuance of the controls in respect of them was unavoidable for some time. For the period up to 31 March 1948 (or earlier date), the committee was of the view that interim arrangements in both the dominions would be well advised to proceed on the advisability of maintaining the status quo as far as possible. Both countries should continue to give or receive these controlled commodities as if there had been no partition. The committee's recommendation, in effect, was that the two countries should take more or less the same measures of control over their production and distribution. The Partition Council on the whole found this approach reasonable and said so.

In regard to the effect of partition on the administration of existing controls, it was emphasised that the inter-dependence of the two dominions was such that any agreement or arrangement based on a sense of distrust would defeat its aim. In their view, the only basis for interim arrangement for its limited period must be goodwill and trust. However, the committee could not agree on various issues and asked the Steering Committee for its guidance on the points given below:

Whether licensing should be separated with immediate effect or with effect from 15 August. If the answer to this question is that separate licensing should be started immediately, whether revalidation of licences which expired on 30 June and have not been revalidated so far, should proceed on the basis of the existing system and be valid for all ports or like new licenses be made valid only for specified ports.

The monetary ceilings in un-licensed as on 15 August or earlier date if so decided have to be allocated between the two countries. What should be the basis of such allocation, population or earnings of foreign exchange or actual requirements of goods for which restricted monetary ceilings have been prescribed or ratio, which the value of imports into Pakistan ports bears to the value of imports into the rest of India during a selected period. If the decision is in favour of earnings of foreign exchange what should be the basis of calculation of earnings of foreign exchange?

The Steering Committee's reply was as follows: The facts of data that the Finance Department have after inclusion of sum of Rs.50 crores for food and Rs.30 crores for other purchases abroad, an earmarked sum of Rs.106 crores for private imports during the current quota period that is July to December 1947 as the possibility of Pakistan not getting its normal share of goods after 15 August 1947, could not be ruled out. It was agreed that the Pakistan government should be permitted to issue licences for the current shipping period. Both governments would, however, follow the present import trade control policy.

In their general observations, this Expert Committee stated that it had proceeded on the assumption that it was desirable to maintain the status quo as far as possible. The Muslim members stated that they would like to make the interim arrangement more rigid for it was their view that in the short period involved there should be no occasion for a change. Unforeseen possibilities would be met by providing for mutual agreement on changes, which may become necessary. The non-Muslim members were, on the other hand, of the view that rigidity was not desirable as between two sovereign states. While they agree that it should be the aim of both the governments to maintain the status quo as far as possible, they felt that even during the short interim period all arrangements should have a certain degree of flexibility.

The Partition Council discussed the recommendations of the Expert Committee and the observations of the Steering Committee as set out in general terms. One of the Pakistan members suggested that the two parties might agree to retain controls on certain important commodities until 31 March 1948. Controls in respect of other items might be modified or lifted by the other party after consultation with the other government. One of the Indian members said that the dominion should be free to do away or modify controls if it considered it necessary to do so in the interest of the country. While India would not lift any existing controls as far as possible but some had already been found to be troublesome by the people and the government would be compelled to respect the wishes of the people. Mountbatten suggested that whenever such issues arose between the two dominions, there should be consultation at the departmental level between the two dominions and this should be followed, if necessary, by a discussion in the Partition Council before either dominion modified or did away with any controls. The formal decision recorded that until 31 March 1948, the status quo should be maintained as far as possible and that modifications in or removal of controls would be made by either dominion only after consultation between the two dominions at departmental level followed, if necessary, by discussion in the Partition Council. The two dominions, however, should do their best to start trade negotiations at a very early date.

The Expert Committee No. VII on Economic Relations (Trade) was asked to examine matters regarding all trade and movement between territories of the two successor governments. Since a separate Expert Committee had been constituted for the purpose of examining economic relations with regard to controls, Expert Committee No. VII confined itself mainly to matters bearing generally on trade and commerce and the movement of goods between the two dominions and has not concerned itself with special arrangements necessary with regard to such commodities as are now under control. The committee, after careful consideration of the various issues involved, recommended that the two governments should agree to maintain, as far as possible, the status quo regarding all matters affecting trade and movements between the two dominions until 29 February 1948, and in particular, they should not (1) impose custom barriers between the two dominions; (2) change existing import and export policies; (3) change existing customs tariffs, excise duties and cesses; (4) impose any restriction on the free movement of goods and remittances including capital equipment and capital; (5) levy transit duty or taxes on goods passing across the territory of the other; (6) interfere with existing trade channels by monopolistic government purchases; (7) modify existing controls or introduce new controls; (8) interfere with contracts between nationals of the two states.

While there was general agreement on the various issues posed, there was one relatively minor point on which accord could not be achieved. The Muslim members insisted that throughout the report the expression 'mutual agreement' should be substituted for the expression 'mutual consultation' wherever it occurred. The non-Muslim members' view was that 'mutual consultation' was a more appropriate expression in all the circumstances. On this point, the members of the Steering Committee also were unable to agree. Although the Steering Committee stated that they agreed that the arrangements for the interim period should be such as to produce the maximum amount of goodwill and understanding, Mohamad Ali felt that the objective could be better achieved in a more satisfactory manner if the two governments were to agree to proceed in regard to all matters dealt within the report by 'mutual agreement'. On the other hand, for precisely the same reasons, I said that I preferred 'mutual consultation'. The Partition Council approved of the recommendations of the Expert Committee's Report as stated in paragraph 13 of the report. Since the recommendations in paragraph 13 made no reference to either expression 'mutual agreement' or 'mutual consultation' it may be presumed that in their view, the difference would not be a matter of any significance in practice. The council had thus found an ingenious way out!

The Partition Council approved the proposals of the Expert Committee but the Pakistan members of the council reserved the right to revise their attitude in view of the stand taken by the dominion of India regarding customs revenue.

The Expert Committee No. VIII on Domicile and Nationality was the first to complete its work and submit its report to the Steering Committee for onward transmission to the Partition Council, which held its first meeting on 27 June 1947. The report was unanimous. The committee concluded that partition by itself would effect no change in nationality and called for no immediate action by the Partition Committee except in regard to the public service if it desired to restrict entry into the public service, but not otherwise. The Steering Committee did not recommend any action for restricting entry into the public service and suggested that it would be advisable to leave it over for the dominion governments to take such action later as they considered suitable. The council was in agreement with this.

A question raised in Expert Committee No. VIII was whether an inhabitant of one dominion would require a passport for entry into the other dominion. The committee further suggested that the term India does not include the French and Portuguese territories, which are foreign states but the passport rules expressly provided for exemption from rule 3 of persons domiciled in India proceeding from any foreign possession in India or from Ceylon, the Federated Malay States, or Burma and also persons domiciled in a foreign enclave in India proceeding to any other foreign enclave in India. Therefore, by suitable adaptation of the passport rules, it would be possible for the inhabitants of each dominion to be exempted from the regulations of the other. It may indeed be convenient administratively at the start to have no passport restrictions between the two dominions. The Steering Committee accepted this recommendation and added that the dominion governments can later carry out such modifications as they consider necessary.

The Partition Council accepted the recommendations of the Steering Committee.

Finally, there was the Report of the Expert Committee No. IX on Foreign Relations. Surprisingly, even this Expert Committee was unable to agree on an important aspect. It found itself in difficulties almost at the outset when considering a basic issue, that of the juridical position concerning the question of international personalities of India and Pakistan and its effect on international obligations. Does India cease to exist because a portion of it had decided to come out of it? Would both the new states have to negotiate fresh treaties? Would they both have to seek membership anew from international organisations of which India was a member?

The Steering Committee prepared a special note on this point for consideration by the Partition Council. I prepared the note based on the correspondence that had been exchanged between the secretary of state for India and His Excellency the Governor General. The note propounded the view that the new dominion India should be regarded as a successor government and inherit the treaty obligations, as also the membership of various international organisations; and likewise for Pakistan. This was not acceptable to Pakistan. Mohamad Ali, the other member of the Steering Committee, was of the view that the present Government of India would disappear altogether as an entity and would be succeeded by two independent dominions of equal international status both of whom would be eligible to lay claim to the rights and obligations of the present Government of India. When the note came before the Partition Council for consideration, Lord Mountbatten informed the Council that he had just received a telegram from the secretary of state pointing out that it was essential for Pakistan to apply for the membership of the United Nations before 10 August so that the application could be considered at the next session in September. His Excellency offered to forward the application, but it would of course have to be ratified by the dominion of Pakistan after 15 August. Without wasting any time on the merits of the different legal interpretations the Pakistan members on the Council thought it best to accept this advice so as to ensure that there was the shortest possible hiatus between the date of the UN membership and 15 August. Lord Mountbatten went on to explain that His Majesty's government were not anxious to interfere with what they considered to be a domestic matter between India and Pakistan but they had felt it necessary to point out that there would be grave objection to India's national identity being extinguished by reason of Partition. To do so would be to create, to say the least, an awkward international precedent. The international community would have to live under the hanging sword, as it were, of an unscrupulous country, which might be borrowing money much in excess of its capacity to repay, then go through a formal partition and claim that neither part of the divided country was responsible for the debt incurred prior to that partition. His Majesty's government, therefore, welcomed India's offer to take over international obligations and liabilities of the country as they existed on 15 August 1947 and expressed the view that this would not, in any way, affect Pakistan's international stature, etc. Practically, the only consequence of the course proposed by the Pakistan side would be that both the countries would have to apply for membership of every international organisation of which undivided India was a member now as also to negotiate separately existing treaties anew with each of them. Not only would there be no advantage, but it is more than conceivable that much loss may have to be faced by both. Anxious as Mountbatten was for an agreed solution, he agreed to Pakistan's raising the constitutional issue, if it finally chose to do so. It was agreed that the constitutional advisor to the Government of India (undivided) would be asked to evolve a possible formula, which would meet the needs of both sides. If it were found possible to evolve such a formula, it would be placed before the governments of both Pakistan and India for their approval. A reasonable view, however, prevailed in the end and the matter was dropped.

# 5

# The Partition Council at Work

IT MIGHT HELP IN OBTAINING A MORE SATISFACTORY IDEA of the spirit, and the speed, with which the Partition Council worked, if a descriptive account were given of the items on the agenda of some of the meetings and the manner in which the Council tackled them. This would also give an idea of the variety of problems that came up for consideration at a meeting, the kind of notes with which each item was presented by the Steering Committee, the availability of the more detailed report or study on the basis of which the Steering Committee's recommendations were formulated and the kind of approach adopted by the Council in considering the items placed before them. Where the matter related to the Armed Forces, there would be similar notes setting out the proposals on which decisions or instructions were sought by the Armed Forces Reconstitution Committee. On almost all the items presented to the council, decisions were taken by it: very rarely did it put off the consideration of any matter. The decisions quite frequently enjoined a certain amount of follow up action by the Steering Committee because in most cases prompt implementation of the decisions was necessary in order that further action at some other level could be carried out. Let me begin with an account of the very first meeting of the Partition Council, which took place on 27 June. (It should be remembered that there had already taken place four meetings of the Special Committee of the Cabinet, whose personnel was virtually identical with that of the Partition Council and which, for all practical purposes, set up the machinery of Partition and got it started on its work.)

There were three items that had been placed on the agenda of that meeting. The first item related to the procedure regarding appointment of governors of provinces. No papers had been circulated in regard to this item. There was neither discussion nor decision as Jinnah wanted it to be postponed because he had not been able to consult his colleagues on this matter. He, nevertheless, gave expression to his personal view, which was that the appointments of governors should be made not on the advice of provincial governments but on the advice of the Central Government.

The second item related to the reconstitution of governments at the Centre and in Bengal, and in connection with this a note had been circulated by the Steering Committee. Lord Mountbatten suggested for the consideration of the Council the following arrangement, so far as the Centre was concerned, namely: that he should in the first instance ask for the resignation of all the existing members of the Cabinet, that he should thereafter invite the leaders of the two future governments to nominate an equal number of men for appointment as members, say a set of nine members from each side, each of whom would hold one or two portfolios. The Congress members would be put in actual charge of the portfolios, their authority extending, however, only to their own future area, that is, the areas that would fall within the dominion of India. The League members holding corresponding portfolios would be allowed to see all papers, but would have overriding power both to refer any matter to the full Cabinet and in the event of disagreement to refer to the viceroy for his decision any proposal, which solely or predominantly affected areas which would become Pakistan and to which they had any objection. They would also have the right to initiate any action required for the Pakistan area, which must be acted upon by the member concerned. In actual fact, it would be the stand still agreement that would be operative over the greater area of governmental activity. The top leaders and the administrative machinery would have to concentrate all their energies on the partition work. Jinnah did not like the arrangement proposed by Mountbatten. He considered it to be illegal and constitutionally wrong and untenable. Lord Mountbatten reiterated his own preference for the continuance of the existing arrangements, but asserted firmly that he could not accept Jinnah's view. He had been advised that he had the authority to appoint anybody and create as many portfolios as he considered desirable and distribute the work among those appointed. Jinnah was advised to prepare a note setting out his views on the legal aspect of the proposal and submit it to the viceroy within forty-eight hours so that it could be transmitted to His Majesty's government and the matter could then be settled by the Cabinet at its next meeting. In the end, Lord Mountbatten's view was upheld, though for all practical purposes, no formal action became necessary, since things moved fast.

In so far as Bengal was concerned, the existing League Ministry was asked to continue in office nominally for the whole of Bengal, but it was arranged for the representatives of the future government of West Bengal to be included in the Ministry and be given overriding powers both to refer to the full Cabinet and in the event of disagreement to refer to the governor any proposal solely or predominantly affecting West Bengal and to which they objected. They would also have the right to initiate any action required for the West Bengal area which must be acted upon by the League Minister concerned. In the case of the Punjab which was under Section 93 (now popularly known as President's Rule), it was agreed that the governor would invite two bodies of advisors, one group from each of the two future parts of the provinces to advise him on matters concerning their respective territories.

The third item was a note by the Steering Committee relating to a request for the transfer of a Printing Press and relating to various types of assistance in the work of setting up the Central Pakistan Government. In regard to the request for the transfer of the Printing Press, Lord Mountbatten said that there were many disadvantages in moving a Printing Press. It would take considerable time to dismantle it, transport it and re-install it. There would thus be a loss to both sides. If the Council agreed, he would send a telegram to His Majesty's Government at the highest level requesting them to arrange for top priority for the supply of two Presses for India, the first off the line to go to Karachi for Pakistan and the second for use in the rest of India. In the meantime, India may be agreeable — as in fact it was — to making one Press in India available for doing work solely for Pakistan: it would be understood of course that the control over the Press would not change, but the Press would be given instructions for its work direct by the Pakistan government.

Two or three other matters were also considered at this meeting. One of these related to the appointment of the Chairman of the Boundary Commission. Both the Congress and the League agreed to the proposal which had been put forward by Lord Mountbatten for the appointment of Sir Cyril Radcliffe as chairman of the two Boundary Commissions, one for the Punjab and the other for Bengal. The second matter that was considered related to the appointment of the president of the Arbitral Tribunal. The Congress did not approve of the proposal that Sir Cyril Radcliffe be invited to be the president after he had completed the Boundary Commission work. After some discussion, both the Congress and the League were invited to submit lists of nominees from which one person could be selected by the viceroy for appointment as president of the Arbitral Tribunal. (In the end, it was agreed to appoint Sir Patrick Spens, who would soon cease to be the head of the Federal Court).

The third matter related to the statement by the viceroy that by special dispensation, it had been arranged for the Draft India Bill to be sent to India in order that the Indian leaders might have an opportunity of studying it. As the Bill could not leave the Viceroy's House it had been arranged for two leaders from each side, accompanied by a legal expert each, to come and study it in the Viceroy's House. In addition, the two members of the Steering Committee were also asked to attend.

At the third meeting of the Council, which was held on 5 July 1947, there were eight items on the agenda:

*Item No. 1:* There was a note by His Excellency the Viceroy regarding the temporary employment of British officers and other ranks with the new Dominions after the 15th of August 1947. The Council approved of the terms and conditions of service to be offered to the British officers and other ranks, who may be invited to serve in the two dominions after 15 August. In view of the importance of persuading as many of the British officers and other ranks to stay on, the Council also agreed to an appeal being issued jointly in the name of the viceroy, Pandit Nehru and Mr. Jinnah to volunteer their services.

*Item No. 2:* Additions of finance officers to the three Armed Forces Sub-Committees. The Council accepted the recommendation of the Steering Committee that two finance officers should be added to each of the three Sub-Committees of the Armed Forces Reconstitution Committee. The Steering Committee had recommended that the four Finance Officers who were thus being appointed on the three Sub-Committees should constitute a Sub-committee of the Armed Forces Reconstitution Committee to make recommendations regarding financial adjustments consequent upon the division of the assets of the Armed Forces. The recommendations of the Sub-Committee would be submitted through the Armed Forces Reconstitution Committee to the main Expert Committee No. II (Assets and Liabilities).

*Item No. 3:* The Position of Royal Indian Air Force Officers. The Honourable Member for Defence stated that he had been warned of the possibility of the Air Force pilots and others taking this opportunity to quit the service and that we would be well advised to take appropriate steps to prevail upon them to remain on in the service. The Council suggested that questionnaires should be issued on a priority basis to ascertain well before 15 August the wishes of the officers whether they wished to continue in service. Further action could be determined on the basis of the outcome of the questionnaires. It was felt that their sense of duty will prove stronger than all other pulls.

*Item No. 4:* Recommendation of the Steering Committee on the Report of the Expert Committee No. VIII on Domicile. The Council approved the recommendation of the Steering Committee in respect of the Expert Committee No. VIII on Domicile. The Expert Committee had come to the conclusion that the partition by itself had no effect on nationality and called for no immediate action by the Partition Council except in regard to the public services and that too, only if it was desired to restrict entry into the public services. The Steering Committee did not recommend any immediate action by the Council to restrict entry into the public services. The dominion governments could, after fuller consideration, take such action as they considered suitable. The Council accepted the recommendations of the Steering Committee that a suitable adaptation of the passport rules should be carried out under which the inhabitants of each dominion would be exempted from the Passport Regulations of the other dominion, so that at the start there would be no passport restrictions between the two dominions. The dominion governments could later carry out such modifications as they found necessary.

*Item No. 5:* Arrangement regarding petrol rationing in the quarter beginning 1 August 1947. This question had arisen out of a Report of Expert Committee No. VI. This Committee had recommended that in view of the special requirements of Delhi, Sind, the Punjab and Bengal consequent on the Partition and the shifting of personnel records, these four areas should be given an additional allotment of 6 ½% to what had been given to them in the previous quarter. The balance available would be distributed among the other provinces and states on the basis of the last allocation plus an additional quota based on a uniform extra percentage of the order of 4%. The Transport Department had also raised the question of the disposal of the reserve of 800,000 gallons of petrol held in India by the oil companies at the disposal of the Central government for allotment by the Centre for special purposes. The Expert Committee No. VI was of the view that this special reserve should be allocated in proportion respectively to the consumers in the last quarter in the areas which were to go under Pakistan on the one hand and in the areas under the rest of India on the other. The Partition Council approved of the proposal of Expert Committee No. VI to allocate an additional 6 ½ % to Delhi, Sind, Punjab and Bengal in addition to the last allocation, and to all other provinces a quota in addition to the last quota not exceeding 4%.

*Item No. 6:* The effect of Partition on the Federal Court of India. The recommendations of the Steering Committee were accepted, namely:

(1) With effect from the date of transfer of power the existing Federal Court of India should continue to function as the Federal Court of the Dominion of India, with powers, authority, and jurisdiction, mutates mutandis, the same as those of the existing Federal Court but with jurisdiction limited to the Dominion of India only.

(2) Provision should be made for the constitution of a separate Federal Court for Pakistan from that date.

(3) (a) Assurance should be given to the present judges, officers and staff that they will be continued in service on existing terms and conditions, and

(b) Assurance should be given to all the officers and staff that they will be given an opportunity to elect to serve in Pakistan on existing terms and conditions, should they wish to do so.

(4) The Pakistan Federal Court should be nominally brought into being on the date of partition with a nucleus of staff

consisting of those of the employees of the existing Federal Court who opt for Pakistan, judges, etc., being appointed in due course.

*Item No. 7:* Effect of partition on the High Courts of Bengal and the Punjab.

The Steering Committee recommended:

(1) That the jurisdiction of the Lahore High Court should, from the date of partition, be limited to the Western Punjab only.

(2) From that date a separate High Court having jurisdiction over East Punjab and Province of Delhi should be constituted.

(3) Appointments to the new High Courts should, as for existing High Courts, be made under Section 220 of the Government of India Act, 1935, by His Majesty after consulting the Central Government of the Dominion of India.

(4) (a) It would be necessary to give an opportunity to the judges, officers and staff of the Lahore High Court to choose which of the High Courts they wish to serve, and

(b) an assurance be given that their salaries and other conditions will not be disturbed as a result of the division of the High Court.

(5) That the East and West Punjab High Courts should be given facilities to continue to have their seats at Lahore and function in the building at present occupied by the Lahore High Court. The temporary arrangement should come to an end before 1 March 1948.

(6) The division of staff and records should be undertaken forthwith and be completed with the utmost possible speed.

Identical procedure should be followed in all its details in respect of the division of the Calcutta High Court also. The East and West Bengal High Courts should be given the facility to function for a temporary period from Calcutta until suitable arrangements are made for the location of the East Bengal High Court in East Bengal.

The Partition Council, while accepting the recommendations of the Steering Committee, directed that both the East and West Punjab

High Courts should have their seats at Lahore and function in the building at present occupied by the Lahore High Court and similarly the East and West Bengal High Courts should function in the building at present occupied by the Calcutta High Court. This arrangement would cease before 1 March 1948.

*Item No. 8:* The composition of the Arbitral Tribunal. Lord Mountbatten reported that he had discussed with Sir Patrick Spens the question of appointment of the Federal Court as Arbitral Tribunal. In Sir Patrick's view, it would be most improper to appoint the Federal Court as Arbitral Tribunal. There was no objection, however, to one or more judges from the Federal Court being appointed to the Tribunal. It was decided that Lord Mountbatten should do his best to persuade Sir Patrick to accept the chairmanship of the Arbitral Tribunal. It was understood that the Central Arbitral Tribunal would also deal with the questions arising out of the partition of the Punjab and Bengal.

At the fourth meeting of the Special Committee of the Cabinet held on 26 June for dealing with Partition matters, the viceroy stated that as the Punjab, Bengal and Sind had all voted in favour of partition, the Partition Council should be set up immediately. It should be composed of three members from the Congress and three from the League, but meetings should be attended by only two members from each party. The viceroy would be in the Chair. It was agreed that the first meeting of the Partition Council should be on the following day, that is, 27 June and that, before this, Sardar Patel and Liaquat Ali Khan should intimate to the Cabinet secretary the names of the members whom their respective parties wished to nominate on the Council.

At this meeting, the question of preliminary arrangements for setting up the Central Pakistan Government in Karachi were considered. Two notes had been submitted for consideration — one by the Steering Committee and another by Mr. Liaquat Ali Khan — in regard to the preliminary arrangements. The viceroy summed up the fairly detailed discussion by observing that the Steering

Committee's note should be accepted and top priority be given both to the consideration of the matters mentioned in it and to the execution of non-controversial items. A revised note should be prepared setting out items, which were considered controversial and the Steering Committee should prepare brief notes on each of these items that would enable the Partition Council to arrive at decisions.

One such matter on which the Steering Committee was asked to prepare a note was that concerning the request for transfer of a printing press which Mr. Liaquat Ali Khan had specifically asked for, as the existing presses in the Pakistan area were not sufficient to cope with the work that they were being and would be called upon to do. The following day, when the first meeting of the Partition Council was held, the question of the printing press was considered. The viceroy initiated the discussion with the observation that there were many disadvantages in moving a printing press. It would take considerable time to dismantle it and then further time would be required to transport and reinstall it and there would be an inevitable loss of efficiency. It would be far better from every point of view if he were instead to request the British government at the highest level to arrange to give top priority for the supply of two printing presses for India, the first off the line to go to Karachi and the second for use in the rest of India. In the meantime, he suggested that India should agree to make available one Press in India solely for Pakistan's work. Sardar Patel was agreeable to this arrangement, it being clear that the control over the Press would not change, but that the Press could be given instructions direct by Pakistan government. This arrangement was acceptable to Mr. Liaquat Ali Khan on behalf of Pakistan. It was clear that this arrangement had been arrived at as a result of considerable behind-the-scene diplomacy. It enabled the Council to arrive at a workable arrangement, putting aside the point of principle that underlay to be resolved at a later date. This point of principle, of course, was whether in regard to plants and machinery it would not be better to leave them undisturbed wherever they already stood installed and give credit to the other side in respect of its share.

The Partition Council then took up the question of laying down broad guidelines for carrying on the work of the division of the Armed Forces. A note was prepared by the viceroy in consultation with Field Marshal Sir Claude Auchinleck, Sir Chandulal Trivedi and other advisors on the subject of the partition of the Armed Forces. After some discussion, the Council decided as follows:

1) That all personnel now serving in the Armed Forces would be entitled to elect the dominion they wished to serve in subject to the condition that, a Muslim from Pakistan serving in the Armed Forces would not have the option to join the Armed Forces of the Indian Dominion and a non-Muslim from the rest of India now serving in the Armed Forces would not have the option to join the Armed Forces of Pakistan. There would be no objection to non-Muslim personnel from Pakistan and Muslim personnel from the rest of India electing to serve in the Armed Forces of the Indian Dominion and of Pakistan respectively. The serving personnel will also have the option to resign if they did not wish to serve the Armed Forces of either Dominion.
2) That for the future it would be for the two Dominions to determine their respective policies for recruitment to their Armed Forces. The Partition Council further directed that the terms of reference of the Armed Forces Reconstitution Committee should be revised on the following lines:

   'In close consultation with the Steering Committee acting under the orders of the Partition Council, to make proposals for the division of the existing Armed Forces of India, namely, the Royal Indian Navy, the Indian Army, and the Royal Indian Air Force (including the various installations, establishments, and stores owned by the present Defence Department of the Government of India), in accordance with the principles enunciated in the note by His Excellency the Viceroy of India and Annexure I thereto.'

The Committee will work on the following assumption:

1) Existing members of the Armed Forces serving in either side will be governed by their existing terms and conditions of service. If, subsequently, new terms are promulgated and if they do not desire to serve on the new terms, they will have a right to terminate their services and proportionate benefits will be admissible to them.
2) Services of any Indian officer or other rank in the Armed Forces between now and the date of the transfer of power could be engaged under existing conditions of terms of service, with the option of resigning from the services, should they not wish to serve under any new terms of conditions which may be imposed by the new dominion government.
3) The liability of unallocated charges in respect of pensions, gratuities, annuities, etc. earned by Indian officers and other ranks of the three Services prior to transfer of authority to the new dominion governments will be undertaken by these governments and publicly so announced. (It was agreed that the allocation of pensionary liability between the two governments would be dealt with by the relevant Expert Committee.)
4) Except as demanded by the processes of reconstitution of the Armed Forces, there shall be no changes in the basic organisation and nomenclature of Formations, Units, Establishments and installations of the three Services and in class compositions of units until such reconstitution is completed.
5) For the successful division of the Armed Forces, the services of a number of British officers, now serving in them, would be required.

It will have been evident from this survey of work done at three meetings of the Special Committee of the Partition Council that the members were called upon to take decisions on a variety of subjects of varying degrees of importance. Whatever the intrinsic degree of importance of each matter that was considered, a decision had to be taken in regard to it. At this early stage, naturally a number of matters related to the setting up of the machinery for partitioning, such as the constitution of the Boundary Commission, the setting up of the Arbitral Tribunal, the basis for the option offered to members of Armed Forces, etc. The question of citizenship, etc., also came up with the studied recommendations of the relevant Expert Committee. It will also have been seen that a decision was taken on every matter that was put before the members. It is true there would have been no point in attempting to evade any issue, for however awkward the issue, some agreement or arrangement would have to be found for it. The issue of the Press was a good example, a thoroughly practical and commonsense view was taken and a solution was found.

The Partition Council and the entire machinery designed to assist its working had been set up and had begun functioning expeditiously and in a businesslike manner within a matter of a couple of weeks. The Council itself had had opportunity to show that it meant to work in a purposive manner and was not going to allow itself to be bogged down in futile casuistry and argumentation.

# *Afterword*

*'The sunlight in the garden hardens and grows cold.*
*We cannot cage the minute within its nets of gold.*
*When all is told*
*We cannot beg for pardon.*

— Louis Mac Neice

With a casual paragraph suggesting that the Partition Council was not likely to be caught up in long-winded bureaucratic niceties, this book ends on an abrupt, upended note. It is an unfinished story, quite unlike the man and his life. When H.M. passed on into the shades in November 1993, his death coincided with the end of an age. He had attained to inner ripeness; his outer work was done insofar as any man's work is ever done. That he intended to finish his memoirs is a fact I observed at first hand. I had watched him struggle from time to time with dictaphones and less than first rate stenographers. But like all public minded men, the life to be lived came first and absorbed him wholly. And so, ironically, the memoirs remained the one venture in his life where his meticulous planning failed him. Time, with its overriding tyranny, defeated him in the end.

The memoirs end at the point when his life as a government servant ends, and leaves him considering setting up shop at Vallabh Vidyanagar in Gujarat. But that covers less than half of his adult life. Something sufficient needs to be said about the remaining thirty-five years. Those years saw the seeding, the flowering and the fruition of his path-breaking work in rural education and healthcare. They were also to witness the emergence of H.M. the political person, whose influence was to grow steadily in New Delhi, culminating in his three years as Cabinet minister holding, in turn, Finance and Home portfolios.

Of these thirty-five remaining years, I had the good fortune to know him at first hand for thirty-two. What follows therefore is a string of personal reminiscences, interspersed with excerpts taken from tributes paid to him by his more eminent colleagues in the civil service, politics and other spheres of public life. He was a public man, first and last. It is not that he had no family life. But it was an area that he was careful to wall off from everyone except a few very close friends... who had, over the years, become family to him.

I have ventured to write this Afterword to the man and his work, because I was, and am, in a privileged and perhaps, unique position. To be adopted into the family of a great public figure is not a particularly easy thing and in the early years at any rate, he himself did not make it any easier. The precision of a trained mind, the encyclopedic grasp of disparate facts, the dispassionate perspective and impersonal attitude that the reader will have found in the material of his book were things that I observed at first hand. These are clear and obvious landmarks of his way of thinking. What is not so obvious and what took me nearly two decades to uncover was the human decency and almost sorrowful compassion for his fellow men that was so carefully concealed behind the probity, the rectitude and the impartiality of a man whose private interests had been disciplined by overriding public concerns.

With his resignation from the civil service, the first half of his career was over. But one cannot simply close this chapter without giving the reader a glimpse of his preeminence in the sphere of government service. He was what he was, and so the material he recorded was with the flat dispassion of a camera, eliminating the personal self. By great good fortune V.P. Menon, ten years his senior in the service and perhaps the only other public servant of comparable stature, has had something to say about him in 1964. One cannot conclude this first half without quoting Menon in full:

> 'I became closely associated with H.M. Patel in 1946, and from then till I retired in 1951 — six of the most critical years in the history of our country — nobody was in a better position than I to see his work at close quarters. At that time he was only in his forties, but he shouldered with brilliant success some of the weightiest responsibilities that could fall to an official under the first Government of free India.
>
> I have never known anybody with such a capacity to get a job done quickly as H.M. possesses. At one.time in 1947 he held simultaneously four jobs, each of which would have been quite enough for an able man. He was Cabinet Secretary, Establishment Officer, Member of the Central Committee for Refugees, the Executive Head of the Delhi Committee for restoring order in the Capital, and the Chief Indian Member of the Steering Committee whose function was to decide the distribution of assets and liabilities between India and Pakistan. Even in those hectic days, when all of us were stretched to the limit of our capacity, nobody else held such a backbreaking collection of responsibilities.
>
> When the final plan for Independence and Partition was announced on 3 June 1947, only ten weeks were left in which to settle the distribution of assets and liabilities between the two Governments and the division of armed forces. It was a gigantic undertaking and I thought the problem was insoluble. But H.M. was put in charge on our side, with Choudhuri Mohammad Ali, and he knew how to get the best out of his assistance. That capacity to organize and inspire

men to do their best is the greatest attribute of the leader. The I.C.S. produced many great men, but I can say without fear of contradiction that H.M. is one of its finest products.

Immediately after partition, the refugees came flooding in, and a large proportion of them camped in Delhi. Inflamed by their miseries and the atrocities they had seen, they inevitably made life difficult for a very large Muslim population. Soon the capital was in a state not far from chaos.

Mountbatten was then at Simla, and I took it upon myself to ask him to come immediately. I said that if the Governor General delayed his return, he might find that he had no capital to return to. Mountbatten asked if the Prime Minister and Deputy Prime Minister would want him, and I said I had no doubt that they would, as they had great confidence in his leadership. He came the very next day. Immediately on his arrival, he met the Prime Minister and Deputy Prime Minister and drew up his plans for dealing with the refugee problem. He constituted a Central Committee, of which he was Chairman, for dealing with the problem as a whole. Under it a special committee was set up for Delhi, with Mr. C.H. Bhabha as Chairman and H.M. was its guiding genius. All the Departments of Government especially concerned were represented, and as Cabinet Secretary. H.M. could secure the cooperation of all the Departments and select the most suitable officers to tackle the problem. We have forgotten that dark period now. For two or three days, Delhi was cut off from the country of which it was the Capital — no trains or planes arrived or departed, and no mail was delivered. Many people in the foreign embassies prophesied the early end of independent India. But the Delhi Committee decided otherwise. Within two weeks, H.M. and his staff were in control of the situation, and in a month the Capital was working more or less normally.

It was a hard job, and not without danger, which required a great capacity for leadership, and very hard work. One secret of H.M.'s ability to do this kind of thing is that he can get on for long periods with only about three to four hours sleep out of the twenty-four. I remember that once when the central budget was being drawn up, a big contribution from the Nizam came in handy, and Rajaji asked me jokingly how we should have balanced it if the Nizam had not been so parsimonious. In the same way it could have been asked how H.M. could perform these prodigies if, like other men, he had to get his eight hours of sleep.

Immediately after this, he was called upon for one of his most remarkable feats of quick improvisation and organization. In October, the raiders from the Frontier entered Kashmir and advanced towards Srinagar. I was sent to get the Maharaja's signature to the accession, and as soon as I came back to Delhi I told H.M. that the plan was going through and we should have to send troops. He was given the job of arranging for their transport and supply. He commandeered all the aircraft within reach, concentrated them where the advance units of our force were to emplace, and the very next day the first battalion had been landed on the airfield at Srinagar. Other units duly followed them, and the force was kept properly supplied. Mountbatten, who is one of world's best experts on this subject, said that it was a job requiring the highest organizational ability and one of the finest feats of the kind he had witnessed.

By the time of the Police Action in Hyderabad, H.M. was Defence Secretary and I had another opportunity to see at close quarters how he could tackle a job of military organization. As we all know, every contingency was foreseen and the operation went though without a hitch. As soon as it was over, H.M., Mr. Shavax Lal, who was then the Secretary to the Governor General, and I flew in to Hyderabad to set up the Military Administration under General Chaudhury. I have merely picked out one or two of the most dramatic episodes in which H.M. showed what he could do. In whichever Department he was appointed to work, he left a record of outstanding achievement. When he was Defence Secretary, he was responsible for an ambitious plan to develop the defence industries; when China became hostile we understood the wisdom of it. When he was in the finance Department, he undertook the nationalization of life insurance.

I can repeat about him the words in which Sir Winston Churchill once paid tribute to a former colleague: 'the only guide to a man is his conscience; the only shield to his memory is the rectitude and sincerity of his actions. With this shield, however the Fates may play, we march always in the ranks of honour.'

So H.M. marches on.'

What was this man in himself, away from the power and the glory of which his public life was so full? I can only open a personal window on this private space and like all such openings it will give one angle on what was clearly a complex man.

I first met H.M in 1961, I was twenty-five, young for the age and shy. H.M. was having breakfast with his great friend A.D. Gorwala, at Gorwala's apartment overlooking a garden on the edge of Malabar Hill. Gorwala must have just crossed sixty and H.M. was pushing it. They greeted the young woman I was with effusively with a cheerful 'Good Morning' and barely glanced at me. I remember thinking then that these silvering dons were the most formidable men I had ever met. I stood there tongue-tied, till Gorwala looked up briefly with a faint smile and said, 'Sit down for god's sake.' I sat obediently, trying to be invisible and stared at my boots. H.M. continued silently with the serious business of demolishing fried eggs.

Looking back across a gulf of forty-three years, I realize that he was in fact, as shy as I was then. I realize also that it must have been a difficult moment for him. Usha, his eldest, had brought me along as a prospective candidate for his future son-in-law. It was to be her second marriage and she already had two children by the first. Difficult, because the polish of a senior Civil Servant and the Oxford degree concealed a very conservative Hindu gentleman, I was mercifully oblivious of the fact at the time. I could only notice as the morning progressed that he was scrupulously correct in his behaviour towards me with a kind of impersonal old-world courtesy.

As I grew into his family, I grew steadily more familiar with his public life, both past and present. He never spoke about himself to me except perhaps in the last decade or so of his life. But there were family stories that I began to grow familiar with, first from my wife, and soon after, his daughter Nisha, who was to become my first real friend in the family. And as the years passed and our professional lives intersected more frequently from my involvement in the electoral campaign for various political parties. I had the opportunity of watching him at first hand as he conducted his public life.

By August 1964, when Usha and I were married, I had barely scratched the steel frame in which he had concealed himself. But Gorwala, (Uncle G to the whole Patel clan) was on his way to becoming a friend. Gorwala must have been the only person as close to H.M. as his five girls. As close to each other as brothers, close perhaps because they were connected by shared values and ideals and an interlinked past rather than by blood. Retired from public life, Gorwala had a vastly cynical attitude to the Government of India. From his point of view, public concerns in that age were a waste of his time, except by way of being a concerned but dispassionate critic. This function was one that he perfected over three decades as editor of *Opinion*, a small monthly magazine whose tiny circulation belied its enormous impact on small intersecting circles of industrial and political power in Bombay and New Delhi.

His self-imposed distance from authority and power made him a much easier man to be familiar with. Three and a half decades of time separated us, but we shared a love of fine sherry and good scotch as well as for good poetry in English and Persian. Besides we were part of the closed Bombay Freemasonry of having being born Zoroastrian Parsees.

I remember vividly that wedding dinner at the Ambassador Hotel Grill Room. Gorwala and H.M., together as ever, determined to seriously unbend and celebrate, donned party hats and blew paper whistles, thoughtfully provided by my father for his guests, and got ceremonially pissed. I watched bemused as they loosened their ties and circulated. Gorwala wandering towards our table, poked me in the ribs and offered me a final drink.

I must be content to let this essay remain loosely strung and largely anecdotal. It is not my business to analyze or evaluate: the reader will have had ample opportunity to exercise his critical faculties on the body of material which H.M. himself has presented. All I will present is an album of family photographs taken over three decades. Being part of the mis-en-scene, there can be no claim to possessing any objective perspective. And whereas my task in this case is to cover all the historical detail spanning thirty-five years, the account is bound to be personally coloured with subjective sentiment. One cannot maintain a journalist's stance in the face of a relationship, which grew progressively closer over the years.

Gaining entry into a family of five strong willed daughters was as difficult as acquiring membership into an elite cabal. There were several requirements, which had to be met before you got past the front door. The putative entrant needed to be highly intelligent and widely read. Other recommendations included alertness, a quick wit, a sense of humour, a voluminous vocabulary and the ability to speak the English language with a fluent county accent. It also helped if you had access to several second languages and if you knew your cheeses, wines and single malts nearly as well as H.M. himself. And oh yes, you were required to be as straight as an arrow.

Those five women were as different from each other as can be imagined. The two things they shared were a great love of good books and an unremitting will, which if crossed, gave way to an explosive temper. Usha, the eldest, was warm, generous, theatrical, friendly and open hearted enough to be sometimes taken in. Usha, fun-loving in her youth, contemplative and searching for meaning as she grew older. Uma, the recluse, preferring the wilderness to the countryside and the country to the city. Good with plants and animals, difficult in general with people. Shy, stubborn Uma, the only one of the five who could not be cowed by a father used to deploying armies and ordering national treasuries. Nisha, the one with the Cambridge tripos, who managed to be the bluestocking even in a family of non-stop readers. The writer Nisha, who in some ways was the antithesis of her father, a straightforward, son-like man with an ordered world-view, where (in the words from the *Gita*) the righteous went to Heaven. Nisha, lunar in her quicksilver changes of mood, a born doomsday child and (in her own words) 'a true believer in the way the world punished the good and let the evil and destructive of the earth reign and get away scot free.' Sharad, the fourth, who appeared in the frost of an early winter. Dear, straight Sharad, born into a family of people so highly individual as to be eccentric, herself determined to be just like everybody else in the world. Sharad, who retired a senior manager in Air-India. And Amrita, the youngest, the quiet one, the most difficult to get to know well, her father's true heir both in terms of her values and her public-minded spirit. Amrita who, after her mother died became her father's close companion for over twenty years. And with whom H.M. could exchange a paragraph of information and opinion with a single glance and a smile across a crowded room. And then, the grand children Rohit, the eldest grandson, soft spoken, laconic, but with a head for business; the responsible one to whom H.M. would turn in terms of managing family affairs. Nayan, his eldest grand daughter, affectionate and stunningly beautiful when young, still able to turn heads at forty-eight. Rahul, the dude, with a pierced ear and a cool, outrageous sense of humour. Maia the youngest, the bright one, who read every bit as much as her aunts did and who shared their explosive temper. It was not a large family, but it filled H.M.'s dining room at the annual late October family reunions in Gujarat. I can see him now sitting at the head of the table, smiling, heaping plates, every inch the affectionate patriarch.

Rummaging about in my memory, two incidents occurring in the late sixties stand out. In July 1965, I undertook a journey to the family home in Vallabh Vidyanagar, Gujarat. The purpose was to discuss a business enterprise in the advertising field and seek H.M.'s advice and help. (In the event, he introduced me to the venture capitalist who financed the project). H.M. himself was largely absent except at meal times. Notwithstanding, it was my first and only insight on what it might mean to be a son-in-law in a relatively conservative Hindu household. Savitaben (Mrs. Patel) overwhelmed me with her kindness and meticulous attention to whatever it was that I might possibly want. I was both charmed and somewhat puzzled by her complete acceptance of a relative stranger, on the basis of family by marriage. It was only decades later that I grew to understand the sacramental attitude to all life, which is the old Hindu way and was to read it overtly expressed in one of the Upanishads ('.... *as a Fire, the Guest enters the house....*'). She went on to give me cautionary warning about her eldest daughter's fiery temper and asked in advance for my understanding, adding by way of explanation that the fire concealed a kind heart. It was an inexpressibly poignant moment for someone who was not yet thirty. I was touched but did not yet have the maturity to appreciate such an openhearted trust in the benign power of life. I knew Savitaben only over a brief five year period till 1970, till she passed away prematurely. But I remember her vividly as the cornerstone of that large house in Vidyanagar and its adjoining gardens full of light and air. A constant, benevolent presence, never intrusive, always caring, always welcoming and warm to all comers.

H.M.'s work over three and a half decades at Vallabh Vidyanagar in rural Gujarat was staggering in its range and scope. Defined by three concentric circles, it consisted of an industrial township (Vithal Vidyanagar), a vast array of institutions of higher learning (Charutar Vidya Mandal) and every sort of health care facility (Charutar Arogya Mandal). The array came finally to resemble the combined wish-list of a Cambridge don and a Harley Street specialist: An Arts and Science College giving bachelors and masters degrees; a college of Fine Arts; an English teaching school and an Institute of English Training and Research; a College of Home Science, a College of Pharmacy, a College of Architecture, a Career Development Centre; degrees in Business Administration, diplomas in Accounts and Banking; a Commerce College; Libraries, workshops, computer laboratories, a Research Institute of Renewable Energy Sources; a large, modern 700 bed hospital, a Medical College, a School of Nursing. The list is endless.

But to return to my personal album of memories. The second snapshot is from 1966 at our Bombay flat. My colleague Ravi Gupta and I were discussing a major presentation to be made by us to the Advertising Club at the Taj Ballroom the following morning. H.M., who had arrived by a late flight from Delhi, was having a pre-dinner drink. Dinner had been delayed on his account, he was tired and appeared to be dozing. About twenty minutes into our discussion, he interrupted with a remark. It was cogent and from a viewpoint neither of us had encountered before. We gaped. He appeared to be familiar with every detail we had discussed. This continued for the next half-hour until dinner was served. I was both impressed and foxed. Years later, in the late seventies, I was to see him repeat the process at his ministerial bungalow in New Delhi late one evening when preparing for a budgetary meeting. I was watching a man, at the end of his tether, apparently half asleep, but able to marshal a vast number of facts. I asked him the following morning exactly what he was doing and just how he managed to do it. He replied that he didn't know how but that it was something he had learnt to do. Life in a tent as a district collector was hard and tiring, he said, but you learnt to keep your wits about you even when you were utterly exhausted.

It was a curious synchronicity that his entry into politics in 1967 as a Swatantra Party member contesting a Gujarat State Assembly Seat, coincided with my own career in electoral advertising. I happened to handle the Swantantra Party campaign on an All India basis that year. H.M. had nothing whatsoever to do with this. Minoo Masani, general secretary of the party was looking for takers, and found us, a small advertising shop at the time. H.M. lost the election. He was to proceed on a winning streak from then onwards starting 1969 in the Lok Sabha elections. In 1988, he lost following Rajiv Gandhi's electoral sweep three months after Mrs. Gandhi was assassinated. H.M. was to bow out of the political arena that year after two decades as sitting member of the Lok Sabha. My parallel life as it were, in political advertising, was to continue with the Janata Party campaign in 1980, an election that was badly lost, and in 1984 in the Karnataka State Elections, when Ramakrishna Hegde re-captured his chief ministership.

H.M. moved camp to New Delhi for part of the year in 1969 to attend his new Lok Sabha schedule. Usha and I had, in the meantime, contracted a powerful bond with a Vaishnav ashram in the Kumaon hills and with the man in charge an Englishman turned Vaishnav sanyasi, who was in 1970 to become our formal guru. Visits to the hills on a six monthly basis were to become a part of our lives for the next three decades and H.M.'s Delhi bungalow became a natural stopover. Observing him in his natural professional environment, I very quickly became aware that he had slipped back into the circle of governmental power as though the intervening eleven years had simply never happened. I was in my mid-thirties then and head of my own successful advertising organization. Watching Gorwala and H.M. operate and getting my own head into the rarified air of business success, it struck me that the whole of upper-class India was in fact a small village scattered geographically in Delhi, Bombay and perhaps three or four other metropolitan cities. Everybody knew everybody else or least someone who knew anybody else who mattered. I was amazed at first and later amused by this small fragile ring of concentric circles, amounting perhaps to ten thousand families, who in point of fact were the real rulers of India. I remarked then to Usha, that 1947 may have ushered in a nominal democracy, but this nation remained, for anybody with eyes to see, a seamlessly functioning triple oligarchy of political power, industrial wealth, and media influence.

Life, even on the fringes of this well-oiled elite, could be extremely comfortable ... to the point of putting you into a sound dreamless sleep. It sounds naïve in retrospect, but I do believe that many of us were convinced that this picnic would never end. Mrs. Gandhi's salutary shock in June 1975 quickly opened our eyes. The Emergency saw every important leader of the Opposition in jail. I believe H.M. was spared because Mrs. Gandhi saw him as relatively apolitical, a non-combatant so to speak. In the event, he saw himself become the formal leader of the Opposition in a depleted Lok Sabha. It was only post 1977 that the minutes of the Lok Sabha Sessions were made public. If you care to look at those records, you will see that H.M. played his part meticulously. Never fudging any issue, always biting the bullet and standing by his principles as well as by the facts. I give an excerpt from one of his speeches in the Lok Sabha during the Emergency's darkest days:

> "If it is your contention that you have (anti-national) elements in control and if it is your contention that you need the Emergency in order to bring them under control, then you will always need the Emergency. Are you then suggesting that the Emergency has to be retained for all time to come?
>
> The Prime Minister ... when she has given interviews to foreign journalists ... has said that she cannot think of lifting the Emergency until the Opposition behaves as it should behave. I would very much like to know precisely how

> the Opposition is expected to behave? How is it behaving? What is its behaviour today, which the Prime Minister does not altogether appreciate? As far as I know, if you could lay any charge against the Opposition today, it is that it has remained completely inactive. Its impassivity is its offence. Of course, it has done one thing, which is that within the parliament it has opposed Government, whenever opposition was called for. That I maintain is its legitimate duty and it will continue to do so."

H.M. was never personally insulting, always correct to the point of being courteous. This attitude, I believe, kept him out of jail. And when elections were declared, he played an important in camera role in bringing together Charan Singh, his party chief in the BLD and Morarji Desai, whom he had known well as a bureaucrat, thereby forming the nucleus of the nascent Janata Party, which was quickly to rope in the leaders of the Jana Sangh. It may be true that cell mates incarcerated in a common cause become good friends. It was certainly true in Allahabad jail, when Nehru and Patel began to understand each others' mindset, two generations prior to Morarji Desai, Charan Singh and Atal Behari Vajpayee.

The Emergency was certainly a time of growing up for us who had till then been entirely apolitical. Clear and present danger is a wonderful stimulus to learning. Reading Machiavelli and Marx, Cohn-Bendit and Tawney untutored and at first hand is a curious and heady mixture. In the five years that followed 1975, I began to realize that either everything is political or nothing is political. It is like the air you breathe, you don't notice it except when it turns bad. And when in 1981, Arun Shourie challenged Mrs. Gandhi to take him to court or jail him, on the front page of *The Indian Express* you realized that politics was everybody's business, unconfined to parties and elections. It was during the last six months of 1975, that politics was to touch us personally. Our friends Romesh and Raj Thapar had to shut down *Seminar* in New Delhi. Gorwala in Bombay refused to submit to any censorship, and decided to cyclostyle *Opinion*, and mail the copies to his former subscribers, without payment, thereby avoiding the label of publisher. He was over seventy-five years old at the time, and when I together with Gauri Deshpande decided to jump in and help him, it was as someone who frequently wrote for the journal. My first political act was an act of friendship as was my second. Gorwala was convinced that Vidya Charan Shukla wanted to jail him. 'They won't find me in bed,' he commented grimly. 'I'll spare myself the indignity of being hustled into my clothes. They'll find me ready'. And so the old gentleman waited night after night, after supper, fully dressed and with his boots on, waiting for a knock that never came. At the time, we lived yards away, down the hill. I used to stroll up to his house very often to keep him company. Gorwala was frugal by nature and switched off the lights as soon as he had eaten and dressed. So we would sit in the dark telling each other stories till two in the morning when he would say: 'I don't suppose they'll come for me now' and would go off to bed, carrying his bottle of sherry or rum or whatever happened to be on hand, which he had unfailingly put out for his guests.

February 1977 was a breathtaking time for those of us who are old enough to remember it. Jagjivan Ram had just walked out of the Congress party to form his own version of the Congress, and had held a press conference on his lawns to announce the fact. The Emergency had not yet been formally lifted, but Mrs. Gandhi's spell was broken. In the space of a few hours, that magical late winter afternoon, everybody was talking and no longer in whispers. All sense of fear had vanished: people in Delhi, Bombay and all over the country were celebrating openly sensing what was to come. Jagjivan Ram and Morarji's Janata Party had yet to come to an electoral arrangement, but everyone everywhere was foreseeing Mrs. Gandhi's electoral defeat. In the event, it was to become a rout. For that short month, the political horizon was drenched in sunlight as it has seldom been before or since. When the results came in through that late March evening and night, it became clear that in every Hindi speaking state in the entire northern belt, the Congress had been wiped out without a trace, without a single seat. I cannot speak of Delhi, but I do not believe that all of Bombay slept that night. Results kept coming in through the night and were posted in lights outside *The Times of India* and *The Indian Express* buildings. That night all of us were roisterers on foot. I remember complete strangers, embracing as they cheered each Janata seat and hooting at Mrs. Gandhi's seats coming in from the southern states. I was eleven years old when Independence was declared and remember nothing of the celebrations, having been tucked into bed by my upper-class Parsee parents. But I have never before or since saw such wild and unambiguous political celebration. We were all Indians that night, every mother's son and daughter and proud of it.

The three years that followed were to be the crown of H.M.'s professional career. First as finance minister and later as minister of Home Affairs, his return to the height of political power was vindication for his family after his shabby treatment at Nehru's hands over the Mundhra affair, and his long decade in political exile. This period of his life is over documented and I do not need to dwell further on it. I was a small and consciously recessive part of the long stream of guests and visitors at his 2 Akbar Road, ministerial bungalow, across the road from 1 Safdarjung Road, which Mrs. Gandhi occupied as the uncrowned leader of the Opposition, and two hops away from 2 Teen Murti Marg, the final house he had occupied in New Delhi as principal finance secretary, before Nehru and TTK decided to fling him to the wolves as scapegoat.

What is there to say about ministerial glory, of a whole acre of flowering garden and official gun toting paraphernalia that has not been fried to a burn and made clichetic? Looking back, I can only observe that the Janata government, in some sense wedded to relative decency, and innocents in political psychology were shorn lambs to Mrs. Gandhi's old wolf. She began to take them to bits, even before they could make a beginning. Three months after coming to power, Charan Singh made the mistake of trying to destroy Mrs. Gandhi by jailing her. This led to the famous scene at the Haryana border, where Mrs. Gandhi, playing her old role of empress of India, got out of the police van touched Indian earth and refused to budge through the night. She was eventually returned safely to Safdarjung. No Inspector General in the land would have dared lay a finger on her.

A more psychologically astute home minister would have taken his time over disassembling her carefully built myth of divine right and done that first before attempting to destroy the woman. Alas, the only guile the Janata Ministers ever displayed was what they used against each other.

The great electoral rout in 1980 and Mrs. Gandhi's triumphant return to power as Durga Redux, was substantially the end of H.M.'s political career. He was to remain in the Lok Sabha for eight years, but in some sense his work in New Delhi was done. In that sense, it is both possible and accurate to see him as a man who rode the political whirlwind without any conscious intention of doing so. A relatively mild storm drove him out of the capital at a time when he was the premier civil servant. The great political upheaval of 1977 blew him back to the pinnacle of power, as the cataclysm of 1980 uprooted him from the government in 1988 and the major typhoon that followed Mrs. Gandhi's death, deprived him of his Lok Sabha seat. He was in his mid-eighties at the time. The Sikh riots that followed made him turn away in shame and disgust and helped him decide to leave politics once and for all. As he was to say ruefully to me at the time, 'I was always proud of my country, now I cannot even say that I understand it.'

An astute astrologer might have remarked that there was great affinity between H.M.'s natal horoscope and the chart for New Delhi midnight, 15 August 1947. It was certainly remarkable how all the major political events of the last half century in India, from Partition onwards were reflected in the major events of his own life. And so he was to return to his roots in Gujarat, to continue the work he had begun in 1958 in pursuance of Sardar's dream of a higher rural education, of first rate rural medical services and the building of agricultural co-operatives and of rural based industry. He believed, as Gandhi did before him, that the soul of India was to be found in her villages. And if you were going to create infrastructure and wealth, it is there that you had to build it.

In the five years between 1988 and his death in 1993, I grew to know him in an entirely different way. As he grew remote from concerns of power, he grew softer and less judgemental. He had always made time for his extended family. He now enjoyed playing Paterfamilias with a small immediate circle of children, grandchildren and now great grandchildren. By another curious synchronicity, a large part of my life in those five years was to be spent promoting the use of organic fertilizers. And so, working with the Gujarat Oilseeds Growers association of which H.M. was chairman, I found myself a frequent weekend guest at his house.

I have referred to that house before in passing, think it necessary now to describe it in some detail. Whenever I think of H.M., I think of large houses, with spacious lawns, ample flower beds, a kitchen garden and a detached outhouse for an army of servants. This is not part of my fantasy. All three houses that come to mind, the one in Gujarat and the two Delhi houses at Akbar Road and Lodhi Estate were mansions, though not all of equal size.

H.M.'s Vidyanagar home was designed on three levels, a ground floor, which contained a master bedroom, living room, dining room, an ample verandah with a swing overlooking the lawns and a wide, well-lit passage, which ran beside a sunken inner courtyard, open to sun and air, with a central, flowering champak tree. An annex on the ground floor contained a guest bedroom with an independent entrance. The top floor had two large bedrooms for the family flanked by another wide verandah. The mezzanine contained H.M.'s library, also a short order bedroom. It was here that I gravitated on every visit. For an omnivorous reader like myself it was an earthly paradise. Plato, Hume, Bentham and Locke rubbed shoulders with Sophocles, Plutarch and Thucidydes. On neighbouring shelves was Shakespeare, The King Jame's Bible, George Eliot and Dickens. Two rungs up you would find Hafiz, Omar Khayyam, Firdausi's *Shah Namah* and Sri Aurobindo's *The Life Divine*. But it was the Penguins and the Crime Club books that simply floored you. H.M. loved detectives, and so Conan Doyle, Edgar Allen Poe and Simenon hobnobbed with Agatha Christie, Rex Stout, P.D. James and Dorothy L. Sayers.

The house had changed subtly over two decades. Amrita was now the presiding genius. And although the guest's needs were as always anticipated and swiftly met, it was brisk, no-nonsense hospitality. Savitaben's easy paced pampering had vanished.

I find it less easy to talk about this last period because it was so much more personal. The common bond of the Gujarati language now came into play. It was as though he was consciously allowing himself to revert to type and touch forgotten roots. And I followed him willingly and playfully. Some of our deepest bonds are made at play, when we are least aware of reaching out. I have a vivid memory of a visit, when Amrita was away on tour and he and I sat alone for the usual pre-dinner drink. After his second Black Label, he began humming an old Gujarati nursery rhyme. It was familiar and I jumped in with the words. He roared with laughter and began singing with me. It was a ludicrous moment, but also poignant. He was suddenly close to tears, as he remarked that he had never really given his daughters a formal education in Gujarati. Then, suddenly quiet he said under his breath 'It's a shame.'

It is not my intention to end on any sentimental note. But one more occasion comes to mind. The flight from Bombay to Gujarat had been delayed and I reached the family house to find him awake an hour before midnight with dinner kept hot on a trolley and a bottle of Black Label, a glass and an ice bucket at his side. When I remonstrated 'Why are you waiting up, Sir.' He chuckled broadly, looked me in the eye and said 'For you, Sir. For you.' All the barriers were down. He, who had been formally correct with me for over two decades, looking all the while into the middle distance as it were was now unabashed about his personal affection, and also I sensed, happy with his new way of being open. I am not the only person who recalls H.M.'s meticulous and caring hospitality. I.G. Patel, who was governor of the Reserve Bank during H.M.'s tenure as finance minister, remembers a late night visit where H.M. put his head around the door, enquired if I.G. was furnished with a thermos of cold water, blankets and other provisions for the night.

I rode beside his flag draped body on the flatbed truck that passed for a gun-carriage in November 1993. Like anybody who had held important Cabinet positions, he was by now a national figure. But all that seemed unimportant in the face of the true local hero he had finally become. Nothing was stage-managed. It didn't have to be. The outpouring of grief and silent respect was spontaneous. Whole villages streamed out to follow the funeral procession as it proceeded to Karamsad, Sardar Patel's village where the cremation was to take place, the women defying tradition and leading the way as a tribute to his long fight for women's equality. He had become Sardar's true political heir, and Sardar's son was coming home for the last time. As Amrita, his youngest daughter and companion for twenty years lit the pyre and as Rohit, his grandson, performed the final obsequies, the military band played the taps on a lone trumpet and the curtains came down on an era. J.R.D. Tata, his great contemporary, had passed on a day earlier.

Much has been written about the Indian Renaissance that began in the late nineteenth century with Gandhi, Aurobindo and Tagore. Dadabhoy Naoroji, and Lokmanya Tilak, Pherozeshah Mehta and Ranade, Jamshedjee Tata, Nehru, Azad and Patel now have their place in the Indian Pantheon. Very little has been said of the generation that followed: men who had lit their torches at the parental flame.

When I remember my three decades with H.M. and his great friend A.D. Gorwala, I feel touched by a sense of latter-day glory.

These men, who died just before the century died, lived impeccable lives. They were touched by greatness if by that word you, mean width and depth of mind, fullness and plentitude of heart, and nobility of spirit, in the sense of noblesse oblige. These men were more than ready to handle the obligation that privilege presents to those who are ready to accept the common burden and try to lift it. To call these people incorruptible goes far beyond any limited fiscal rectitude, for they have learnt to guard their minds, bridle their emotions and discipline their lives in a way that puts them beyond contagion from the viruses of hate, anger, prejudice and despair that corrupt our air today. They are the salt of the earth of whom Christ spoke and it was for them that Dryden wrote his final lines:

*'From Harmony to Harmony a span*
*Which like an octave all through Nature ran.*
*The final chord and diapason in Man.'*

**Kersy Katrak**

# *Chronology*

1904 Born in Bombay on August 27, 1904, the second son of Shri Muljibhai Dwarkadas Patel and Smt Hiraben of Dharmaj, Gujarat.

Studied with gifted teachers, Shri Karunashanker Pandya, Shivabhai Jethabhai and Bhulabhai Dwarkadas, his uncle, and later went to St. Xavier's High School, Bombay, where he took Sanskrit as his second language.

1920 Married Savitaben Patel of Sojitra, Gujarat, in May.

1920-1926 Left for England and studied at Felixstowe (Suffolk) under private tutors and passed the London Matriculation Examination in early 1922 with a First Class. Took Latin and French.

Received a BA (Modern Greats) from St Catharine' College, Oxford, and a B.Com degree from London University where he was enrolled as an external student.

1926-1927 Passed the I.C.S. examination and stayed on for a year's training as required by service rules.

1927 Returned to India in October and began work as a Supernumerary Assistant Collector in Larkana, Sind.

1928-1934 Assistant Collector and Sub-Divisional Magistrate, later Collector and District Magistrate at Sukkur,

Mirpur Khas (Tharparkar District) and Larkhana (Sind). Appointed by the Government of India on special duty to investigate silver smuggling on the borders of Sind and Kutch.

1935 Sind Separation Officer with headquarters at Bombay and Poona.

1936 Nominated by the Government of Bombay to receive special training, organized by the Government of India, in the management of ways and means and allied matters connected with the control of currencies. Worked partly in Calcutta with the Controller of Currencies and partly in Bombay with the Accountant General. Appointed Deputy Secretary, Department of Finance, Government of Bombay. Also appointed Secretary of the Morrison Stock Exchange Inquiry Committee.

1937 In May, went to the UK and later to Hamburg as the Government of India's Trade Commissioner for Northern Europe.

1939 The Second World War broke out on 3rd September. Sent to London as Deputy Trade Commissioner and later as Trade Commissioner.

1940-1945 Returned to New Delhi in September 1940 and joined the Government of India as Deputy Secretary, Department of Supplies (a new, wartime department).

Between 1940 and 1941, also served as Deputy Secretary to the Eastern Supply Council composed of representatives from Great Britain, Australia, New Zealand, South Africa and India.

1943 Appointed Deputy Director General of Supplies, Government of India.

Took charge as Joint Secretary of the new Department of Industry and Civil Supplies in 1944.

Involved, among other things, with drafting and implementing legislation on price controls.

Towards the end of 1945, appointed Secretary, Department of Industry and Civil Supplies. Awarded the C.I.E. in appreciation of his services.

1946 Appointed Joint Cabinet Secretary in April.

1947 In March, became Cabinet Secretary and, on the partition of the country, held additional responsibility as Partition Secretary.

1947-1953 In October 1947, took charge as Secretary, Ministry of Defence, Government of India, and organized the defence of the Kashmir valley. During this period, oversaw the reorganization of the armed forces and development of ordnance factories, services' training schools, and other institutions. On one of several visits to the UK, appeared before the British Cabinet in order to explain the Kashmir situation and India's approach and policy.

Appointed Secretary, Ministry of Food and Agriculture, Government of India, in November 1953.

In November 1954, joined the Ministry of Finance as Secretary, Department of Economic Affairs and later as Principal Secretary. During this period, life insurance was nationalized, the company law administration was reformed, coinage was decimalised and the Imperial Bank of India was nationalized. He was appointed first Chairman of the Life Insurance Corporation of India in 1956.

1958 Retired from government service.

Became Chairman, Charutar Vidya Mandal, Vallabh Vidyanagar, Gujarat, with responsibility for the management and expansion of educational institutions.

1960-1966 Appointed Honorary Chairman, Gujarat Electricity Board by the government of Gujarat. Rapid execution of the Dhuvaran project undertaken.

1964 Charutar Vidya Mandal honoured him on his 60th birthday and H.M. Patel commemoration volume, a collection of essays by his admirers, was presented to him along with a purse. He donated the purse to the Mandal for setting up an institute of English and a badminton hall.

Wrote a report for the Government of India on a scheme for the utilization of the waters of the Narmada river.

Unable to accept offer to assume chairmanship of the Gujarat State Fertilizer Company but agreed to join the company board and remained a director until 1977.

1962-1964 Sarpanch of Vallabh Vidyanagar Gram Panchayat.

1966 Joined the Swatantra Party and was in charge of organizing the party's election campaign in Gujarat.

1967 Lost elections to the Anand Assembly and Parliament seats. The Swatantra Party emerged as a major opposition force winning 66 seats to the Gujarat Assembly. (The party held 21 seats earlier).

Won Gujarat Assembly by-election from Dhrangadhra.

1968-1969 Appointed Chairman, Public Committee of the Gujarat Legislative Assembly.

1968 Sardar Patel University conferred on him Degree of Doctor of Letters (Honoris Causa)

1968 President, Gujarat Swatantra Party.

1969 President, Gujarat Khedut Sangh.

1970 Savitaben, wife, passed away on 30 October.

1971 Elected to the Lok Sabha from Dhandhuka constituency in Gujarat.

President, All-India Swatantra Party.

| | |
|---|---|
| 1974 | Chairman, Reception Committee, Gujarati Sahitya Parishad, 27th Convention at Vallabh Vidyanagar in January. |
| 1976 | Elected leader of the Janata Front in the Lok Sabha during the Emergency (The Front consisted of all Opposition groups barring the left parties). |
| 1977 | Elected to Parliament on a Janata Party ticket from Sabarkantha (Gujarat) in March and appointed Finance Minister in Morarji Desai's Cabinet. Major concerns were containing inflation, price stabilization and the removal of food zones.<br>Appointed Chairman, Indian Board of Wild Life (post held until the Janata government fell in July 1979). Also Chairman of the Steering Committee on Project Tiger. |
| 1979 | Home Minister, Government of India, from January to July. |
| 1979 | Charutar Arogya Mandal honoured him by presenting him H.M. Patel commemoration volume to mark his 75th birthday. The volume is a collection of articles by his many admirers. |
| 1980 | Lost mid-term election from Sabarkantha. |
| 1981 | Chairman, Charutar Arogya Mandal and Chairman, Charuta Vidya Mandal.<br>Received the Albert Schweitzer Award of the Animal Welfare Institute, U.S.A. First Asian to win this honour. |
| 1981-1986 | Elected to Parliament from Sabarkantha. |
| 1983-84 | Chairman, SPRERI (Sardar Patel Renewable Energy Research Institute). |
| 1986 | Chairman, D.C. Patel School of Architecture. |
| 1988-89 | Founder-Chairman of Film Foundation. |
| 1990 | Chairman, Hindustan Oil-Seeds Growers' Association. |

1993 Initiated the production of a feature film, *Sardar*, on the life of Vallabhbhai Patel.

Died November 30, 1993.

Awarded the Nargis Dutt Award (posthumously) for the production of *Sardar*.

H.M. Patel was associated at various times with the following institutions in an honorary capacity:

Chairman, Charutar Vidya Mandal, Vallabh Vidyanagar
Chairman, Charutar Arogya Mandal, Vallabh Vidyanagar
Chairman, Jyoti Solar Energy Institute, Vallabh Vidyanager
Chairman, Sastu Sahitya Trust, Ahmedabad
Chairman, Saraswati Kelavani Mandal, Ahmedabad
Chairman, Kelavani Mandal, Dharmaj
Chairman, Gujarat Education Society, New Delhi
Chairman, Lotus Hospital Trust, Bombay
Chairman, Lotus Ayurvedic Research and Hospital Trust, Lambha
Chairman, Observatory, Ahmedabad
Vice-President, Indian Institute of Public Administration, New Delhi
Vice-President, Executive Committee, Sardar Patel Institute of Economic and Social Research, Ahmedabad
Trustee, Modasa Education Trust
Member, Sardar Patel Memorial Trust, Ahmedabad
Served as a member of various committees and bodies of Sardar Patel University, including the Senate, Syndicate, Academic Council, Finance Committee and Board of Sports. Set up the Agro-Economic Research Centre at the University in July 1961.

Established a number of institutions at Vallabh Vidyanagar
June 1959: Nalini & Arvind Arts College

June 1960: Kala Kendra, College of Fine Arts
June 1961: Rajratna P.T. Patel Science College
June 1964: A new arts college (later named the T.V. Patel Arts College)
July 1964: A new high school (later named the Smt. S.D. Desai High School)
July 1965: H.M. Patel Institute of English
June 1970: An English-medium high school
June 1971: S.M. Patel College of Home Science
June 1977: Commerce Polytechnic for diploma courses in Accounts & Banking (at the B.J. Commerce College)
August 1978: G.I. Patel Institute of Industrial Chemistry (at the V.P. Science College)
January 1979: Jyoti Solar Energy Institute
August 1980: School of Nursing under the auspices of Charutar Arogya Mandal
1986: D.C. Patel School of Architecture

# III

# Appendices

# Appendix 1

# The Mundhra Affair

### *Extracts from* My Submissions *by H.M. Patel,* The Lies of T.T.K. *by A.D. Gorwala and Personal Reminiscences of Contemporaries*

#### A. Extracts from *My Submissions* by H.M. Patel, Bombay, n.d., for private circulation only.

"In these past months, it has become painfully evident how easy it is for prejudice to be created against a civil servant and how powerless he is to dispel it. Nevertheless, where it is a question of doing justice, it is obviously desirable that all the proprieties are scrupulously observed. And in this case, where the morale of the Civil Service is also at stake, the utmost importance should be attached to seeing to it that not only justice is done but to making it abundantly clear that justice was going to be done". (Prefatory Note).

"Briefly stated, the charges held by the President [of the Board of inquiry — SM] to have been proved against me as the Principal Secretary, Finance Ministry, are:

a) That I caused Mr. Kamat and Mr. Vaidyanathan to enter into an 'improper' transaction, which transaction was un-businesslike and resulted in loss;

b) That I was 'negligent' in not giving a clear indication of the price and thereby caused a loss.

2. The charges have been framed in respect of the purchase of certain shares of Joint Stock Companies held by Mr. Mundhra. The purchase, hereinafter referred to as the 'Mundhra deal', was the culmination of certain events which followed the 'Wealth and Expenditure Tax' Budget of 15th May 1957". (p. 3).

"8. The Board has held that the transaction entered into by me was to help Mr. Mundhra and not for any legitimate LIC purpose; that its purpose was not to relieve the Calcutta market of the Mundhra drag; that the deal was presumably in pursuance of the assurance of one or more Ministers of the Government of India to Mr. Mundhra to give him monetary assistance in consideration of his having subscribed funds to the Congress Party, and of his having kept the Kanpur Mills open, thereby assisting the U.P. Government to escape undesirable political consequences". (pp. 4-5)

"12. ....It is not for me to draw attention to my past record or to recount the services I rendered to government in more than one responsible position. These must speak for themselves. I venture to think that nothing in my long career as a public servant can give countenance to the suggestion that I am capable of substituting a political or personal motive for the right course of action as I saw it or the public interest as, in the given circumstances, I conceived it". (p. 5)

"270. ....But even Homer is known to nod, and, to my regret, in this case has nodded heavily". (p. 110)

"380. I admit that I have always acted with expedition (and it has never been suggested that I should have acted otherwise) in dealing with whatever important matters I was entrusted with in different contexts ranging from Partition, Delhi disturbances and Defence to Food and Finance. But never have I done things, however important, at any cost, if by that is meant, improperly or dishonestly". (p. 155)

"I have sought in the course of this unavoidably lengthy submission to show that the Board's approach to this enquiry has been vitiated by its obsession with a pre-conceived theory. As a result, it has failed to weigh the evidence fairly. It has found it difficult to resist the temptation to fit certain facts into the theory it favoured rather than let all the facts lead to the only conclusion they justify.

Had this not been the case, had the evidence on record been properly assessed and had natural and legitimate inferences been drawn, only one conclusion would have been possible, namely, that the Mundhra deal had been entered into with the full knowledge and approval of the Minister and there had therefore been no abuse of authority, that the deal was proper and that the price formula had been fixed in a businesslike manner.

I submit that on merits I should be acquitted on all the above charges". (Conclusion) (p. 161)

**B. Extracts from A.D. Gorwala, *The Lies of T.T.K*, Bombay *1959*.**

"Of Mr. T.T. Krishnamachari, it has been said by:

Mr. Justice Chagla

"It is most unfortunate that in answering the question the Minister did not think it proper to place all the facts fully and frankly before the Lok Sabha".

"I would prefer to accept the positive evidence of Shri Patel and Shri Bhattacharya" (to that of Mr. Krishnamachari)." (p. 3)

"The U.P.S.C. Says:

"21. The Commission have, therefore, come to the conclusion that:

a) The Minister was aware of the antecedents of Shri Mundhra;
b) In the context of the Knowledge that the Minister had of Shri Mundhra and his doings, Shri Patel adequately apprised the Minister about the transaction:
c) Shri Patel, with good reason, honestly believed that the Minister approved of the deal being entered into; and
d) The fact that the Minister's approval was not reduced to writing was in keeping with the 'informal' procedure that was followed between him and his Principal Finance Secretary." (pp. 11-12)

"The U.P.S.C. says:

"20. The Commission are satisfied that the facts mentioned above, particularly those emerging from the evidence of Shri A.K. Roy and Shri Nehru, clearly establish that Shri Patel had reasonable grounds for honestly believing that he had the Minister's authority for the transaction. It is significant, as pointed out by Shri Patel in his explanation to the charges-sheet, that at no time did the Minister "even suggest that I had, in the part which I took in regard to the Mundhra deal, gone beyond my authority'." (p. 14)

## C. Personal Reminiscences of Contemporaries about the Mundhra Affair.

*Shri K.M. Munshi, eminent political leader*

"During the tragic days when he was singled out for being responsible for the "Mundra deal", I appeared for him at the enquiry held by Justice Chagla, the then Chief Justice of Bombay, and prepared his statement when the enquiry was held by Justice Vivian Bose. I also prepared his statement of defence before the Union Public Service Commission.

Day after day we sat down to scrutinize and marshal the evidence. I discovered that H.M. was a man of great integrity and sincerity, who was more sinned against than sinning.

It was a trying time for him. For weeks on end, he fought bravely against heavy odds and against the antipathy of some highly placed persons in the land. The Mundra affair had become a great scandal and someone's blood had to be shed, and it was his blood that was shed.

I had innumerable occasions to elicit all facts from H.M. and others. If anyone connected with the Mundra deal was innocent, it was H.M. Patel.

The U.P.S.C., by a majority of 4 to 1, exonerated H.M. Patel of any negligence or dereliction of duty in the Mundra affair. The Government thereupon decided to drop the charges against him and he was asked by the Cabinet Secretary to report for duty at New Delhi. He, however, decided to submit his resignation. He gave as reasons that having regard to his seniority, Government would have to place him in a position where he could discharge his duties with efficiency and satisfaction only if he enjoyed the fullest confidence of the Prime Minister and other Ministers of the Government. In view of what had happened, that was unlikely. With rare sense of self-respect, he felt it best not to embarrass the Government nor to place himself in an unedifying situation".

*Shri B.K. Nehru, former ICS Officer*

"H.M. was not a financial expert, but it took no time for him to learn his job. Like every other job that he handled, he did it with enthusiasm and did it very successfully. It was this enthusiasm of his which finally resulted in his break with T.T. Krishnamachari and many undeserved months of agony. One of our peculiar contributions to democracy is that it is the civil servant who must suffer for the wrong-doings of the politician.

I was out of India when the Mundhra Deal which caused the crisis actually took place. But I was well aware of the background. The Mundhra Deal was part of an effort by the Finance Minister to restore confidence in the business community after his staggering and unbelievably unrealistic budget of 1957. Every single senior officer of his (including H.M. and myself) as well as the Governor of the Reserve Bank and the Chairman of the State Bank had advised him strongly against taking the foolish decision which not only harmed the economy of India that year but continued to harm it, because of the pattern it set, for a quarter of a century. The immediate consequence of the budget was a disastrous fall in the stock market. It was this that T.T. was trying to correct by giving orders for the purchase of shares by the newly established Life Insurance Corporation of India following on the nationalization of the Life Insurance business. He disregarded the fact that he had no authority to do so. The L.I.C. was an autonomous body with its own investment procedures; the Minister had no authority to order it to do so to get out of his political difficulties. H.M.'s fault was that with his usual enthusiasm to get things done, he had T.T.'s orders carried out.

T.T.'s statement before the Chagla Commission that he had nothing to do with these orders was totally false. There was not an iota of doubt that he had given those orders. Why that man of great ability and character should have told such a lie is something that I cannot explain. I am convinced that there was no financial corruption involved at all; why, then, did he lie? It is not generally known that immediately after giving his false evidence (which Chagla did not believe) T.T. himself went to H.M.'s house (where he was lying ill) and said to him "I am sorry, H.M. I have let you down".

My own evidence before the Vivian Bose Commission helped in clearing H.M.'s honour. But the nit-picking pursuit of the man for having broken this rule or that, continued to plague him till he was finally cleared by the Public Service Commission."

*K.B. Lall, former ICS Officer*

"It is tragic that one who had done so much to develop healthy conventions on relations between Ministers and Civil Servants should have been caught up in a web of misunderstanding and misrepresentation. It is not feasible for all that passes between Ministers and Senior Civil Servants to be recorded in writing. Surrounding circumstances have often proved to be insufficient to sustain definitive findings in regard to the contribution made by the

Minister and the concerned Civil Servant to a particular decision or event. It could not be judicially established in the Mundra case that the Minister had approved the impugned decision. H.M. had therefore to bear responsibility for it. His conduct throughout the enquiry was correct and dignified. He did not stoop down to mobilize evidence in support of his version. He chose finally to retire prematurely."

*Maurice Zinkin, former ICS Officer*

"His love of action in due course got him into trouble. The Mundhra group of companies found itself in financial difficulties. Mundhra was one of the less attractive of the new capitalists who had bought out old British firms, but his group had an important place in the economy, and there were fears that its collapse might have wide ripple effects. It was decided to save the group and H.M. given the job of doing it. This he did with his usual speed and efficiency. Then, when questions arose about the propriety of the rescue, his Minister left him to carry the can.

In the subsequent enquiry, I gave him some assistance in the preparation of his evidence and was much struck by his innocence. He had done what he was told to do, and he had totally failed to cover his back. He had not made sure that everything was in writing on the file, he had not even, immediately questions were asked, taken the precaution of locking up the relevant files. So it was easy for one crucial file to disappear and for everybody else concerned to deny or play their part.

It was not pretty, and he alone came out with honour unstained, though he had to retire."

## Appendix 2

# Emergency Committee Meeting Extracts

SECRET AND IMMEDIATE
COPY NO. 40

6th September, 1947 E.C. 1st Meeting

EMERGENCY COMMITTEE MEETINGS
FIRST MEETING

MINUTES

The 1st meeting of the Emergency Committee was held in the Council Chamber at Government House, New Delhi, at 5 p.m. on Saturday 6th September, 1947....

PRESENT

| | |
|---|---|
| The Viscount MOUNTBATTEN OF BURMA | Governor General of India |

---

Minutes and Papers of the Emergency Committee of the Cabinet, *Mountbatten Papers*, microfilm, rolls 29 and 30, Nehru Memorial Museum and Library, New Delhi.

| | |
|---|---|
| Sardar BALDEV SINGH | Minister of Defence |
| Dr. JOHN MATTHAI | Minister of Railways |
| Mr. K.C. NEOGY | Minister of Refugees |

ALSO PRESENT

| | |
|---|---|
| General Sir ROB LOCKHART | C. in C. of the Indian Army |
| General the Lord ISMAY | Chief of the Governor General's Staff |
| Rao Bahadur V.P. MENON | Secretary, Ministry of States |
| Mr. K.V.K. SUNDARAM | O.S.D. Ministry of Law |
| Captain R.V. Brockman, R.N. | Private Secretary to the Governor General |
| Mr. A. CAMPBELL-JOHNSON | Press Attache to the Governor General |

SECRETARIAT

| | |
|---|---|
| Mr. H.M. PATEL | Cabinet Secretary |
| Mr. V.H. COELHO | Under Secretary to the Cabinet |
| Lieut.-Colonel V.F. ERSKINE-CRUM | Conference Secretary to the Governor General |

The items discussed were:-

ITEM 1. THE SETTING UP OF AN EMERGENCY COMMITTEE OF THE CABINET
ITEM 2. THE MINISTRY OF REFUGEES
ITEM 3. THE DELHI NEWSPAPERS
ITEM 4. THE IMPOSITION OF MARTIAL LAW.
ITEM 5. THE FREEZING OF BANK ASSETS IN WEST PUNJAB
ITEM 6. LIAISON WITH PAKISTAN
ITEM 7. DISCIPLINE IN THE ARMY
ITEM 8. SETTING-UP OF A RELIEF COMMITTEE
ITEM 9. ROAD AND AIR TRANSPORT
ITEM 10. RAF TRANSPORT AIRCRAFT
ITEM 11. DISPOSALS FOR REFUGEES
ITEM 12. LEAFLETS

ITEM 1. THE SETTING-UP OF AN EMERGENCY COMMITTEE OF THE CABINET.

THE GOVERNOR GENERAL expressed his great sense of honour at having been invited by the Cabinet to join the Emergency Committee. He pointed out that it would be quite legal and proper to make this a Committee of the Cabinet on the condition that the membership consisted of only himself and Cabinet Ministers. By doing this, the Committee would be able to derive its power from the Cabinet; and also benefit from the use of the Cabinet Secretariat.

A paper entitled "The Setting-up of an Emergency Committee of the Cabinet" was then considered. Certain amendments to this paper were made. It will be circulated separately as amended (as E.C.P.1.). It was stated that Major General Rees would probably be appointed Head of the Military Emergency Staff.

THE GOVERNOR GENERAL stated that the proposals in this paper had been based on an organisation for speed; a similar principle to that which had been used in the United Kingdom during the emergency of the war had been suggested.

THE COMMITTEE:

(i) approved the paper entitled "The Setting-up of an Emergency Committee of the Cabinet", as amended in discussion;
(ii) directed the Conference Secretary to the Governor General to circulate this paper, as amended;
(iii) directed the Cabinet Secretary to arrange for those concerned to be invited to a meeting at 11 a.m. the following day, at which the Governor and Ministers of East Punjab would be present;
(iv) directed the Commander-in-Chief of the Indian Army to appoint the Head of the Military Emergency Staff; and to set up a map room in Government House;
(v) directed the Commander-in-Chief of the Indian Army to attempt to obtain the services of Colonel Nayar as his representative on the Public Relations Committee. …

ITEM 7. DISCIPLINE IN THE ARMY.

SIR ROB LOCKHART reported that the feeling among the troops had recently become much worse. There had been what almost amounted to a mutiny in one Pakistan battalion the previous day in Gujranwala. It had been necessary to remove the non-Muslims element of this battalion immediately.

ITEM 8. SETTING UP OF A RELIEF COMMITTEE.

THE GOVERNOR GENERAL suggested that a Relief Committee of representatives of non-official organisations should be set up for overall co-ordination purposes. He stated that Lady Mountbatten had offered to organise such a Committee, which could work under the Minister of Refugees.

THE PRIME MINISTER said that he understood that there was at present a local Relief Committee functioning in Delhi. There were probably also local ones in some of the East Punjab cities. He agreed that a high-level Committee, as suggested by His Excellency, would be most useful.

THE COMMITTEE:

(1) approved the setting-up of a Relief Committee of representatives of non-official organisations, with which the Health Minister would be associated and which would work under the Minister of Refugees.

SECRET AND IMMEDIATE
COPY NO. 34

7th September,1947 E.C. 2nd Meeting

EMERGENCY COMMITTEE MEETINGS
SECOND MEETING

MINUTES

The 2nd Meeting of the Emergency Committee was held in the Council Chamber at Government House, New Delhi, at 11 a.m. on Sunday 7th September, 1947....

The items discussed were:

ITEM 1. THE SITUATION IN DELHI
ITEM 2. OUTSTANDING ITEMS
ITEM 3. CHOLERA.
ITEM 4. STANDING CROPS IN THE PUNJAB.
ITEM 5. HOSPITALS IN LAHORE.
ITEM 6. COURT OF ENQUIRY AT AMBALA.
ITEM 7. ESCORTS FOR TRAINS
ITEM 8. THE NORTH-WEST FRONTIER PROVINCE.
ITEM 9. THE SITUATION IN EAST PUNJAB.
ITEM 10. PUBLIC HOLIDAYS. ......

ITEM 1. THE SITUATION IN DELHI

THE GOVERNOR GENERAL stated that the situation in Delhi had worsened very considerably during the previous 24 hours. There had been a large number of incidents; these included employees of his estate having been stabbed. In his opinion, the trouble had grown up through refugees arriving in such very large numbers before any refugee organisation was ready to receive them.

The Banning of Fire-arms.

THE GOVERNOR GENERAL suggested the possibility of issuing an ordinance making the carrying of any form of weapon illegal. This would be a temporary measure. The question arose whether it should include the banning of the carrying of kirpans by Sikhs.

THE DEPUTY PRIME MINISTER said that any suggestion to ban kirpans would raise very great difficulties, as they had been recognised by the Government as religious weapons for many years. The Punjab Government had never been able to introduce such a ban; Bombay and other places had failed also.

SARDAR BALDEV SINGH stated that there was no restriction on the carrying of kirpans even in West Punjab.

RAJKUMARI AMRIT KAUR stated that, although a certain number of casualities in the Delhi hospitals were suffering from bullet wounds, the majority were victims of stabbing and slashes.

THE GOVERNOR GENERAL said that, whereas religious tenets were obviously to be respected, if a general ban on the carrying of arms were ordered, it would be out of the question to make exceptions in the case of one community. He asked whether it would be possible for the Sikhs to carry a very small emblem, sufficient to satisfy religious tenets. SIR ROB LOCKHART confirmed that kirpans had been strictly limited in size in 1922-3. He believed that in Calcutta the Sikhs had themselves agreed to limit the size. Another possibility was that kirpans should be sealed up to render them incapable of being drawn.

THE GOVERNOR GENERAL stressed the world-wide effect that continued disturbances in Delhi, the capital city, would have. Possibly kirpans could be kept in houses and not be taken out except to a specified area. The question was which decision would result in most people being killed — the banning of kirpans or the safe-guarding of the Sikh religious feelings by letting them continue to carry them.

THE GOVERNOR GENERAL asked Sardar Baldev Singh whether he could consult the religious leaders of the Sikh community in Delhi and ask them voluntarily to accept restrictions on the carrying of kirpans by Sikhs.

THE PRIME MINISTER suggested that another step which might immediately be imposed would be an ordinance making it an offence for anybody to be seen in public with an unsheathed weapon; or with any weapon of the category of firearms, explosives and bombs.

THE COMMITTEE:

(i) directed the Minister of Defence to consult the Sikh leaders in Delhi with a view to their voluntarily inducing the Sikhs in Delhi not to carry kirpans except in a specified area.

(ii) directed the Deputy Prime Minister to form a sub-committee consisting of himself, the Minister of Defence and the C. in C., further to consider the question of banning the carriage of arms in Delhi.

<u>Refugees in Delhi.</u>

THE DEPUTY PRIME MINISTER suggested that measures might be taken to prevent the influx of refugees into Delhi. RAJKUMARI AMRIT KAUR said that a further influx would result in the health administration of Delhi collapsing. THE PRIME MINISTER stressed the desirability of making proper arrangements in any other cities to which they might be sent. He stated that the Prime Minister of Madras had already offered to take 10,000 refugees.

THE COMMITTEE:

(iv) decided that the Prime Minister should telegraph the Prime Ministers of Provinces (excluding West Bengal and Assam) to ask whether they could accept refugees;

(v) directed the Ministry of States to enquire from various States the number of refugees they could accept;

(vi) directed the Ministry of Railways, on receipt of the information in (iv) and (v) above, to make arrangements for the movement by train of refugees from the disturbed areas to the various destinations;

(vii) directed the Ministry of Communications to examine the possibility of diverting aircraft carrying refugees to places other than Delhi;

(viii) directed the C. in C. of the Indian Army to find out what military barracks were available throughout India and the States for use by refugees.

<u>Police and Military Action</u>

THE GOVERNOR GENERAL stated that it had been reported to him that there had been two cases in the last few days in Delhi of Police firing over the heads of crowds. He pointed out that it was a rule, which had been proved in every riot during the last 50 years, that, if any firing took place, in such circumstances, it should be directed with the object of killing.

LORD ISMAY suggested that possibility of reinforcing the existing police force in Delhi in a manner similar to what had been done in London during the General Strike of 1926 — that was to draw on reliable and reputable citizens to volunteer for "special constable" duties. Such persons might be given armlets and armed with pistols. He had some of the older students in mind. He suggested that they should get no pay but should, if necessary, receive a subsistence allowance.

RAJKUMARI AMRIT KAUR stated that certain citizens had already asked her whether they could not help in this respect. THE PRIME MINISTER said that he considered that it was an excellent idea.

On SIR ROB LOCKHART's suggestion, the PRIME MINISTER also agreed that the provision of patrols of armed officers from the military Headquarters would also be most useful.

RAJKUMARI AMRIT KAUR also suggested the use of motor-cycle squads, particularly for reconnaissance patrols.

THE COMMITTEE:

(ix) directed the Minister of Home Affairs to ensure that the Chief Commissioner of Delhi gave orders that any firing on crowds should be "shooting to kill";

(x) directed the Minister of Home Affairs to take steps to increase the subsidiary police force of volunteers in Delhi.

(xi) directed the C. in C. of the Indian Army to make arrangements, in conjunction with the civil authorites, for the provision of armed patrols of officers from military Headquarters in Delhi. ......

<u>ITEM 6.</u> <u>COURT OF ENQUIRY AT AMBALA.</u>

THE COMMITTEE:

directed the Commander-in-Chief of the Indian Army to report, when received, the results of the Committee of Enquiry which had been set up at Ambala to examine the behaviour of some Pakistan troops who were said to have opened fire from a train on non-Muslims and killed or wounded some 60 persons.

ITEM 7. ESCORTS FOR TRAINS

THE PRIME MINISTER asked whether trains were still being run without proper escorts. In his opinion, train services should be suspended if proper escorts could not be provided.

DR. MATTHAI said that the latest suggestion was that in areas which were not generally disturbed trains should run with police escorts; in those areas which were generally disturbed they should have armed military escorts.

SIR ROB LOCKHART advocated the adoption of the principle that no train should run which was not adequately guarded. He suggested that passengers should be searched before being allowed to board the train. He went on to say that the Quarter-Master General at Supreme Headquarters held a conference every day to decide which trains should or should not run.

THE GOVERNOR GENERAL reiterated his opinion expressed at the previous day's meeting, that the only final answer to attacks on trains was that, whenever a train arrived at a station after a massacre, those guards who were not wounded should be immediately shot.

DR MATTHAI pointed out that the Railway police were under the jurisdiction of provincial governments.

THE COMMITTEE:

(i) directed the Ministry of Law to prepare legislation empowering the search of intending passengers on trains;
(ii) directed the Ministry of Law further to consider the means of introducing legislation to enforce discipline among those whose duty it was to protect trains;
(iii) directed the Commander-in-Chief of the Indian Army to issue orders to ensure that military escorts on trains who did not do their duty would be court-martialled;
(iv) directed the Cabinet Secretary to arrange for the Quarter-Master General, Supreme Headquarters, to attend the meeting the following day. .....

ITEM 10. PUBLIC HOLIDAYS.

THE COMMITTEE:

Directed the Minister of Home Affairs to consider the desirability of cancelling all public holidays during the present emergency.

SECRET
E.C.P.2.
COPY NO.63

EMERGENCY COMMITTEE PAPER NO.2

OUTSTANDING ITEMS

The attached list of items, on which action has been ordered by the Emergency Committee, will be reported on at the meeting of the Committee at 11 a.m. on Sunday, 7th September.

Sd/-
V. ERSKINE CRUM
Lieut-Colonel.
<u>Conference Secretary to the Governor-General</u>

## OUTSTANDING ITEMS

| Serial | Meeting at Which Ordered. | Action | Detail |
|---|---|---|---|
| 1. | 1st | Principal Private Secretary to the Prime Minister | To report whether the leaflets, which he and Mr. Mahomed Ali had been directed (at the Lahore J.D.C. meeting on 29th August) to draft, had yet been dropped. |
| 2. | 1st | Ministry of Refugees | to examine the possibility of making available to refugees some of the assets of the Disposals Board. |
| 3. | 1st | Ministry of Refugees | To set up an Information Bureau for Refugees. |
| 4. | 1st | Ministry of Law | To draft, for consideration by the Committee, an ordinance "stiffening" the Acts at present in force in East Punjab, particularly so as to enable military as well as civil courts summarily to try offenders. |
| 5. | 1st | Ministry of Law | To draft, for consideration by the Committee, an ordinance extending the Punjab Acts to Delhi. |
| 6. | 1st | Ministry of Law | To draft, for consideration by the Committee, an ordinance under which civilian road transport could be requisitioned. |

| | | | |
|---|---|---|---|
| 7. | 1st | Ministry of Law | To draft, for consideration by the Committee, an ordinance under which aircraft belonging to private civil lines could be requisitioned. |
| 8. | 1st | Commander-in-Chief, Indian Army | To appoint the Head of the Military Emergency Staff; and to set up a map room in Government House. |
| 9. | 1st | Commander-in-Chief, Indian Army. | To attempt to obtain the services of Colonel Nayar as his representative on the Public Relations Committee. |
| 10. | 1st | Commander-in-Chief, Indian Army. | To report further on the possible provision of Army officers to act as civil magistrates in East Punjab, or in military courts. |
| 11. | 1st | Commander-in-Chief, Indian Army. | To report to the Committee the circumstances in which the R.A.F. transport aircraft, which were supposed to be ferrying personnel between Delhi and Lahore, had returned empty from Lahore on 6th September. |
| 12. | 1st | Cabinet Secretary | To arrange for the preparation of a brief on the freezing of bank assets in West Punjab, for Chief of Governor-General's Staff to discuss this matter with the Pakistan Government. |

| | | | |
|---|---|---|---|
| 13. | 1st | Cabinet Secretary | To inform the Committee of the name of the person appointed to be Secretary of the Ministry of Refugees. |
| 14. | 1st | Public Relations Committee. | To attempt to improve the reporting by the Delhi newspapers of the communal situation; and to report. |

SECRET AND IMMEDIATE
COPY NO. 34

7th September, 1947 E.C. 3rd Meeting

EMERGENCY COMMITTEE MEETINGS
THIRD MEETING

MINUTES

The 3rd Meeting of the Emergency Committee was held in the Council Chamber at Government House, New Delhi, at 6 p.m. on Sunday, 7th September,1947. .....

The items discussed were:

ITEM 1. REFUGEES — THE UNITED PROVINCES
ITEM 2. THE SITUATION IN DELHI
ITEM 3. THE MOVEMENT OF TROOPS
ITEM 4. THE SITUATION IN THE PUNJAB
ITEM 5. DRAFT ANNOUNCEMENT REGARDING EVACUATION
ITEM 6. THE APPOINTMENT OF HIGH COMMISSIONER IN THE N.W.F.P. ... ....

ITEM 1. REFUGEES — THE UNITED PROVINCES

THE COMMITTEE:
directed the Minister of Refugees to avoid, in principle, sending refugees to Cawnpore and other cities and large towns in the United Provinces.

ITEM 2. THE SITUATION IN DELHI

THE GOVERNOR GENERAL said that requests for protection had been received from the United States Ambassador and the Australian and Pakistan High Commissioners. There was no need to stress how embarrassing it would be to India if anything happened to these diplomatic representatives.

The importance of guarding the All-India Radio transmitter was also stressed.

THE DEPUTY PRIME MINISTER stated that an Order had been promulgated that day making it an offence to carry any arms in Delhi, including kirpans of greater length than nine inches; all kirpans under this length would have to be sheathed and concealed. An Order for requisitioning civilian transport had also been promulgated.

THE COMMITTEE:

(i) directed the Commander-in-Chief of the Indian Army to place guards forthwith on the residences of the American Ambassador and the Australian and Pakistan High Commissioners;

(ii) directed the Commander-in-Chief of the Indian Army to place a guard on the All-India Radio transmitter;

(iii) decided to issue forthwith an Ordinance extending the Punjab Acts to Delhi;

(iv) directed the Public Relations Committee to put a notice in the Press asking the owners of motor cycles to volunteer at Police Headquarters for patrols under police auspices. .......

<u>ITEM 5.</u> <u>DRAFT ANNOUNCEMENT REGARDING EVACUATION</u>

A draft statement to be issued by the Governments of India and Pakistan, was handed round at the meeting. A copy, as amended in discussion, is attached as Appendix A to these minutes.

THE COMMITTEE:

directed the Cabinet Secretary to arrange for a copy of this draft announcement to be given to Sardar Nishtar at the Partition Council meeting the following morning, so that he might discuss it with the other members of the Government of Pakistan.

APPENDIX "A"

## DRAFT ANNOUNCEMENT REGARDING EVACUATION

(To be Agreed with the Government of Pakistan)

The situation in the Punjab has developed in such a way that mass movement of Muslims from East Punjab and of non-Muslims from West Punjab has become inevitable.

The Governments of India and of Pakistan have therefore decided that the movement of these people from East to West Punjab and vice versa is to have first priority. They have agreed to cooperate with each other on this matter to the fullest extent and to take all steps to ensure that the movements in both directions are completed with the greatest possible speed and with the fullest measure of security.

Both Governments appeal for the co-operation of every member of the public in this matter. Violence begets violence and it cannot be too strongly emphasized that any interference with the movement in either direction will inevitably delay and imperil the movement in the opposite direction. Consequently, any persons who may attempt such interference will, in effect, grievously injure their own people.

The Governments of India and Pakistan are resolved to use all available resources to expedite and secure the safety of these movements; and they have armed themselves with the most drastic powers to ensure that wrongdoers are summarily dealt with in the severest manner.

SECRET AND IMMEDIATE
COPY NO. 45

8th September, 1947 E.C. Fourth Meeting

EMERGENCY COMMITTEE MEETINGS
FOURTH MEETING

MINUTES

The 4th meeting of the Emergency Committee was held in the Council Chamber at Government House, New Delhi, at 10 a.m. on Monday 8th September, 1947. ....

The items discussed were:

ITEM 1. Situation in East Punjab
ITEM 2. Situation in Delhi
ITEM 3. Outstanding Items (E.C.P.3)
ITEM 4. Movement of trains.
ITEM 5. The supply of arms to Provinces
ITEM 6. The supply of uniform for Police in East Punjab
ITEM 7. The Chief Commissioner, Delhi
ITEM 8. The Prime Minister's visit to SONEPAT. ...... .....

ITEM 1. THE SITUATION IN EAST PUNJAB

It was reported that the general situation in East Punjab was quiet. No reports had been received of major incidents during the last 24 hours. The process of evacuation was going smoothly.

ITEM 2. THE SITUATION IN DELHI

It was stated that Delhi had been fairly quiet the previous night. Minor looting had taken place in Connaught Circus that morning. There was criticism that the police and soldiers had not been very active and had shown a tendency to await orders rather than to take immediate action.

Reference was made to the necessity for guarding the houses of all foreign representatives in New Delhi.

RAJKUMARI AMRIT KAUR emphasized the need for all hospitals in Delhi being properly protected.

THE COMMITTEE:

(i) directed the Ministry of External Affairs and Commonwealth Relations to provide the Commander-in-Chief of the Indian Army with a list of all foreign representatives in Delhi and their addresses, so that the protection of these persons might be ensured; this protection was also to include the Nawab of Chhatari, who was at present at Hyderabad House.

(ii) directed the Commander-in-Chief of the Indian Army to make arrangements for the protection of all hospitals in Delhi.

ITEM 3. OUTSTANDING ITEMS.
(E.C.P.3)

The meeting considered a list of items on which action had previously been ordered by the Committee.

In connection with Serial 5 of this list, it was stated that a public appeal for volunteers to augment the subsidiary police force in Delhi was being issued that day. It was suggested that some ex-soldiers among the refugees who had come to Delhi would make suitable volunteers.

In connection with Serial 6, it was agreed that the special motor-cycle squads to be formed in Delhi would be under the Command of the police, but would be available to the military authorities.

In connection with Serial 6,

THE COMMITTEE:

(i) directed the Ministry of Home Affairs to issue a notification cancelling public holidays during the present emergency.

(ii) directed the Ministry of Home Affairs to arrange for the Chief Commissioner of Delhi to lay on a service of requisitioned buses to get Government servants (who would have to work for longer hours during the emergency) to work; and to obtain from all other Ministries a list of those persons who wished to make use of this bus service.

In connection with Serials 8 and 9, the DEPUTY PRIME MINISTER stated that he had summoned the Sikh leaders in Delhi to an interview that morning. Sardar Baldev Singh had also been present. He had told the Sikh leaders that, if the present state of affairs persisted, a number of Sikhs would find themselves in concentration camps. The Sikh leaders had asked why it was suggested that the Sikhs were the people primarily responsible for the present trouble; he had replied that the answer to this would be made apparent if all trouble stopped when the Sikhs desisted.

Incidents of bands of Sikhs visiting various bungalows in Delhi were quoted.

SIR ROB LOCKHART gave his opinion that the Order prohibiting the carriage of weapons should include lathis.

THE COMMITTEE:

(iii) directed the Ministry of Home Affairs to ensure that the Order forbidding the carriage of weapons in Delhi was extended to include lathis.

(iv) directed the Ministry of Information and Broadcasting to take every possible measure (including use of loud-speaker cars, beats of drums and broadcasting, etc.) to publicise the Order forbidding the carriage of weapons in Delhi.

(v) directed the Commander-in-Chief of the Indian Army and the Ministry of Home Affairs to issue an Order to the military and the police in New Delhi authorizing them to search houses from which shooting took place.

(vi) directed the Commander-in-Chief of the Indian Army and the Ministry of Home Affairs to instruct the Delhi Area Commander and the Chief Commissioner to set up a Joint Headquarters. ........

In connection with Serial no. 23, the CHIEF OF STAFF, INDIAN ARMY HEADQUARTERS, stated that a Court of Enquiry into the behaviour of certain Pakistan troops who were said to have fired from a train on non-Muslims near Ambala had been held. The train containing these troops had been permitted to proceed with those who had been judged guilty under arrest. The Commander-in-Chief, Pakistan, had been requested to take immediate and severe action against these persons immediately he received the proceedings of the Court of Enquiry.

THE COMMITTEE:
(xii) directed the Commander-in-Chief of the Indian Army to report on the punishment awarded to the Pakistan troops who had been found guilty of firing from a train on non-Muslims near Ambala.

RAJKUMARI AMRIT KAUR reported the details of casualities admitted to hospitals in Delhi the previous night. A copy of the report is attached as Appendix A to these minutes. ……..

ITEM 8. THE PRIME MINISTER'S VISITS TO SONEPAT

The PRIME MINISTER stated that he intended to visit Sonepat the following afternoon. He would address a mass meeting there. It would doubtless include numbers of people who had been involved in incidents of arson and murder in that area.

APPENDIX 'A'

Casualties admitted to Delhi Hospitals up to 10 p.m. on 7th September, 1947

| | |
|---|---|
| Muslim Male | 243 |
| Non-Muslim Male | 89 |
| Muslim Female | 38 |
| Non-Muslim Female | 1 |
| Muslim Children | 21 |
| Non-Muslim children | 4 |
| Unknown | 5 |
| <u>Gun-shot wounds</u> | |
| Muslim | 20 |
| Non-Muslim | 45 |
| Unknown | 1 |
| <u>Died in Hospital</u> | |
| Hindus | 10 |
| Muslim children | 3 |
| Muslim females | 3 |
| Unknown | 17 |
| | 33 |

| | | | | |
|---|---|---|---|---|
| Dead admitted | to hospital on | | 7th September 1947 | ....... 40 |
| Casualties | -do- | -do- | 6th September 1947 | ....... 200 |
| -do- | -do- | -do- | 7th September 1947 | ....... 136 |
| -do- | -do- | -do- | 8th September 1947 | .......Numerous |

SECRET
E.C.P.3.
COPY NO.30

EMERGENCY COMMITTEE PAPER NO.3.

OUTSTANDING ITEMS

The attached list of items, on which action has been ordered by the Emergency Committee, will be reported on at the meeting of the Committee at 10 a.m. on Monday, 8th September.

Sd/- Erskine Crum
Lieut-Colonel.

7th September, 1947

Conference Secretary to the Governor-General

## OUTSTANDING ITEMS

| Serial | Meeting at Which Ordered. | Action | Detail |
|---|---|---|---|
| 1. | 2nd | Private Secretary to the Governor-General | To draft a telegram to the Governor General of Pakistan concerning protection for the hospitals and girls' institution in Lahore, which the Minister of Health had mentioned. |
| 2 | 1st | Principal Private Secretary to the Prime Minister | To report whether the leaflets which he and Mr. Mahomed Ali had been directed (at the Lahore J.D.C. meeting on 29th August) to draft, had yet been dropped. |
| 3 | 2nd | Principal Private Secretary | To report when replies were received to the Prime Minister to the telegrams which had been dispatched to Prime Ministers of Provinces, asking them how many refugees they could accept. |
| 4 | 2nd | Ministry of Home Affairs. | To ensure that the Chief Commissioner of Delhi gave orders that any firing on crowds should be "shooting to kill". |

| | | | |
|---|---|---|---|
| 5 | 2nd | Ministry of Home Affairs. | To take measures to increase the subsidiary police force of volunteers In Delhi. |
| 6 | 2nd | Ministry of Home Affairs | To examine the possibility of using motor-cycle squads for reconnaissance purposes in Delhi. |
| 7 | 2nd | Ministry of Home Affairs | To consider the desirability of cancelling all public holidays during the present emergency. |
| 8 | 2nd | Deputy Prime Minister | To form a sub-committee consisting of himself, the Minister of Defence and the C.in C., further to consider the question of the banning of arms in Delhi. |
| 9 | 2nd | Minister of Defence | To consult the Sikh leaders in Delhi with a view to their voluntarily inducing the Sikhs in Delhi not tocarry kirpans except in a specified area. |
| 10 | 2nd | Ministry of States | To enquire from various States the number of refugees they could accept. |
| 11 | 2nd | Ministry of Railways | On receipt of the information in serials 3 and 10 above, to make arrangements for the movement by train of refugees from the disturbed areas to the various destinations. |
| 12 | 2nd | Ministry of Communications | To examine the possibility of diverting aircraft carrying refugees to places other than Delhi. |

| | | | |
|---|---|---|---|
| 13 | 1st | Ministry of Refugees | To examine the possibility of making available to refugees some of the assets of the Disposals Board, in conjunction with the Ministry of Industries and Supplies. |
| 14 | 1st | Ministry of Refugees | To set up an Information Bureau for Refugees. |
| 15 | 1st | Ministry of Law | To draft, in conjunction with C. in C.'s staff, and the Governor of East Punjab, for consideration by the Committee, an ordinance "stiffening" the Acts at present in force in East Punjab, particularly so as to enable military as well as civil courts summarily to try offenders. |
| 16 | 1st | Ministry of Law | To draft, for consideration by the Committee, an ordinance extending the Punjab Acts to Delhi. |
| 17 | 1st | Ministry of Law | To draft, for consideration by the Committee, an ordinance under which civilian road transport could be requisitioned. |
| 18 | 1st | Ministry of Law | To draft, for consideration by the Committee, an ordinance under which aircraft belonging to private civil lines could be requisitioned. |
| 19. | 2nd | Ministry of Law | To prepare legislation empowering the search of intending passengers on trains. |

| | | | |
|---|---|---|---|
| 20 | 2nd | Ministry of Law | Further to consider the means of introducing legislation to enforce discipline among those whose duty it was to protect trains. |
| 21 | 1st | Commander-in-Chief Indian Army. | To attempt to obtain the services of Colonel Nayar as his representative on the Public Relations Committee. |
| 22 | 1st | Commander-in-Chief Indian Army | To report further on the possible provision of Army officers to act as civil magistrates in East Punjab, or in military courts. |
| 23 | 2nd | Commander-in-Chief Indian Army | To report, which received, the results of the Committee of Enquiry which had been set up at Ambala to examine the behaviour of some Pakistan troops who were said to have fired from a train on non-Muslims and killed or wounded some 60 persons. |
| 24 | 2nd | Commander-in-Chief Indian Army | To find out what military barracks were available throughout India and the states for use by refugees. |
| 25 | 2nd | Commander-in-Chief Indian Army | To issue orders to ensure that military escorts on trains who did not do their duty would be court-martialled. |
| 26 | 2nd | Commander-in-Chief Indian Army | To examine the possibility of moving the Headquarters of East Punjab District from Lahore to Amritsar, leaving a liaison mission in Lahore. |

| | | | |
|---|---|---|---|
| 27 | 2nd | Commander-in-Chief Indian Army | To make arrangements, in conjunction with the civil authority, for the provision of armed patrols of officers from Military Headquarters in Delhi. |
| 28 | 2nd | Ministry of Health | To dispatch a telegram to the Minister of Health, Pakistan, drawing his attention to the insanitary conditions in refugee camps in Pakistan, and particularly to a reported case of cholera. |
| 29 | 2nd | Ministry of Food | To discuss the question of standing crops in East Punjab with representatives of the Provincial Governments, and to report any further action that was required. |
| 30 | 1st | Cabinet Secretary | To arrange for the Partition Council to take up the question of the freezing of bank assets in West Punjab. |
| 31 | 1st | Cabinet Secretary | To inform the Committee of the name of the person appointed to be Secretary of the Ministry of Refugees. |
| 32. | 2nd | Cabinet Secretary | To convene a meeting of Secretaries to discuss the provision of staff (including a Financial Adviser) and accommodation for the Ministry of Refugees. |

| | | | |
|---|---|---|---|
| 33. | 1st | Public Relations Committee | To attempt to improve the reporting by the Delhi newspapers of the communal situation; and to report. |
| 34 | 3rd | Public Relations Committee | To put a notice in the Press asking the owners of motor cycles to volunteer at Police Headquarters for patrols under police auspices. |
| 35 | 3rd | Commander-in-Chief Indian Army | To convey the request of the Committee to the Supreme Commander that the units of the Indian Army at present stationed in the N.W.F.P. should be moved to India forthwith. |
| 36 | 3rd | Commander-in-Chief Indian Army | To issue executve orders for the move of Indian Army Units stationed in Hyderabad. |
| 37 | 3rd | Deputy Prime Minister | To discuss with Sardar Nishtar, with a view to the latter taking the matter up with the other members of the Pakistan Government, the appointment of a Deputy High Commissioner for India In Lahore. |
| 38 | 3rd | Principal Private Secretary to the Prime Minister | To telegraph to the Deputy High Commissioner for India in Lahore, asking whether it was true that the West Punjab Government had issued an order forbidding refugees to take their arms with them. |

| | | | |
|---|---|---|---|
| 39 | 3rd | Ministry of Defence | To investigate the circumstances in which an order had been issued by the Ministry as coming from the Joint Defence Council, stopping all movement of troops from Hyderabad. |
| 40 | 3rd | Ministry of Defence | To arrange for the Ministry of Defence constabulary to be armed. |
| 41 | 3rd | Ministry of Refugees | To appoint a representative to the Government of East Punjab |
| 42 | 3rd | Ministry of Information and Broadcasting | To erect a transmitter at Jullundur, so as to improve communications between there and Delhi. |

SECRET AND IMMEDIATE
COPY NO. 50

9th September,1947 E.C. 5TH MEETING

EMERGENCY COMMITTEE MEETINGS
5TH MEETING

MINUTES

The 5th meeting of the Emergency Committee was held in the Council Chamber at Government House, New Delhi, at 10 a.m. on Tuesday 9th September,1947. .....

The items discussed were:

ITEM 1. THE SITUATION IN EAST PUNJAB
ITEM 2 THE SITUATION IN DELHI
ITEM 3 DELHI COMMITTEE
ITEM 4 OUTSTANDING ITEMS (E.C.P.4)
ITEM 5 EVACUATION FROM SIND
ITEM 6 THE MOVEMENT OF MEOS FROM DELHI
ITEM 7 THE MOVEMENT OF FOOD
ITEM 8 THE UNITED PROVINCES
ITEM 9 MOVEMENT OF REFUGEES BETWEEN EAST AND WEST PUNJAB
ITEM 10 MARTIAL LAW
ITEM 11 DELHI UNIVERSITY ........

ITEM 1. THE SITUATION IN EAST PUNJAB

The cities were reported quiet, but tension was high in the rural areas. Evacuation of refugees was continuing despite attacks on refugee columns. It was stated that cholera had broken out among refugees.

ITEM 2. THE SITUATION IN DELHI

It was reported that many incidents, including arson and looting, had taken place during the previous day. On two occasions, bands of Muslims opened fire on troops. During the night the city was quiet.

ITEM 3. DELHI COMMITTEE

It was decided to set up a Committee to deal with the local situation in Delhi, so that the Emergency Committee might confine itself more to issues affecting India as a whole. The members of the Delhi Committee were to be the Chief Commissioner, the Sub-Area Commander and the I.G. of Police. Subsequent to the meeting it was decided to request Mr. Bhabha to act as Chairman of this Committee. It would report daily to the Emergency Committee of the Cabinet.

THE COMMITTEE:

(i) directed the Delhi Committee to consider the following matters and report the following day:-
   (a) the possibility of concentrating, for purposes of better protection, the Muslim officials of the Government of India;
   (b) arrangements to get Government Servants to work, including possibly a system whereby special constables would be dropped off to guard the officials families;
   (c) the protection of the storage and movement of petrol;
   (d) movement of food from depots to ration shops and protection for this movement;
   (e) the provision of food for hospitals;
   (f) the disposal of persons let out of hospitals;
   (g) the burial of the dead, including those in hospitals;
   (h) measures to make full use of private enterprise, including special constables;
   (i) ways and means of getting the Meos at present in a camp in Delhi to trains, when these were available to move them;
   (j) measures to be taken in connection with the arrival that day of 100 R.S.S. young men, who were reported to have come by train from Amritsar with the object of creating further disturbances in Delhi;
   (k) the setting-up of an Information Room of its own;

(ii) directed the Public Relations Committee to arrange publicity for the Delhi Committee, and to appoint a representative to the latter;
(iii) directed the Public Relations Committee to accord publicity to the fact that special constables and volunteers for duty on motor cycles might enlist at any Police Station……….

ITEM 6. THE MOVEMENT OF MEOS FROM DELHI

Rajkumari AMRIT KAUR stated that she could not guarantee the health of Delhi if the Meo camp, in which upto 20,000 refugees had gathered, was not moved in the near future. It was stated that the majority of these Meos were States' subjects and had come from Bharatpur and Alwar. Dr MATTHAI said that the movement of the number involved would mean arranging for seven special refugee trains. It was suggested that the Meos should be sent direct to Bahawalpur.

THE COMMITTEE :-
(i) directed the Minister of Railways to arrange for the provision of seven (or the requisite number) of trains to move the Meo refugees from Delhi;
(ii) directed the Ministry of States to ask the Nawab of Bahawalpur to receive these refugees and also 10,000 Muslim refugees who were in Bikaner. …..

ITEM 8. THE UNITED PROVINCES

The PRIME MINISTER stated that he had received a telegram from the Prime Minister of the United Provinces, saying that reinforcements of police and military were required on the Western border.

The COMMITTEE:
directed the Principal Private Secretary to the Prime Minister to ask the Prime Minister of the United Provinces to take this matter up with General Tuker. ……

APPENDIX "C"

Casualties admitted to Delhi Hospitals
upto 10 p.m. on 8th September,
1947

| | | | |
|---|---|---|---|
| Total casualties | ...... | 153 | |
| | | | |
| Muslims | ...... | 67 | |
| Non-Muslims | ...... | 72 | |
| Muslim females | ...... | 10 | |
| Muslim children | ...... | 1 | |
| Non-Muslim children | ...... | 1 | |
| Unknown | ...... | 2 | |
| | | | |
| <u>Gun-shot wounds</u> | ...... | 56 | |
| | | | |
| Muslims | ...... | 11 | |
| Non-Muslims | ...... | 48 | |
| Deaths | ...... | 34 | |
| Non-Muslims | ...... | 86 | stabbings |
| Dead bodies | ...... | 80 | |
| lying in the hospital since 5 days waiting to be cleared. | | 34 | |
| | | 114 | |

SECRET AND IMMEDIATE
COPY NO. 50

10th September, 1947 E.C. 6TH MEETING

EMERGENCY COMMITTEE MEETINGS
SIXTH MEETING

MINUTES

The 6th meeting of the Emergency Committee was held in the Council Chamber at Government House, New Delhi, at 10 a.m. on Wednesday 10th September, 1947. .....

The items discussed were:

ITEM 1. SITUATION IN PUNJAB
ITEM 2 SITUATION IN PESHAWAR
ITEM 3 SITUATION IN DELHI
ITEM 4 THE DELHI EMERGENCY COMMITTEE
ITEM 5 CHOLERA
ITEM 6 OUTSTANDING ITEMS
ITEM 7 PAKISTAN HIGH COMMISSIONER
ITEM 8 PASSES FOR IMPORTANT PERSONS
ITEM 9 HEALTH CONDITIONS IN EAST PUNJAB
ITEM 10 THE PRIME MINISTER'S VISIT TO SONEPAT
ITEM 11 MOVEMENT COMMITTEE
ITEM 12 THE RELATIVE PRIORITY OF EVACUATION OF REFUGEES AND THE MAINTENANCE OF LAW AND ORDER. .....

<u>ITEM 1.</u> <u>SITUATION IN THE PUNJAB</u>

(a) <u>EAST PUNJAB</u>

It was reported that incidents had continued during the previous day. There had been several attacks on trains, the escorts of which had inflicted casualties on the attackers in some cases. Details from Army H.Q. sitrep are attached at Appendix A.

(b) <u>WEST PUNJAB</u>

It was stated that there had been a number of incidents on the previous day, but that Lahore was quiet.

ITEM 2. SITUATION IN PESHAWAR

It was stated that the cantonment was quiet but tension prevailed outside. The city was not yet quite under control and there had been some looting by Afridis. Reports that the city was in flames and that there had been incidents between Hindu and Muslim troops were not true.

ITEM 3. SITUATION IN DELHI

It was reported that all parts of the city were under control and that vigorous patrolling by military continues. Details from Army H.Q. sitrep are attached at Appendix A.

The GOVERNOR GENERAL reported an incident which had occurred the previous evening, and in which his Deputy Military Secretary had been wounded and the driver of the car in which the latter was travelling had been killed. This had occurred when troops had opened fire on the car without challenging.

THE COMMITTEE:
directed Commander-in-Chief, Indian Army, to ensure that orders were given to the troops in Delhi not to open fire on cars without first challenging them.

ITEM 4. THE DELHI EMERGENCY COMMITTEE

The GOVERNOR-GENERAL stated that he had asked Mr. Bhabha to undertake the appointment of Chairman of the Delhi Emergency Committee. It had also been agreed that Mr. H.M. Patel should be Deputy Chairman.

It was stated that the United Council for Relief and Welfare had nominated Sir Usha Nath Sen and Mrs. Kirpalani to be their representatives with the

Delhi Emergency Committee; and that Dr B.N. Khan would be the representative of the Ministry of Health.

Mr. BHABHA said that he had only received the information that he was to be Chairman of the Delhi Emergency Committee late the previous evening. He had already summoned one informal meeting at which, however, there had been no military representation. It had been decided that a Joint Headquarters should be set up in the Town Hall. .......

ITEM 6. OUTSTANDING ITEMS (E.C.P.5.)

The Meeting considered a list of items on which the Committee had given orders at its previous meetings. .....

In connection with Serial 49, Mr. MOZUNDAR stated that official communiqués were being issued to the Press at 5 p.m. and 9 p.m. each evening. Editors had been requested to submit to the Public Relations Committee any news referring to the communal situation and not included in these communiqués. He went on to say that the only newspapers which were at present being produced in Delhi were "The Statesman" and "The Hindustan Times". These were having difficulty in maintaining publication. All-India Radio was also experiencing difficulty in keeping going and required protection of movement for its employees.

Lt. General BUCHER stated that the main military difficulty in Delhi at present was the shortage of transport. All available spare transport companies had been ordered up.

The COMMITTEE:-

(xiv) directed the Public Relations Committee to arrange for Press Conferences to be held in the Map Room at 4 p.m. each day;

(xv) directed the Delhi Emergency Committee to take measures to keep at least two newspapers and All-India Radio running in Delhi. ......

ITEM 10. THE PRIME MINISTER'S VISIT TO SONEPAT

THE PRIME MINISTER said that he visited Sonepat the previous day and addressed two meetings — one of Muslim refugees and one of Jats. On his way there and back, he had met several small groups carrying loot of all kinds. He had seen several large concentrations of Muslims who had evacuated the smaller villages. There had been relatively little killing in the area, but the situation was dangerous. There were in his opinion only three ways of dealing with it — first to evacuate all the Muslims; secondly to arrange protection on a large scale for all the big camps; and thirdly to take effective military action against attacking groups. He was of the opinion that unless this third course was taken, the situation would deteriorate rapidly; and then Meerut, which was a similar type of district, was bound to be similarly affected. THE PRIME MINISTER added that he had just received reports that looting had started by communities inter-se. LIEUT. GENERAL BUCHER said that a regiment of armoured cars, which would be useful for the purposes which the Prime Minister had in mind, was due to arrive in Delhi the following day. He explained that reinforcements to Delhi were delayed because the trains carrying them had to return empty on each occasion to bring the next unit.

THE COMMITTEE:
directed the Minister of Railways to investigate the movement of troop trains, particularly in view of the present necessity for trains bringing troops from Southern India to return there empty; and to report. .......

<u>ITEM 12.</u> <u>THE RELATIVE PRIORITY OF EVACUATION OF REFUGEES AND THE MAINTENANCE OF LAW AND ORDER.</u>

MAJOR GENERAL CHIMMI said that he had been appointed head of the Military Evacuation Organisation in East Punjab on 29th August. He had set up his Headquarters in Amritsar with a forward link at Lahore. A number of convoys had been running, using civilian transport. He had collected information in various ways of the conditions in West Punjab – and this information was most disturbing. He was clear that the evacuation of refugees was by no means the only commitment at the present time. He pointed out that there was never a military situation in which there were sufficient resources to meet every contingency - the relative importance of the several tasks had to be considered. In this particular case, he had no desire to minimise the importance of internal security, but he considered that the very existence of the large majority of non-Muslim inhabitants of West Punjab was now in danger and felt that internal security should take a secondary place to evacuation and that risks in the sphere of internal security should be accepted. The harrowing tales which he had heard about

West Punjab had brought him to the conclusion that it was imperative that the refugees there should be evacuated within three or four weeks. Otherwise, there might be none to bring. Whatever the intentions of the Pakistan Government itself, there was no doubt that the lower grades of officials were not obeying their orders. He dreaded to think of the political repercussions that a wholesale massacre would have.

MAJOR GENERAL CHIMMI went on to say that he had suggested that the resources required to improve the rate of evacuation of refugees could be obtained from certain sources; but Lieut. General Bucher had informed him that many of these were already tapped. He had in mind particularly 123 Brigade who had recently arrived in East Punjab. Many of the troops in East Punjab were employed in collecting Muslim refugees from small pockets to larger camps. There were not sufficient Pakistan troops for this purpose. He required altogether two Brigades. He had so far been given a battalion less a Company and a Platoon, and one more Battalion was due to be put at his disposal that day.

MAJOR GENERAL CHIMMI also suggested that there should be but one Commander to deal with question of internal security and of evacuation. He gave his view that most of the refugees in East Punjab would have to come out on foot. To protect this movement, armoured car patrols would be most useful. He suggested that more civilian transport should be requisitioned and formed into Companies on a military basis. He had also asked for a workshop element, which might be provided by the Armoured Division.

LIEUT. GENERAL BUCHER said that he personally agreed with the general ideas put forward by Major General Chimmi. Acceptance of these ideas was, however, a matter for the Government. He also agreed that one over-all Commander for both evacuation and internal security should be appointed. He explained that all Units which could be spared from Eastern Command had already been ordered up. Lieut. General Tuker had said that he would send no more unless he was ordered to do so. Southern Command would be able to provide some more Units. He pointed out that it was impolitic to take away the transport of units employed on internal security. Decreased mobility required further forces.

THE GOVERNOR GENERAL gave his opinion that no reinforcements should be sent to East Punjab at the expense of Delhi. In his view, Delhi should remain the over-riding first priority.

THE PRIME MINISTER said that he agreed that Delhi should continue to have first priority. It seemed to him that the questions of evacuation of refugees and the maintenance of law and order were closely inter-related. To relax on law and order might well increase the refugee problem – new districts might be affected. In his view, however, so far as East Punjab was concerned, the evacuation problem should have priority. The extent to which this was done would be a matter for those on the spot. He emphasized the necessity for tackling the problem with this in mind. Apart from this undertaking, the presence of Muslims waiting to be evacuated in East Punjab — for example 200,000 in Jullundur was a constant irritant. Each factor reacted upon the other. It came down to a requirement of further troops. THE PRIME MINISTER also agreed that the separate military evacuation organisation should be abolished and that one Commander should be appointed to deal with problems of both law and order and evacuation.

THE COMMITTEE:

(i) decided in principle that the evacuation of refugees, on a mutual basis, should have priority over the maintenance of law and order in East Punjab.

(ii) decided that one Commander should in future deal with evacuation of refugees and law and order in East Punjab.

## APPENDIX A

### INCIDENTS — 9TH SEPTEMBER 1947

1. EAST PUNJAB

| | |
|---|---|
| (a) Ambala. | Situation in Rupar, Chamkaor, Bharatgarh and Karauli tense. One Muslim stabbed fatally in City. |
| (b) Rohtak | Tenseness in Kharkaoda and Sonipat. Situation in Gohana deteriorated. Gharwal village set on fire. 30 Muslims killed and 50 converted. |
| (c) Simla | Tension decreased. More Goondas arrested. |
| (d) Karnal | 400 Muslims of Pipli attacked Hindu village of Barumajri and set on fire. Casualties were 2 Hindus killed. 50 small arms were recovered from city and neighbouring villages. Sikhs looted a Nawab's house. |
| (e) Hissar | Rioting in Sirsa and Hissar reported. Situation now under control. |
| (f) Gurgaon | On the 6th September, Chilhar was attacked by a mob of over 10,000. Raiders were beaten off by military patrol and suffered 70-80 casualties. |
| (g) Trains Incidents | The 25 up was attacked on 8th September, and the escort killed 10 and wounded 18 of the attackers. The 4 down was attacked at Khana on the 7th September, the escort killing one. Special refugee train down was attacked at Habud Garh on the 8th September by Muslims. The escort killed 5 and wounded 6.<br><br>The Red Trunk Express was attacked near Nizamuddin Railway Station by Sikhs and Hindus. Casualties to Muslims were 12 killed and 7 injured, including 12 lying in the fields nearby. |

2. DELHI

| | |
|---|---|
| (a) Sabzi Mandi | Tension prevails. 15 looters were killed by military. There were sporadic rifle fire from alleged Muslim strongholds. A number of arms were captured. |
| (b) Karol Bagh | Situation improved. Some looters were fired on but casualties not known. One muslim was burned. |
| (c) Pathargani | Under control. Several looters shot. Some fires still burning and some corpses to be recovered. |
| (d) Delhi Junction | 15 Muslims killed by stabbing. The Pakistan baggage bogies were looted and fired at. |
| (e) New Delhi | 5 looters were killed in Connaught Place. 6 Muslims were assaulted and killed in Southern, New Delhi. |
| (f) Chandni Chowk | 3 looters killed. |

APPENDIX B.

Casualties admitted to Delhi Hospitals
upto 10 p.m. on 9th September,
1947

| | | | |
|---|---|---|---|
| Total casualties | .... | 110 | |
| Hindus | | 35 ) | |
| Sikhs | | 12 ) | non-Muslims |
| Muslims | | 63 | |

Except three all bullet wounds — 12 died.

25 women and 5 children

| | |
|---|---|
| Muslim | 22 |
| Non-Muslim | 3 |

SECRET AND IMMEDIATE
COPY NO. 51
11th September, 1947 E.C. 7th MEETING

EMERGENCY COMMITTEE MEETINGS
SEVENTH MEETING

MINUTES

The 7th meeting of the Emergency Committee was held in the Council Chamber at Government House, New Delhi, at 10 a.m. on Thursday 11th September,1947. .....

The items discussed were:

ITEM 1. SITUATION IN THE PUNJAB
ITEM 2 SITUATION IN DELHI
ITEM 3 MILITARY COMMANDS
ITEM 4 CHOLERA
ITEM 5 OUTSTANDING ITEMS
ITEM 6 THE JOINT DEFENCE COUNCIL
ITEM 7 HEALTH CONDITIONS IN EAST PUNJAB
ITEM 8 THE MOVEMENT OF REFUGEES ON FOOT
ITEM 9 THE PROVISION OF MILITARY OFFICERS FOR EAST PUNJAB
ITEM 10 KAPURTHALA
ITEM 11 CUSTODIANS OF REFUGEES' PROPERTY
ITEM 12 THE TELEPHONE SYSTEM IN DELHI
ITEM 13 THE CARRIAGE OF WEAPONS IN DELHI
ITEM 14 THE CONTROL OF LAND TRANSPORT BETWEEN INDIA AND PAKISTAN (EAST AND WEST PUNJAB)
ITEM 15 BRITISH OFFICERS ........

ITEM 1. SITUATION IN THE PUNJAB

It was reported that the situation in East Punjab remained much the same, except at Simla where it was deteriorating. A request had been received for reinforcements to be sent to Simla. Sir ROB LOCKHART said that one Company was already there; he believed that a second Company was on its way; and it might be possible to send still further reinforcements provided that a battalion which was due in Ambala that day arrived.

It was stated that so far as West Punjab was concerned, the movement of outgoing refugees continued strongly. Major General REES stated that Sheikupura and Montgomery districts had, on the whole, been evacuated by now.

The COMMITTEE:
directed the Commander-in-Chief, Indian Army, to report the following day on the reinforcements sent to Simla.

ITEM 2. SITUATION IN DELHI

It was stated that the situation continued to show improvement. There had been a number of small incidents which included looting and firing on police and military. …..

ITEM 5. OUTSTANDING ITEMS

The meeting considered a list of items on which orders had been given by the Committee at previous meetings.

In connection with Serial 49 (a), Mr. BHABHA stated that arrangements were being made to concentrate the Muslim officials of the Government of India in the Sher Shah Mess.

In connection with Serial 49 (k), THE COMMITTEE:-

(1) directed the Head of the Military Emergency Staff to assist the Delhi Emergency Committee in the setting up of an Information Room.

It was stated that the milk supply for hospitals in Delhi was very bad; and that there was fear that the dairies would be attacked by Muslims and their cows slaughtered. Arrangements had, however, been made to provide tinned milk which was about to arrive.

THE COMMITTEE:-

(ii) directed the Delhi Emergency Committee to make arrangements for the protection of dairies in Delhi.

Sir ROB LOCKHART stated that an extended operation had commenced the previous day to round up persons carrying arms in the open. However, the Area Commander had reported that the "gaff had been blown" before this operation took place; as a result it was less successful than had been hoped.

The PRIME MINISTER handed in a list of persons who were suspected of having taken part in organising the recent disturbances in Delhi.

The COMMITTEE:

(iii) directed the Delhi Emeregency Committee to take action to round up the persons mentioned in the Prime Minister's list.

Sir ROB LOCKHART asked whether more could not be done to stop continual rumour-mongering. He suggested that the more obvious rumous might be denied.

THE COMMITTEE:-

(iv) directed the Public Relations Committee to consider measures of reducing rumour-mongering; and to issue prompt denials of the more obvious rumours.

The PRIME MINISTER said that reports had been received that there were considerable stores of arms in the Purana Qila, where 12,000 Muslims, including servants of the Pakistan Government, were concentrated. SARDAR PATEL said that the Pakistan High Commissioner had asked that the Government of India should take over responsibility for running Purana Qila Camp.

THE COMMITTEE:-

(v) directed the Delhi Emergency Committee to consult the Pakistan High Commissioner on when the running of the Purana Qila Camp could be taken over by the Government of India.

(vi) directed the Ministry of Railways to report on the arrangements made for moving the Muslims at present in the Purgana (Sic) Qila Camp to Lahore;

(vii) directed the Commander-in-Chief, Indian Army, to issue orders for all refugees entering the Purana Qila Camp to be searched;

(viii) directed the Chief of the Governor General's staff to include the Purana Qila Camp in the tour of the city which he was going to make, so that he could report on conditions there first-hand to the Government of Pakistan.

In connection with Serial 75, Dr MATTHAI stated that a train carrying Meos from Delhi to Lahore was due to leave at 10.30 a.m. that day; and two further trains that afternoon.

In connection with Serial 3, the PRIME MINISTER stated that he had received a telegram from the Prime Ministers of Bihar and the C.P., each offering to take 10,000 refugees.

## ITEM 6. THE JOINT DEFENCE COUNCIL

THE GOVERNOR GENERAL said that at a Joint Defence Council Meeting the previous day, representatives of both Governments had confirmed the principle that the Reconstitution of the Armed Forces, as planned, should have priority over refugee movement by train. The Pakistan representatives had also agreed with the principle, discussed in the Committee the previous day, that the provision of troops for the evacuation of refugees should take priority over the maintenance of law and order in the Punjab. Lieut. General Messervey had also undertaken to provide proper guards for the Pakistan airfields (especially Lyallpur), from which air evacuation took place.

## ITEM 7 HEALTH CONDITIONS IN EAST PUNJAB

THE COMMITTEE:
directed the Ministry of Health to report on the results of the meeting between the Director General of Health Services and the Prime Minister of East Punjab, to discuss health conditions in East Punjab.

## ITEM 8 THE MOVEMENT OF REFUGEES ON FOOT

Major General REES drew attention to the dangers which existed to marching columns of refugees. These were easily ambushed and required considerable numbers of troops for adequate protection. It had been suggested to him the previous day that a column of 35,000 refugees should set forth with one Company of troops of their own community. He had agreed to this suggestion provided that an adequate additional "floating" guard was arranged. As only two tanks were available for that, the movement had not been able to begin. There had been one incident in which 400 people of a refugee column moving out of Faridkot had been killed (in East Punjab territory) within ten minutes. This column had been sent back to Faridkot.

In discussion it was pointed out that the risks liable to be faced by columns on the march had to be balanced against those which they would face — attacks on their camps, cholera and starvation — if they were not moved. The PRIME MINISTER pointed out that the local authorities were the only people who could judge in each individual case which was the greater risk and take decisions.

It was stated that no reply had yet been received to the message, which had been sent to the Pakistan Government by Sardar Nishtar, suggesting that both Governments should put out a joint appeal to the effect that they recognised that mass evacuation must take place, and asking that refugees should be allowed to go in peace.

The MEETING:
directed the Chief of the Governor-General's Staff to discuss this draft statement with the Pakistan Government.

ITEM 9. THE PROVISION OF MILITARY OFFICERS FOR EAST PUNJAB

The GOVERNOR-GENERAL read out a telegram, which had been received from the Governor of East Punjab, asking for the services of 40 military officers to work as additional District Magistrates and additional Superintendents of Police in East Punjab. These officers would be required for at least six months. Those of the rank of Captain or Major would suit best. He asked for as many as possible to be sent urgently.

The COMMITTEE:
directed the Commander-in-Chief, Indian Army, to report whether or not he could comply with the Governor of East Punjab's request for 40 military officers to serve as additional District Magistrates and additional Superintendents of Police.

ITEM 10. KAPURTHALA.

The PRIME MINISTER read out a telegram which he had received from the President of the Kapurthala State Council, asking for reinforcements — three Companies if possible.

The COMMITTEE:
directed the Commander-in-Chief of the Indian Army to report whether he could send reinforcements to Kapurthala.

ITEM 13. THE CARRIAGE OF WEAPONS IN DELHI.

THE DEPUTY PRIME MINISTER stated that the Order banning the carriage of weapons in Delhi of any sort, including kirpans of whatever length, had caused much bitterness among the Sikhs. He suggested the possibility of rescinding this Order and going back to the Order which allowed Sikhs to carry kirpans of a length not more than 9".

SARDAR BALDEV SINGH said that the issue of this Order had made his own position extremely difficult. He also made reference to a broadcast which had suggested that all stabbing in Delhi had been done by kirpans.

THE PRIME MINISTER gave his view that the Order banning the carriage of arms of any sort, including kirpans of any length was at present essential. He pointed out that this only applied to people going about in the open. Even lathis were prohibited in public streets. He considered that those who felt that they could not come out without their kirpans would have to remain at home, even at the expense of Government service. He did not feel that this Order could at the present time, be relaxed in the slightest, whatever the consequences. ....

ITEM 15. BRITISH OFFICERS

SIR ROB LOCKHART said that there had been a campaign in certain places to circulate propaganda to the effect that British officers were not doing their jobs. He ventured to put forward that this suggestion was, on the whole, unfounded. In particular, he had received a report from an officer who had been on tour in the Punjab and had received the impression from many people that the general opinion was that the British officers were doing nothing and did not care. Everybody who repeated this story said that they had heard it from someone else. It sounded as if there was a definite attempt to spread this story. It was having a bad effect, because, both in India and Pakistan, British officers were coming to the conclusion that they were not wanted. SIR ROB LOCKHART said that from all that he had seen and from all the dealings that he had had with Ministers, he had come to the conclusion that this was not the policy of the Government. He added that the propaganda was spreading to South India.

SIR ROB LOCKHART asked whether both Governments could put out a statement, preferably simultaneously, to the effect that the British officers were serving at the request of and under the Dominion Governments. If it was intended to keep the Army as a solid body it was most desirable to keep up the morale of the British officers.

THE PRIME MINISTER pointed out that the feeling against British officers was the result of past events and difficult to expunge at once. There was a tendency when difficulties arose for this feeling to function even more powerfully. He agreed that a statement of some sort should be made, but suggested that it should be made in the right context – possibly in connection with a statement of the Government's policy as regards Indianisation.

LORD ISMAY suggested that the Prime Minister might be able to give the requisite assurance in one of his speeches (which were so widely read), instead of by a Government statement.

THE GOVERNOR GENERAL said that he would talk to the Prime Minister and the Deputy Prime Minister further on this question after the meeting.

THE COMMITTEE:
directed the Chief of the Governor General's staff to discuss with representatives of the Pakistan Government the possibility of that Government making, simultaneously with the Government of India and possibly in speeches by the Prime Ministers, a statement to the effect that British officers were serving at the request of and under the Dominion Governments.

APPENDIX: A

## DETAILS OF CASUALTIES ON THE 10TH SEPTEMBER, 1947

| | | | |
|---|---|---|---|
| Hindus | — | Males | 52 |
| | | Females | - |
| | | Child | 1 |
| | | | 53 |
| Muslims | — | Males | 34 |
| | | Females | 2 |
| | | Child | 1 |
| | | | 37 |
| Unknown | | | 3 |
| Christians | | | 1 |
| Grand TOTAL | | | 94 |

| | | |
|---|---|---|
| Bullet wounds | 42 | |
| Stab wounds | 13 | (All Hindus) |
| Bomb explosion | 1 | (Probably) |

SECRET AND IMMEDIATE

12th September, 1947 COPY NO.49

E.C.8th Meeting

EMERGENCY COMMITTEE MEETINGS
EIGHTH MEETING

MINUTES

The 8th Meeting of the Emergency Committee was held in the Council Chamber at Government House, New Delhi, at 10 a.m. on Friday, 12th September, 1947.

The items discussed were :-

ITEM 1 SITUATION IN DELHI

ITEM 2 SITUATION IN THE PUNJAB

ITEM 3 REFUGEES IN DELHI

ITEM 4 OUTSTANDING ITEMS

ITEM 5 PRISONERS IN THE PUNJAB

ITEM 6 THE PROVISION OF VEHICLES FOR DISPOSALS

ITEM 7 CARRIAGE OF WEAPONS THROUGHOUT INDIA

ITEM 8 THE MOVE OF HEAD QUARTERS,INDIAN ARMY

ITEM 9 THE NORTH-WEST FRONTIER PROVINCE .......

ITEM 1. SITUATION IN DELHI

It was reported that the city was now much quieter. There had been one incident reported during the night when the military were fired upon by unidentified attackers. It was stated that the police were in some cases reluctant to enforce the curfew.

ITEM 2. SITUATION IN THE PUNJAB

(a) East Punjab

It was reported that incidents had continued to occur duirng the past 24 hours. In Simla, there had been some stabbings and looting by Hindu and Sikh refugees, but the situation was now under control. Large scale looting was reported from Jullundur. It was also stated that the Muslim refugees in the Province were less cowed and were becoming more aggressive: they had attacked one village.

(b) West Punjab

The movement of refugees was continuing in both directions. Cholera was spreading and had been reported in Ferozepur, Sheikhupura and Montgomery District. Tension was reported in the rural areas of Sialkot.

ITEM 3. REFUGEES IN DELHI

Lord ISMAY handed round a note on refugee camps in Delhi, which he had prepared as a result of visits paid by him to these camps the previous day. A copy of this note is attached as Appendix 'A'.

The GOVERNOR-GENERAL emphasised the particular necessity for appointing Camp Commandants and staff in these camps; and for providing loudspeaker equipment. It would also be necessary to make a census of everybody in the camps, as families were in many cases divided and in different places. Concerning the reports of people having difficulty in entering the Purana Qila camp, he suggested that this difficulty would be overcome by a proper approach. Lady Mountbatten would, he was sure, offer to go down with representatives of the United Relief and Welfare Council to arrange this. The GOVERNOR-GENERAL pointed out that a large number of the inhabitants of the Purana Qila camp were Pakistan Government employees. On their treatment would largely depend the reports of events in Delhi which were taken back to Pakistan.

Sir ROB LOCKHART said that he had visited the camps with Lord Ismay the previous day. He had found that many people there were anxious to help; and a general desire that the Government of India should take over the running of the camps. The guard on the Purana Qila camp was only

25 men. He personally had seen no signs of hostility amongst the inmates. He emphasised that a very large staff would be required to make the camps run properly. He went on to say that many people of all types had been ordered to go to these camps; and instanced the case of a Major in the Pakistan Army on his way to Quetta who, on arrival at Delhi, had been told to go to the Purana Qila camp.

Mr. NEOGY said that he had spoken to the Pakistan High Commissioner the previous day about the Purana Qila camp being taken over by the Government of India. The Pakistan High Commissioner was in agreement with this proposal — in fact keen on it — on the condition that a Muslim guard was retained.

Dr. MATTHAI stated that 14,500 people had already left Delhi for Pakistan in special trains. He hoped to be able to provide two trains on the following day for those in the Purana Qila camp, provided that guards were available. After discussion it was agreed that these trains, so that they could travel throughout the journey from Delhi to Lahore in day-light, should not leave until dawn on Saturday, 13th September.

The GOVERNOR-GENERAL suggested that those in the Purana Qila camp should be segregated into two lots – those who wished to leave for Pakistan and those who wanted to stay on in Delhi. The latter could then be brought out and either sent to their homes if they wished to go, or accommodated together in some place of safety. In this connection Mr. BHABHA mentioned that not one tenth of the Sher Sheh Mess was yet occupied.

The COMMITTEE:

(i) directed the Ministry of Railways to arrange for the two special trains carrying persons from the Purana Qila camp, to leave Delhi for Lahore on Saturday, 13th September; these trains should leave sufficiently early in the morning to ensure that they arrived at Lahore in day-light;

(ii) directed the Commander-in-Chief of the Indian Army to ensure that adequate guards were provided for these trains; and to instruct East Punjab Area to inform Lahore District of the time of their arrival;

(iii) directed the Delhi Emergency Committee to arrange for a Camp Commandant and staff to be appointed for the refugee camps in Delhi; to instal loudspeakers in these camps; to arrange that censuses were taken of the inmates of the refugee camps; to arrange for those in the Purana Qila camp to be separated into those who wished to stay in Delhi and those who wished to go to Pakistan; and to report when the administration of the Purana Qila camp was taken over by the Government of India.

ITEM 4 OUTSTANDING ITEMS

The meeting considered a list of items on which orders had been given by the Committee at previous meetings. ……

In connection with Serial 88, it was stated that 54 persons, suspected of organising the disturbances in Delhi, had been arrested since the previous day.

In connection with Serial 84, the PRIME MINISTER stated that a large number of leaflets — including some which had never appeared before — were now coming out in Delhi. Many of these were highly objectionable.

THE COMMITTEE:

(ii) directed the Ministry of Home Affairs to take steps to stop the production of objectionable leaflets in Delhi; all publications must be licensed before circulation.

Mr. BHABHA also reported that he had visited Willingdon airfield, the previous day, and was on the whole satisfied with the arrangements there. On the other hand,he understood that Palam airport had an all Muslim staff. Sir ROB LOCKHART said that according to his information,all was in good order at Palam. He suggested that it might be helpful to appoint a Pakistan officer as the Liaison Officer at Palam.

THE COMMITTEE:

(iii) directed A.M.C., R.I.A.F. to report the following day on the situation at Palam, particularly with a view to stopping arms' traffic through that airport;

(iv) directed the Commander-in-Chief of the Indian Army to arrange for the appointment of an officer of the Pakistan Army as Liaison Officer at Palam airport.

Sir ROB LOCKHART said that it had been suggested to him by local Military Commanders that it would be of advantage to re-introduce the Whipping Act for goondas; and to include youths and boys who were doing a lot of looting. The GOVERNOR GENERAL said that he considered this usually to be a retrograde step; but agreed that the present circumstances demanded it.

THE COMMITTEE:-

(v) directed the Ministry of Home Affairs to arrange for the Whipping Act to be re-introduced in Delhi. ….

On Serial 93, it was stated that the Information and Broadcasting Ministry had stationed a staff at the Town Hall, Delhi, which had been made the Clearing House of local news. Rumours were being checked up. This staff passed on information collected four times a day for broadcasting on the four news services, which were fixed points in the radio programme. Further, a non-official body had taken on the charge of moving about the city in motor transport with loud speakers, giving the news, contradicting rumours and speaking to the people generally.

<u>ITEM 5.</u> <u>PRISONERS IN THE PUNJAB</u>

Sardar BALDEV SINGH stated that he had received reports of non-Muslim prisoners in jails in West Punjab being attacked immediately they were released. He suggested that all prisoners due for release should be exchanged, where applicable, to the Province in which their community was in a majority.

THE COMMITTEE :-

(i) directed the Ministry of Home Affairs to investigate the possibility of all prisoners in jails in East and West Punjab being transferred, where appropriate, to the Province in which their community was in the majority, before release;

(ii) directed the Chief of the Governor-General's Staff to take this matter up with the Pakistan Government. ……

APPENDIX'A'

## NOTE BY THE CHIEF OF THE GOVERNOR GENERAL'S STAFF ON REFUGEE CAMPS IN DELHI

1. The immediate necessity is to get into personal touch with each individual in the camps. This can be done only by loud speaker and must be done at once.
2. The first speech on the loud speaker should include the following :-
   (a) Everything possible will be done to improve conditions in the camp and to take care of you'
   (b) We shall find out from each one of you what your wishes are about evacuation:
   (c) We will try to carry out these wishes as quickly as possible;
   (d) This loud speaker will be kept here and we will give you periodical messages about arrangements and plans.
3. Camp staffs must be appointed for each camp as quickly as possible. These staffs will live in the camp and establish their permanent offices therein. They will include:
   Camp Commandant
   Food Officer
   Transport Officer
   Medical Officer
   Welfare Officer
   Information Officer
4. The inhabitants of every camp must be divided into units of, say 100 or perhaps 200. This grouping should be on the voluntary system and each group will elect its own leader. The groups will be serially numbered for convenience of identification. They will also appoint their own parties for different types of work — drawing, rations, cooking, and so forth.
5. The above deals only with immediate necessities and no attempt has been made to eleborate arrangements. Ultimately much could be done to relieve the monotony and reduce the despair of the refugees, e.g. by the installation of a radio set from which all stations in India could be heard, the provision of literature, and so forth.

## APPENDIX B

Details of Casualties on the 11th September, 1947

| | | | | |
|---|---|---|---|---|
| Hindu | - | Males | 20 | (bullet wounds 11) |
| Muslim | - | Males | 38 | (bullet wounds 11) |
| | | Females | 31 | (These are old cases but received in Hospital |
| | | Children | 7 | on the 11th ) |
| | | Total | 96 | |

Muslims were in majority of those who were stabbed.

15 deaths.

In addition, 6 non-Muslim wounded from Paharganj area crawled into the Lady Hardinge Hospital yesterday:

| | | |
|---|---|---|
| 1 Sikh | - | male |
| 3 Hindu | - | males |
| 1 Hindu | - | woman |
| 1 Hindu | - | boy aged about 10 or 12. |

13th September, 1947 SECRET AND IMMEDIATE

COPY NO. 49

E.C. 9th Meeting

EMERGENCY COMMITTEE MEETINGS
NINTH MEETING

MINUTES

The 9th Meeting of the Emergency Committee was held in the Council Chamber at Government House, New Delhi, at 10 a.m. on Saturday, 13th September,1947. ……

The items discussed were:

ITEM 1. SITUATION IN DELHI
ITEM 2 SITUATION IN THE PUNJAB
ITEM 3 DELHI EMERGENCY COMMITTEE
ITEM 4 EVACUATION OF REFUGEES FROM EAST PUNJAB
ITEM 5 OUTSTANDING ITEMS (E.C.P.8)
ITEM 6 THE NORTH-WEST FRONTIER PROVINCE. ……..

ITEM 1. SITUATION IN DELHI

It was reported that there had been some incidents of firing and of looting. Arms and ammunition had been found near the Delhi Gate and some cases of shot-guns were found at Delhi Main Station.

ITEM 2. SITUATION IN THE PUNJAB

(a) East Punjab

It was stated with regard to the general situation that there was some tension in the rural areas but that movement of refugees continued satisfactorily.

In Ambala district the situation was reported to have deteriorated greatly and in Rohtak district heavy killing was reported at Babona. Cholera continued to spread in the Ferozepore district and four cases had been reported in the Dogra Regiment. Two cases of Smallpox were reported from the non-Muslim refugee camp at Pathankot.

(b) West Punjab

Some incidents were reported from Sialkot district but most of the Province had nothing to report.

ITEM 3. DELHI EMERGENCY COMMITTEE

Mr. PATEL said that Mr. Sulaiman Sait had been appointed to be in charge of the Purana Qila camp. This officer was going there that morning with a supply of foodstuffs. From that day onwards all food arrangements would be made by the Government of India. A local non-official committee had offered to give all possible assistance. The officer in charge would also be given all the assistance he needed by the Delhi Emergency Committee. He had been provided with three experienced assistants.

Sir ROB LOCKHART undertook also to provide every possible military assistance in the running of the Purana Qila camp.

Mr. PATEL went on to say that a police guard was due to take over the protection of the Purana Qila camp that day. The whole problem would be eased by the reduction in numbers in the camp consequent upon the departure of two trains the following day. He stated that the Pakistan Government had expressed the desire that these first two trains should, so far as possible, be filled up with Pakistan Government officials.

Major General REES said that two loudspeakers for use in the Purana Qila camp had been located; but their operators had disappeared. The GOVERNOR-GENERAL suggested that the Royal Indian Navy or the Royal Indian Air Force might be able to produce operators. Mr. BHABHA said that there was only one movable loudspeaker van in Delhi which was being used to restore confidence throughout the city.

Miss WATSON stated that the refugees in the Purana Qila camp had already appointed a Committee of their own.

The PRIME MINISTER agreed that the first two trains taking persons from the Purana Qila camp to Lahore should be filled up with officials of the Pakistan Government. The GOVERNOR GENERAL pointed out that the larger question of whether Muslims normally resident in Delhi should be sent to Pakistan was one of high policy and for the Cabinet to decide upon. Dr. MATTHAI said that the first two trains were due to leave the following morning at 7 a.m. and 7.30 a.m. The GOVERNOR GENERAL stressed the necessity of providing sufficient food in the trains; and for the Chief Commissioner being responsible for seeing that the right people were sent from the camp to the trains in time.

The GOVERNOR GENERAL said that he had, the previous day, seen some 10,000 refugees gathered together on the Ridge. He pointed out that if these people were not soon moved to a proper camp, there was likely to be trouble. Mr. BHABHA said that the general policy was to concentrate these refugees in the Purana Qila camp. Sardar BALDEV SINGH pointed out that there would be room for this as trains left.

Sir ROBERT LOCKHART said that he believed that there were a number of Afghan subjects in the refugee camps in Delhi.

The COMMITTEE:

(i) directed the Delhi Emergency Committee to find out how many persons there were of nationalities other than of India and Pakistan in the refugee camps in Delhi;
(ii) directed the Delhi Emergency Committee to arrange for the refugees on the Ridge to be moved to the Purana Qila camp as soon as conditions in the latter allowed this;
(iii) directed the Ministry of Health to report whether there were any cases of cholera among the refugees on the Ridge;
(iv) directed the Ministry of Health to report on the progress made in inoculating refugees against cholera in the camps in Delhi.

Sir ROB LOCKHART said that he had seen officials travelling in cars in Delhi with their escorts poking their rifles out of the windows of the cars. This, he suggested, induced panic and fear. The PRIME MINISTER said that his own escort had insisted on doing this.

The COMMITTEE:

(v) directed the Delhi Emergency Committee to issue orders that escorts in cars in Delhi should not show their weapons in a provocative manner.

Mr. PATEL said that there were no supplies whatever of charcoal in Delhi; and supplies of fire-wood to last only ten days. He had asked the Railway Board to provide trains for bringing in these commodities from outside.

The COMMITTEE:

(vi) directed the Ministry of Railways to ensure that arrangements were made for supplies of charcoal and fire-wood to be brought into Delhi by train.

Rajkumari AMRIT KAUR drew attention to the serious shortage of ambulances in Delhi. Sir ROB LOCKHART undertook to order to Delhi half a Field Ambulance Unit.

The PRIME MINISTER emphasized that the Delhi Civil Administration retained their responsibility despite the formation of the Delhi Emergency Committee.

The PRIME MINISTER said that almost every morning, after the curfew was raised in Delhi, there were cases of looting and arson. He considered that something should be done immediately to prevent this state of affairs in the area immediately around the Town Hall and Station. Mr. SANJEVI said that he had already made arrangements for mobile patrols for this purpose.

The PRIME MINISTER also stated that he understood that the Delhi University Officers Training Corps was having difficulty in obtaining arms.

The COMMITTEE:

(vii) directed the Delhi Emergency Committee to investigate the supply of arms for the Delhi University Officers Training Corps.

The GOVERNOR-GENERAL stated that about one thousand of the more important Muslims residents of Delhi were gathered together at Hyderabad House.

The COMMITTEE:

(viii) directed the Delhi Emergency Committee to ensure that food was sent to Hyderabad House that day.

Sir ROB LOCKHART said that he was proposing to get as many as possible members of the Pakistan armed forces out of the refugee camps in Delhi and perhaps form a unit of them.

A Reuter's report, to the effect that 50,000 Muslims had been killed in Delhi, was quoted.

The COMMITTEE:
(ix) directed the Public Relations Committee to investigate this report.

## ITEM 4. EVACUATION OF REFUGEES FROM EAST PUNJAB

The Meeting considered two telegrams which General Messervy had sent to General Lockhart; and a telegram sent by the Governor of West Punjab to the Governor General of Pakistan, with a copy to the Governor General of India.

This last telegram contained the following sentence:-

'Tara Singh finished discussion by saying "This is war". Major General REES stated that he had rung up the Governor of West Punjab and Major General Thimayya in order to clarify the telegrams received and this sentence in particular. The report of Master Tara Singh's remark had been made by Major General Thimayya to Major General Gain, and by the latter to Sir Francis Mudie. Major General Thimayya had asked Master Tara Singh to undertake that the Sikhs would not attack a column of Muslim refugees due to go through Amritsar from Jullundur to Lahore. Master Tara Singh had not been able to give this guarantee as Amritsar city, through which the road ran, was full of Sikh refugees from West Punjab in ugly temper. Major General Thimayya had accordingly arranged to bulldoze a road round Amritsar city and to impose a curfew there. The conversation between Major General Thimayya and Master Tara Singh had finished on a more general note, discussing how the present situation would end. Major General Thimayya had understood Master Tara Singh to say that the only real solution appeared to be war. Therefore the telegram from Sir Francis Mudie, who had received a report of this conversation second-hand, definitely created a false impression.

Major General REES said that he understood the Governments of East and West Punjab both to desire to ensure safety for refugees on the move on foot. He himself had pointed out to representatives of both Governments that the three essentials were first, to provide adequate escorts; secondly, to induce the right atmosphere among the local population; and thirdly, for the Governments themselves to be aware of the situation and to decide whether each move was justified by the risks involved. Major General REES pointed out that most of the biggest incidents had taken place in connection with marching columns of refugees. He explained that this road was going to be allotted to either side for three or four days in turn. The first move under this scheme which had been worked out by Major General Chimini, was that of the Muslim refugees from Jullundur through Amritsar to Lahore. Both Major Generals Thimayya and Chimini were hopeful that these moves would be successful. Major General REES stated that the Sikhs and Hindus had decided to postpone their departure from West Punjab. He pointed out that the responsibility for guarding them was that of the West Punjab Government, which he understood to be confident that there would be no major incident.

The GOVERNOR-GENERAL asked whether it was fair to say that, on both sides, the Muslims and Hindus were comparatively well controlled by their respective Governments; and that Master Tara Singh had not got the same degree of control over the Sikh jathas. The PRIME MINISTER pointed out that there were jathas and bands of all three communities in both Provinces which were not under the control of any Government.

In connection with the two telegrams received by General Lockhart from General Messervy, it was pointed out that the word "Sikhs" was being used loosely, instead of the word "non-Muslims". The PRIME MINISTER also queried General Messervy's statement that there were many more Muslim refugees to bring to West Punjab than non-Muslims to move to East Punjab. He asked on what data this statement could be based. The GOVERNOR GENERAL suggested that the award of the Boundary Commission had resulted in more Muslims being left in East Punjab than non-Muslims in West Punjab. The PRIME MINISTER also queried General Messervy's statement that the movement of refugees from West to East was organised and unmolested. He pointed out that many incidents in the course of this movement had been reported. Sir ROB LOCKHART suggested that there had probably been more non-Muslim soldiers, when the movement had started, available for protection duties in West Punjab than vice versa.

The GOVERNOR GENERAL emphasized the desirability of asking Master Tara Singh to come to Delhi for discussions at an early date.

ITEM 5. OUTSTANDING ITEMS
(E.C.P.8.)

The Committee considered a list of items on which action had been ordered at previous meetings. ……

In the course of a discussion on priorities, the Committee made it clear that they considered that measures to restore the situation in Delhi must continue to have top priority. As already decided, the evacuation of refugees would continue to have priority over the maintenance of law and order in East Punjab. So far as the choice of priority between the evacuation of refugees from Delhi, and the restoration of law and order in the surrounding districts, was concerned, it was pointed out that the former was closely connected with law and order in Delhi, the paramount priority. ……

Serial 111 (the decision taken the previous day to introduce the Whipping Act in Delhi) was cancelled.

On Serial 110, the COMMITTEE:-

(vii) directed the Public Relations Committee to ensure that adequate publicity was given to the fact that kirpans of 9" and under, which were now allowed to be carried in the streets of Delhi, must be concealed. ……..

APPENDIX 'A'

Details of Casualties on the 12th September,1947

| | | | | |
|---|---|---|---|---|
| Hindu | - | males | 16 | |
| | - | females | 4 | |
| | - | child | 1 | 21 |
| Muslim | - | males | 30 | |
| | - | females | 2 | |
| | - | child | – | 32 |
| Unknown | - | | 1 | 1 |
| Total | - | | | 54 |

1 Fatal case of stabbing at Lady Hardinge — Muslim.

SECRET AND IMMEDIATE
COPY NO. 50

14th September, 1947 E.C. 10TH MEETING

EMERGENCY COMMITTEE MEETINGS
10th MEETING

MINUTES

The 10th meeting of the Emergency Committee was held in the Council Chamber at Government House, New Delhi, at 10 a.m. on Sunday 14th September, 1947. .....

The items discussed were:

ITEM 1. SITUATION IN DELHI AREA
ITEM 2 SITUATION IN THE PUNJAB
ITEM 3 OUTSTANDING ITEMS (E.C.P.9)
ITEM 4 SPEECHES BY THE PRIME MINISTER AND THE DEPUTY PRIME MINISTER ......

ITEM 1. SITUATION IN DELHI AREA

It was reported that there had been some incidents of stray looting in the city, and some firing between military and unknown attackers. Some arms were recovered. In Gurgaon area there was fear amongst the people of a Meo attack and in Palwal area both communities were in panic. A quantity of arms was recovered from a village in Hodal area.

ITEM 2. SITUATION IN THE PUNJAB

(a) East Punjab

It was stated that the movement of refugees continued. Some convoys were being attacked by Sikhs in the vicinity of Fatehgarh. Cholera cases were reported from Ludhiana and Jagraon.

(b) West Punjab

There was little to report other than the continual movement of refugees. In the Multan district a military patrol contacted an armed Sikh Jatha which was 300 strong. They engaged them and afterwards recovered 9 guns.

ITEM 3. OUTSTANDING ITEMS (E.C.P.9)

The meeting considered a list of items on which orders had been given at previous meetings of the Committee. ……

The Deputy Prime Minister said that the continual incidents, particularly firing, which were going on in Delhi, day and night, were having a very demoralizing effect. One engagement the previous day had lasted for six hours and it appeared that the operation eventually arranged to clear a house from which firing was taking place had not been carried out completely. He was willing to give authority that houses from which continual firing took place should be blown up. He suggested that if a full-scale operation to cover the whole of Delhi was not possible because of a shortage of troops, the city should be cleared area by area. …..

Lady MOUNTBATTEN said that there were many rumours in the Purana Qila camp that Muslims were being shot down by soldiers on their way to the camp. It was agreed that denials of such rumours should be put out over the loudspeaker there.

In connection with Serial 134, Mr. BHABHA stated that 50 jeeps and 40 trucks had been put at the disposal of the Delhi Emergency Committee through requisition. A large number of vehicles, which would otherwise be available for requisition in Delhi, had been sent to the East Punjab before the trouble in Delhi started. He said that he understood that the Army possessed 25,000 brand new vehicles; and suggested that some of these should be released. Mr. PATEL added that he had received a report that 25% of these vehicles were "runners". He emphasized the extreme importance and urgency of the provision of adequate transport in Delhi.

The GOVERNOR-GENERAL suggested that now that the principle of evacuating refugees on foot had been established and in view of the fact that it had been agreed that the restoration of the situation in Delhi should have top priority, no more vehicles should be sent from Delhi to East Punjab. …….

The GOVERNOR-GENERAL referred to the death of Mr. K.S. Misra, a magistrate in Delhi, who had been killed by a sniper. He pointed out that this officer had been killed in the course of his duty, and suggested that a tribute should be paid by the Committee to the example which he had set.

The COMMITTEE:

(x) directed the Public Relations Committee to issue, on their behalf, a statement paying tribute to the courage of and example set by Mr. K.S. Misra; saying that provision would be made for his family; and going on to pay a more general tribute to all officers who were carrying out their duty bravely.

Sir ROB LOCKHART said that the departure of a refugee train from Delhi had been reported in a broadcast four hours after it had left.

The Committee:

(xi) directed the Ministry of Information and Broadcasting to find out why this had been broadcast; and to ensure that no publicity was in future given to the movements of refugee trains. ......

<u>ITEM 4.</u> <u>SPEECHES BY THE PRIME MINISTER AND THE DEPUTY PRIME MINISTER</u>

Sir ROB LOCKHART stated that the speeches made during the last few days by the Prime Minister and the Deputy Prime Minister had gone down very well with the troops.

The GOVERNOR GENERAL suggested that the Prime Minister and Deputy Prime Minister might wish to make a special broadcast to the Armed Forces. These could perhaps best be put out at 7-45 p.m. as part of the Forces Programme.

The COMMITTEE:

Invited the Prime Minister and Deputy Prime Minister to make special pre-arranged broadcasts to the Armed Forces in the near future.

APPENDIX 'A'

Casualties figures on the
13th September, 1947

| | | | Total | Bullet and gun shot cases | Burns |
|---|---|---|---|---|---|
| Hindu | - Males | 11 | | 10 | |
| | - Females | – | | | |
| | - Child | – | 11 | | |
| Muslim | - Males | 26 | | 8 | 1 |
| | - Females | 2 | | | |
| | - Child | 3 | 31 | | |
| Grand Total - | | 42 | | | |
| Deaths | - | 2 | | | |

SECRET AND IMMEDIATE
COPY NO. 51

15TH September, 1947 E.C. 11th MEETING

EMERGENCY COMMITTEE MEETINGS
11TH MEETING

MINUTES

The 11th meeting of the Emergency Committee was held in the Council Chamber at Government House, New Delhi, at 10 a.m. on Monday, 15th September, 1947. .....

The items discussed were:

ITEM 1. CHOLERA AND SMALL-POX
ITEM 2 SITUATION IN DELHI AREA
ITEM 3 SITUATION IN THE PUNJAB
ITEM 4 OUTSTANDING ITEMS (E.C.P.10)
ITEM 5 POSTAL ARRANGEMENTS
ITEM 6 PRIME MINISTER'S VISIT TO LAHORE
ITEM 7 THE UNITED PROVINCES
ITEM 8 THE NORTH-WEST FRONTIER PROVINCE
ITEM 9 SIND AND QUETTA
ITEM 10 MUSLIM NEWSPAPERS IN LAHORE
ITEM 11 VISIT OF THE CHIEF OF THE GOVERNOR-GENERAL'S STAFF TO KARACHI ........

<u>ITEM 1.</u> <u>CHOLERA AND SMALL-POX</u>

Major General REES said that cases of cholera and small-pox were on the increase. Details are given in Appendix A attached.

ITEM 2. SITUATION IN DELHI AREA

(A) Delhi City

Major General REES reported that during the past 24 hours there had been further incidents in which a number of looters had been shot and others arrested. The evacuation of Mehrauli was proceeding satisfactorily until a shot was fired by an unknown attacker, which fatally injured the Magistrate. During the past 24 hours, 137 bad characters had been rounded up by police and military.

(B) DELHI RURAL AREAS

Tension was reported from Ballabgarh area, and also from Jhajjr and Sonepat in Rohtak district. In Hissar the situation was improved. Mobs were dealt with by the military in Gurgaon and in Karnal District. In Simla there was no improvement in the situation; when the curfew was relaxed on the morning of 13th, a bomb exploded, killing five and injuring twenty. Intensive patrolling by the military and police continues there.

ITEM 3. SITUATION IN THE PUNJAB

(A) East Punjab

Major General REES reported that there was little change in the general situation and attacks on refugees were continuing. At Jullundur and Ludhiana, troops fired on Sikh jathas who were attacking Muslim refugee trains and inflicted casualties in both cases. In Gurdaspur city, the situation was improved and the static military guard had been withdrawn.

(B) West Punjab

It was reported that an attack in Sialkot district on non-Muslim refugees was beaten off by the P.A.P. Some women and children had been abducted but a military patrol recovered 200 of them. The movement of non-Muslim refugees from Lyallpur has started.

ITEM 4. OUTSTANDING ITEMS (E.C.P.10).

The Meeting considered a list of items on which orders had been given at previous meetings of the Committee. .....

Mr. PATEL stated that there was in existence a Central Office in the Town Hall which was open 24 hours a day, and to which the commandants of the various camps put in their applications. Food, Medical and Transport officers were always on duty at this Central Office.

Mr. BHABHA drew attention to the fact that many of the inmates of the refugee camps were not real refugees at all. He pointed out there was always a large floating population in Delhi; many of the people comprising this had taken advantage of the present situation to enter the camps, and were increasing the disorder there.

On the question of supplying military personnel to help run refugee camps, Sir ROB LOCKHART said that it would be possible to provide the half Battalion of the Mahar Regiment, which had been brought as reinforcements to Delhi. Another possibility would be for the Headquarters of the Armoured Division to be put in charge of organising the two main Muslim refugee camps under Mr. Bhabha. He pointed out, however, that further calls on the Indian Army in this respect would react on and delay the operations to clear the city.

The GOVERNOR-GENERAL said that it had been suggested that some of the British troops, at present stationed in Delhi cantonment, should offer their services as volunteers to help in the running of the camps of both communities during their spare time. It should be made quite clear that these British troops would not be used for escort or military duties of any kind. They would not take their weapons with them. The Prime Minister said that he agreed that this offer should be accepted. Sir ROB LOCKHART pointed out that the British soldiers so employed would require interpreters; but it was not considered that there would be any difficulty in the supply of these from amongst the refugees themselves.

The COMMITTEE:-

(ii) invited the representative of Supreme Headquarters to arrange for the Commanding Officers of the two British Battalions stationed in Delhi Cantonment to contact Mr. Bhabha or Mr. Patel with a view to volunteers from these Battalions helping in the camps at Humayun's Tomb and Kingsway; this help would be on a volunteer spare time basis; the troops would not carry arms nor be employed on escort or other military duties. ….

Mr. Bhabha stated that the two refugee trains carrying persons (particularly Pakistan Government employees) from the Purana Qila camp, had left at 1.20 p.m. and 1.55 p.m. the previous day. These trains had carried 2,000 and 2,500 persons, respectively There had been some empty carriages, but this had been unavoidable. Mr. Patel confirmed that this had not been because the refugees concerned had been unwilling to go; rather, time had been too short to bring sufficient (sic) along. He also stated that most of the food which had been arranged for these trains had never arrived, although it had been despatched by the non-official organisation responsible. It had probably been delivered to the Purana Qila camp. .....

ITEM 6. THE PRIME MINISTER'S VISIT TO LAHORE

The PRIME MINISTER said that he had visited Lahore the previous day. There he had held long discussions with the Prime Minister of Pakistan on various matters. They had investigated certain complaints which had been made by both the West Punjab and the East Punjab Governments. These complaints had been strikingly similar. He had discussed the telegram from Sir Francis Mudie which had quoted Master Tara Singh as saying "This is war"; it had become obvious that this quotation was based on a misconception of what Master Tara Singh had, in fact, said.

The Prime Minister stated that two convoys of refugees on foot had already started. These stretched for as much as 40 miles; he had flown over one of them on his way back. There were perhaps 100,000 people in this convoy. The one (of Muslims) which was to have marched from Jullundur to Lahore via Amritsar had been held up because of the difficulty of passing through Amritsar, where there were 70,000 refugees from West Punjab in an excited state and where the atmosphere was not wholesome. The process of bull-dozing a road round Amritsar would take a week. The representatives of the West Punjab Government had considered that this would involve too long a delay , because the refugees from that province would meet trouble if it was learnt that those from East Punjab had been delayed. If this report went around, the police escort of the convoy from West Punjab would, it was felt, prove inadequate. The possibility of sending the East Punjab lot by a canal road was being investigated — the difficulty about this was that the two convoys might meet. After considerable discussion, it had been left to Major-Generals Cariappa and Chimini to make the best possible arrangements, and it was hoped that the convoy from Jullundur would start that day or the following day. .....

The PRIME MINISTER went on to say that another matter which had been discussed at Lahore was the vast number of women who had been abducted and how these could be restored to their families. According to his own information, there had been a fairly large number of abductions in East Punjab, but a very much larger number in West Punjab. Some women had already returned. He had suggested that this was largely a question for the military and the police; but that women helpers might be associated in their efforts. He had offered to accept in East Punjab any such women helpers nominated by the Pakistan Government. The main duty of such helpers would be to introduce the human element.

Lady MOUNTBATTEN undertook to examine this question in the United Council for Relief and Welfare. On Mr. Neogy's suggestion that the services of the Red Cross should be obtained to help with a Missing Persons Organisation, she explained that the International Red Cross set-up for such a purpose only came into play when there was war. She added that Pakistan were already appealing to the Indian Red Cross Society for help.

The COMMITTEE:-

(ii) directed the Principal Private Secretary to the Prime Minister to draft a statement to the effect that measures to restore abducted women had been discussed between the two Prime Ministers at Lahore; and were being further considered.

Dr. MOOKERJEE asked what arrangements were being made to bring officials of the India Government from West Punjab and Sind. The GOVERNOR GENERAL said that so far as Hindu officials in the Sind Government Service were concerned, Mr. Jinnah had given him an assurance that he wanted to keep them. The PRIME MINISTER said that many India Government officials had come and were coming from West Punjab and Sind. It was of interest to note that both the Punjab Provincial Governments had expressed a hope that officials of the opposite community would at a later stage come back and serve in their Provinces. .......

The PRIME MINISTER also stated that the representatives of West Punjab at the previous day's meeting had complained that refugee trains had arrived at Lahore without their having been informed in advance of their arrival. They had protested particularly about the arrival of Meos. They had also made complaints about certain Sikh States in East Punjab, particularly Patiala, Faridkot and Nabha.

ITEM 7. THE UNITED PROVINCES

The PRIME MINISTER stated that two Parliamentary Private Secretaries from the United Provinces had come to see him the previous day from Saharanpur. The question arose what measures should be taken to avoid the extension of trouble to the United Provinces. For example, four refugee trains were arriving there daily, carrying vast groups of people. Dr. MATTHAI stated that no refugee trains were being run to the United Provinces. The trains concerned were presumable (sic) ordinary passenger trains on which refugees were traveling.

The PRIME MINISTER went on to say that there were already 250,000 refugees in the Northern districts of the United Provinces. A dangerous situation was now being created. At Hardwar, for example, the normal population was 25,000; and there were now 60,000 Sikh and Hindu refugees. There were also some 20,000 Muslim refugees. Incidents were gradually developing from the individual to the group stage. There had been trouble in the Luxor area. The reports received from there were of great credit to the police and military. In one incident, fifteen police constables had stopped a group of 10,000 persons possessing sten guns from crossing a bridge for 24 hours.

THE PRIME MINISTER said that the measures which appeared necessary were — (a) to stop a further influx of refugees; (b) to remove some of the large number in the Luxor-Dehra Dun area; (c) to send to West Punjab the 20,000 Muslim refugees; and Muslim railway employees, who included 1,500 Baluchis; and (d) to make available, if possible, the barracks at Chakrata, possibly for Sikh refugees.

The PRIME MINISTER added that he had received a reply to his telegram to the United Provinces Prime Minister, asking whether he could accept further refugees. This was to the effect that, while the United Provinces Government was ready to take any number that was considered necessary and to help in any way, they had 2 lakhs of refugees already and hoped that a further influx would be stopped.

The COMMITTEE:-

(i) directed the Commander-in-Chief of the Indian Army to investigate the possibility of making available the barracks at Chakrata for refugees;
(ii) directed the Minister of Refugees, in consultation with the Minister of Railways and the Minister of Communications to examine points (a), (b) and (c) mentioned above by the Prime Minister.

ITEM 8. THE NORTH WEST FRONTIER PROVINCE.

The PRIME MINISTER said that he had met the Governor and the Prime Minister of the North West Frontier Province at Lahore the previous day. They had informed him that there had been two major incidents in the Province in each of which some 250 Hindus and Sikhs had been killed. The situation was completely in control; there was considerable tension and a further exciting event might lead to further incidents. They had had very exaggerated reports of what was going on in Delhi. They had informed him that there were approximately 45,000 Sikhs and Hindus left in the Province itself – one third of this number was in Peshawar, one third in Bannu, and one third in refugee camps. It was proposed kthat these last should be sent to Wah, and thence into India. They hoped that the remainder would stay on.

Lord ISMAY said that he had received identical information about the North West Frontier Province from Mr. Jinnah. He had asked that the latter should send on reports from the N.W.F.P to the Government of India; Mr. Jinnah had replied that he believed that this was already being done.

ITEM 9. SIND AND QUETTA

The PRIME MINISTER said that Mr. Liaquat Ali Khan had informed him that the situation in Sind was on the whole quiet and under control. There was a certain amount of tension and needless panicking. It was hoped and expected that the large majority of the Hindu population there would not move. Stabbings in Karachi had not exceeded about a dozen. There had been one big bomb explosion in the Headquarters of the R.S.S.S.

So far as Quetta was concerned, a certain number of non-Muslim refugees had left for Hyderabad (Sind). Otherwise the situation was quiet.

ITEM 10. MUSLIM NEWSPAPERS IN LAHORE.

The PRIME MINISTER stated that some of the Muslim newspapers in Lahore contained daily headlines urging that the Sikhs should be exterminated. He had brought this to the notice of Mr. Liaquat Ali Khan and had instructed the Indian Deputy High Commissioner in Lahore to bring further cases to the notice of the Government of West Punjab.

ITEM 11. VISIT OF THE CHIEF OF THE GOVERNOR GENERAL'S STAFF TO KARACHI

Lord ISMAY stated that he had gone to Karachi on Friday, 12th September and returned on Sunday 14th September. He had had conversations with the Governor General of Pakistan. The latter had not understood why the evacuation of Muslims from East Punjab had been so slow. He had explained the difficulties of this evacuation and informed Mr. Jinnah of the instructions which had been given to Major General Chimini.

Lord ISMAY said that he has asked Mr. Jinnah about the Draft Appeal, which was to be issued by both Governments, recognizing the necessity for mass evacuation, and undertaking to assist this. Evidently Sardar Nishtar had believed that the copy of this Appeal which he had been asked to discuss with the Pakistan Government, was only a rough draft. Mr. Mohd. Ali had sent a telegram to the Government of India, asking if they still wanted to issue it.

The PRIME MINISTER said that he had received this telegram and undertook to get into communication with Mr. Liaquat Ali Khan about the matter again.

The COMMITTEE:-
directed the Principal Private Secretary to the Prime Minister to draft a telegram from the Prime Minister to the Prime Minister of Pakistan, concerning the joint Appeal which it was suggested that both Governments should issue, saying that they recognised that mass evacuation of minorities in the Punjab was necessary and would assist it.

Lord ISMAY said that Mr. Jinnah had also asked why evacuation of refugees from Delhi had not been quicker. He (Lord Ismay) had explained the difficulties and dangers of this movement, and had informed Mr. Jinnah of the number of trains which had left. He had also told Mr. Jinnah of the tremendous efforts which were being made in connection with the refugee camps in Delhi.

Lord ISMAY went on to say that Mr. Zahid Hussain had, in his presence, complained to Mr. Jinnah that officials in Delhi had disobeyed orders given by Ministers to help him. He (Lord Ismay) had suggested that a liaison officer might be appointed to the Pakistan High Commissioner, but Mr. Zahid Hussain was at the present ill (and it was no diplomatic illness) and an Acting High Commissioner had been appointed.

The PRIME MINISTER pointed out that there was no question of officials having disobeyed orders, but rather that some of the demands which Mr. Zahid Hussain had made were so big that they were still being tackled. He added that Mr. Liaquat Ali Khan had expressed himself opposed to the suggestion that all Muslim residents in Delhi should be sent to Pakistan. Lord ISMAY said that Mr. Jinnah had expressed a similar opinion. Complaining of the slowness of evacuation from Delhi, he had been referring mainly to officials of the Pakistan Government.

APPENDIX 'A'

## CHOLERA AND SMALL-POX

LAHORE AREA
Outbreak of Cholera among Muslim refugees SHEIKHUPURA CITY.

SHEIKHUPURA DISTRICT
Cholera reported both SHEIKHUPURA and CHUHA KANA

LYALLPUR DISTRICT
Cholera Outbreak reported. Cholera vaccine provided but supply inadequate.

PAKPATAN DIPALPUR
150 cases Cholera reported. (25 miles N.E. PAKPATAN).

AMRITSAR
Likelihood imminent danger of Cholera outbreak.

FEROZEPORE DISTRICT
Cholera... 230 Muslims died 13 September in Muslim refugee camp FZR.

SITREP EAST PUNJAB AREA
Cholera increasing.

INDEP EASTERN PUNJAB AREA
Cholera increasing.

SITREP AMRITSAR
Likelihood imminent danger of cholera outbreak.

EASTERN PUNJAB AREA
Cholera and small pox reported from refugee camp Ludhiana Ferozepore

FATEHGARH CHURIAN
10 cases small pox Muslim refugee camp (18 miles N. Amritsar) evacuated to Lahore.

FEROZEPORE CANTONMENT
4 cases cholera

APPENDIX 'B'

Casualties on 14th September, 1947:

| | | | |
|---|---|---|---|
| Irwin Hospital | | Total 23 | |
| 10 Non Muslims – all men | | Bullet wounds | 5 |
| | | Stab wounds | 1 |
| | | Gun shot wounds | 4 |
| | | | 10 |
| 13 Muslims – Men | | Stab wounds | 7 |
| | | Gunshot | 1 |
| (from explosion of their own bomb) | | Burns | 1 |
| | women | Stab wounds | 1 |
| | children | stab wounds | 2 |
| | children | bullet wound | 1 |
| | | | 13 |
| | | Deaths – 1 | |

Lady Hardinge Hospital — Total 11

6 Non Muslim men, wounds dressed and wounded discharged

| | | |
|---|---|---|
| 5 Muslims – | 4 Muslim males | – stab wounds |
| | 1 Muslim girl | – stab wounds |

These say they had lain wounded for 3 days.

APPENDIX 'C'

## DECISION TAKEN AT THE CONFERENCE BETWEEN THE PRIME MINISTERS OF INDIA AND PAKISTAN AT LAHORE

Irrespective of any controls or previous administrative orders to the contrary, no convoys of evacuees and no temporary camps of evacuees about to move from West to East Punjab and from East to West Punjab will be subjected to any kind of search either by the police or the military.

Both Governments reiterate their previous decision that evacuees will be permitted to take away at their discretion and within the limits of transport available, movable property, including licensed weapons, food, domestic animals, carts and motor vehicles which are not licensed for public use.

16th September, 1947 SECRET AND IMMEDIATE
E.C.P. 12th MEETING

COPY NO. 66

EMERGENCY COMMITTEE MEETING
12TH MEETING

MINUTES.

The 12th Meeting of the Emergency Committee was held in the Council Chamber at Government House, New Delhi, at 10 a.m on Tuesday, 16th September, 1947. .....

The items discussed were:

ITEM 1. THE SITUATION IN DELHI
ITEM 2. THE SITUATION IN EAST PUNJAB
ITEM 3. CHOLERA
ITEM 4. FOOD SITUATION
ITEM 5. FUTURE MEETINGS OF THE EMERGENCY COMMITTEE
ITEM 6. REFUGEES IN DELHI
ITEM 7. OUTSTANDING ITEMS (E.C.P.11)
ITEM 8. STATEMENTS BY PAKISTAN MINISTERS
ITEM 9. DELHI AND EAST PUNJAB COMMAND

16th September, 1947. GOVERNMENT HOUSE,
NEW DELHI .......

ITEM NO. 1. THE SITUATION IN DELHI

(a) Delhi City

Major General REES stated that, on the whole, the previous 24 hours had been quiet and that the chief difficulty now as in obtaining foodstuffs, particularly for hotels and hostels. These had been some stray shooting incidents and stabbings and while the curfew was lifted there had been some looting in Chandni Chowk. At the Kadan Sharif Graveyard in Pahar Ganj hand-to-hand fighting between mobs of the two communities had been broken up by troops firing. In New Delhi, panic and tension had been reported from the Bengali Market.

(b) Delhi Rural Areas

Troops had broken up mobs near Asaoti and Sarsa Railway Stations. A patrol ws fired on by civilians near Kheri Kalan and had returned fire, inflicting casualties on their attackers. In Rohtak District, the general situation was reported to be worsening, and in Karnal District great tension was prevailing. In Simla, the situation was under control, owing to intensive patroling by the police and military.

ITEM 2. THE SITUATION IN EAST PUNJAB

Major General REES stated that the general situation had improved and that no major incidents had been reported……

ITEM 5. FUTURE MEETINGS OF THE EMERGENCY COMMITTEE

The Governor General suggested that the stage had now been reached at which action had been initiated on most of the immediate matters; and at which other matters which came before the Committee for co-ordination required a further period between meetings for action to be taken. Therefore, he proposed that meetings should be held every second day in future. The Delhi Emergency Committee would carry on as heretofore. Mr. Bhabha would ask representatives of the various Ministries concerned to attend his daily meetings in the Town Hall. Other Cabinet Meetings would, of course, be held as necessary.

THE COMMITTEE:

(i) decided that in future it would meet on every even date. (The next meeting would be at 10 a.m on Thursday, 18th September; the one after that at 10 a.m on Saturday, 20th September; and so on);

(ii) decided that Ministries need in future only send representatives to meetings when they had specific problems to be dealt with.

ITEM 6. REFUGEES IN DELHI

Rear Admiral HALL said that six loud hailers, for use in Delhi, were due to arrive that day or the day after. He undertook to obtain six more and to be responsible for their maintenance.

The GOVERNOR GENERAL suggested that the floodlights, which were being made available for use in refugee camps in Delhi, should not be permanently installed in one position, but should be made portable so that they could be used anywhere in emergency.

Dr. ZAKIR HUSSAIN made a statement on the refugee camps in Delhi, at the Prime Minister's invitation. He suggested that these places could not properly be called camps, but rather areas in which humanity was dumped. Disease was breaking out. The suggestion that he wished most to emphasise was that the present influx of refugees into the camps must be stopped. There were some 50,000 already in the Purana Qila. 16,000 had been moved from the Ridge to Humayun's Tomb but 10,000 more had turned up there. The previous day (and that morning) there had been a stream of Muslims to the Purana Qila without escort. He could see no reason why these people should have moved. There had been no incidents in some of the predominantly Muslim areas of Delhi City to impel their movement. They were evidently being advised to move by officials. He suggested that they should repeatedly be told not to move. In this matter speed was essential. He further suggested that uniforms should be provided for volunteers from among the refugees themselves to help organise the camps.

THE COMMITTEE :-

(iii) directed the Delhi Emergency Committee to investigate the possibility of providing uniforms for volunteers among the refugees in camps, to help run the camps.

MR. BHABHA said that he agreed that there had been confusion in the refugee camps, but was sure that Dr. Zakir Hussain would appreciate that the Administration had been taken by surprise by a vast mass movement. He pointed out that the Purana Qila had been run by the Pakistan High Commissioner until two days previously. He suggested that all that was possible was in fact being done. One of the main difficulties was that many of the refugees did not obey the Camp Commandants or their own leaders. It should be appreciated that until the people started to help themselves, it would not be possible to get a satisfactory organisation running.

Dr. ZAKIR HUSSAIN said that he fully agreed that much had been done for the refugee camps; his above remarks had not been intended to imply criticism.

On the suggestion that the Headquarters of the Armoured Division should be placed at the disposal of the Delhi Emergency Committee to help organise the camps, Mr. BHABHA stated that he did not consider that this would be necessary at present, particularly in view of the fact that British troops were being made available to help on a voluntary basis.

It was pointed out that these British troops would not, as had been recorded the previous day, go without arms; but they would not use their arms nor be employed on escort duties. It was further pointed out that the employment of British troops was not limited to the camps at Humayun's Tomb and Kingsway.

The PRIME MINISTER pointed out that if the mass migration of Muslims from their homes to refugee camps continued, the whole organisation would collapse. Furthermore, protection and feeding of these people in their own homes ought to be easier than in camps. The queston facing the Government was whether the migration should be approved of or not. The alternative to taking measures to stop the migration was mass evacuation.

The DEPUTY PRIME MINISTER suggested that it was probably agreed by all that those refugees who wished to leave Delhi, should be enabled to do so. It would be best to sort out those who wanted to go and to remove them as soon as possible. As for those who desired to stay, they should be advised to go back to their homes. The Government could surely not, however, take responsibility for telling people to stay and guaranteeing them protection if they did.

Major General CARIAPPA related incidents in which, as a result of prompt military action, thousands more of the Muslim inhabitants of Delhi had been stopped from going to Purana Qila, large number of those who had gone to the camps would return to their homes if some measures to ensure their security were taken. In this connection he considered that propaganda work by the leaders would be most useful.

The GOVERNOR GENERAL pointed out that the loud hailers, being produced by Rear Admiral Hall, would be most useful as a means of enabling leaders to address large masses of people.

The GOVERNOR GENERAL said that the Muslim Police at Government House had all left the previous day, in the belief that they had been offered safe transport to Pakistan and immediate employment when they arrived there. It was pointed out that these men must have been under a misapprehension, as the Pakistan Government had already declared its inability to employ more Police.

MR. SANJEVI said that he had explained this position clearly to the Muslim Police in Delhi, and had done his best to assure them that they would be safe if they remained. However, 75% had deserted; and the balance were likely to leave that day or the following day. A total of 1,600 men were involved. The GOVERNOR GENERAL suggested that , when the Cabinet considered the problem of the future of the Muslim refugees in Delhi, they should also bear in mind the question of whether or not the Muslim Police were to be re-employed. He also emphasised that, before measures were taken to induce those people at present in camps to return to their homes, arrangements for visible security and, if possible, for the provision of food in the areas to which they were to be returned, should be made.

THE COMMITTEE:

(iv) directed the Delhi Emergency Committee to consider ways and means of stemming the movement of the Muslim inhabitants of Delhi from their homes to refugee camps.

Mr.PATEL said that he had seen, the previous day, a large number of military trucks and lorries carrying refugees to the Purana Qila.

THE COMMITTEE:

(v) dirrected the Commander-in-Chief, Indian Army, to take measures to stop the use of military vehicles (probably offered on an unofficial basis by Muslim officers) to carry Muslims to refugee camps in Delhi.

Mr. PATEL said that he understood that there were a large number of wounded people in the Pahar Ganj and Ridge areas. Rajkumari AMRIT KAUR said that the Irwin Hospital was prepared to accept all these.

Mr. PATEL suggested that as many as possible of the Hindu and Sikh refugees at present in Delhi should be sent to East Punjab — particularly those who came from West Punjab.

THE COMMITTEE:

(vi) directed the Minister of Refugees to consider, in conjunction with the Government of East Punjab, the possibility of sending to that Province the Hindu and Sikh refugees from West Punjab and at present in Delhi; and of sending to other Provinces Hindu and Sikh refugees from Sind and the North-Wast Frontier Provinces at present in Delhi.

MR.PATEL stated that there was still a number of Pakistan Government officials in the Purana Qila camp.

THE COMMITTEE:

(vii) directed the Minister of Railways to arrange for two more special trains to be run on Thursday, 18th September, carrying Pakistan Government Officials from the Purana Qila camp to Lahore. ….

ITEM 8. STATEMENTS OF PAKISTAN MINISTERS.

Dr. MOOKERJI drew attention to a statement made by Mr.Liaquat Ali Khan, an account of which had appeared in that morning's newspapers. The PRIME MINISTER said that he was proposing to communicate with Mr. Liaquat Ali Khan concerning this statement; and also to issue a brief public statement himself about it.

Dr. MOOKERJI also drew attention to an extract of a statement made by Mr.Ghazanfar Ali Khan to the effect that only 10,000 people had been killed in West Punjab, as opposed to 100.000 in East Punjab.

THE COMMITTEE :-

(x) directed the Commander-in-Chief, Indian Army, to request Commander 4 Division to forward estimates of the number of people killed in East and West Punjab respectively; and of the number of refugees who had crossed the border from one Province to the other in each direction; these figures to be agreed, if possible, with Commander Lahore District.

…….

CASUALTY FIGURES FOR 15TH SEPTEMBER, 1947.

Irwin Hospital

| | | | Bullet and gun-shot cases | Stab Cases |
|---|---|---|---|---|
| Hindu | Males | 6 | 5 | 1 |
| ” | Child | 1 | 1 | |
| Muslim | Males | 6 | 2 | 4 |
| Total | | 13 | | |

No deaths

Lady Hardinge Hospital

| | | |
|---|---|---|
| Hindu | Child | 1 |
| Muslim | child | 1 |
| Total | | 2 |

No deaths

18th September,1947 SECRET AND IMMEDIATE

Copy No.68

E.C. 13th MEETING

EMERGENCY COMMITTEE MEETINGS

THIRTEENTH MEETING

MINUTES

The 13th Meeting of the Emergency Committee was held in the Council Chamber at Government House, New Delhi, at 10 a.m. on Thursday 18th September, 1947. ……..

The items discussed were:

ITEM 1. THE SITUATION IN DELHI
ITEM 2 THE SITUATION IN THE PUNJAB
ITEM 3 OUTSTANDING ITEMS
ITEM 4 THE DALMIA OFFER
ITEM 5 THE REPORT BY THE GOVERNOR OF EAST PUNJAB
ITEM 6 MEETINGS OF THE EMERGENCY COMMITTEE ……

ITEM 1. THE SITUATION IN DELHI.

The PUBLIC RELATIONS OFFICER stated that New Delhi was rapidly returning to normal and that from Old Delhi only a few cases of attempted looting and curfew breaking had been reported.

ITEM 2. THE SITUATION IN THE PUNJAB

The PUBLIC RELATIONS OFFICER reported that there was little change in the general situation and that large-scale evacuation was in progress. Near Rawajpur the military opened fire on a mob estimated at 3-4,000 and beat them off, inflicting casualties. The situation was reported to be deteriorating in Dujana, Ambala and Simla areas. Refugee escorts beat off attacking mobs at Barnala and Kaithal.

Major General REES stated that there were many rumours circulating on both sides of the border. One, in particular, alleged that the Pakistan authorities were holding up a large column of Sikh refugees because they believed that the East Punjab authorities were doing the same to Muslim refugees. He stated that there was some delay in the evacuation of Muslim refugees, owing to the water-logged nature of the country since the recent heavy rains, but it was untrue to say that the West Punjab authorities had delayed Sikh refugees, and they were, in fact, on the move.

Mr. SHANMUKHAM CHETTY and Dr. MOOKERJI expressed the opinion which was generally accepted, that insufficient information was being obtained from West Punjab; and that there was a possibility that the reports of incidents from West Punjab were being minimised.

Sir ROB LOCKHART pointed out that there was already a Brigadier of the Indian Army attached to Headquarters, Lahore Area. However, it was agreed that arrangements should be made for more observers to be exchanged between East and West Punjab on a reciprocal basis.

The COMMITTEE:
invited the Prime Minister to discuss at his next meeting with the Prime Minister of Pakistan, the possibility of an exchange of observers, including civil representatives and Press men, between East and West Punjab, with the object of improving the standard of reports of incidents in one Dominion sent to the other.

ITEM 3. OUTSTANDING ITEMS (E.C.P.12)

The meeting considered a list of items on which action had been ordered at previous meetings by the Committee.

Refugees in Delhi

On Serial 151, Mr. BHABHA stated that a Sub-Committee, especially convened to consider the matter, had reported that it considered that there was no necessity for plans for a further refugee camp in Delhi to be formulated at the present stage. The GOVERNOR GENERAL said that it was estimated that there were about 95,000 persons in the two existing Muslim refugee camps.

On Serial 170, it was suggested that members of the police force who had deserted to the Muslim refugee camps in Delhi should be given back their uniforms on the condition that they helped to organise the camps. Mr. PATEL stated that this proposal was opposed by the Police authorities. He added that caps and armlets had been issued to volunteers among the refugees helping to run the camps; and undertook at the Prime Minister's suggestion, to look into the possibility of providing these volunteers with at least half a suit of uniform.

On Serial 171, Mr. BHABHA said that the movement of the Muslim inhabitants of Delhi from their homes to the refugee camps had greatly diminished. Muslim leaders had been going round asking them not to leave their homes.

On the Prime Minister's suggestion, the COMMITTEE:-

(i) directed the Ministry of Information & Broadcasting give publicity to the fact that it was the object of the Government to stem the exodus of the Muslim inhabitants of Delhi from their homes to refugee camps.

The GOVERNOR-GENERAL emphasized the importance of sufficiently guarding those Muslims who were asked to stay in their homes. Cordons should be put round the areas concerned; unruly elements should be stopped from entering these areas; and illegal occupants of houses should be ejected. ....

Mr. PATEL stated that the refugees were still arriving at Delhi by train. The recrudescences of trouble which had occurred in the last few days might well be due to these arrivals. Dr MATTHAI pointed out that the only way to stop any refugees arriving by train in Delhi was to cancel all passenger trains from West Punjab. He proposed that this should be done as from 20th September.

The PRIME MINISTER emphasized the enormous importance of improving the sanitary conditions in the refugee camps in Delhi. If this was not done, he considered that the health of the city of Delhi as a whole would be imperiled. Apart from this, it was evident that the present conditions in the camps were being used for propaganda purposes, as many Press correspondents were visiting them regularly. Dr MOOKERJI suggested that Press correspondents should be stopped from taking photographs in these camps; Sardar BALDEV SINGH considered that it might be better if, rather than stopping facilities for the Press in India, an improvement was made in facilities for them in Pakistan. Mr. CAMPBELL JOHNSON pointed out that the difficulty arose from the fact that the majority of the correspondents were based at Delhi. Sir ROB LOCKHART stated that Miss Bourke-White a photographer from Life, had expressed herself very anxious to visit the Punjab.

The COMMITTEE:-

(vi) directed the Public Relations Committee to examine methods of facilitating tours by Press correspondents to West Punjab, with particular reference to the Press camp which it had been decided (at a Joint Defence Council Meeting on 29th August) to set up at Lahore.

The PRIME MINISTER asked what arrangements were being made to provide the refugee camps in Delhi with doctors. Dr MEHTA stated that there was great difficulty in obtaining doctors because of the fear of danger within the camps. Lady MOUNTBATTEN gave her view that the hostility which had at first been displayed by the refugees in the camps, had subsided. The GOVERNOR GENERAL suggested that the doctors already in the camps should be consulted by Dr Mehta and asked if they wanted help.

Dr. MEHTA stated that some sweepers, who had been brought over from Meerut, had refused to work in the camps. He pointed out that there were a number of Muslim servants already there. Mr. BHABHA said that these sweepers had been brought in by the Chief Commissioner to help clear up Delhi city. He added that the Muslim servants in the camps were not at all keen to work.

The PRIME MINISTER said that he would be grateful if Dr Mehta would inform him what progress was made in medical arrangements at the camps. In particular, screens or tents should be provided for labour cases. Mr. PATEL said that 200 tents had been sent to the Purana Qila, intended for use in the hospital there, but all except 10 had been misappropriated for other purposes.

The PRIME MINISTER also asked that ambulances should be made available to take casualties from the camps to hospitals. Brigadier MADHUV SINGHJI undertook to provide one ambulance or lorry, equipped to take stretcher cases, for this purposes.

The PRIME MINISTER said that he also understood that barbed wire was urgently required. Sir ROB LOCKHART undertook to provide this.

The PRIME MINISTER then stated that he had received complaints about the food supplied in the Hindu/Sikh camp at Kingsway. It had been reported that food was being brought into the camp from neighbouring villages. Mr. BHABHA said that all indents received from the Kingsway camp had been met.

Mr. BHABHA said that many unjustified complaints were being received that no food or medical supplies had been sent to the refugee camps. He instanced particularly a letter which he had received from a European lady. He suggested that more publicity, of what had been to the camps, should be given.

The COMMITTEE:-

(vii) directed the Delhi Emeregency Committee to report at the next meeting on the conditions in the refugee camps in Delhi, with particular reference to measures taken to improve sanitation and medical arrangements.

(ix) directed the Delhi Emergency Committee to issue publicity daily on the food, medical, etc. supplies which were being sent to the refugee camps.

<u>Other matters concerning Delhi</u>

Sir ROB LOCKHART produced a list four pages long of the static guards which the Army was having to find in Delhi. The PRIME MINISTER suggested that the soldiers guarding Ministers' residences should be removed. The GOVERNOR GENERAL pointed out that, if this was done, police guards on their residences must be retained.

Mr. PATEL reported an incident which had just occurred at Delhi Station. A military guard from the Pakistan Army had arrived to escort back a refugee train. Certain soldiers, who had opted for India, had been left at the station. A Muslim had been stabbed by a Sikh and ten minutes later another Sikh had been shot by one of these soldiers.

The COMMITTEE:-

(x) directed the Commander-in-Chief, India, to report at the next meeting on this incident at Delhi station.

<u>"Non-Delhi" Items</u>

On Serial 163, the PRIME MINISTER stated that he had received information from the Indian Deputy High Commissioner in Lahore that searches of refugees passing from there to East Punjab had been stopped. He had not yet, however, received a reply from Mr. Liaquat Ali Khan to his telegram suggesting that the ban on searches of refugees should be extended.

The DEPUTY PRIME MINISTER said that he had received a report that 10,000 refugees waiting to be evacuated from Hyderabad (Sind) had been searched and robbed. Dr MOOKERJI also quoted reports of licenced arms having been taken away from refugees.

The COMMITTEE:

(xi) invited the Prime Minister to bring these reports to the notice of the Prime Minister of Pakistan……

On Serial 179, the PRIME MINISTER stated that there were 250,000 Hindu and Sikh refugees in the Western United Provinces. More than half of these had arrived over the last fortnight. It was for consideration whether some of them could be moved to East Punjab. Sir CHANDULAL TRIVEDI pointed out that, since 15th August, East Punjab had received more than a million refugees from West Punjab. Another two million might be coming. He did not consider that East Punjab would be able to absorb more than that number. The PRIME MINISTER pointed out that at least an equivalent number of Muslim refugees would have left or be leaving East Punjab. Sir CHANDULAL TRIVEDI said that there were one million Muslims in Ambala Division, the movement of whom had not yet started. The total Muslim population in East Punjab was four million. There was a difference of one lakh between that and the total non-Muslim population of West Punjab. Moreover, refugees from the North-West Frontier Province had come to East Punjab. Whereas he agreed that any further movement into the United Provinces should be stopped, he said that he would much prefer to leave those who were already in the United Provinces there, until East Punjab had a chance of clearing up their own mess…….

ITEM 5. THE REPORT BY THE GOVERNOR OF EAST PUNJAB

SIR CHANDULAL TRIVEDI reported that collective fines had been imposed in four cases on non-Muslims in East Punjab. He pointed out that it required great courage on the part of his Ministers to agree to these impositions. Three had been in Ambala District and three in Hoshiarpur District.

The COMMITTEE:

(i) invited the Prime Minister to inform the Prime Minister of Pakistan of these impositions of collective fines, and to ask whether it was intended that the Government of West Punjab should impose collective fines.

SIR CHANDULAL TRIVEDI said that he had (in accordance with the decisions of the Joint Defence Council meeting held at Lahore on 29th August) issued ordinances for the setting up of concentration camps and making illegal congregations of more than five persons.

The COMMITTEE:-

(ii) invited the Prime Minister to find out from the Prime Minister of Pakistan whether the West Punjab Government had issued similar ordinances.

SIR CHANDULAL TRIVEDI recalled that he had been asked to consider the re-arming of the Muslim Police in Ambala District. As most of these had now opted to go to West Punjab, he considered that such a step would be inadvisable.

SIR CHANDULAL TRIVEDI emphasized that he still wanted more troops — particularly in the Ambala sub-Area and in Hissar and Rohtak. SIR ROB LOCKHART said that all possible reinforcements were being brought from the rest of India to Delhi and East Punjab. He understood to inform Sir Chandulal Trivedi what units would be sent to East Punjab.

SIR CHANDULAL TRIVEDI went on to say that he understood that only one or two sections of each battalion at present in the East Punjab Area were available for the maintenance of law and order. Over 90% of the soldiers were engaged in guarding Muslim refugee camps and escorting Muslim refugee convoys. He recalled that the Joint Defence Council had, on the 29th August, decided that Muslim refugee camps in East Punjab should be guarded by troops of the Pakistan Army. He considered that the Pakistan Army were not providing their proper quota of escorts.

SIR ROB LOCKHART said that it had been agreed that it would be impracticable for all Muslim refugees in East Punjab to be guarded by troops of the Pakistan Army; each case was to be taken on its merits. It had also been laid down by the Emergency Committee that the first priority in East Punjab was to be the movement of evacuees, even at the expense of law and order.

MAJOR-GENERAL CARIAPPA said that he had been personally assured by Lieutenant-General Gracey that all the non-Muslim convoys leaving West Punjab were adequately protected. He went on to point out that the number of companies sent by either Dominion to guard their refugees in the other was equal.

The PRIME MINISTER said that he understood that one convoy of 100,000 non-Muslim refugees was protected by only 40 policemen. He also drew attention to a telegram from Major-General Chimini saying that a convoy of four lakhs of non-Muslim refugees was in a very vulnerable position and asking for two further Infantry Battalions and an Armoured Car Regiment.

The COMMITTEE:-

(iii) directed the Ministry of States to convene a conference of representatives of the Punjab States and the East Punjab Government to consider the re-settlement of non-Muslim refugees in those States.

Mr. DESAI said that the Government of Bikaner had drawn attention to the fact that there were 50,000 Muslim refugees wanting to pass through Bikaner on the way to Bahawalpur. Their way would lead through an area in which there was a very large number of Hindu and Sikh refugees, and this was very liable to lead to trouble. THE GOVERNOR GENERAL asked Sir Chandulal Trivedi to bear in mind the possibility that these Muslim refugees might have to move through East Punjab.

SARDAR BALDEV SINGH said that he intended to send to the Government of East Punjab within the next few days his proposals on the raising of Home Guards of a semi-military character in East Punjab. .........

Casualty figures for the 16th September 1947

## IRWIN HOSPITAL

| | | Bullet and gun Shot cases | Stab cases | Lathi | Burns |
|---|---|---|---|---|---|
| Hindu | | | | | |
| Males | 10 | 7 | 2 | 1 | - |
| Females | - | - | - | - | - |
| Children | - | - | - | - | - |
| Muslim | | | | | |
| Males | 27 | 7 | 18 | 2 | - |
| Females | 2 | - | - | 2 | 2 |
| Children | 10 | 1 | | 6 | 3 |
| Total | 49 | | | | |
| Deaths | 7 | | | | |

## LADY HARDINGE HOSPITAL
(Out patients Department)

| | | | |
|---|---|---|---|
| Hindu | Males | 4 | (ordinary injuries) |
| Muslim | Female | 1 | |
| | | 5 | |

(Admissions)

| | | | |
|---|---|---|---|
| Hindu | Males | 3 | (2 gun shot wounds) |
| Muslim | Child | 1 | (old stab wound) |
| | Total | 4 | |

No deaths.

APPENDIX B

Casualty figures for the 17th September, 1947

## IRWIN HOSPITAL

| | | Bullet and gun shot cases | Lathi cases | Stab cases | Burns |
|---|---|---|---|---|---|
| Non-Muslim | Males | 3 | 2 | 1 | 6 |
| | Females | - | - | - | - |
| | Child | 1 | - | - | 1 |
| | | | | | 7 |
| Muslim | Males | 7 (all old) | 7 | 10 (5 old) | 24 |
| | Females | - | 1 | - | 1 |
| | Children | - | 1 | 1 | 2 |
| | | | | | 27 |
| | | | | Grand Total | 34 |

Deaths - 6

## LADY HARDINGE HOSPITAL

| | | Bullet and gun shot cases | Lathi cases | Stab cases | Burns |
|---|---|---|---|---|---|
| Non-Muslim | Males | 1 | - | - | 1 |
| Muslim | Female | - | 1 | - | 1 |
| | | | | Total | 2 |

No.245\CF\47
14th November 1947

SECRET AND IMMEDIATE
COPY NO. 63
E.C. 27TH MEETING

EMERGENCY COMMITTEE MEETINGS
TWENTY-SEVENTH MEETING

MINUTES

The 27th Meeting of the Emergency Committee was held in the Council Chamber at Government House, New Delhi at 10 a.m. on Friday, 14th November 1947.......

The Items discussed were:

<u>ITEM No.1</u> OUTSTANDING ITEMS (E.C.P 25)
<u>ITEM NO.2</u> REHABILITATION POLICY

14th November, 1947

GOVERNMENT HOUSE
NEW DELHI .......

<u>ITEM NO.1</u> <u>OUTSTANDING ITEMS (E.C.P. 25)</u>

<u>Refugee Camps in Delhi</u>

On Serial 270, Mr. DHARMA VIRA handed in a report, of which a copy is at Appendix A to these Minutes. Mr. DHARMA VIRA undertook, at Dr.MEHTA'S request, to arrange for an ambulance to be sent to Humayun's Tomb.

<u>Movement of Muslims from Delhi</u>

MR. NEOGY stated, in connection with Serial 310, that a train had been laid on to remove 8,000 Pakistan Government personnel and their families from Delhi the previous day. This had, however, had to be cancelled because a large number of ordinary Muslim refugees, of whom there were, 20,800 from Delhi city, Gurgaon District and elsewhere, had reached the station first and prevented the right people from being loaded. Arrangements would now be made to lay on another train; and special precautions would be taken to prevent unauthorized people reaching the platform. Mr. NEOGY stated that he understood that the difficulty which prevented more trains being supplied for movement from Delhi was that the rakes which had gone to Pakistan had not been returned as quickly as had been anticipated.

The MINISTER OF HEALTH gave her view that trains should be arranged for all the Muslim refugees in Delhi; they were all suffering and they all wanted to go to Pakistan.

The PRIME MINISTER pointed out that many Muslims who had not previously desired to leave had now changed their minds. There appeared to be no end to the process of sending Muslim refugees by train from Delhi. The feeling of insecurity continued. This was mainly a psychological problem; and the present Committee was not the place to discuss this.

The COMMITTEES:

(i) directed the Minister for Relief and Rehabilitation to report further, at the next meeting, on the progress of evacuating Pakistan Government personnel and Muslim refugees in general from Delhi. .........

28th November 1947 SECRET AND IMMEDIATE

COPY NO. 62

EMERGENCY COMMITTEE MEETINGS
TWENTY-EIGHTH MEETING

MINUTES

The 28th Meeting of the Emergency Committee was held in the Governor-General's room at Government House, New Delhi at 10.30 a.m on Friday, 28th November, 1947. ……

The items discussed were:

ITEM 1 - OUTSTANDING ITEMS (E.C.P.26)

ITEM 2 - THE MILITARY EMERGENCY STAFF

28th November 1947 Government House New Delhi ……..

ITEM - 1 OUTSTANDING ITEMS (E.C.P 26)

Delhi Refugee Camps

On Serial 270, Mr. DHARMA VIRA handed in a report of which a copy is at Appendix A to these Minutes.

Movement of Muslim Refugees from Delhi

In connection with Serial 316, Mr. NEOGY stated that, of the total of 28,000 Muslim refugees in Delhi, some 4,000 were Pakistan Government personnel. Many of the remainder had come to Delhi from Gurgaon, presumably in the hope of being sent by train thence to Pakistan. In practice, it so happened that trains were running from Gurgaon itself but not from Delhi, to Pakistan.

Mr. GOPALASWAMI AYYANGAR said that the provision of trains to carry Muslim refugees from Delhi to Lahore would present little difficulty.

The COMMITTEE:-

(i) directed the Minister for Relief and Rehabilitation to examine, as a matter of urgency, ways and means of clearing Delhi completely of Muslim refugees, and of closing down, after they had all left, the Muslim refugee camps there.

The Number of Muslims left in East Punjab.

Sir CHANDULAL TRIVEDI stated that 137,000 Muslims were left in Ambala District, 120,000 in Karnal District, and 53,000 in Gurgaon District. This total of over 3 lakhs might, however, by now have been reduced to 2½ lakhs. He understood that some Muslims wished to remain in Karnal and Gurgaon districts.

The Number of non-Muslims to come to East Punjab

Sir CHANDULAL TRIVEDI stated that the number of non-Muslims still to come to East Punjab was 61,000 from West Punjab (which number did not include those in pockets, but only those in concentrations); 50,000 from the North West Frontier-Province; and 20,000 from Bahawalpur. He said that from comparison with census figures, 160,000 non-Muslims had so far not been accounted for. Mr.NEOGY pointed out that the numbers not accounted for were probably higher than this, because of the undoubted increase in population since the last census.

Non-Muslims in the N.W.F.P.

The CHAIRMAN OF THE UNITED COUNCIL FOR RELIEF & WELFARE said that Mr.Kirpalani had informed her that there were a number of non-Muslims in Bannu who wanted to stay there. The PRIME MINISTER said that he, on the other hand, was every day receiving large numbers of telegrams from non-Muslims in Bannu asking for arrangements to be made to evacuate them from India.

The GOVERNOR GENERAL said that Lieut.Colonel Iskander Mirza had informed him that he had met in Delhi some Hindu evacuees from

Bannu and Dera Ismail Khan who wanted to return there. The PRIME MINISTER said that he had never heard such fantastic nonsense; he was surrounded by evacuees from these places asking him to make arrangements to bring the remainder out. There was no doubt but that the non-Muslims in the N.W.F.P were even more frightened now since the Kashmir affair.

Mr.GOPALASWAMI AYYANGAR said that he had asked Mr.Liaquat Ali Khan why the Premier of the N.W.F.P was allowed to prevent non-Muslims leaving that Province. Mr.Liaquat Ali Khan was now awaiting a reply on this subject from the Premier of the N.W.F.P and had given an assurance that he would not stand in the way of allowing every single non-Muslim who wished to leave Pakistan to depart. Mr.GOPALASWAMI AYYANGAR added that the M.E.O.S were ready to provide trains as soon as clearance was received.

Sir CHANDULAL TRIVEDI gave his view that these non-Muslims were probably being kept in the N.W.F.P. as hostages.

The COMMITTEE:

(ii) directed the Minister Without Portfolio to continue his efforts to make the Prime Minister of Pakistan induce the Premier of the N.W.F.P no longer to prevent the evacuation of non-Muslims from that Province.

The Kurukshetra Camp

In connection with Serial 320, the MINISTER OF HEALTH stated that almost 3 lakhs of refugees were now in Kurukshetra Camp. There was no shelter for about one third of this number.

Sir CHANDULAL TRIVEDI undertook to issue a public notification to the effect that no further refugees would be permitted to enter Kurukshetra Camp; and to take the necessary measures to put this decision into effect. He pointed out that batches of refugees were already leaving the camp for rehabilitation at different places.

The COMMITTEE:

Directed the Minister Without Portfolio to arrange for the fact that this notification was going to be issued to be immediately publicized.

Movement of Refugees into the United Provinces

The PRIME MINISTER recalled that the Premier and Home Minister of East Punjab had both agreed, at a meeting a fortnight previously, to take steps to stop the further movement of refugees into the United Provinces. It had been agreed that a permit system should be introduced in order to keep this movement down to an absolute minimum. This was intended primarily for the benefit of business men. He understood that 3,000 permits a day were now being given to people to enter the United Provinces from East Punjab. He did not consider that this was in accordance with the policy which the East Punjab Ministers had agreed to.

Panepat

The PRIME MINISTER recalled that when Mahatma Gandhi had visited Panepat some three weeks ago he had found a deplorable state of affairs there. However, the leaders of all communities, including non-Muslim refugees who had arrived there, had given their pledge to Mahatma Gandhi that peace and order would be maintained and that the Muslims would not be pushed out. The total of non-Muslim refugees had then been 10,000. The East Punjab Ministers had undertaken not to send any further non-Muslim refugees there. Since then, however, another 20,000 had been sent in.

Mr.GOPALASWAMI AYYANGAR stated that the total number of Muslims in Panepat was 30,000. Practically the whole lot , in view of these recent developments, now wanted to move to Pakistan. Accordingly registration was proceeding for those who insisted on going and train facilities would be made available. The COMMITTEE agreed, though with regret, that there was no alternative now to the arrangements which had been made by the Minister Without Portfolio.

Movement of Muslim Refugees from Gurgaon

Mr.GOPALASWAMI AYYANGAR stated, in connection with Serial 319, that it had been intended that the last foot convoy of Muslim refugees should leave Gurgaon two days previously. This was to have consisted of 50,000 persons. But 45,000 had decided to take the opportunity of going by train instead. Trains had been arranged accordingly. He understood .: at 120,000 Muslims remained in Gurgaon.

Rehabilitation Policy

In connection with Serial 312, Mr.Neogy said that the Premier and Home Minister of East Punjab had given him the impression that, apart from those non-Muslim refugees who had already gone to other Provinces from East Punjab, there was a further requirement for 750,000 to be moved outside that

Province. The Government of India did not agree with this view, and considered that East Punjab had plenty of room to absorb even more than this number. He pointed out that the unit of land (10 acres) which was being allotted to non-Muslim refugees in East Punjab was larger than the Muslim evacuees had ever had and much larger than the average allotment in other Provinces. The accommodation question was also closely involved, because, if so large allocations of land were made, a considerable amount of accommodation would not be utilized. It was considered impracticable that it should be utilized temporarily, because of the difficulty of turning people out again.

The PRIME MINISTER pointed out that there was an agitation for the land allotment in East Punjab even to be increased to 15 acres. Sir CHANDULAL TRIVEDI pointed out that the refugees had had much larger allotments in West Punjab.

Mr.NEOGY said that the Punjab States were not co-operating fully in the rehabilitation of refugees. They were applying a highly selective process before acceptance. In Patiala 600,000 Muslims had left, but only 90,000 non-Muslims had been taken in. How, in these circumstances, was it possible to ask Provinces like Bombay and Madras to accept more refugees?

Sir CHANDULAL TRIVEDI said that he agreed that the States were not cooperating fully. He had asked representatives of those concerned to a conference at Jullundur on 3rd December.

The PRIME MINISTER said that so far as urban refugees were concerned the Central Government was doing everything possible to help the Government of East Punjab solve this problem.

The COMMITTEE:

(iii) agreed that land should be provided in East Punjab and the East Punjab States for all the non-Muslim agriculturist refugees who had come there; and directed the Minister for Relief and Rehabilitation in consultation with the East Punjab Government to calculate what the average land allotment should be, taking into account the total figures of refugees who had entered the area in comparison to those who had left. .........

Abducted Women

The CHAIRMAN OF THE UNITED COUNICL FOR RELIEF AND WELFARE said that a considerable number of abducted women were now being restored from Pakistan. The numbers that had been restored from

East Punjab were not so high. A proposal had been made that funds should be made available to liaison officers in Pakistan to assist in the recovery of abducted women. She personally was very apprehensive at the suggestion of introducing monetary transactions into this matter. Mr.NEOGY said that the practice of paying "ransoms" for abducted women had been started by the relatives of some.

Sir CHANDULAL TRIVEDI said that he had been informed that the total of abducted women in West Punjab was 28,000 and in East Punjab 5,026.

The COMMITTEE:

(iv) agreed that no funds should be made available in connection with the recovery of abducted women.

Smallpox

Sir CHANDULAL TRIVEDI undertook to investigate reports of smallpox at Ambala; and to inform the Minister of Health of the results of his investigation.

Organisation for Tracing Missing Persons

The CHAIRMAN FOR THE UNITED COUNCIL FOR RELIEF AND WELFARE mentioned that machinery had now been set up in Pakistan for tracing missing persons.

The Displacement of Harijans and Christians

Sir CHANDULAL TRIVEDI undertook to look into reports of Harijans and Christians having been displaced, in certain areas in East Punjab by Sikhs; and to inform the Minister of Health of the result of his investigation.

Welfare Workers

The CHAIRMAN OF THE UNITED COUNCIL FOR RELIEF AND WELFARE recalled that the Government of East Punjab had asked for a large number of welfare workers. She had now received an unofficial message that these were not after all wanted. Sir CHANDULAL TRIVEDI undertook to investigate this.

ANNEXURE – A

CHIEF COMMISSIONER'S OFFICE
CENTRAL CONTROL ROOM
TOWN HALL
DELHI

November 27, 1947

MUSLIM REFUGEE CAMPS

Humayun' Tomb Camp

The number of refugees at the Humayun's Tomb camp today is 28,000 as against 26,000 on the 20th November 1947. In addition, about 4,000 Pakistan Government servants are staying in Isa Khan Tomb.

There is a steady increase in population. The Medical Authorities are pressing us for a special train to carry patients, hospital staff and other voluntary workers to Pakistan.

Food

The stock position of food grains at the Humayun's Tomb Camp is satisfactory. 75 bags of atta were supplied today and the camp had a balance of 20 bags yesterday. 20 bags of dal and 3 bags of salt were supplied yesterday.

Health

The medical and sanitary arrangements at the camp are satisfactory.

Security

Security arrangements are satisfactory and there is no incident to report.

Non-Muslim Camps

The population at the Kingsway camps is over 13,000. Arrangements are being made to expand those camps to take about 30,000 refugees. A canteen is being started at these camps.

Two N.C.Os have been engaged for the physical training of refugees at the Kingsway camps. The transit camps at the Wavell Canteen and Willingdon aerodrome are functioning satisfactorily.

Food

There are adequatc stocks of food grains, ghee, masalas, oils etc., at these camps. Arrangements are being made to start a central store where foodstuffs for at least a fortnight will be stocked.

Vegetables are being supplied to the refugees twice a week.

It is also proposed to start a number of cottage industries at these camps to provide remunerative work for the refugees.

Health

Health and sanitary arrangements are most satisfactory.

Sgd. A.S. Bhatnagar, Secretary to the
Chief Commissioner and Secretary,
Central Control Room, Delhi

SECRET

# REPORT ON THE EMERGENCY COMMITTEE OF THE CABINET

## Introduction

1. This report does not attempt to deal in detail with the decisions reached and action taken by the Emergency Committee of the Cabinet; but rather with the way in which that Committee might prove useful if similar events ever necessitated the establishment of a similar body.

## The setting up of the Committee

2. The Emergency Committee was set up on 6th September 1947, when events in the Punjab and in Delhi were such as to make necessary emergency measures to deal with the situation. Owing to the then Governor-General's considerable personal experience of similar crises in the war, and of the functioning of similar bodies to deal with such crises, he was invited by the Government of India to be Chairman of the Committee; and his Chief of Staff, Lord Ismay, probably the most experienced man in the world on this type of set up, attended nearly every meeting.

## Composition and attendance

3. It was decided that the Emergency Committee should consist of the following full members:

The Prime Minister (who was also Minister for External Affairs and Commonwealth Relations)

The Deputy Prime Minister (who was also Minister for Home Affairs; States; and Information & Broadcasting)

The Minister for Defence.

The Minister for Transport and Railways.
The Minister for Relief and Rehabilitation (whose appointment was new, resulting from the crisis).

4. Nearly all meetings of the Emergency Committee were also attended by the Minister without Portfolio (whose appointment was also new and who had special duties with regard to refugees, particularly vis-à-vis the East Punjab Government); and by the Minister for Health,. These two Ministers were virtually treated as full members.

5. The Minister for Commerce also attended nearly all meetings, not so much in his ministerial capacity as in his capacity as Chairman of the Delhi Emergency Committee (see paragraph 18 below).

6. It was laid down that other Ministers would attend as necessary. Those who came most often were the Minister for Education (who, as the senior Muslim member of the Government, represented Muslim interests); the Minister for Communications: and the Minister for Industries and Supplies.

7. It was also laid down that certain Ministries would nominate representatives to attend all meetings and be responsible for ensuring that executive action, decided upon, was taken. The original list of these Ministries was soon out of date, because of the changing situation and also on account of the fact that certain Ministers held more than one portfolio. Similarly, a list of Ministries which would nominate representatives to attend when specifically summoned soon became out of date. The compilation of these lists, in future, would depend upon circumstances and the portfolios held by Ministers who were full members of the Committee.

8. It was also laid down that certain other persons would attend meetings either regularly or when specially required. These included the Commander-in-Chief of the Indian Army (who, in the later stages, usually sent a representative; Commanders of subordinate Commands and Areas also attended on occasion); the two other Defence Service Chiefs; the Chairman of the United Council for Relief and Welfare (which co-ordinated the work of various voluntary bodies); and others.

Terms of Reference

9 The terms of reference given to the Committee were wide.

They read:-

> "Within the general framework of Cabinet policy, the Emergency Committee will issue all the necessary executive orders to meet the situation. The Emergency Committee has been given by the Cabinet overriding authority and priority in dealing with the Emergency".

Frequency of Meetings

10. The Committee usually met at 10.am. From 6th to 16th September 1947 inclusive it met daily; thence until 30th September on an average every other day; thence until 10th October twice weekly; thence until 14th November once weekly; and finally on 28th November.

Secretariat

11. The Governor-General's staff was able to help with secretarial arrangements for the Committee. His Conference Secretary was available to attend and take the minutes of the meetings, and there were up to five stenographers to whom the minutes were dictated and who typed and reproduced them.

This number was not excessive in view of the fact that the minutes of some meetings (which often took over three hours) exceeded 20 pages.

Method of Working

12. Lord Hankey, predecessor to Lord Ismay, (who was Secretary to the British Cabinet and Defence Committee and later Chief of Staff to the Prime Minister) wrote in his book "Diplomacy by Conference":-

> "If we had any success in the Committee of Imperial Defence and the War Cabinet systems of the two wars, it was because we worked on the principle that time, even minutes of time, count. The rule was that the conclusions.... had to be circulated the same day — not three weeks

later, as was only too common in some Departments, and I expect is not unknown today….. Action always had to be followed up. A system of "chasing" was adopted and is essential".

13. So far as speed was concerned, the full minutes of meetings and the consequent papers for the following day were usually issued within four hours of the end of each meeting. It was fortunate that an extra secretarial staff was available, as the same speed could not otherwise have been maintained without a considerable expansion of the Cabinet Secretariat. (On the other hand, it is undeniable that accuracy was occasionally sacrificed in the interests of speed; and it must regretfully be recorded that the Prime Minister's name was spelt wrong on the "cover sheets" of the minutes of the first seven meetings!).

14. The system of "chasing" adopted by the Committee was as follows. The decisions reached under each item were crystallized into "directions" to the Minister or Ministry concerned. At the same time as the minutes containing these "directions" were sent out, a list of all "directions" which had been issued up to date, and on which action was not known to have been completed, was circulated. This list was called "Outstanding Items". At the next meeting, the list was considered item by item, and the Minister or representative of the Ministry concerned reported what had been done in the matter.

15. The list of Outstanding items was made out under four column headings:

(a) Serial Consecutive serial numbers were used throughout. The figure 320 was reached — indicating that this number of "directions", on which "chasing" action was considered necessary, was issued.

(b) Meeting at which ordered, Item number and date
The object of this was to facilitate reference to the minutes concerned, and to show the number of days that the completion of action on any serial had been pending.

(c) Action The Minister or Ministry concerned was shown.

(d) Detail The "direction" itself was shown.

16. The maximum number of items for report on one day exceeded forty. The minimum number, towards the end of the Committee's existence, was six.

Order of business

17. The normal order of business was:-

(a) Report in the Map Room (See paragraph 24 below).
(b) "Outstanding Items"(see paragraph 14 above).
(c) Reports of visits or tours undertaken by Ministers or others.
(d) Unforeseen items (any points which Ministers or others wished to raise).
(e) Agenda papers (of which there were but few).

Delhi Emergency Committee

18. A special Committee was set up to co-ordinate measures to deal with the local situation in Delhi when it was at its worst. The Minister for Commerce was appointed Chairman of this Committee and the Cabinet Secretary (who later became Secretary, Ministry of Defence) was appointed Deputy Chairman.

19. It was made clear that the establishment of this Committee did not affect the ultimate responsibility of the local administration.

Liaison with East Punjab

20. East Punjab was, of course, the Province most affected by the emergency. The Minister without Portfolio had special liaison duties vis-à-vis the East Punjab Government (see paragraph 4 above). The Governor, the Premier, and other Ministers and officials of the East Punjab Government attended Executive Committee meetings periodically.

21. An East Punjab Emergency Committee was also set up, copies of the minutes of the meetings of which were made available to the members of the Executive Committee itself, and vice versa.

The Military Emergency Staff:

22. The Military Emergency Staff, set up to assist the Emergency Committee, was an organization mainly to provide as up to date and accurate information as possible, and also to provide liaison between the Emergency Committee and the Navy, Army and Air Force.

23. The Military Emergency Staff operated from a Map Room and offices adjacent to the Cabinet Room at Government House. The Map Room contained maps, charts, graphs, and statistics of current importance. The maps included large scale maps of the disturbed areas — East and West Punjab, Junagarh, Kashmir, etc — also maps showing troops dispositions of Indian and Pakistan troops Charts and graphs showed the incidence of casualties, hospital admissions, cholera and small pox statistics, inoculations, movements of refugees by train, road or on foot and so on. The Map Room also displayed current newspapers, photographs, and weapons captured during the disturbances.

24. A verbal situation report was rendered before each Emergency Committee meeting in the Map Room. Cabinet Ministers who did not attend the actual meetings often came to the Map Room, so as to be in possession of the latest information. There were also Map Room expositions for representatives of the Diplomatic Corps (originally two sessions a week) and the Press (Originally daily meetings).

25. Many distinguished visitors came to the Map Room, such as the Congress Working Committee; the British Secretary of State for Commonwealth Relations; the Prime Minister of Burma; and Indian Princes.

26. In the matter of liaison the Military Emergency Staff acted as a link between the Emergency Committee and the Headquarters of the Fighting Services — the Navy, the Air Force and the Army (including Army Headquarters, India; Headquarters of the Supreme Commandeer; Pakistan Army Headquarters; and Headquarters Lahore Area).

27. An officer remained on duty in the Map Room from 8. a.m to 8.p.m daily for this purpose, and arrangements were made for dealing with work arising during the remainder of the twenty-four hours.

28. Examples of the matters in which the Military Emergency Staff was employed were: Intelligence (day to day, and periodical summaries); obtaining information, statistics and maps; putting Civil Departments correctly in touch, in given problems, with the right Department of the Fighting Service concerned; obtaining personnel and equipment for Refugee Camps; evacuation of special refugees (e.g. the family of the Prime Minister of Pakistan); liaison

with Civil and Service Air Departments; and arrangements for flights for representatives of the Press.

29. The peak Establishment strength of the Military Emergency Staff was:-

1. Major General
   1 Lieutenant Colonel (C.S.O.1)
   1 Squadron Leader (R.I.A.F) attached.
2. Majors (G.S.O.II)
   4 Captains(G.S.O.III)
   1 Lady Typist A/B Grade P.A.
   2 Stenographers
   2 U.D.C
   2 Peons
   2 Draughtsmen (Geographical Survey)

Publicity

30. A Public Relations Committee consisting of a representative of the Ministry of Information and Broadcasting, the Press Attache to the Governor General and a Public Relations representative from the Commander-in-Chief of the Indian Army was set up to co-ordinate the Emergency Committee's publicity.

## DECISIONS ARRIVED AT A MEETING HELD IN THE TOWN HALL, DELHI, ON FRIDAY THE 26TH SEPTEMBER, 1947, AT 5 P.M.

PRESENT.

1. The Hon'ble Pandit Jawahar Lal Nehru. (In Chair).
2. Mr. H.M. Patel.
3. Mr. M.S. Randhawa.
4. Mr. K.B. Lal.
5. Mr. K. Ram.
6. Captain Ranjit Singh.
7. Mr. V.Krishnaswami.
8. Mrs. Indira Gandhi.
9. L. Deshbandhu Gupta. )
10. Mr. Raghunandan Saran. )
11. Dr. Yudhvir Singh. )
12. Mr. Onkar Nath. ) Representatives of the Delhi
13. Mr. Braham Prakash. ) Provincial Congress Committee.
14. Ch. Sher Jang. )
15. Mr. Radhe Raman. )
16. Mr. A.S. Bhatnagar. )

The meeting discussed ways and means of mobilizing local public opinion for the maintenance of peace in Delhi, and the following decisions were arrived at.

(1) It was decided that a publicity van be placed at the disposal of Dr. Zakir Hussain who should be requested to organize, in consultation with other Muslim leaders, a publicity campaign in the various Muslim *mohallas* of the City, primarily with a view to stemming the exodus of Muslims from the city to the various relief camps.

(2) It was decided that leaflets should be published in Urdu and Hindi exhorting the general public to assist in the restoration of normal conditions in Delhi. The first of the leaflets should be drafted by Mr. Shafiq-ul-Rehman Kidwai. Mr. Raghunandan Saran was made responsible for arranging this and for sending the draft to Pandit Jawahar Lal Nehru by the 27th evening.

(3) It was decided to hold mass meeting in different parts of the city. The first meeting in this series was fixed for the 4th October, 1947 at 4 P.M. at Gandhi Grounds. Pandit Jawahar Lal Nehru, Sardar Vallabh Bhai Patel and other leaders should be invited to address this meeting.

(4) It was decided that *mohalla* meetings in the different non-Muslim areas should be held daily. The first *mohalla* meeting at Katra Neel will be addressed by Pandit Jawahar Lal Nehru on the 27th September, 1947, at 4 P.M.

(5) It was also decided that Pandit Jawahar Lal Nehru should discuss the immediate.problems concerning the maintenance of peace in Delhi with selected groups of Delhi citizens. The first group will meet the Prime Minister on Sunday the 28th September, 1947 at 4 P.M. at the Town Hall. All mass and *mohalla* meetings will be arranged by the Delhi Provincial Congress Committee.

(6) It was decided to arrange for talks by prominent citizens on the local broadcasting system at the Hardinge Library. The District Magistrate was asked to find out if the system was in working order and if so, Pandit Jawahar Lal Nehru should give the first talk of the series on the 28th September, 1947, at 3-30 P.M.

(7) PRESS

(a) The District Magistrate was asked to submit a list of all the newspapers published from Delhi to Pandit Jawahar Lal Nehru.

(b) At the suggestion of Lala Deshbandhu Gupta it was decided to form a committee of three non-official journalists (one each for Urdu, Hindi and English newspapers) to assist and help the Provincial Press Adviser who was asked to arrange for the immediate contradiction of any false news that appeared in the newspapers. Lala Deshbandhu Gupta was requested to suggest names of journalists who will serve on this committee. The District Magistrate was also asked to take necessary action against the newspapers who persisted in publishing false and inflamatory news.

(c) Newspapers published in Pakistan should be properly scrutinized with a view to ensure that no miscievous news is allowed to be circulated in Delhi.

(8) It was decided to arrange bi-weekly radio broadcasts from the A.I.R. by eminent persons, such as Sardar Vallabh Bhai Patel, Maulana Abdul Kalam Azad and Dr. Zakir Hussain.

(9) It was decided that Bakhshi Tekchand and his Committee should be asked to conduct propaganda among the West Punjab refugees in Delhi. Lala Deshbandhu Gupta was asked to request Bakhshi Tek Chand to see Pandit Jawahar Lal Nehru in this connection.

(10) It was also decided to request Bakhshi Tek Chand's Committee to get a list prepared of the various non-Muslim institutions, such as hospitals, colleges, schools etc., located in West Punjab.

(11) The District Magistrate was asked to get a list made of the Muslim factories and large commercial establishments in Delhi which have been abandoned by their owners but have not yet been looted or burnt.

(A.S. BHATNAGAR)

Copy to :-

1. Hon'ble Pandit Jawahar Lal Nehru, together with a list of newspapers published from Delhi.
2. Mr. H.M. Patel.
3. Mr. K.B. Lal (with one spare copy) with reference to items 1 and 8 above.

4. Mr. M.S. Randhawa, District Magistrate, Delhi, with reference to items 6, 7 and 11 above.
5. Lala Deshbandhu Gupta, with reference to items 7, 9 and 10 above.
6. Mr. Raghunandan Saran, with reference to item 2 above.
7. Secretary, Delhi Provincial Congress Committee, with reference to item 3, 4 and 5 above.
8. Mr. Radhe Raman.

ASB/SBL

## MINISTRY OF HOME AFFAIRS SUMMARY NO. 16 FOR THE MONTH ENDING THE 14TH OCTOBER, 1947

1. Communal situation in Provinces. (Second half of August)

(a) MADRAS - *[* 15/1/(a) *]*

Nothing of importance to report, except that there was some misunderstanding between Hindus and Muslims in a few places in connection with the hoisting of the National Flag.

First half of September
The communal situation was satisfactory.

Second half of September.
Report not received.

(b) BOMBAY - *[*15/1/(b)*]*

First half of September.
There was a flare-up in Bombay city on 2nd September with sporadic knife attacks resulting in 6 killed and 13 injured. Next day 15 persons were stabbed of whom 6 died. Thereafter there were stray cases of stabbing, crude explosions and acid-throwing. The districts were generally quiet, except for Ahmedabad where the communal situation flared up on 5th September and 3 Muslim were stabbed of whom one died. Collective fines were imposed on the localities affected.

Second half of September
In Bombay city, the situation showed marked improvement, there being only a few incidents of stabbing and acid-throwing. The tension was, however, still high. The total number of casualties from the 30th March to the 30th September 1947 was 200 dead and 603 injured.

Collective fines amounting to Rs. 33,150 were imposed on several localities. In the Districts the situation was quiet, except for Ahmedabad, Deolali and Khed where there were minor incidents.

(c) WEST BENGAL. - *[* 15/1/(c)*]*

Second half of August.
The communal situation had greatly improved.

First half of September.
In Calcutta, communal trouble started on the night of the 31st August; with cases of stabbing, free use of firearms, arson, loot and attacks on the police etc. The casualties reported were 43 killed and 152 wounded but actual casualty figures were probably considerably higher. The disturbances ended following Mahatma Gandhi's fast but there was still need for strict and constant vigilance by the authorities.

Second half of September.
In Calcutta, communal peace continued. Santi Senas and Ward Peace Committees did valuable work. In the Districts there were no incidents of note to report.

(d) UNITED PROVINCES. 15/1/(d).

Second half of August and first half of September.
As a result of alarming news of disturbances in the Punjab and the tales of non-Muslim refugees, the communal situation deteriorated in the western and northern Districts. The concentration of Muslim refugees from East Punjab complicated the situation. There were numerous cases of attacks on railway trains and of passengers being thrown our of railway trains. Additional police and troops were drafted to the disturbed areas and this had a salutary effect.

Second half of September.
Report not received

(e) EAST PUNJAB. *[*15/1/(e)*]*

Second half of August.
The transfer of power was accompanied by a wave of lawlessness in the Province. Serious trouble broke out in Lahore town on the 11th

August and it had its repercussions in towns of the East Punjab. Amritsar was the first town in East Punjab to have trouble and widespread rioting, arson and murder in Gurdaspur, Jullundur, Hoshiarpur, Ludhiana and Ferozepur districts followed very soon. The trouble also spread to rural areas and there were attacks and counter-attacks in almost all districts of the Jullundur division on a large scale. The number of persons killed would probably never be correctly ascertained but it is likely to run into several thousands. Muslim losses are likely to be heavier in life but it is the other way about in property. Control of the situation was almost gained by the 20th August but the news of atrocities committed on non-Muslims in West Punjab led to fresh outbreak in several places, and it was with the greatest difficulty that the situation was brought and kept under control.

First half of September.

Communal trouble continued to spread eastward. The distressing destruction of life and property also continued, though on a much reduced scale. Non-Muslim Refugees carried stories of unspeakable brutalities perpetrated on them in West Punjab and this poisoned the atmosphere. The main theatre of trouble during the fortnight was the three districts of the Hariana tract — Karnal, Rohtak and Hissar. Trouble on a lesser scale occurred in some districts of the Jullundur Division. Even Simla and Kangra districts were affected. There was a large number of casualties in the Rupar Division of the Ambala District. The incidents in West Punjab, the speeches of Muslim League leaders and the writing in Hindustani Press made it difficult for District Officers to maintain effective law and order. The conduct of the minority community was far from satisfactory and they invited trouble on themselves by staging attacks on non-Muslim villages. Several such incidents took place in Doaba districts. In Karnal there were instances of Muslims attacking Hindus and after inflicting casualties crossing over the Jamuna into United Provinces as "refugees" from East Punjab.

Second half of September

Report not received

f) BIHAR. *[15/1/(f)]*

Second half of August.

There was acute communal tension as a result of widely published stories of atrocities and mass murders in the Punjab. The Hon'ble the Prime Minister convened a conference of military and police officers and special measures were adopted to prevent breaches of the peace. The emergency police scheme was put into operation in all the urban areas of the Province. There was no major communal incidents.

First and second halves of September.

There were no major communal incidents, though tension continued undiminished. The Prime Minister and other Ministers addressed public meetings throughout the Province appealing to the public to preserve peace and this had a sobering effect.

(g) CENTRAL PROVINCES. [15/1/(g)]

Second half of August.

Communal relations continued to be satisfactory on the whole except in Jubbulpore where there were two or three isolated instances of stabbing. The usual precautions were taken and the situation reverted to normal.

First and second halves of September.

The atrocities perpetrated in the Punjab inflamed public opinion to a dangerous extent and strained communal relations. There was however no incidents.

The highlight of the news was the discovery of what appears to be a deep-laid conspiracy to distribute clandestinely arms and ammunition to Muslims with the object of destroying the country's newly-won independence. Certain British Officers were involved. They were arrested and an enquiry was instituted. Searches of Muslim houses in various parts of the Province led to the recovery of considerable amount of arms and ammunition. This added to the panic caused by the Punjab happenings and led to an exodus of Muslims to Hyderabad and Bhopal. The Prime Minister at an

All-Parties Conference assured Muslim Leaguers of full protection and the number of people leaving the Province consequently fell considerably.

(h) ASSAM [15/1/(h)]

First and second halves of September.
Nothing of importance to report.

(i) ORRISA [15/1/(i)]

Second half of August.
Relations between the two principal communities were satisfactory on the whole despite communal disturbances elsewhere in the country.

First half of September.
The news that Government had agreed to accept a number of Hindu and Sikh refugees from the Punjab caused some flutter among the local Muslims but they were reassured that their honour, life and property would be safeguarded.

Second half of September
Report not received.

(j) COORG [15/1/(j)]

First and second halves of September.
Nothing of importance to report.

(k) DELHI [15/1/(k)]

First and second halves of September.
The communal tension burst into an orgy of murder loot and arson which spread to rural areas as well. In the city, Qarol Bagh, Subzimandi and Paharganj were scenes of bitter communal fighting. In Subzimandi, Muslims, who had illicit arms in their possession, caused a good deal of damage by firing with automatic weapons from their houses. A pitched battle was fought between the military and Muslims and it was after great difficulty that pockets of resistence were cleared. Strong action by the military and imposition of strict curfew brought the situation under control. Searches for arms were conducted and a number of illicit weapons were recovered from many houses. A few wireless transmitters were also recovered from some Muslims houses.

A burnt Signal Corps radio transmitter was recovered from the remains of the *DAWN PRESS*. A number of Muslim Police Officers and constables deserted with some arms and ammunition, and all but about 200 (out of about 1600) have since resigned their posts on being given an option to do so. The situation is now almost completely under control, though stray assaults and stabbings are reported occasionally. Cabinet is directly seized of the situation in Delhi through its Emergency Committee.

(1) AJMER-MERWARA. [15/1/(1) ]

First and second halves of September.
Ajmer became a temporary halt for Muslim and non-Muslim refugees going to and coming from Pakistan (some of whom detrained at Ajmer). The presence of refugees of both communities caused deep uneasiness in Ajmer-Merwara, and newspapers and extremist elements of both communities increased the tension. Steps were taken to preserve communal peace, *e.g.* banning of meetings and carrying of arms, detention of undesirables, suspension of a number of licenses for arms, together with action against the press. The Muslim public were sending their families to Pakistan. Many of the Muslim lower ranks in the police have resigned.

Persistent attacks on railway trains running through Alwar, Bharatpur and Jaipur States to Ajmer were a baffling feature of the period. The British heads of the Railway Police did not function properly and Mr. Shankar Prasad, Chief Commissioner, was put in charge of the police force. The States Ministry invoked the assistance of the three States in maintaining order. The Chief Commissioner also maintained close contact with the Home and State Ministries. Military assistance had also to be invoked and the situation is now comparatively better.

## VOLUNTEER ORGANISATIONS

2. RASHTRIYA SWAYAM SEWAK SANGH. [15/2/a]
The strength of this organisation increased in Bombay and O.P. "Rakshabandhan Day" was observed on August 31 in several districts of Bombay province: main features being rallies, flag salutations and private meetings. Arrangements are in train to hold a mammoth rally

in Poona District on November 1st and 2nd - the object being to gauge the strength of the Sangh leaders in Maharashtra and the extent of the leaders' control over their volunteers. In Bombay province the volunteers have been busy carrying on propaganda through public meetings with a view to extending R.S.S. activities. "Guru Pournima" day celebrated in Poona on 31st August was largely attended; a rally was also held there under the presidentship of the Provincial organiser of the Sangh urged the volunteers to strive for the resurrection of the Hindu nation. It is reported that efforts are being made to extend Sangh activities to village in Bombay province. In Central Province increased Sangh activity has been reported. In the United Provinces Sangh members took prominent part in Raksha Bandhan celebration in many parts. In East Punjab R.S.S. workers were reported to have collected funds at Kaithan in Karnal district to purchase arms and to have instigated Hindus in Rohtak to start large scale disturbances.

MUSLIM LEAGUE NATIONAL GUARDS. *[ 15/2/b]*
In Bombay the strength showed some decrease. It is reported that in some parts of Bombay province Guards are being systematically trained and organised with a view to protecting Muslims in case of communal riot. The activities of the Guards in Bombay were directed towards helping Muslim refugees and railway servants on their way to Karachi. In Bengal Muslim League Guards have been touring about preaching disloyalty to the Indian Dominion.

RASHTRA SEVA DAL *[15/2/b]*
The strength of the Dal has further decreased in Bombay. A training class for women volunteers and a physical culture class for males have been started in Poona. The anniversary of the "Mahad Moroha" was celebrated in Kolaba on September 10th and a procession was taken out with flag Salutation ceremony.

AZAD HIND DAL *[15/2/d]*
Nothing to report.

SMATA SAINIK DAL *[15/2/e]*
Nothing to report.

<u>KHAKSARS.</u> [15/2/f]
Nothing to report.

<u>SIKH ORGANISATIONS</u> [15/2/g]
Nothing to report.

<u>CONGRESS SEVA DAL.</u> [15/2/h]
The membership of the Dal increased slightly. The volunteers have been helping the refugees in Bombay. The All-India Congress Seva Dal Organisers' Camp was inaugarated at Dharavi on the 5th September where the necessity of discipline among the volunteer corps for the maintenance of the freedom of India was urged.

<u>OTHER ORGANISATIONS.</u>
In Beawar in Ajmer-Merwara it is reported that the Town Congress Committee have decided to start a quami Seva Dal volunteer organisation to help in looking after refugees.

## MINISTRY OF HOME AFFAIRS SUMMARY NO. 18 FOR THE MONTH ENDING THE 14TH DECEMBER, 1947

1. Communal situation in Provinces.

(a) Madras. 17/1/(a).

Second half of October.
There were minor clashes between Muslims and Hindus at Kurnool and Guntur during the Dasara festival, resulting in injuries to five persons at the former place and to six at the latter.

First and second halves of November.
Reports not received.

(b) Bombay. 17/1/(b).

(First and second halves of November).
In Bombay city there was only one serious incident of bomb-throwing during the first half of the month in which one person was killed and 28 injured; and only two cases of bomb-throwing during the second half of the month, in which 4 persons were injured. The total number of casualties in Bombay City from the 30th March to 30th November 1947 was 224 dead and 744 injured. Collective fines amounting to Rs.79,165 were imposed on different localities during the month.

The districts were generally quiet except for stray minor incidents in Kaira, Ahmedabad, Thana, Belgaum, Ratnagiri, Sholapur Dharwar Panch Mahals, West Khandesh and Nasik districts. The Mohurrum festival passed off peacefully all over the Province.

(c) West Bengal. 17/1/(c)

(First and second halves of November).
Except for tension in the districts on the Indo-Pakistan border the communal situation throughout the Province was generally quiet. The *Kali Puja*, *Jagadhatri Puja*, and *Mohurram* celebrations passed off peacefully

everywhere, except in Malda district, where a *Kali Puja* procession was attacked by several hundred Muslims on the 14th November, and the police had to open fire injuring six persons. There were some minor incidents in the industrial areas of Hooghly district and Kharagpur but prompt action by the authorities prevented any trouble. In Calcutta there was no communal incident of any kind and the city was perfectly normal in this respect.

(d) United Provinces. 17/1/(d).

Second half of October.

The improvement in the occurrence of overt acts of hostility was maintained. Dashera and Id passed off peacefully throughout the Province with the exception of a few districts, where there were incidents on account of cow-sacrifice. Isolated stabbing cases continued, though on a diminishing scale, and train incidents too were fewer.

First half of November.

There were sporadic attacks on unwary persons in certain districts and there were also some organised incidents involving both communities. Vigilance by the police and local officers kept violence under check. There was trouble in Saharanpur, as a result of a procession taken out by Hindu refugees. Quick intervention by the police and the imposition of curfew saved the situation. Homeless Muslims were found operating as criminal gangs and attacking Hindus in the rural areas of Dehra Dun. In general, the western districts were still the danger spots. Bomb explosions took place in some of these, but no major losses in life or property were caused.

Second half of November.

Report not received.

(e) East Punjab. 17/1/(e).

Second half of October.

The massacre of more than 2,000 refugees, who were on their way to India from Sialkot on 23rd October 1947, caused a sudden and serious deterioration of the situation in Amritsar District, and its effects were also felt elsewhere. Huge mobs collected at Amritsar to attack Muslim refugees in retaliation but close vigilance and energetic action by the district officers prevented the situation from taking an ugly form, and the situation rapidly improved again. Karnal was the only district where, on account of the proximity of Muslim and non-Muslim refugees, incidents continued to occur.

The border with Pakistan remained as disturbed as before.

First and second halves of November.
Reports not received.

(f) Bihar. 17/1/(f).

(First and second halves of October)
The Dusserah and Id festivals passed off peacefully in the Province, except for a solitary overt incident in Muzaffarpur district where a Muslim was killed for sacrificing a cow against village custom. There was tension in some other places also but nothing untoward happened. Communal tension eased considerably after id and there were sign of communal harmony in several districts.

First and second halves of November.
Reports not received.

(g) Central Provinces. 17/1/(g)

First and second halves of November.
Except for a number of incidents on the border with Hyderabad State, in which Muslims who had migrated to Hyderabad are reported to have taken part, there was nothing of importance to report.

(h) Assam 17/1/(h).

(First and second halves of November)
Except for a case of stone-throwing at Gauhati where Sikhs pelted a Tazia procession at Moharram, the communal situation was peaceful.

(i) Orissa. 17/1/(i)

Second half of October.
Communal relations were strained at Khariar Road in Sambalpur district. A rumour that while migrating to Hyderabad Muslims of Raipur had been taking away Hindu girls by train led to organised searches of Muslim women in railway compartments by local Sikhs

and members of the Rashtriya Swayam Sewak, and Muslims in their turn started to attend the trains to counter these activities, and police intervention became necessary.

First half of November.
Nothing to report.

Second half of November.
Report not received.

(j) Coorg. 17/1/(j).

(First and second halves of November).
Communal relations continued to be normal.

(k) Delhi. 17/1/(k).

(First and second halves of November).
During the first half of the month, minor incidents of stray assaults and hold-ups, in which refugees were concerned, continued to occur. On the 23rd November, some Hindu and Sikh refugees entered a Muslim house and a scuffle ensued, resulting in injuries to some of them, and on this a rumour started that a number of Hindus and Sikhs had been stabbed. The situation became tense and some stabbing incidents took place. Curfew restrictions were immediately imposed in affected areas, patrolling was intensified and the situation was quickly brought under control.

(1) Ajmer-Merwara. 17/1(1)

First half of November.
Communal tension had somewhat eased but Muslim exodus continued. Propaganda work of the Peace Committee and frequent patrols by the police had a good effect in counteracting wild rumours. Muslim Leaguers were making propaganda that the Durgah would be attacking during the Pushkar Fair. One Muslim was thrown out of a train on 7th November, and sustained minor injuries.

Second half of November.

There was much communal excitement because of Moharrum to be quickly followed by the big Pushkar Fair. Wild rumours had gained currency that the Durgah would be attacked by the pilgrims, but both Moharrum and Pushkar fair passed off peacefully, Both the communities were, however, in a bad state of nerves.

First half of December.

On the 6th December a communal riot broke out in Ajmer following a petty altercation between some Muslims and Sindhi refugees, resulting in 36 injured and 3 killed. Curfew was imposed, and there was patrolling by police and military. Prompt action was taken by the magistracy and the situation was brought under control, but trouble again broke out on the evening of 13th December when the corpse of a police constable murdered by a Muslim mob was being taken for cremating. The situation worsened and armed police and troops were called out. ____________ were burnt and looted and many other small Muslim shops ____________ rifled. Three mosques were damaged one being set on fire which was put out. At two places Muslims fired at the Public and also at the police who returned the fire, killing three and injuring two. Police and Military fired at the looters and the Chief Commissioner himself headed a party which fired forty rounds at rioters and looters. Curfew was enforced rigorously and there was rigorous patrolling by military and police who had orders to shoot at sight any person indulging in looting, arson and murder. The situation is reported to be in hand and expected to improve.

2. VOLUNTEER ORGANISATIONS.

RASHTRIYA SWAYAM SEWAK SANGH. 17/2/a.

The strength of this organisation increased in Madras, Bombay and the United Provinces. Increased activities of the Sangh were noticed in Madras and the United Provinces. The main feature of the activity of the Sangh in Bombay was intensive propaganda throughout the Province particularly in the districts of Maharashtra and Karnatak with a view to consolidate their position vis-a-vis the attacks on the Hindu community and religion. In his speeches in Bombay Mr. M.S. Golwalkar, the chief organiser, while refuting the charge that the Sangh was a communal body, considered the present independence of the country unreal. The Sangh was steadily growing in strength and in importance in the East Punjab and it is reported that the members of the Sangh were noticed exhorting people to proceed to Kashmir and take part in organising defence there. New branches of the Sangh have been formed in the Central Provinces. In Jubbulpore a procession of 20,000 volunteers was taken out headed by a jeep and motor cycles. The "Guru Dakhshna" collections in Delhi lasted from the 2nd to the 11th instant and Rs. 2½ lacs were collected. The Sangh workers decided to join the Gurmukteshwar Fair with the intention of spreading communalism amongst the visitors and to preach their own cult in the rural area from village to village. Mr. M.S. Golwalker, addressed his followers in New Delhi and deprecated the selfishness of the Hindus and urged them to unite.

MUSLIM LEAGUE NATIONAL GUARDS. 17/2/b
In Bombay the strength of the Guard decreased. The activities of the Guards in Bombay were directed towards helping Muslim refugees and railway servants on their way to Karachi and Hyderabad.

RASHTRA SEVA DAL. 17/2/c.
The strength of the Dal has increased in Bombay. A rally of the Dal volunteers was held at Ratnagiri. The Dal volunteers in Bombay have been busy in collecting blankets, clothes and cash for refugees. An anti-communal propaganda campaign was launched by the Dal Volunteers under the instruction of the Socialist Party. In order to counteract the propaganda of communal bodies, particularly the Rashtriya Swayam Sevak Sangh the Dal under the instruction of the Socialist Party took a lead in forming an organisation of non-communal volunteer bodies, known as 'Samyukta Yuvak Sanghtana' with the assistance of the Lok Sena, Lok Natya (Communist) Lal Bawta (Communist) Samata Sainik Dal (Scheduled Castes Federation).

OTHER ORGANISATIONS

In East Punjab a new organisation called 'Desh Sewak Saina' was inaugurated on 21st October, 1947 and is sponsored by the ex-I.N.A. personnel. It is stated to be a non-political and non-communal body of selfless workers organised with the object of helping the authorities in stabilising conditions in the province and assisting in rehabilitation work. The organisers were thinking of opening branches in rural areas also.

3. As a fresh outbreak of communal disturbances in Delhi occurred on 23rd November 1947, the Deputy Commissioner Delhi on 25th November 1947 issued an order sub-clause (b) of clause 4 of the Press (Special Powers) (2) Ordinance, 1947 directing the printers, publishers and Editors of all daily newspapers — English, Urdu and Hindi published in Delhi Province to submit for scrutiny before publication during the period from 25th November to 1st December 1947 all matter, including news, comments, photographs and cartoons relating to the Communal disturbances or incidents in Delhi Province except official communiques.

S_E_C_R_E_T

No. 132/C.M/48
GOVERNMENT OF INDIA
CABINET SECRETARIAT

New Delhi, the 16th January, 1948

In continuation of Cabinet Secretariat memorandum of even number and date circulating minutes and decisions of the Cabinet meeting held on the 14th January, 1948, the undersigned is directed also to circulate to the Ministers a copy of the minutes on the following item discussed at the same meeting and approved by the Prime Minister:

Financial settlement between India and Pakistan.

(D.R. Kohli)
Under Secretary to the Cabinet.

To,
All Ministers.

Copy with three copies of the enclosure forwarded to the Principal Private Secretary to the Prime Minister for information.

(D.R. Kohli)
Under Secretary to the Cabinet.

Copy No. 10 S_E_C_R_E_T

MEETING OF THE CABINET HELD ON
WEDNESDAY, THE 14TH JANUARY,1948
AT 4.30 P.M.

Case No.31/4/48. Financial settlement between India and Pakistan.

P R E S E N T.
The Prime Minister.
The Deputy Prime Minister.
The Minister for Education.
The Minister for Transport and Railways.
The Minister for Commerce.
The Minister for Communication.
The Minister for Health.
The Minister for Finance.
The Minister for Industry & Supply.
The Minister for Relief and Rehabilitation.

The Prime Minister stated that both he and the Deputy Prime Minister had seen Mahatma Gandhi who had taken his fast that day. The Government was anxious to do all in its power to improve the communal situation and steps were being taken to that end.

One particular matter was in Gandhiji's mind and he had referred to it. This was the question of payment of Rs.55 crores, in terms of the financial agreement, to Pakistan. He felt that it would have been better for us to pay this, although legally and on other grounds we might have been justified in refusing to implement the agreement till other settlement had been arrived at. He felt strongly on this question and suggested that even now we should pay this sum. This would remove one cause of illwill and bitterness between the two states.

The Deputy Prime Minister gave an account of his talks with Gandhiji on this question.

The Cabinet discussed the matter fully and were of opinion that on the merits their previous decisions are completely justified, but in the new context that had arisen and more especially because of Gandhiji's wishes in the matter and his fast they were prepared to reconsider their previous decision. It was made clear that this question had nothing to do with Gandhiji's fast. In fact, it had arisen in his mind after he had decided on the fast. Nevertheless Government's decision in regard to it would no doubt affect Gandhiji and might have a considerable effect on the communal situation.

After full discussion it was decided that four members of the Cabinet viz., the Prime Minister, the Deputy Prime Minister, the Transport Minister and the Finance Minister should meet Gandhiji and place all the facts before him. If after full consideration Gandhiji was definitely of opinion that Government should revise its previous decision and direct payment of the Rs.55 crores to Pakistan, then Gandhiji's advice should be accepted and steps should be taken accordingly, that is to say, that a communique on behalf of Government should be issued.

MINISTRY OF HOME AFFAIRS
SUMMARY FOR THE MONTH ENDING THE
14TH JULY, 1948.

1. Communal situation in Provinces.

(a) M A D R A S. 24/1/(a)

Second half of May.
Nothing of importance to report, except that prohibitory orders had to be issued in order to avert Hindu-Muslim clashes over the playing of music before a mosque at a place in Chittoor District.

First half of June.
Nothing of importance to report.

Second half of June.
Report not received.

(b) B O M B A Y. 24/1/(b)

First half of June.
The communal situation in Bombay was well under control except for a minor incident of rioting at Nawabbwadi area in Begumpura, Surat. In Godhra town, a powerful section of Hindus think in terms of preventing Muslims from returning to Godhra in large numbers. Local agitation in regard to this has subsided, but the undercurrent of communal feelings is as high as before.

Second half of June.
There was some deterioration in the communal situation in Bombay and Kurla, as a sequel to some stabbing cases involving Hindu and Muslim residents. The Police took elaborate precautions and the situation was brought under control.

(c) <u>WEST BENGAL.</u> 24/1(c)

<u>First half of June.</u>
Nothing of importance to report.

<u>Second half of June.</u>
There was one incident in Murshidabad District following a trifling incident in which a Hindu slapped a Muslim boy for breaking the branch of a tree, with the result that a number of houses belonging to both communities were looted and some Muslim houses were also burnt. The District Magistrate was directed to take strong action against those responsible. The situation is now quiet.

(d) <u>UNITED PROVINCES.</u> 24/1/(d)

<u>Second half of May.</u>
Except for a few minor incidents, communal relations remained peaceful, but the Hyderabad question had an unsettling effect on the minds of both the communities. At places, the Muslims provoked some minor incidents.

<u>First half of June</u>.
Apart from a few minor incidents, the communal situation remained satisfactory. There was some uneasiness due to a whispering campaign, almost throughout the province, that after a specified date in this month, there would be wide-spread communal trouble in India. District officers were in readiness for forestalling any breach of the peace. They also took steps for counteracting such rumours and restoring confidence.

<u>Second half of June</u>.
Report not received.

(e) <u>EAST PUNJAB.</u> 24/1/(e)

<u>Second half of May.</u>
Nothing important to report., except a slight worsening of Hindu-Sikh relations at some places. The basic cause was the demand of

certain sections among the Sikhs for grant of a greater voice in the affairs of East Punjab than their numerical strength entitled them to. This was naturally resented by the Hindus, and and there has been, on this account, some fairly acrimonious criticism in the Hindu Press of Master Tara Singh and other Sikh leaders of his way of thinking.

First half of June.
Nothing of importance to report.

Second half of June.
Report not received.

(f) BIHAR. 24/1/(f)

Second half of May.
Nothing to report.

First and second halves of June.
Reports not received.

(g) CENTRAL PROVINCES AND BERAR 24/1/(g)

Second half of May.
Communal peace prevailed in the province.

First half of June.
Communal situation in the province was quiet and the relations between the two major communities were outwardly cordial, although Hyderabad affairs were proving a powerful irritant to the Hindus, which, if continued, might add to the difficulties of preservation of peace and tranquillity in the province.

Second half of June.
Report not received.

(h) ASSAM. 24/1/(h)

Second half of May and first half of June.
Nothing to report.

Second half of June.
Report not received.

(i) ORISSA. 24/1/(i)

First and Second Halves of May.
Nothing of importance to report.

First and Second halves of June.
Reports not received.

(j) C O O R G 24/1/(j)

First and Second halves of June.
The communal relations remained normal.

(k) D E L H I. 24/1/(k)

Second half of May.
Wild rumours were afloat that serious communal trouble would break out in Delhi with the departure of Lord Mountbatten from India. The Local Administration took all possible precautionary measures.

First half of June.
But for a few trivial incidents, the communal situation continued to be satisfactory, and tension subsided.

Second half of June.
Report not received.

(1) AJMER–MERWARA. 24/1/(1)

First half of June.
Disquieting rumours about wide-spread trouble on 15th June gained currency, and some nervousness prevailed amongst the local Muslims. Apprehending trouble, about 50 Muslims of Railway workshops, Ajmer, obtained leave and proceeded to Pakistan and other places. Precautionary measures were taken. There were two minor incidents in Ajmer: one on the 4th June, in which a few Sindhis mobbed a Muslim boy suspecting him to be a miscreant, and the other on the 9th June, when a country-made bomb exploded in the house of a Hindu and caused fatal injury to a woman.

Second half of June.

There was some uneasiness owing to the wide rumour which gained wide currency that the 15th June was the critical date for a general flare-up in the country.

The Sindhi refugees generally kept communalism alive, but there were no overt incidents, except that an abortive attempt was made by an unknown person at Beawar to set fire to a Muslim shop.

2. VOLUNTEER ORGANISATIONS.

RASHTRIYA SWAYAM SEWAK SANGH

In the United Provinces, the R.S.S. workers tried to regain public support by preaching that the Sangh had nothing to do with the assassination of Mahatmaji. At Meerut they circulated copies of a leaflet which lays down a code of conduct for the Sangh workers who visit villages to enrol volunteers and also contains instructions about methods of approaching the prospective candidates. Secret activities of the Sangh were on a much reduced scale as compared with earlier periods.

In the Central Provinces and Berar, the Sangh was outwardly quiet, though reports of secret meetings continued to come in. In Amraoti, a meeting was reported to have been held for help to the accused in the Mahatma Gandhi assassination case. Some activity was also reported from Bhamberi in Akot taluq.

In the East Punjab, Sangh volunteers and their sympathisers continued to hold secret meetings in order to take decisions about their future programme. They also maintained contact with each other under the cloak of games. A rumour went round that the top organisers of the Sangh were carrying on negotiations with Government of India to reach a settlement. This rumour contributed to put more life into their activities.

In Delhi some suspected active workers of the Sangh were taken into custody.

In Ajmer, the actvities of the Sindhi Sangh volunteers were on the increase. Certain restrictions were imposed on Shri Lokman Jetly, formerly a District Organiser of the Sangh, who had gone underground after his release.

MUSLIM LEAGUE NATIONAL GUARDS (24/2/b).

Nothing to report except the efforts in Raipur (C.P. & Berar) to send 12 Muslim League National Guards for the assistance of Razvi, if needed.

KHAKSARS (24/2/c)

Nothing to report.

CONGRESS SEVA DAL (24/2/d)

In Bombay the strength of the Dal decreased. As regards its activities two Dal workers gave a talk on May 16 and 17 to the Dal volunteers at Ahmedabad, urging upon them to maintain discipline, and not to be misled by party propaganda of the Socialists. In Bombay, training classes for Dal volunteers were held from the 12th to 26th June, where the volunteers were trained in drill and lectured on discipline and handling of crowds at meetings.

OTHER ORGANISATIONS 24/2/e

There was no appreciable activities by other volunteer organisations.

3. A revised scheme for the reorganisation and reinforcement of the Central Secretariat and proposals for the constitution of a new Central Secretariat Service to man adequately the posts at present classed as Under/Assistant Secretary, Superintendent, Assistant-in-Charge, Assistants, and also to serve as a feeder service for higher posts in the Secretariat such as Deputy Secretary etc., were drawn up and circulated to the various Ministries for their views and comments before being finalised. A meeting of all Secretaries was held on the 12th and 13th July 1948 to discuss the proposals. The meeting arrived at the unanimous conclusion that the Scheme should be accepted subject to certain detailed amendments which were specified. The Scheme as thus amended is now under further consideration of this Ministry.

4. It has been decided that in addition to first or second class graduates in Arts and Science, First or Second Class Graduates in Commerce will also be eligible for appointment to the Indian Administrative and Police Services and gazetted posts in the Central Secretariat under the Emergency Recruitment Scheme. A Press

Communique announcing this decision was issued on the 7th July, 1948.

5. Employment of lawyers and highly qualified middle class refugees.

The Employment Co-ordination Committee have been asked to carry out a proper grading and to recommend 100 names from lawyers and other highly qualified middle class refugees with a view to their placement mainly in the Assistants' grade through the Transfer Bureau, as and when vacancies are available. As these people will be unfamiliar with the work of the Government of India offices, it is essential that they should be given some preliminary training. It has accordingly been decided that they should be given training for a period of three months (two months in the Secretariat Training School and one month by supernumerary attachment to Secretariat Sections) and that during this period of training they should be paid a stipend of Rs.100/-/- p.m. each.

List of posts to which appointments of non-Indians have been concurred in by the Ministry of Home Affairs during the month ending 14th July 1948.

. . . . . . . . . . .

| Name of Ministry | Designation of post | Duration of appointment |
|---|---|---|
| Ministry of Industry & Supply. | Director, Metallurgical Laboratory of India. | Three years. |
| Ministry of Defence. | Works, Manager, Cordite Factory, Aruvankadu. | Three years. |
| Ministry of Railways. | Assistant Transportation Superintendent (Movement) G.I.P. Railways. | One year. |
| -do- | -do- Liaison Officer in the United Kingdome. (*sic*) | Not exceeding three years. |

Vidhani/45/19.7.1948

# Index